QUACKONOMICS!

The Cost of Unscientific Health Care in the US and Other Fraud Found along the Way

E T H A N   L .   W E L C H   M . D .

PAGE PUBLISHING, INC.
Conneaut Lake, PA

First originally published by Page Publishing 2020

ISBN 978-1-64584-515-7 (pbk)
ISBN 978-1-64584-516-4 (digital)

Printed in the United States of America

This book is dedicated to the integrity of science.

CONTENTS

INTRODUCTION

Man knew little more at the end of the
18ᵗʰ century than the ancient Greeks.
—Sir William Osler

EALTH-CARE EXPENDITURES IN the United States
are at the center of the debate on the role of government.
US health care spending grew 3.9 percent in 2017, reaching $3.5 trillion or $10,739 per person. As a share of the nation's gross domestic product, health spending accounted for 17.9 percent.[1] This tells the story of the annual aggregate cost of provision of scientific health care, but what is the cost of nonscientific health care? Along with the examination of all the costs of health care, a closer look at the nonscientific segment may reveal areas of cost savings and serve to educate and assist people in making better health-care decisions. It is certainly worth a try.

At the outset, it is necessary to distinguish between nonscientific health care and health care based upon credible science. I submit that a definition of quackery by Stephen Barrett, MD,[2] is useful:

> All things considered, I find it most useful
> to define quackery as *the promotion of unsubstan-*
> *tiated methods that lack a scientifically plausible*
> *rationale.* Promotion usually involves a profit
> motive. Unsubstantiated means either unproven

9

or disproven. Implausible means that it either clashes with well-established facts or makes so little sense that it is not worth testing.

Nonscientific medicine is health care based upon unsubstantiated methods that lack a scientifically plausible rationale. The inclusion of "promotion" in the definition of quackery introduces a new spectrum that considers potential overpromotion to outright fraud. It may seem harsh or abrasive to use the word "quackery," but clear definitions are necessary to outline terms and generate a useful discourse toward the truth and the resultant benefit to all consumers of health care.

William Helfand suggests that the origin of the term "quack" was probably from the Dutch *Quacksalber*, a charlatan or itinerant seller of medicine.[3] He further traces the term to the seventeenth-century reference in *The Oxford English Dictionary* as "an ignorant pretender to medical skill, one who boasts to have a knowledge of wonderful remedies, an empiric or imposter in medicine." However defined, the fact is that up until the later part of the nineteenth century, the history of medicine was, in retrospect, the history of quackery. Helfand, quoting Pickard and Buley,[4] notes:

> In the 1880's in the American Midwest, one could distinctly identify different kinds of "doctors" in addition to the regulars including eclectic, botanic, homeopathic, uroscopian, Thomsonian, hydropathic, electric, faith, spiritual, herbalist, electropathic, vitapathic, botanico-medical, physio medical, physioelectric, hygeo-therapeutic and traveling.

Most recently, any definition that applies to the area of nonscientific medicine must recognize the term "alternative medicine" as it has been used since the 1990s. Wikipedia[5] states that:

Alternative medicine is any healing practice that does not fall within the realm of conventional medicine. It is based on historical or cultural traditions, rather than on scientific evidence.

The web article goes on to conclude:

Claims about the efficacy of alternative medicine tend to lack evidence and have been shown to repeatedly fail during testing. Alternative Medicine is now often grouped under the term, Complementary Alternative Medicine (CAM). Some researchers state that the evidence-based approach to defining Complementary Alternative Medicine (CAM) is problematic and that the terms "complementary" and "alternative" are deceptive euphemisms meant to give the impression of medical authority. Thus, boundaries between CAM and mainstream medicine, as well as among different CAM systems, are often blurred and are constantly changing.

It is this confusion among different CAM systems that the National Center for Complementary and Alternative Medicine (NCCAM) was established under the National Institutes of Health in Bethesda, Maryland. The mission of NCCAM is to define, through rigorous scientific investigation, the usefulness and safety of complementary and alternative medicine interventions and their roles in improving health and health care.[6] Medlineplus,[7] a website service of the US National Library of Medicine and the National Institutes of Health (NIH) explains further that:

Complementary and alternative medicine (CAM) is the term for medical products and practices that are not part of standard care. Standard care is what medical doctors, doctors of osteop-

athy and allied health professionals, such as reg-
istered nurses and physical therapists, practice.
Alternative medicine means treatments that you
use instead of standard ones. Complementary
medicine means nonstandard treatments that
you use along with standard ones. Examples of
CAM therapies are acupuncture, chiropractic
and herbal medicines.

The claims that CAM treatment providers
make about their benefits can sound promising.
However, researchers do not know how safe many
CAM treatments are or how well they work.
Studies are underway to determine the safety and
usefulness of many CAM practices.

(The term *CAM* has evolved into the term "functional medicine," but more on that later.)

It is the intention of this book to take a critical, unbiased look
at the quackery currently practiced in this country. I hope that an
in-depth examination of the costs will result in a more rational spending of our health-care dollars. Finally, the better understanding of
science as the basis of medicine will clarify the place of science in our
education and make us all more informed citizens and consumers.

A word about references: Throughout the book, there are a few
short quotes, but for the most part, rather than quotation marks,
numbered citations are in indented margins and refer to exact sources
in books, newspapers, magazines, and websites rather than original
medical literature, which is often difficult for a consumer to track
down. My purpose was not only to avoid plagiarism in making a
point but also to provide quick access to internet material, allowing
the reader easy extended browsing for their own research.

Endnotes

Introduction

[1] https://www.cms.gov/research-statistics-data-and-systems/statistics-trends-and-reports/nationalhealthexpenddata/nationalhealthaccountshistorical.html.

[2] Stephen Barrett, MD. http://www.quackwatch.com/01QuackeryRelatedTopics/quackdef.html.

[3] Helfand, W. H., *Quack, Quack, Quack* (New York: The Grolier Club, 2002), 14.

[4] Ibid., Pickard and Buley, *The Midwest Pioneer, His Ills, Cures and Doctors*, 169.

[5] Wikipedia, http://en.wikipedia.org/wiki/Alternative_medicine.

[6] http://nccam.nih.gov/.

[7] http://www.nlm.nih.gov/medlineplus/complementaryandalternativemedicine.html.

Historical Perspective

CHAPTER 1

Science

*Science is the attempt to discover by means of
observation and reasoning, particular facts about
the world and then laws connecting facts with one
another and making it possible to predict future
occurrences.*

—*Bertrand Russell.*[1]

UNDERSTANDING AND MAKING decisions on health
care is difficult, if not impossible, without the basic understanding of science. Understanding science requires knowledge of the scientific method. Our modern world is divided between
scientists and nonscientists. Scientists, particularly those involved
in research, know about and understand the scientific method.
Nonscientifically trained people may have a variable understanding
or none at all.

The scientific method is best understood in the context of
history. Prior to the emergence of science, all progress was by trial
and error. Plato believed that all knowledge could be obtained from
reasoning, and it took a long time before observation and recording of knowledge preceded experimentation. The ancient Egyptians
had knowledge of setting fractured bones, draining abscesses, tooth

extraction, and trephine of the skull and had a code of ethics long before the Hippocratic Oath. Carlo Rovelli, a professor of theoretical physics and a historian, calls Anaximander, the sixth-century BC Greek philosopher the first scientist because "he was the first to suggest that order in the world was due to natural forces, not supernatural ones."[2] Anaximander's influence put Western culture on the path toward the dawn of science.

Aristotle had a method. He gathered what others knew about a topic, looked for relationships between topics or subjects, and then developed a system of study by subdividing and naming things into different branches such as biology, physics, zoology, and even poetry. Hippocrates, in the fifth century BC, provided the foundation of early medicine and gained great credence by simply observing and recording symptoms and signs provided by his patients. These early Greek physicians were empirical humanists and recommended treatments such as herbal remedies rather than appealing to the gods. The people of the Greco-Roman era were limited, however, by the extent to which their "method" understood the nature of the human body, believing that their bodies were made up of four humors: blood, phlegm, yellow bile, and black bile, each identified with a natural element: air, fire, water, and earth. Although the science was rustic, the Greeks laid the foundation for the art of medicine as well, traveling through Egypt, Persia, and Southern Italy.

With the fall of Rome in the fifth century CE and the emergence of the Dark Ages, evolution of the scientific method was halted by the focus on religion. The writings of St. Augustine of Hippo, converted to the Christian faith in AD 387, directed the faithful to see only the hand of God behind every and all aspects of nature. Christian teaching saw disease as punishment by God for the sins of man. Curiosity was thwarted and reason banished. It was not until the Crusades in the late eleventh century that the Western world had any exposure to the next phase of prescience as it was progressing in the Muslim world, a dominion that spread from the Atlantic to Afghanistan. Arabic became the language of inquiry and discourse, as the Arabs had found and translated Greek libraries and, together with Persian and Sanskrit sources, molded the early essentials of

Arab science. Schools of higher education were formed in cities from Cordoba to Baghdad. The first teaching hospital was established in Damascus in AD 707.[3] The early Arab astronomers and seafarers were keen observers of the heavens and named many of the brighter navigational stars in their own Arabic language. Islamic science was closely aligned to the Quran, and all knowledge needed to fit into the Muslim worldview. The principles of science and medicine were synthesized in a twelfth-century publication, *Cannon of Medicine*, by the Persian genius Avicenna, better known by his Muslim name Ibn Sina. Although this vast compendium, describing the diagnosis and treatment of many ailments together with a collection of drugs, was translated into Latin and served as a text well into the seventeenth century, it was still a long way from our modern scientific method. Ill health was still considered an imbalance of the body's four humors and their associated opposites—blood (hot vs. moist), phlegm (cold vs. moist), the yellow bile (hot vs. dry), and black bile (cold vs. dry). Although it is easy to dismiss the contributions of the earliest Islamic world, focus on scholarship and the belief that knowledge of science provides man with a unique power over the forces of nature without abrogating a belief in their God is a legacy tilted toward progress.

Emerging from the Dark Ages in the Western world, one of the earliest contributions to the notion of the scientific inquiry came in the thirteenth century. The English Franciscan friar Roger Bacon and a number of his contemporaries, during the time of the founding of universities at Oxford and Paris, described the importance of observation, hypothesis, and experimentation. They stressed the need for independent verification and less emphasis on theology. Bacon wrote of optics, mathematics, and alchemy. His inquiring mind often put him at odds with the church and his own order. He fought reliance on translations of Aristotle, superstition, and magic. His writings are a brilliant marker on the road to the scientific method.

Throughout the second millennium, there were several forces that contributed to the evolution of the scientific method and, hence, the growth of science in the Western world. The founding of the great universities, a gradual abridgment of the divine right of Kings, the emergence of a parliamentary system of government, the questioning of the writings of the Ancients, and the fall of Constantinople to the Turks (1453) all contributed in their own way to the growing emergence of reason as a basis of knowledge.

Leonardo da Vinci (1452–1519) trained himself to be an intense observer and experimenter as Walter Isaacson points out[4]:

> Leonardo became one of the major Western thinkers, more than a century before Galileo, to pursue in a persistent hands-on fashion a dialogue between experiment and theory that would lead to the modern Scientific Revolution.
>
> Leonardo da Vinci, had he published his scientific writings during his lifetime, would have been considered the father of modern science, rather than Galileo born 112 years after.

The mathematical and the philosophical writings of Descartes (1596–1650) marked a turning point. Discoveries through the mid-millennium, such as the Davis back staff in 1594 for navigating at sea, the microscope in Holland in 1595, and the telescope in 1608, accelerated the ability to make observations, hypotheses, and experiments previously considered impossible. Copernicus and Galileo upset papal authority by showing the sun to be the center of our galaxy based purely on observation. Art and science marched together. Just as the Romans empirically used applied mathematics to build their marvelous aqueducts, the architects of the Middle Ages embellished the principles of mathematics further in building their magnificent cathedrals.

Observations and trial and error eventually led to advances in experimentation. Benjamin Franklin understood the basis for attracting lightning. It was not, however, until the discoverer of oxygen, Joseph Priestly (1774), and the genius Michael Faraday (1791–1867) introduced experimentation and the notion of an experimental laboratory that the concept of the scientific method was clearly advancing. It may seem a simple evolutionary process, but the development of the scientific method was a very long and tedious effort over many centuries—the work of many brilliant contributors in many fields of endeavor, including chemistry, physics, astronomy, and medicine. The advancement became sophisticated and accelerative to the extent that the sixteenth through early eighteenth centuries are referred to as the Scientific Revolution. The Scientific Revolution, it must be emphasized, was primarily the creation of Western civilization. The Chinese, as pointed out by the eminent scholar Joseph Needham,[5] from antiquity spent centuries developing many quite elegant and sophisticated products and inventions in many fields of undertaking but never really understood or, in the end, developed and used the scientific method until the twentieth century.

Bernard Lewis, the eminent Arabic scholar, wrote that up until the eighteenth century, with a few exceptions, no European books were translated into Arabic or Turkish or Persian languages.[6] He went on to comment:

> It was military necessity, even more than the need for political intelligence that drove Muslims to undertake venturing into infidel lands, even worse, the distasteful task of learning infidel languages.

The self-imposed isolation of the Ottoman Empire, together with the near-continued state of war between the Western world and the Muslim from the late sixteenth century (the Ottoman-Hapsburg Wars) to 1920, goes a long way to account for the failure of progress of the scientific method and science in general in Islamic culture. The Treaty of Sèvres in August of 1920 itemized the dismemberment of the Ottoman Empire by the victorious Western powers, including their Russian and Greek allies. As Lewis[7] further summarizes:

> The Turks finally came to barriers which they could not cross or remove, posing grave problems to a society and polity that for centuries had been shaped and maintained by a process of continuous conquest (jihad).

The paralyzing effect of fundamentalist demonology upon objective learning and the scientific method may be coming to an end in the twenty-first century. The uprisings in the Islamic world referred to as the "Arab Spring" may see a return to learning and a rebirth of Islamic efforts toward science. With revolution and evolution, the Middle East may again find a renewed age of science. Let us hope. In the meantime, it suffices to say that the development of the scientific methodology was *primarily a European accomplishment*, as noted by Thomas Kuhn[8]:

Every civilization of which we have records has possessed a technology, an art, a religion, a political system, and laws and so on. In many cases those facets of civilizations have been as developed as our own. But only the civilizations that descend from Hellenic Greece have possessed more than the most rudimentary science. The bulk of scientific knowledge is a product of Europe in the last four centuries. No other place and time have supported the very special communities from which scientific productivity comes.

As we highlight key developments from the Age of Enlightenment (eighteenth century) to the present, the research by James Lind on scurvy (vitamin C deficiency) is a true early advancement. Lind, a Scottish physician, conducted the first ever clinical trial confirming the value of a controlled experiment as an essential part of the scientific method. In 1753, Lind published his experiments on seamen in the British Navy at sea using different agents in separate groups and pointed to the value of "citrus." Yet it was not until after 1800 that lemon juice was provided in sufficient supply to be part of the daily ration in the British Navy. That delay may seem absurd, but comparing it to the fact that the efficacy of citrus fruits in preventing scurvy was known by John Woodall (1557–1643), surgeon to the British East India Company two centuries prior, propagation of scientific information was slowly improving. Science was not served by any recognized means of sharing new discoveries. Although there were early scientific and philosophical publications—journals, they were not disseminated in significant numbers, and so discoveries were most often simply ignored. The first edition of Philosophical Transactions of the Royal Society was published in 1665, and it was not until the early nineteenth century that the rigor of research and wide dissemination became a mark of the scientific method. Today we take for granted the abundance of peer-reviewed journals, with the near-instant transmission of information on the internet.

During the twentieth century, the diversity of science makes the description of the history of the scientific method more complex. The application of the scientific method in a variety of fields generated the growth and specialization in a wide range of disciplines such as chemistry, physics, medicine, and astronomy. Each discipline in its turn generated new branches of learning, both basic and applied. Chemistry divided into organic and inorganic chemistry; physics into areas of matter and energy; medicine into pharmacology, surgery, and psychiatry as examples. Each specialized area of science begot other areas of specialization, and a cascading growth beyond the wildest imagination of pioneer contributors attested to the value of the scientific method.

In addition to the exponential growth in scientific information was the increasing sophistication across all aspects of the scientific method itself. For example, the development of blind and double-blinded experimentation in testing various hypotheses added to the certainty of the effectiveness of various procedures, drugs, and medications. A deeper understanding of the placebo effect is another example of the diversity of sophistication in many fields of medicine. Further expansion of technology led to the Hubble Telescope and a new appreciation of the origins of the universe. Later this decade, NASA will launch the Webb Telescope that will bring further observations and speculation on the "Big Bang" event.

Perhaps the most astounding development in both the sophistication of the scientific method and the march of technological instrumentation and the storage and dissemination of information is the building of the computer. The first computers in the late 1940s, emerging from the attempt to make calculators more useful, were as large as a room. It was a long way from 1801 when Joseph Marie Jacquard made an improvement to the textile loom by introducing a series of punched paper cards as a template which allowed his loom to automatically weave intricate patterns. Even the developers of the first large computers in the early 1950s had no idea that they would need more than a few. Sometimes our scientists did not understand what they had developed. Scientists at Xerox in Palo Alto, California, had the first PC (personal computer) and did not understand what to do with it. Others did, and although it may not be a linear story to tell, an astounding acceleration in the use and application of the computer has brought us to the age of the internet with all its glitter and "twitter."

Neither time nor space will allow a comprehensive review of the history of the scientific method. I do not have time to tell you about Galen of Pergamum in the first century, whose writings on anatomy were held sacrosanct into the sixteenth century, nor of Andreas Vesalius's *De Humani Corporis Fabricant (On the Structure of the Human Body)*—1543, nor of Isaac Newton's contributions to the scientific revolution—*Philosophiae Naturalis Principia Mathematica*—1687, nor of William Harvey's *On the Motion of the Heart and Blood in Animals*—1628. The lives of these great and courageous contributors and others can be found in other references.[9, 10, 11] The purpose of this sketchy review is to emphasize the fact that the birth and development of the scientific method was a very long, tedious, and hard road: long in taking twenty-five centuries, tedious in the plodding progress in the thought processes, and hard in the trial and error of technological developments and tardy evolution in the dissemination of results. It was only possible by the perseverance of the essentials of the method—the *observation* the *hypothesis*, the *testing*, the *verification*, the *dissemination*, and the *application*. We, at the start of the twenty-first century, take this all for granted. We need to have this history in mind when considering our science today and keep in mind how much is involved in gaining one single new fact and what it means to verify that it is true.

Endnotes

Part I
Chapter 1: Historical Perspective
[1] Bertrand Russell, *Religion & Science* (Oxford University Press, 1935), 8.

2   Carlo Rovelli, *The First Scientist, Anaximander and His Legacy* (Yardley, PA: Westholme Publishing, 2007).

3   Jonathan Lyons, "Early Islamic Medicine," *Latham's Quarterly* II, no. 4 (2009), 191.

4   Walter Isaacson, *Leonardo da Vinci* (Simon & Schuster, 2017), 173–6.

5   Joseph Needham and Ling Wang, *Science and Civilization in China: History of Scientific Thought* (Cambridge University Press, 1956).

6   Bernard Lewis, *Islam and the West* (New York: Oxford University Press, 1993), 34. See Fatma Müge Göçek, *East Encounters West: France and the Ottoman Empire in the Eighteenth Century* (New York and Oxford, 1987), 69–70, 80.

7   Ibid., 28.

8   Thomas S. Kuhn, *The Structure of Scientific Revolutions*, 3rd ed. (Chicago, IL: University of Chicago Press, 1996), 167–168.

9   John Gribbin, *The Scientists: A History of Science Told through the Lives of Its Greatest Inventors* (New York: Random House, 2002).

10   Roy Porter, ed., *Cambridge Illustrated History of Medicine* (Cambridge University Press, 1996).

11   A. McGee Harvey et al. *A Model of Its Kind: A Centennial History of Medicine at Johns Hopkins* I (Baltimore: The Johns Hopkins University Press, 1989), 50.

CHAPTER 2

The American Scene

No one can really feel at home in the modern world and judge the nature of its problems—and the possible solutions to these problems—unless one has had some intelligent notion of what science is up to.

—*Isaac Asimov, 1987*[1]

The Scientific Illiteracy of the American People

Native American Medicine

THE AMERICAN INDIANS had their physicians. They were called shamans. In addition to treating wounds and administering herbs, the shamans were trained in complex rituals sometimes involving the entire community using chants, drums, rattles, and dancing. In the Navajo culture, healing ceremonies often lasted a week or more. Patients paid the shaman, who often became quite wealthy. The Apaches believed that the shaman's power came directly from a god or through the application of some sacred relic.

Early American Folk Medicine

In the backwoods of early rural America, various folk cures were called "simples." The remedies included salves, teas, tonics, ointments, and poultices. There is little record of what worked as the following ditty recounts.

> For every illness under the sun,
> There is a cure or there is none.
> If there is a cure, go and find it.
> If there is none, never mind it.

Mothers and grandmothers were most often the family's folk healers. One example is a cure for both asthma and hay fever using tea made from sumac leaves. All was not ignorance. Some advice made sense, for example:

> After breakfast work a while;
> After dinner set a while;
> After supper walk a mile.

Because there wasn't much science, there wasn't much medicine. It was not until the middle of the twentieth century that antibiotics became available. Prior to the twentieth century, it was not a question of the public's lack of understanding of medical science. There was simply not that much medical science. In 1899, the *Merck Manual* for practicing physicians had 192 pages. (Latest twentieth edition has 3,250.)

The Patent Medicine Age

Patent or proprietary medicine peddlers were common in the nineteenth century. This was the age of Lydia Pinkham's Vegetable Compound, Hamlin's Wizard Oil and Kick-a-poo Indian Sagwa. Most were useless, but many were responsible for contributing to alcoholism, drug addiction, and mercury poisoning. One of the leading muckrakers was Samuel Hopkins Adams,[2] who wrote a series of articles in *Collier's Weekly* magazine bashing the false claims made by patent medicine manufacturers and in a book called *The Great American Fraud*. Through such efforts, President Theodore Roosevelt signed the Pure Food and Drug Law in 1906.

Recent History in the United States—Scientific Illiteracy

The Flexner Report: Bringing Science to Medicine

In examining the origins and extent of the public's lack of understanding of science, Chris Mooney, in his book *Unscientific America*,[3] states:

> 80 percent of Americans can't read the *New York Times* science section and only half of the adult populace knows the earth orbits the sun once per year.

One can blame a deficient public education system or the elitist element in the scientists themselves for not being able to connect or the ready availability of bad science or the fact that science competes with an array of interests including crime, sports, and religion. All four may be contributing causes of scientific illiteracy. The underlying cause, however, is much deeper. It is simply the failure to comprehend the meaning of the scientific method. Many people may have and talk about scientific knowledge. They may have a wealth of scientific facts, but that does not mean they understand the fundamental notion of the scientific method. This state of affairs is a salient symptom of anti-intellectualism in the United States in general and the lack of basic curiosity and a questioning mind. As a consequence, science fails to become a disciplining force in our political or cultural life.

The lack of scientific understanding was splendidly illustrated in the course of the Republican primaries for president in 2012. Contender Newt Gingrich, attempting to sway voters in Florida, proposed a Moon colony and even extended the argument in predicting that it would become the next sate in the union. The tragedy is that no one in the NASA community seemed to object to such an absurd proposal. There was little or no debate—not even a sturdy journalist with the courage to question openly or to question the motivation of the candidate who was attempting to gather votes among NASA employees and engineers who would not want to be seen as questioning their budget objectives. A nation that understood science would not tolerate this level of discourse in such an important arena.

According to the National Science Foundation, only 15 percent of the people follow science.[4] Perhaps this is a consequence of a lack of journalists, suitably interested and educated not only in the nature of science but in the ability and skills necessary to propagate a sufficient level of understanding. The National Association of Science Writers was founded in 1934 and, for several decades, enjoyed a growing number of accomplished communicators. The trend in the recent past is that newspapers, in a frantic attempt to save their bottom line and compete with the internet, have greatly reduced their staff dedicated to science journalism. As the British scientist and author C. P. Snow noted, "science was not being translated." In a speech in 1959[5] entitled "The Two Cultures and the Scientific Revolution," in lamenting the gap between science and the humanities, he pointed out that the two not only failed to communicate but distained each other, yielding a "gulf of mutual incomprehension." It may very well be this gulf of incomprehension is because scientists and the public cannot speak the same language. The public never learned it.

In spite of the widely acclaimed growth of liberal education curricula, there continues to be misunderstanding. Many colleges and universities allow graduation without any intention whatsoever to assigning a discipline in one of the sciences. There are only a few colleges and universities which require, as part of the core curriculum, some minimum science education. Requirements for teaching science at primary and secondary levels are extremely minimal. The recent No Child Left Behind Legislation is an effort in the right direction, requiring minimum standards in the subject being taught. There is no evidence, however, that this part of the legislation has been properly funded or rigorously assessed. It is possible to continue with a litany of various aspects of our failure to generate a scientifically literate public, but it is more important to proceed to pursue some viable solution.

There is a solution for the problem of science illiteracy. It is very simple. Everyone must be a scientist by some minimal standard. That standard should include fundamentals of the scientific method. It should start in the first grade of every school. It should be continuous until the completion of the education at whatever level. It should be like learning to read with continuous improvement in reading skills throughout life. Understanding should be the new life skill. In short, to our education system, we must add science to the three *R*s, making a universal commitment to a new quadrate: reading, writing, arithmetic, and science. We must do this not simply to avoid the perils of quackery but to understand the place of science in our survival in the twenty-first century—on this planet—in this universe. As a citizen of our neighborhood, of this nation, of Western culture, as an inhabitant of this planet with seven billion others, we cannot reach our goals of understanding and survival without an improved understanding of science—without being scientifically literate. Democracy will not survive without an informed electorate, indeed, no form of government will.

The twentieth century opened with a number of developments that sponsored the growth of sound science, the emergence of the United States as a leader in science and a trusting public that began to appreciate the value of science. In 1901, funded by oil tycoon John D. Rockefeller, the Rockefeller Institute of Medicine (now since 1965 Rockefeller University) opened in New York City. This was the first American institution dedicated to biomedical research and, through the years, has fostered many Nobel Prize recipients in medicine. The Rockefeller Institute contributed to medical science in many ways. The institute's first medical director was William Henry Welch, founding dean of the Johns Hopkins Medical School (1893) and responsible for bringing Simon Flexner to New York to be the institute's first director of laboratories. World-class research led to many signal discoveries, including the first cultures of the causative agent of syphilis, the role of viruses in disease, the identification of blood groups which allowed safe transfusion, showing that genes were made of DNA, among so many others. The Rockefeller Institute also published several journals for the dissemination of discoveries, notably the *Journal of Experimental Medicine*, and supported the founding in 1896 of Johns Hopkins School of Medicine.

In 1910, Abraham Flexner, brother of Simon Flexner, funded by another great philanthropic power, the Carnegie Foundation, published his report, *Medical Education in the United States and Canada*. This landmark study was a "scathing indictment of American medical education" of the time.[6] Of the 150 medical schools then standing, Flexner had mild approval for but five. Flexner's critical observation was that the intellectual basis of modern medicine was not being incorporated into the teaching and research curriculum, that the scientific method was not being employed. It is hard to imagine the disarray and haphazardly practiced medicine in the early years of the twentieth century, but following the Flexner Report, and following the efforts of several of the great philanthropic foundations in the early quarter of the century, order and discipline of the scientific method was brought to medical education. Such progress brought about the concept of full-time teaching, research, and practice which saw the development and growth of the great teaching hospitals and clinics on this continent and the undisputed reputation of world leadership formerly belonging to France and Germany. The system of residency training postmedical degree started in the first part of the twentieth century flourished in the later half and proved the foundation of specialty research and training that became a model worldwide.

The funding for atomic research and the development of the atomic bomb gave science a new prominence in the public's mind during and shortly after WWII. The place of scientists, particularly physicists, gained recognition earned by the understanding that it was their work that provided the convincing victory. Enter another report[7] entitled *Science, the Endless Frontier* by Vannevar Bush, president of the Carnegie institution of Washington, emphasizing the importance of science to the future of America. The report reasoned:

> The government should invest heavily in basic scientific research conducted at US Universities, and in turn, the knowledge produced would lead to technological advances that would enrich our lives—improving health and medicine, spurring economic growth and the creation of jobs, and strengthening the national defense. A generation of scientific talent would be trained in the process.

Unfortunately, the vision got blunted by the fog of reality. Federal funding of research and development did increase substantially after the war and into the decade of the fifties, but two unforeseen forces became notable. The first was that funding was largely provided through elite networks between various government agencies created during those years and what was then considered the top universities. The second development was that the US military co-opted an accelerating amount of funding for extensions of wartime technologies. As a result, little trickled down to the education system throughout the country. Little, that is, until the Russians launched Sputnik in 1957, and the realization that we were apparently a second-rate country hit the fan.

Federal R&D in 1940 was about $74 million. For fiscal 2012[7]:

President Obama had requested $147.911 billion for research and development (R&D) in FY2012, a $772 million (0.5%) increase from the FY2010 actual R&D funding level of $147.139 billion. Congress plays a central role in defining the nation's R&D priorities, especially with respect to two overarching issues: the extent to which the federal R&D investment can grow in the context of increased pressure on discretionary spending and how available funding will be prioritized and allocated. Below is a historical chart from the American Association for the Advancement of Science (AAAS):

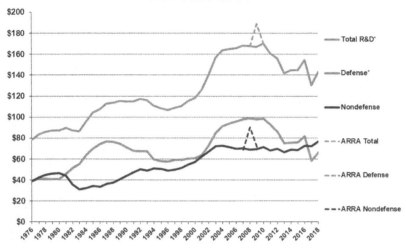

Trends in Federal R&D, FY 1976-2018

in billions of constant FY 2018 dollars

*Note: Beginning in FY 2017, a new official definition of R&D has been adopted by federal agencies. Late-stage development, testing, and evaluation programs, primarily within the Defense Department, are no longer counted as R&D.
Source: AAAS analyses of historical budget and agency data and FY 2018 omnibus legislation. R&D includes conduct and facilities. © AAAS | 2018

Permission to reproduce this chart was granted by the American Association For the Advancement of Science, Matt Hourihan, Director of R&D Budget and Policy Program.

Under President Obama's request, six federal agencies would receive 94.8% of total federal R&D spending: The Department of Defense (DOD, 51.8%), Department of Health and Human Services (largely the National Institutes of Health, 21.9%), National Aeronautics and Space Administration (6.6%), Department of Energy (DOE, 8.8%), National Science Foundation (NSF, 4.3%), and Department of Agriculture (1.5%). The Department of Energy would receive the largest R&D dollar increase for FY2012 of any agency, $2.153 billion (19.9%) above its FY2010 funding level. Nondefense R&D has been relatively constant 2004–2018 as noted.

Failure of the Education System

Level of Preparedness of Teachers Lacking

From my perspective as a citizen member of a public-school board of education back in the 1980s, I believed that one of the major failures of our system was the level of education of teachers in the United States. A look at most of the four-year programs to gain a degree was not even up to standard for most liberal arts programs, and mostly bare minimums in the subjects they were to teach. A load of "fluff" education courses was notable. A second observation was the apathy of the general public in participation in improving the system. This reality, together with the political force of the teacher unions, together with underfunding of poorer school districts in the country, contributed to the charter school and voucher movements.

Although there has been progress since the shock of Sputnik, there is a large gap between our level of science education and the rest of the world. Derek Bok, former president of Harvard,[8] points out the detrimental effects of commercialization in the institutions of higher learning. He also points to the eroding effect of big-time college athletics on academic values.[9] The jury is still out on the net benefits to the education system from the development and acceleration of the internet, but most feel they are positive, but we are way behind the potential. Most educators feel that the Bush administration's No Child Left Behind Legislation has been positive, but test scores are highly variable. In fact, the question of testing in our public schools has come into question. Although the legislation mandated the requirement that teachers prove proficiency in the subject they teach, there remains a gap to that goal.

Anti-Intellectualism a Feature of Early American Education

Anti-intellectualism has been a detrimental force against raising the level of understanding of science and the scientific method. Richard Hofstadter,[10] an American mid-twentieth-century historian, pointed to the great irony "that the United States was founded by intellectuals; for throughout most of our political history, the intellectual has been an outsider, a servant, or a scapegoat." He pointed out that "while most of the Founding Fathers were still alive, a reputation for intellect became a political disadvantage." Hofstadter[11] reviews the several causes of anti-intellectualism in the United States, including fundamentalist religions attacking the public-school education system. He quotes William Jennings Bryan, three-time candidate for the presidency in a speech before Seventh-Day Adventists in 1924, declaring,

> All the ills from which America suffers can be traced back to the teaching of evolution. It would be better to destroy every other book ever written and save just the first three verses of Genesis.

He reminds us that the time of our founding fathers was a zenith in intelligent leadership in our political history—John Adams, George Mason, Alexander Hamilton, Thomas Jefferson, and Benjamin Franklin as examples. Yet the system deteriorated quickly. Tocqueville in 1835[12] observed the "vulgar demeanor" of members of the House of Representatives. In 1850 Francis Bowen in the *North American Review* found both Houses of Congress had been "transformed into noisy and quarrelsome debating clubs." "Furious menaces and bellowing exaggeration take the place of calm and dignified debate; the halls of the capitol often present scenes which would disgrace a beer-garden; and Congress attains the unenviable fame of being the most helpless, disorderly, and inefficient legislative body which can be found in the civilized world."[13]

Hofstadter argues that President Theodore Roosevelt and the Progressive era went a long way to close the gap between intellectuals and power.[14] "In this he did more to restore mind and talents to public affairs than any president since Lincoln, probably more indeed than any since Jefferson." Other than the presidency of Woodrow Wilson and the candidacy of Adlai Stevenson in 1952, our political system did not resonate with intellectuals in either party until the presidency of Barak Obama. The full impact of his ability to meld a brilliant intellect with the craft of political leadership will certainly be the cornerstone of his legacy.

From our earliest history, education has always been the force against anti-intellectualism. Samuel Eliot Morison, eminent American historian commenting on early New England, notes, "One trait in which the New Englanders excelled the old country was their emphasis on education. Free popular education has been the most lasting contribution of early New England to the United States, and possibly the most beneficial."[15] "The first college was founded at Cambridge in a small house in a cow-yard given by the town and named after its earliest benefactor, the Reverend John Harvard, who dying at the age of thirty, left the college half his fortune and a library of 400 volumes. In 1650 Harvard College was given a charter by the Bay Colony, which declared its purpose to be 'the advancement of all good literature, arts and *sciences*.'" By the first half of the eighteenth century, there were other colleges in the colonies: The College of New Jersey (Princeton, 1746), King's College (Columbia 1754), and the University of Pennsylvania at Philadelphia (1749).

The high road to respect for learning was not an even one, however. From 1828 to the Civil War, Andrew Jackson and his brand of democracy brought us to what Morison called "the great American tragedy,"[16] traces of which linger to this day. He further argues, "Jacksonian Democracy catered to mediocrity, diluted politics with the incompetent and the corrupt, and made conditions increasingly unpleasant for gentlemen in public life." It must be pointed out, however, that Jackson did support free public education.[16]

How is it that the American people with a dedicated history toward education allowed such a coexisting tendency to anti-intellectualism? We began our history establishing free common schools as emphasized by George Washington in his *Farewell Address*. We had excellent leaders who understood the value of good education. Jefferson warned in 1816:

> If a nation expects to be ignorant and free
> in a state of civilization, it expects what never was
> and never will be.

The dream was quick to come up short. Horace Mann, from his seat as secretary of the Massachusetts Board of Education in 1837, was an early forceful critic. He was afraid that "neglectful school committees, incompetent teachers, and an indifferent public, may go on degrading each other" until the whole idea of free schools would be abandoned.[16] There have been many indications of failure, but Hofstadter[17] comes to defend the system.

> If the American public Educational system is measured not by some abstract standards of perfection but by the goals for which it was originally established, must it not be considered a success? On this count there is undoubtedly much to be said. The American System of common schools was meant to take a vast, heterogeneous, and mobile population, recruited from manifold sources and busy with manifold tasks and forge it into a nation, make it literate, and get at least the minimal civic competence necessary to the operation of republican institutions. This much it did; and if in the greater part of the 19th century the United States did not astound the world with its achievements in a high culture, its schools at least help to create a common level of opinion and capacity that was repeatedly noticed with admiration by foreign observers.

Hofstadter concluded that the prime benefits of mass education were primarily political and economic resulting in "forging an acceptable form of democratic society".

Herein lies the answer to the problem of congruent anti-intellectualism as simply the gap between the good and competent as the school system was designed to accomplish and the next level of education necessary to understanding the more complex—and it is the complex that we must strive to understand in the current world. Throughout the twentieth century and into this twenty-first century, there have been valiant efforts to close the gap between the good and the excellent. Perhaps it would be easier on us to refer to this gap, not as anti-intellectualism but the complexity gap or the excellence gap, and I could accept that except for one thing. The ardent anti-intellectual forces at work today in the United States refuse to accept the truth of science and the scientific method, and what is worse, they generate a troglodytic ignorance through their religious beliefs and corrupt partisan politics that is incompatible with progress and possibly even survival.

The Rise of Charter Schools

The rise and growth of charter schools in the United States is offered as further evidence of failure of the public-school system. Charter schools receive public funding but operate independently of the public-school district wherein they are located. Since Minnesota first legislated charter schools in 1991, forty-three states have followed, and by 2011, there were over two million students attending.[18] By 2009 school year, the majority of New Orleans schoolchildren were in charter schools.[19] This movement has been a combination of several forces: (1) dissatisfaction with performance, (2) perceived bureaucracy of the system, (3) dissatisfaction with teacher unions and their political influence.

As a product of public education, I have been a strong supporter of public education, having served three terms on a public-school board. I am skeptical of the charter school movement, mostly because the effort to generate for-profit schools exposed the effort to the greed of Wall Street. A significant number of charter schools are for-profit, and the drive to make a profit will run the danger of compromising quality. Even non-for-profits are paying their administrators high salaries and squeezing costs at all other levels. There is even the criticism that non-for-profits are the child of corporate sources which, in turn, are hired by the nonprofits to run them, wherein lies their profit.

The for-profit schools and their stocks in the college-level category have had their day in the sun and have plunged, according to a recent *Barron's* article.[20] Five years ago, the for-profit education industry was the darling of Wall Street. The University of Phoenix operator Apollo Education Group (symbol APOL) had revenue growing at 25% annually, but by 2009, federal regulators reined the industry's high-pressure sales tactics and loading of students with government-backed student loans and questioned the value of the degrees sold. The stock is down 41%, as is many in the same category— Strayer Education (ESI) is down 64%, ITT Educational Services (ESI) is down 90%. Only two others have beaten the NASDAQ average.

As to whether charter schools are better, the jury is still out and the debate rages.[21] I can only speculate that if all the money and effort that went into the charter school movement were applied to the public-school system, the result would have been better. I can only hope that perhaps the competition between the two systems, public schools vs. charter schools, will result in an improved understanding of science and one of its most import applications—a critical approach to people's choice of health options.

The Political Force of Teachers Unions

In the meantime, there is ample room for teachers, through their unions or professional organizations, to foster improved preparation standards, generate an internship of perhaps two years between college and job entry, and improve proficiency in the subject they teach, accept the concept of merit pay, and like other professions, aspire to continuing education programs. Continued progress will not only strengthen our public education system but inoculate us against the shock of another Sputnik event revealing our deep deficiencies.

Rise of the Religious Right and the Anti-Science Movement

The Religious Right, or the "Moral Majority" as they liked to call themselves, formed in the early 1970s. Essayist Amanda Marcotte, in a recent article,[22] quoted Randle Balmer, a Dartmouth professor writing on the origins of the Moral Majority:

> It wasn't Roe vs. Wade that woke the sleeping dragon of the evangelical vote. It was Green vs. Kentucky a 1970 decision stripping tax-exempt status from the "segregation academies"— private Christian schools that were set up in response to Brown vs. Board of Education, where the practice of barring black students continued.

The article further states that anger about forced desegregation of private schools galvanized Conservative Christians. Bob Jones University stalled and resisted admitting black students, forcing the IRS to strip its tax-exempt status in 1976, an event that spurred evangelical leaders to action. Jerry Falwell and Paul Weyrich, two Conservative activists who had been seeking a way to marshal evangelicals into a Republican voting bloc, led the movement. They realized, however, that a larger force could be mobilized by adding anti-abortion as an issue. They were also quick to add anti-Darwin positions in their education policy, even to the extent of preventing the purchase of biology textbooks teaching evolutionary theory. Rev. Jerry Falwell wrote:

> I hope to see the day when, as in the early days of our country, we don't have public schools. The churches will have taken them over again and Christians will be running them.[23]

This is not to say there is anything anti-intellectual in fundamentalist, Pentecostal, or charismatic churches. They help people of such persuasion and offer a sense of belonging. But when religious zealots bring governance by "the Bible" and the inerrancy of scripture into the public square, forcing anti-abortion law, ostracizing homosexuals, excluding the science of evolution in public schools, debunking the evidence for global warming, and denying the basic tenants of science and the scientific method, then anti-intellectual is hardly a strong-enough criticism. It must be recognized that the Republican Party is now strongly influenced, if not controlled, by the Christian Conservatives and based mostly in our southern states. President George W. Bush furthered the agenda with his "faith-based initiative" which blurred the lines between church and state, between secular social service programs and religious activities. The political war against women and women's rights by the Republican representatives in Congress is a matter of public record and needs no references. Anti-intellectualism is alive and well in Texas. Witness the Texas Republican Party Platform 2004:

> The Republican party of Texas affirms the
> United States of America is a Christian Nation…

The very fact that, according to Pew Research,[24] the three issues—evolution, homosexuality, and global warming—are the outstanding points of friction between secular governance and the Conservative Christian voting is an indictment of our level of discourse and understanding of science. But to be fair, it must be pointed out that anti-science is not the exclusive province of the far right. As science writers Alex Berezow and Hank Campbell, according to an Amazon review of their book *Science Left Behind*, have drawn open the curtain on the left's fear of science.[25] As the book reveals:

Vague inclinations about the wholesomeness of all things natural, the unhealthiness of the unnatural, and many other seductive fallacies have led to an epidemic of misinformation. The results: public health crises, damaging and misguided policies—and worst of all, a new culture war over basic scientific facts—in which the left is just as culpable as a right.

Predating anti-science in politics was the challenge to science by radical academics starting in the early thirties, discussed in detail by Timothy Ferris in his book *The Science of Liberty*[26]:

> Rather than investigate how science interacts with liberal and illiberal political systems, radical academics began challenging science itself, claiming that it was just one among many truth games and could not obtain objective knowledge because there was no objective reality... These recondite theories went by a variety of names— deconstructionism, multiculturalism, science studies, cultural studies: which Ferris sums up under the umbrella term *postmodernism.*

Most of these academics were in philosophy departments and had no record of training or accomplishments in any branch of science. Ferris further points out that the foundations of this endeavor were laid, to some extent unwittingly by the Viennese philosopher Karl Popper and the American historian of science Thomas Kuhn.[27]

Failure of Critical Health Journalism

Not Enough Journalists with Science Background

Hardly a day passes without a report on a health item of some kind. One day is a study on how coffee drinking causes pancreatic cancer. Another reports on margarine being better for you than butter and another that saccharin causes bladder cancer. As Berezow and Campbell point out[28]:

> The media do an enormous disservice to the public by reporting every study that suggests that any chemical-of-the-week is bad for you. Most likely, within a month or two, another study will show the exact opposite. By reporting every twist

and turn, the media causes the public to become jaded and distrustful of the information they receive. Perhaps that is the biggest reason we live in a society full of chemophobes.

The result is confusion. There is little attempt on the part of the reporter to lend a critical eye to the information. Indeed, the number of reporters and broadcasters with any knowledge of science or the scientific method is limited. This is not to say that we have not made progress in public policy regarding health issues. The mandatory legislation on seat belts, bans on smoking, and crackdowns on drinking and driving can be attributed in part to reporting the science behind the need for change.

Lack of Discrimination

There are many thousands of publications in hundreds of scientific journals every year from nearly every country in the world. Only a very few reach the level of "critical new" information, and they are usually reported as sound bites from a reporter called by an author of a paper and often appear in the tabloids at the supermarket checkout line first. What is not reported is that science, and medical science in particular, is best interpreted by seasoned observers and results are usually only of significance after repeating studies and reaching consensus. But that is not our lifestyle. Worst of all is misinformation tucked into print and TV advertising or reports that are produced by the pharmaceutical companies with obvious bias declaring "revolutionary" or "breakthrough" treatments, often with small-print footnotes de-emphasizing the absence of FDA approval. The so-called anecdote or a spectacular cure is a common journalistic trademark.

We would expect the heavy hitters in the media—*the New York Times*, *Washington Post*, and *Time*—would be more dependable, but as Jane Hu[29] reported last year that *The Times* reporter Nicholas Kristof wrote about hurricanes:

> Americans expect male (named) hurricanes to be violent and deadly, but they mistake female (named) hurricanes as dainty or wimpish and don't take adequate precautions.

This, after the original report had been investigated, was reevaluated and clearly debunked as bad science in several sources. Other bad science reporting by *the Post* and *Time* were cited as well.

We cannot expect all reporters to be educated in science and medical science in particular. The Australian Science Media Center maintains a valuable website (www.scijourno.com.au) inspiring science journalism training. It serves up to six modules to educate media students. Since 1938, the Neiman Foundation for Journalism at Harvard has sponsored yearlong fellowships dedicated to improving the standards of journalism in all fields. Many leading newspapers including *The New York Times* dedicate a science section weekly usually containing a goodly amount of information on medical and health science. Reporters Nicholas Bakalar, Jane Brody, Gina Kolata, C. Claiaborne Ray, John Markoff, George Johnson, and Abigail Zuber MD are among the best. Dr. Perri Klass, professor of pediatrics and journalism at NYU, is an example of a physician writing about evidence-based medicine in her specialty. There is, however, a trend away from the traditional print sources, radio and news broadcasts toward online web sources and blogs. Berezow and Campbell note[30]:

> A new generation of science bloggers—many of whom are scientists—is communicating complex issues to the public. Therefore, we have hope that a new era of science is dawning.

Googling "medical science journalism" brings forth a batch of institutions working to improve medical information reporting. There are science and medical journalism programs at the University of North Carolina, Boston University, and Arizona State University and a new program at the Walter Cronkite School of Journalism, to name a few. Eric Topol, MD, an internist and leader in medical information technology, is blazing the trail in reporting on how the new information systems are altering the practice of medicine.[31] The bottom line is that science journalism and health areas in particular have been wanting, but there is reason to believe that it is improving. The lesson is that, as readers and listeners and watchers, we need to learn about our sources and constantly question the validity of advice.

The Story of CERN

Lack of Scientific Understanding Brings a Missed Opportunity

An excellent example of anti-intellectualism and anti-science and missed academic and business opportunities occurred in the late 1980s in Upstate New York. On January 14, 1988, *The New York Times* reported that then governor Mario Cuomo had withdrawn a proposal to make Wayne County near Rochester, New York, the home of a $4.4 billion atom smasher (supercollider). The European Organization for Nuclear Research, known as CERN, is a research organization that operates the largest particle physics laboratory in the world, established in 1954 and based in the northwest suburbs of Geneva under Franco-Swiss border. The organization sought to enlarge their operation by building a large superconducting super-collider (SSC) in a twenty-seven-kilometer (fifty-three-mile) circumference tunnel underground and had pledged to a portion of the funding. Several sites in the United States were in the running. Wayne County had most favorable geologic stability and was, among seven other sites, a leading contender for the massive project which would have meant thousands of jobs and enormous prestige for the University of Rochester and surrounding colleges, particularly their physics departments, not to mention the sustainability of such an endeavor and keeping the US at the frontier of particle physics. The distinguishing aspect of the story was the instant opposition by the citizens. They formed CATCH, "Citizens Against the Collider Here." President Reagan had even approved the proposal for submission to Congress in January 1987 and included funds in his budget for fiscal year 1988 to initiate the SSC project. I recall a public hearing in which a farmer dressed in his overalls, red suspenders, and manure-tipped boots declared in a loud voice, "I ain't gonna tolerate no electrons running under my cows." And our elected representatives caved. Representatives Frank Horton and Louise Slaughter (one of the few members of Congress with a scientific degree) came out against it. Senator Daniel Patrick Moynihan followed, and Governor Mario Cuomo withdrew the application. The project was awarded to Waxahachie, Texas. It died in 1993 midway through construction when Congress withdrew funds after spending $2 billion of an estimated $10 billion. In the end, an uninformed public and economic arguments trumped scientific curiosity. As one blogger pointed out, the cost of completing the SSC would be the equivalent of fighting four months of the Iraq War.

The Medicalization of Everything

The Need of Pharma to Create Markets

Peter Conrad, a professor of sociology at Brandeis University in Boston, has studied and written on the medicalization of so many aspects of life.[32]

> The key to medicalization is definition. That is, a problem is defined in medical terms, described using medical language, understood through the adoption of a medical framework, or "treated" with a medical intervention.

He notes that medicalization results in conditions that are not ipso facto illness or disease and *making them medical.* Examples cited are homosexuality, sexual and gender differences, child abuse, emotions (e.g., shyness), stress, athletic underperformance, and aging. The result is creation of new medical consumer markets exploited by corporatized health systems, pharmaceutical companies, and members of the health professions and television. The use of direct to consumer (DTC) advertising has exploded and is very much an integral part of medicalization. As Conrad points out, Big Pharma creates markets by promoting "diseases."[33] Promotion of the aging male body as a disease ("low T") is another excellent example and has resulted in increased treatment with testosterone, disregarding the complications from cardiovascular events. Dr. Lisa Schwartz,[34] a professor at Dartmouth Institute for Health Policy and Clinical Practice, wrote:

> We're giving people hormones that we don't know they need, for a disease we don't know they have, and we don't know if it will help or harm them.

There is a corresponding "disease" called Hypoactive Sexual Desire Disorder (HSDD) for which clinical trials of a drug are underway for premenopausal women. Indeed, in the spectrum of medicalization, women are targeted far more than men. Conrad sees the marketing of diseases and then the selling drugs to treat is now common in the "post-Prozac era."

Exploitation of Athletic Performance

Athletes, from the time of ancient Greek games, have sought substances that would improve performance. These so-called ergogenic or performance-enhancement aids have infiltrated nearly every sport. In the early 1950s, steroids were the ergogenic drugs of choice. The International Olympic Committee (IOC) initiated testing in 1968 and banned steroid use in 1975.[35] The drive to take drugs to win has no limits.

> In a survey of 100 top runners, each was asked if he could take a pill that will allow him to be an Olympic champion but kill them in a year, over half the runners said they would take the pill.[36]

Athletes would rather die than find themselves on the short end of an uneven playing field and strive desperately to have the edge up on an even playing field. They gladly treat the lack of an edge as a disease, which is clearly absurd. There is no reason to believe that there will be any end to the medical competition to beat the athletic competition. Note the scandals in bike racing Tour de France. Wikipedia[36] records use of ergogenic agents starting in 1903—as long as the tour existed. Hence the quip "No dope, no hope." Lance Armstrong has become the poster boy of doping on the tour.

The medicalization of athletic performance has been insidious, dishonest, and destructive of our human and American values. When it tainted field and track, it was a scandal, but when it touched baseball and threatened golf, it became a national moral issue.

Targeting Women

Julie Holland, a psychiatrist in New York, notes how women are being targeted more than men.[37] She discerns how women's feelings are twisted into a form of disease. She notes in a recent *New York Times* opinion page:

> By evolutionary design, women are hard wired to be sensitive to our environments, empathetic to our children's needs and intuitive of our partner's intentions. Women's emotionality is a sign of health, not disease; is a source of power. We are under constant pressure to restrain our emotional lives. We have been taught to apologize for our tears, to suppress our anger and to fear being called hysterical. The pharmaceutical industry plays on that fear, targeting women in a barrage of advertising on daytime talk shows and in magazines. More Americans are on psychiatric medications than ever before, and in my experience, there stay on them far longer than ever intended. Sales of antidepressants and anti-anx-

iety meds have been booming in the past two decades, and they're recently been outpaced by an antipsychotic, *Abilify*, that is the number one seller of all drugs in the United States, not just psychiatric ones. As a psychiatrist practicing 20 years, I must tell you this is insane.

The lesson is clear. Big Pharma has made emotion a sign of disease.

Exploitation of Health Care Technology

Technological innovation is part of every field of health care, and it is clearly accelerating. Becker's Review, a med-tech website, offers the ten biggest advancements in health-care technology in the last ten years[38]:

1. Electronic health record
2. Mobile health devices
3. Telemedicine
4. Portal technology
5. Self-service kiosks
6. Remote monitoring tools
7. Sensors and wearable technology
8. Wireless communication
9. Real-time locating services
10. Pharmocogenomics / genome sequencing

In addition, each medical specialty has undergone remarkable technological advances: endoscopic surgery, arterial stents, endovascular repair of aneurysms of the aorta, ophthalmic lasers, and numerous radiological procedures, to name but a few. The growth in pharmaceutical companies bringing new drugs and devices before the FDA is truly astounding. There are over 170 pharmaceutical manufacturers listed in the US alone.[39] It is a challenge for each provider to keep up, let alone the public at large. The options available for any single condition can be paralyzing.

Moreover, innovation is the turbulence caused by the changes in health-care financing at both state and federal level. That, on the patient side, is accompanied by the revolutionary policy on the physician side, to change the delivery system from a fee-for-service to a results-oriented system. "Change" seems too simple a word to apply to our health-care system.

Medicalization of Food

Until the modern era, the major consideration was whether enough food was available. Indeed, in major portions of the world today, food insecurity is still a major issue. In developed countries, issues center on quality, pesticides, and biotechnology, plus issues of health and nutrition. There are even issues of social status. The Duchess of Windsor once remarked, "You can never be too rich or too thin," emphasizing the cultural forces at work.

Medicalization of obesity emerged in the 1950s. Obesity went from badness to sickness, from gluttony to eating disorder, from the personal responsibility realm to the responsibility of medical science. Obesity became a disease. International Classifications of Disease provided official sanction with the designated code (ICD-9-CM1990). The Metropolitan Life Insurance Company promulgated standards of ideal body weight in 1959 and revised upward in 1983 and 1990. Societies and journals were formed to address the new disease: the American Society of Bariatric Physicians, the Association for the Study of Obesity (1966), the *International Journal of Obesity, Obesity Research*, and *Obesity and Metabolism*. Numerous surgical procedures were performed and many abandoned. Laparoscopic gastric bypass is currently a procedure of choice.[40] Pharmacology companies came out with specialized products such as Metrical and various diets emphasizing low calories or high protein. Psychiatrists tried hypnosis, and behavioral modification programs in various national organizations were formed such as Weight Watchers. Millions of dollars are now being focused on research on obesity.

One cannot go grocery shopping in the United States today without being confronted with medicalized labeling of nearly every item. Food manufacturers claim an array of products that have health-promoting and disease-preventing attributes. As Germov and Williams[41] point out:

> Food manufacturers claim that developments in biotechnology and nutritional science allow them to produce so-called "functional foods," which allegedly have health promoting and disease preventing qualities. Marketing food with therapeutic properties effectively *treats food as drugs* and is likely to have significant public health implications. Examples of functional foods include breakfast cereals containing psyllium fiber which allegedly helps lower cholesterol levels and margarines which contain phytochemicals that allegedly help lower cholesterol.

They go on to cite the following example:

> Claims about the benefits of functional foods can easily be exaggerated or misleading, adding further to public confusion and anxiety. For example, some years ago, the Heart Smart Egg with omega-3 fatty acids was promoted to Australian consumers. The food company producing the egg claimed that consuming it would reduce blood pressure and alleviate the symptoms of arthritis and asthma. The claims were unproven and had to be retracted, with the company agreeing to change the name and abandoning such advertising.
> Conclusion—there is a lot of bad science in the functional food industry. They want you to

believe that good health comes from the Pharma, not from the farm.

Selling of Pharma on TV

There are only two countries in the world that allow direct-to-customer (DTC) television advertising. They are the United States and New Zealand. DTC started in the United States in 1997. The process was approved by the FDA, but they do not approve or pass judgment upon content except in egregious situations in which complaints are filed. Their standards for listing risks or allowing the public to know about risks are low and incomplete. Before 1997, spending for DTC was $220 million. By 2016, spending exceeded $6.4 billion, up 5 percent from 2015.[42] One notorious example was Vioxx, a pain reliever produced by Merck. Vioxx became a blockbuster of income for Merck primarily due to DTC's television advertising, but it turned out to be a failed drug causing 140,000 cardiac events, including 60,000 deaths. It took five years to have it removed from the market. Recall cost $5.5 billion in judgments.

There is clearly a downside to DTC drug advertising. Such advertisements may provide incomplete and biased information that leads to inappropriate prescribing and consumes valuable time during a physician-patient encounter.[43] Lipsky and Taylor[44] reported that 71 percent of family physicians surveyed felt pressured by patient request to use drugs that they would not ordinarily use. The blitz of advertising creates an unbalanced view because the average American TV viewer watches as many as nine drug ads a day, totaling sixteen hours per year, which far exceeds the amount of time the average individual spends with their primary care physician.[45] Nielsen, the TV rating agency, estimates an average of eighty drug ads air every hour of every day on American television.[46] The top five companies are Pfizer, Eli Lilly, AbbVie, Merck, and Amgen. Arguments that prescription drug ads are educational and encourage medical consultation for all sorts of conditions can be considered, but the downside is clearly a preponderance of confusing information on many drugs whose long-term safety profiles are not always known and, finally, clearly have led to overuse of perception drugs worldwide. According to STATNEWS,[47] nine prescription drugs are on pace to break $100 million worth of TV ad time in 2012.

Of the $300 billion a year, the US pharmaceutical industry spent $3.1 billion on advertising directly to the consumer in 2012.[48] There are more ads every year. According to Kantar Media,[49] a firm that tracks multimedia advertising,

> 771,368 such ads were shown in 2016, THE LAST FULL YEAR FOR WHICH DATA IS AVAILABLE, AN INCREASE OF ALMOST 65 PERCENT OVER 2012.
>
> "TV ad spending by pharmaceutical companies has more than doubled in the past four years, making it the second-fastest-growing category on television during that time," quoting Jon Swallen, Kantar's chief research officer.
>
> "The drug companies aren't generally marketing to people in their 30s; they're marketing to the 65-plus, and that's the population that tends to still be watching television," said Allen Adamson, a brand strategy consultant.

The results for Big Pharma must be good, or they would not continue. As of May 2011, the average number of prescriptions for new drugs with DTC advertising is nine times greater than prescriptions for new drugs without DTC ads.[50] The arguments for DTC advertising are that they encourage consumers to seek medical advice, that they inform patients about medical conditions, that they help remove stigma associated with certain diseases, that they generate R&D revenue for research, and finally that they are to be considered protected by free speech—First Amendment protection. The arguments against DTC advertising are that they misinform patients, that drugs are promoted long before safety information is known, that normal conditions and bodily functions are medicalized and stigmatized by DTC prescription drug ads, that they encourage over-medication, that they pressure health professionals to treatment not in the best interest of the patient, that they weaken the patient-doctor relationship, that they add unnecessarily to health-care costs, and that they cause the pharmaceutical industry to spend excessive lobbying money to influence congressional approval of their already-uncontrolled activities. The reader must be the judge.

Endnotes

Chapter 2
The American Scene

[1] Isaac Asimov, *Asimov's New Guide to Science* (London: Penguin), 1987.

[2] Samuel H. Adams, *The Great American Fraud: Articles on the Nostrum Evil and Quacks*, 4th ed (New York, NY: P. F. Collier & Sons, 1911).

[3] Chris Mooney, *Unscientific America: How Scientific Illiteracy Threatens Our Future* (New York: Basic Books, 2009), 13.

[4] Ibid., 19.

[5] Ibid., 20.

[6] http://archive.carnegiefoundation.org/pdfs/elibrary/Carnegie_Flexner_Report.pdf.

[7] Chris Mooney, ibid., 26.

[8] Derek Bok, *Universities in the Marketplace* (Princeton, NJ: Princeton University Press, 2003), 15.

[9] Ibid., 56.

[10] Richard Hofstadter, *Anti-intellectualism in American Life* (New York: Alfred A. Knopf Inc., 1963), 145.

[11] Ibid., 125. From Maynard Shipley, *The War on Modern Science* (New York, 1927), 130.

[12] Alexis de Tocqueville, *Democracy in America* I (New York, 1898), 66.

[13] Ibid., 166.

[14] Hofstadter, ibid., 207.

[15] Samuel Eliot Morison, *The Oxford History of the American People* (New York: Oxford University Press, 1965), 70–72. It should be noted that Morison would have added the name of John Fitzgerald Kennedy to the list of "intellectual presidents." When American winners of Nobel Prizes (never before given official recognition in Washington, together with writers, scholars, and artists of many races) were given a dinner and reception in the White House, conducted with a good taste that no European court could have surpassed, he set a gay note by announcing, "This is the most extraordinary collection of talent...that has ever been gathered together at the White House—with the possible exception of when Thomas Jefferson dined alone!" (ibid., 1120–1121).

[16] Ibid., 423.

[17] Hofstadter from Horace Mann, *Lectures and Annual Reports on Education* I (Cambridge, 1867), 396.

[18] https://en.wikipedia.org/wiki/Charter_schools_in_the_United_States.

[19] Ibid., Wikipedia, "The Times-Picayune" (Dec. 18, 2009).

[20] "For-Profit Schools' Stocks Still Get Failing Grades," *Barron's* (Jan. 5, 2015), 12.

[21] Chris Potter, "Charter Schools Debate Continues—Are They about Money or Education?" *Pittsburgh Post-Gazette* (Jan. 5, 2015).

[22] Amanda Marcotte, "It Wasn't Abortion that Formed the Religious Right. It Was Support for Segregation," *XX Magazine* (May 29, 2014).

[23] *America Can Be Saved* (Murfreesboro, Tenn.: Sword of the Lord Publishers, 1979), 52–53.

[24] "Religious Groups' Views on Global Warming," Pew Research, Religion & Public Life Project (April 16, 2009).

[25] Alex Berezow and Hank Campbell, *Science Left Behind, Feel-Good Fallacies and the Rise of Anti-Scientific Left* (Public Affairs, 2012).

[26] Timothy Ferris, *The Science of Liberty: Democracy, Reason, and the Laws of Nature* (Harper Collins, 2010).

[27] Ibid., Ferris, 403.

[28] Ibid., Berezow and Campbell, 124.

[29] June C. Hu, "Falling for Familiar Narratives," *The State of the Universe* (June 17, 2014).

[30] Ibid., Berezow and Campbell, 206.

[31] Eric Topol, MD, *The Creative Destruction of Medicine: How the Digital Revolution Will Create Better Health Care* (New York: Perseus Book Group, 2012), www.medscape.com.

[32] Peter Conrad, *The Medicalization of Society: On the Transformation of Human Conditions into Treatable Disorders* (Johns Hopkins University Press, 2007).

[33] Ibid., Conrad, 19.

[34] Well.blogs.nytimes.com/2014/weighing-testosterone-benefits-and-risks.

[35] Ibid., Conrad, 85.

[36] Thomas Sanaras, "Short Is Beautiful: So Why Are We Making Kids Grow Tall?" *Futurist* 29:26-3en (1995), Wikipedia.org/wiki/Doping_at_The_Tour_de_France.

[37] Julie Holland, *Moody Bitches: The Truth about the Drugs You're Taking, the Sleep You're Missing, the Sex You're Not Having, and What's Really Making You Crazy* (New York: Penguin Press, 2015).

[38] www. Becker's hospital review.com/healthcare…technology.

[39] www.rxlist.com.

[40] H. Risstad et al., "Five-year Outcomes After Laparoscopic Gastric Bypass and Laparoscopic Duodenal Switch in Patients with Mass Index of 50 to 60: A Randomized Clinical Trial" (JAMA Surgery, Feb. 4, 2015).

[41] M. Lawrence and J. Germov, "Functional Foods and Public Health Policy," in J. Germov and L. Williams, eds., *A Sociology of Food and Nutrition: The Social Appetite*, 3rd ed., (Melbourne: Oxford University Press, 2008).

[42] https://www.usatoday.com/story/money/2017/03/16/prescription-drug-costs-up-tv-ads/99203878/.

[43] M. B. Rosenthal, E. R. Burnett, J. M. Donahue, P. G. Frank, A. M. Epstein, "Promotion of Prescription Drugs to Consumers," *N Eng. J Med* no. 346498 (2002), 505.

[44] M. S. Lipsky and C. A. Taylor, "The Opinions and Experiences of Family Physicians Regarding Direct-to-Consumer Advertising," *J Fam Pract* no. 45495 (1997), 499.

[45] www.ncbi.nlm.nih.gov//pmc/articlesPMC3278148.

[46] https://www.statnews.com/2016/03/09/drug-industry-advertising/.

[47] www.fearcepharma.com.

[48] Prescription Drug Ads ProCon.org.p1.

[49] https://nytims/2pmLbcw.

[50] Ref. no. 48, ibid. 2/10/15.

Knowledge and Trust

*It is easier to fool people than to convince them that
they have been fooled.*

—*Mark Twain*

How Good Is the American Consumer in Judging Science from Bunk?

THE NATIONAL SCIENCE Foundation, which is used to gauge US scientific literacy annually, surveyed 2,200 in 2014 who were asked ten questions about physical and biological sciences. The disturbing news was that one in four Americans were unaware that the earth orbits the sun. The poll further showed that a majority of Americans think astrology is a science.[1] In January of 2014, Chris Kirk, reporting in www.slate.com, documented the publicly funded schools that are allowed to teach creationism—that is, thousands of schools across the country that can use public taxpayer money to cast doubt on basic science.[2] In fairness, it should be noted that the largest concentration of such schools is in Tennessee and Louisiana and, third, Florida, with a scattering about Texas. In Indiana, at least thirty-seven schools teach creationism while participating in the state's voucher program for children from low-income families. This lack of separation of church and state is clearly impeding the teaching of science and the scientific method.

Writing in 2002, Jon Miller,[3] in broad terms, classified as civic scientifically literate a citizen who displayed (1) an understanding of basic scientific concepts and constructs, such as the molecule, DNA, and the structure of the solar system; (2) an understanding of the nature and process of scientific inquiry; and (3) a pattern of regular information consumption. This is a rather complex issue, and there are various levels of scientific literacy. From Miller's classification, I would extract the most important of the three issues, and that is an understanding of the nature and process of scientific inquiry. Progress has been made in increasing requirements for scientific courses in our colleges and universities in the United States. I hope the time has passed when one could graduate with a degree from college without a single course in science. That being said, the question is, How good is our teaching of the scientific method at any level?

If you google "How good is the teaching of the scientific method?" you get quite a hodgepodge of sites, mostly aimed at teachers at all levels trying to find a good teaching technique. There are a number of sites that state that there are several scientific methods. I found one site particularly good because it gives an accurate summary of the scientific method, and that is www.sciencebuddies.org/. It properly defines the scientific method as a process for experimentation used to explore observations and answer questions and further notes that scientists use the scientific method to search for cause-and-effect relationships in nature; in other words, they design an experiment so that changes to one item cause something else to vary in a predictable way. The schematic for this method is as follows:

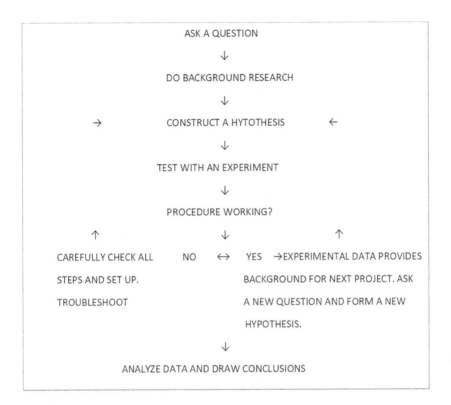

ASK A QUESTION

↓

DO BACKGROUND RESEARCH

↓

→ CONSTRUCT A HYTOTHESIS ←

↓

TEST WITH AN EXPERIMENT

↓

PROCEDURE WORKING?

↑ ↓ ↑

CAREFULLY CHECK ALL   NO ↔ YES →EXPERIMENTAL DATA PROVIDES

STEPS AND SET UP.   BACKGROUND FOR NEXT PROJECT. ASK

TROUBLESHOOT   A NEW QUESTION AND FORM A NEW

HYPOTHESIS.

↓

ANALYZE DATA AND DRAW CONCLUSIONS

This is a clear-cut summary of the essence of the method. There are not several methods as so many teachers' websites broadcast. Yet as central as this method is to our entire progress and civilization, it is sad to note that the Ohio state legislature has introduced legislation to specifically prohibit a discussion of the scientific process. The legislation states, "The standards in science…shall focus on academic and scientific knowledge rather than scientific process."[4]

The landscape of teaching science and the scientific method has a few bright spots. Pearson Publishing[5] has introduced an interactive science and technology curriculum pre-K–12, combining text sources and online inquiry all based on the fundamentals of the scientific method. The content is superbly illustrated and provided by experts in various fields. The effort serves as an example of what can be accomplished when we set our minds to the task. The challenge is there. Americans have major holes in our knowledge of science, but efforts now underway will generate the needed level to make the important decisions, not only for public policy, but as the core of this book urges, in their health-care choices as well.

Loss of Trust in Authority

It is difficult to tell exactly when the American public began to lose trust in medical science and in medical practitioners in general. I contend that it was part of the loss of trust in authority that occurred because of the Vietnam War and the tumultuous times immediately leading to our withdrawal from that war. Post-World War II America had faith in their government, faith in their future, faith in their institutions, and faith particularly in the profession and integrity of the field of medicine. Once they were lied to, once they had been deceived by their public leadership by the so-called best and brightest, once they learned that Vietnam was a manufactured war by President Lyndon Johnson and the US Navy, they never recovered that trust. They became aware of the growing fraud and deceit that marked an eroding pervasive characteristic of our culture.

According to the Pew Research Center, public trust in government is nearing all-time lows.[6]

> Only 18% of Americans today say they can trust the government in Washington to do what is right "just about always" (3%) or "most of the time" (15%).

The erosion of trust in governance affects the professions at every level. Sanjay Gupta, MD, and his website MedPage Today[7] note that physicians in the US experience a lower level of public trust than physicians in any of the countries that the US health-care system is normally compared against. He notes that only 58 percent of US adults agree with the statement "All things considered, can doctors in your country can be trusted." That puts the US at twenty-fourth among the twenty-nine industrial countries where the survey was carried out, above only Chile, Bulgaria, Russia, and Poland and tied with Croatia. In other countries (Turkey, France,

Finland, Britain, the Netherlands, Denmark, and Switzerland), more than 75 percent of adults agreed that doctors could be trusted. In citing the primary reference, Dr. Gupta goes on to say that the lack of public trust in leaders in the medical profession undermines the confidence in physicians making decisions involving national health policy. In short, the literature on trust in public institutions suggests that groups that are not trusted are more susceptible to having the public pay less attention to them. It makes sense. You don't tend to follow anyone you do not trust!

Of more disturbing concern is a statement by Dr. Robert J. Blendon's Harvard study that shows that poor people in the US have a substantially lower level of trust in the entire health-care system than people in higher income levels. Adults from families earning less than $30,000 are significantly less trusting of physicians and less satisfied with their own medical care than adults not from low-income families.[8]

From the Woodrow Wilson School of Public and International Affairs, Susan Fiske, the Eugene Higgins professor of psychology and professor of public affairs, recently stated, "Scientists have earned the respect of Americans but not necessarily their trust. But this gap can be filled by showing concern for humanity and the environment. Rather than persuading, scientists may better serve citizens by discussing, teaching, and sharing information to convey trustworthy intentions."[9] I'm a bit suspicious for the consensus of her remarks seems to be that a little more humanism engenders a little more trust. I'm more likely to suspect that people who do not want to hear the truth of science do so because they simply do not want to believe it regardless of how "warm" the presentation.

A recent Pew Research Center study showing opinion differences between the public (American adults) and scientists (members of the American Association for the Advancement of Science [AAAS]) was most revealing.[10] About 88 percent of AAAS scientists said it's safe to eat genetically modified foods, as opposed to 37 percent of US adults. About 98 percent of scientists versus 65 percent of adults on the question of humans evolving over time. About 86 percent of AAAS scientists said childhood vaccines should be required versus 68 percent of adults. There were similar differences in climate change considered being caused by human activity, growing world population as a major problem, and those favoring nuclear power plants. More scientists than adults favored offshore drilling, but more adults than AAAS scientists said that astronauts were essential for the future of the US space program, about the same difference favoring fracking. The least difference was over the question of whether the space station has been a good investment for the United States: 68 percent of scientists said yes versus 64 percent of adults, a difference of only four points. The significant point is, differences in trust of scientific information profoundly affect public policy.

The Vaccine Mess

In 1998 in the respected British Journal *Lancet*, a former surgeon and medical researcher named Andrew Wakefield published a paper claiming a link between the administration of MMR (measles, mumps, and rubella) vaccine and the appearance of autism and bowel disease.[11] Subsequently, the claim was discredited when other investigators were unable to reproduce Wakefield's findings.[12]

The narrative is well summarized in Wikipedia, which goes on to note that it was not only a matter of bad science but that an exposé by reporter Brian Deer in the London *Sunday Times* identified financial conflicts of interest on Wakefield's part.[13] In summarizing the next events, Wikipedia states:

> On 28 January 2010, a five-member statutory tribunal of the GMC (General Medical Council) found three dozen charges proved, including four counts of dishonesty and 12 counts involving the abuse of developmentally challenged children. The panel ruled that Wakefield had "failed in his duties as a responsible consultant," acted both against the interests of his patients, and "dishonestly and irresponsibly" in his published research *Lancet* fully retracted

the 1998 publication on the basis of the GMC's findings, noting that elements of the manuscript had been falsified. *The Lancet's* editor-in-chief Richard Horton said the paper was "utterly false" and that the journal had been "deceived." Three months following *The Lancet's* retraction, Wakefield was struck off the UK Medical Register, with a statement identifying deliberate falsification in the research published in *Lancet* and was barred from practicing medicine in the UK.

But the damage was done! Skepticism followed and led to decline in vaccination rates in Great Britain and the United States and subsequent return to higher rates of measles! Skepticism followed and led to a mumps and consequent deaths. In 2012, more than forty-eight thousand cases of whooping cough and twenty deaths were reported by the Centers for Disease Control.[14] Reports of recurrence of measles starting in Disneyland affecting over one hundred were noted in the same article.

Bipartisan politics in 1993 resulted in the passage of federal legislation, Vaccines for Children, which subsidized immunization for children uninsured or on Medicare—all the result of the 1989–91 epidemic, the most disturbing since the introduction of measles vaccine in 1963. But with the death of bipartisanship, the science of vaccinations became politicized.[15] Examples cited were:

1. On Fox News, Sean Hannity declared that he wasn't "trusting President Obama to tell me whether to vaccinate my kids."
2. On CNN, Senator Rand Paul, a candidate for President and a doctor spewed, "I've heard of many tragic cases of walking, talking, normal children who wound up with profound mental disorders after vaccines."

And further to show that a medical degree does not immunize against scientific ignorance, Dr. Ben Carson argued in an early Republican candidate's debate that it was safer to give lower dosages in longer time frames for which there is *no evidence to support this view*. Candidate Governor Chris Christie got in the act by declaring that parents must have a choice. I wonder if he holds the same need for choice when it comes to car seats for tots and the use of seat belts for children.

MMR (measles, mumps, and rubella) vaccines are not alone. In 2015 the science behind the vaccines for prevention of meningitis in teens came under fire from Robert F. Kennedy Jr., who spoke against a New York State bill saying that "it would make our children dumber."[16] He referred to mercury thimerosal, a preservative that he said causes autism. This is despite the fact that two of the three available meningococcal vaccines do not contain thimerosal and the third contains a trace amount only when administered in multidose form, according to the Center for Disease Control. Kennedy has been a strong environmentalist in the Hudson Valley, but not a scientist. The CDC, the American Association of Pediatrics, the organization Autism Speaks, and the Institute of Medicine agree, Kennedy's contention is not supported by science. The contention of a causal relationship between vaccines and autism has been long rejected, and the bill was supported by Medical Society, the March of Dimes, and the Association of County Health Officials.[17]

We can talk "backward states" all we want, but the state of Mississippi had a 99.9 percent inoculation rate against measles.[18] The real hotbed of anti-science in the vaccine market is the state of California, not in impoverished neighborhoods, but in the sophisticated zip codes of Hollywood progressives. Frank Bruni of the *New York Times*[19] quotes the Hollywood reporter newspaper revealing that 57 percent of the children at a Beverly Hills preschool and 68 percent of one in Santa Monica had filed personal-belief exemptions from having their children vaccinated. Who has been fanning the flames of panic? Celebrities like actress, part-time actress, former Playboy playmate, and part-time immunologist Jenny McCarthy,[20] who has put in numerous appearances on talk shows and, incidentally of late, has been showing her total disregard for health by working as a pitch-woman for electronic cigarettes.[21] Perhaps her most famous quote was on the *Oprah Winfrey* TV show, "The University of Google is where I got my degree from."[22]

Which brings us full circle back to Andrew Wakefield, who now lives in the United States and has a following led by none other than celebrity anti-vaccinationist Jenny McCarthy and a cadre of chiropractors to whom he has given lectures to their continuing education programs sponsored by Life Chiropractic College West.[23] Wakefield is not licensed to practice medicine in the United States but lobbies for the Oregon Chiropractic Association.[24]

The Evolution of Alternative or Complementary Medicine

The evolution of what came to be called Complementary and Alternative Medicine (CAM), or Complementary Integrative Medicine (CIM), and eventually functional medicine began in the turbulent 1960s growing out of the anti-authority or counterculture forces unleashed during and after the Vietnam War era. Rapid changes in social norms contributed to questioning nearly all aspects of Western life, including science-based medicine. Up until that time, various unproven or unscientific medical treatments were referred to as "irregular practices" and fraudulent ones as quackery. Even the forces of vigilance caved to the mass marketing efforts growing exponentially at the time. Even the American Medical Association (AMA) could not hold the line on quackery and abolished its Department of Investigation in 1975.[25]

The TV program *Frontline* on PBS[26] has archived a program called "Countercultural Healing: A Brief History of Alternative Medicine in America" by historian James Whorton, MD. He makes the following historical points:

> 1. Current CAM (Complementary and Alternative Medicine) is history repeating itself—the most recent of three "waves"

was preceded by the first two waves in mid-1800's and early 1900's.

2. Irregular or alternative medicine was justified in the late 1700's because medicine was based upon bloodletting and purging containing mercury, which "left patients often in horrible condition.".

3. In mid-1800's, hydrotherapy, hypnotism and homeopathy prevailed.

4. A second wave after the Civil War included osteopathy, chiropractic and naturopathy.

5. Hostility has often marked the line between alternative and traditional.

6. The tendency of the human body to heal itself has been the common basis of alternative methods in this history.

7. The placebo effect has been the common response to alternative treatments by scientific medicine.

8. In 1998, the office of Alternative Medicine at the National Institutes of Health became the National Center for CAM suggesting that alternative would be complementary to standard care henceforth.

9. CAM supports envisioned a grand integration of alternatives and tradition medicine.

In a link to the *Frontline* piece,[27] Stephen Straus, MD, then director of the National Center for Complementary and Alternative Medicine at NIH, traces the progress in more spending and more resources and people dedicated to research since 1992 when there was a budget of $2 million and a handful of people. According to Dr. Strauss,

This has grown to $105 million plus collaborating funding of $120 million and a staff of seventy. Dr. Straus points out that there has been only one funded NIH clinical trial conducted so far and that has been on the efficacy of St. John's Wort for depression, and that failed to show a difference with a placebo effect. At this rate we will be forever sorting out any science in CAM.

Marcia Angell, MD, senior lecturer at Harvard Medical School, testified several years ago at the White House Commission on Complementary and Alternative Medicine[28]:

> I know of no good study that has shown an alternative remedy to work.

It should be noted that in the same link to the *Frontline* piece quoted above, four links that commented on evidence of CAM had been taken down and were nowhere to be found. This was disturbing particularly in the light of the fact that accompanying Dr. Angell's comments noted above was the observation of Dr. Angell that,

> "The White House Commission consisted of people the majority of whom had financial ties to complementary and alternative medicine. They had vested interests. They owned businesses that offered complementary and alternative medicine." It could be said that they had a conflict of interest that had the potential of obstructing objectivity.
>
> In historically tracing the key elements of CAM versus regular medicine note the emergence and dependency of regular medicine on science and the scientific method whereas CAM depends on listening to nature for inspiring cures and the natural tendency of the human body to cure itself as well as a commitment to holism or the holistic approach in the treating process. It is

easy to comprehend how little regular medicine had to offer in the beginning of the 19th century and how logical irregular methods must have appeared as attractive solutions, but with the stethoscope (1816) emergence of understanding the germ theory of disease, ether anesthesia (1846), antibiotics, applied genetics, advanced scientific imaging devices and a literal explosion of scientific knowledge in every field of medicine that is evolving, how can it be that there would be any cause for entertaining the use of the non-science of CAM?

The second controversial aspect of the rise of complementary and alternative medicine is the recent infusion of money into the payment systems of health care at all levels. It could be said that there was little money in medicine's payment systems until Medicare and other government-sponsored payment systems were introduced in the 1960s. My father, who graduated from medical school (the University of Buffalo in 1925), practiced for forty years of two-dollar office visits and retired in 1968 when they were five dollars. The public insists on insurance covering all treatments, regular or irregular, and therein lies the core of the second controversy—are we going to pay for unproven and unscientific and possibly fraudulent therapies? Will we allow *quackonomics* as a matter of course? I submit that it would be reasonable to allow payment for any CAM therapies that have been *proven scientifically effective* by the National Center for CAM in Washington, DC, and a reliable third party, not just any listed on their website.

Oprah and the Rise of Celebrity Medicine—Dr. Oz

Google "Oprah Winfrey (history)" and it notes 689,000 results. Oprah Winfrey is, by any measure, one of the most remarkable women in the world. Born in poverty in Mississippi in 1954, she took charge of a daytime chat program in 1976[29] and grew an empire that made her the first black woman billionaire and a cultural icon on a global scale. From talk show host to author, book promoter, philanthropist, political operative, actress, and world media personality, she has been a leader and role model. It is fair to say she has enormous influence on American culture, and of these avenues, health is certainly of prime importance.

From TV shows to magazine to website, Oprah has been influential in furthering better health through tips on eating, fitness, vitamins, weight control, thyroid health, cancer diagnosis, to name but a few. Her endorsements of medical personalities have not been so stellar. As an example, in 2006, one of Oprah's favorites, Dr. Christiane Northrup,[30] pushed a study that concluded that large doses of vitamin D "might" decrease the risk of breast cancer. Later research did not confirm plus dosages recommended were twice recommended allowance, thus increasing risk of complications.

The so-called Oprah Effect—namely, that just because it is claimed on her show has the result of validity—has become controversial. Oprah is dismissive of such criticism and has stated[31]:

> For 23 years, my show has presented thousands of topics that reflect the human experience, including doctors' medical advice and personal health stories that have prompted conversations between our audience members and their health care providers. I trust the viewers, and I know that they are smart and discerning enough to seek out medical opinions to determine what may be best for them.

So the controversy extends. Are we dealing in truth or show business? Perhaps her greatest Oprah Effect is Dr. Oz, the Columbia University cardiac surgeon. She put him on the map, as well as Jenny McCarthy and her anti-vaccination program.[32] Mehmet Oz, MD, has become a national oracle on various medical conditions and products notably in the area of weight control, now well beyond the launchpad of Oprah Winfrey's TV show. But it has not been without controversy. In April 2015, a letter authored by ten physicians at Columbia University College of Physicians and Surgeons[33] asked for his resignation from his faculty appointment and his vice chairmanship of the Department of Surgery, citing his "disdain for science and for evidence-based medicine," his "baseless opposition to genetically modified foods," and his promotion of "quack treatments" for financial gain. So are we dealing with conflicts of interest and flawed judgment or, as Dr. Oz responded, "I bring the public information that will help them on their path to be their best selves"?

Dr. Oz now has his own "show." The *British Medical Journal*, in an online article, found that of eighty randomly selected health-care recommendations made on the show, roughly half *lacked believable evidence or else the evidence contradicted them.*[34] A *New York Times* article on April 26, 2015, by author Bill Gifford[35] attempted a more balanced view on criticism of Dr. Oz. He sees criticism of Dr. Oz rather picky and declares, "This is daytime television, not the Journal of the American Medical Association." He further lets Dr. Oz off the hook, concluding that,

> Progress in medicine and science is a messy, contested affair. It can be hard to know who's right or wrong until the dust has settled and time has passed. Without people pushing the boundaries of accepted treatments and conventional wisdom—and fostering dialogue, which Dr. Oz see as part of his mission—there would be no advancement. Here in America, rightly or wrongly, we have clearly chosen a wild and wooly marketplace where free speech comes before regulation and expert ruling. That means that, as patients and consumers, we need to do our own homework.

So, readers, only in America, or as the show tune goes, "There's no business like show business like no business I know." So three

cheers for dialogue and skip over the scientific method. This is enter-
tainment, folks.

The Effect of the Internet

The effect of the internet on medical practice has been profound. Dr. John Oro at the University of Missouri concluded that the
most fundamental change has been health-care consumer empowerment.[36] As early as 2000, he estimated that seventy-two million adult
Americans had used the internet to seek health-care information. He
further concluded that 40 percent seeking health information on the
internet were very satisfied with the web versus 25 percent satisfaction
with magazine/newspaper information and only 13 percent satisfied
with TV information. Other marks of empowerment reported were
the rapid growth of disorder-specific websites and chat rooms, the
development of supersites by medical centers such as Johns Hopkins
and the Mayo Clinic, online pharmacy and prescription services,
the development of evidence-based medical information, as well as
online personal chart services.

The proliferation of the smartphone allows a growth of applications (apps) covering everything from fitness to diagnosis of skin
pathology. *Medical Economics* magazine (2013) summarized five tech
trends[37]: (1) PCPs (primary care physicians) will act more as a cura-
tor of information than as a gatekeeper, and physicians will have to
scamper to keep up or lose the image or "informed"; (2) Personal
Health Records will grow as security issues are solved; (3) electronic
health records (EHR) will be cloud based, increasing functionality,
convenience, and security with reduction of cost; (4) reorganization
of support staff, and the EHR will allow efficiencies in the use of
nurse practitioners and physician assistants; and (5) remote monitoring (and I add telemedicine) will allow greater saving in time and
convenience. In summary, we are evolving a different model.

Most recently, social media has become a dominant force in the
future of medical information.[38] As of January 20, 2018, 95 percent
of American adults own a cell phone, and nearly 85 percent have
at least one type of mobile device, according to the Pew Internet

Project.[39] Thus the emergence of the e-patient, who actively gathers and compares health-care information of multisources. And it is not just young users. Nearly 50 percent of those over the age of sixty-five are also daily users of a least one social medial outlet.[40] The conclusion? The impact is that social media "provides a wide level playing field of physicians, nurses, patients and other providers for a less formal interaction outside traditional clinic and hospital settings."[41] Integrity of information and keeping up with the latest, whether it be Facebook, Twitter, or blogs, is going to be a sine qua non in strategies for hospitals and health professionals in areas of patient satisfaction and in practical economic considerations such as maintaining market share for all services.

The year 2015 was the year of growth in the number of health-care apps.[42] These start-ups also included telehealth, prescription management, physician reference, patient portal, and virtual house call categories. Among those going public was Teladoc (trading symbol TDOC),[43] the largest national telehealth platform providing 24-7 consultation by board-certified physicians on the internet. Prescriptions as necessary can be sent to your pharmacy of choice. The Apple iOS and Google's Android have, through growth and branding, become the dominant phone operating systems, and Epic and Cerner[44] hold the largest market share in their large health system EHRs (electronic health records).

What we are seeing on the American scene, and indeed globally to variable degrees, is an explosion in managing health care from the experimental laboratory to the physician-patient interphase. Verification, integrity, and transparency will build the tripod of success while preserving patient privacy will always be a challenge. It must be the intention of all parties involved in this progress, to eschew false information, the unnecessary, secondary conflict of interest, and quackery.

Understanding the Placebo Effect

Before embarking on the examination of cost of quackery in the United States, it is necessary that the reader be comfortable with a good understanding of the placebo or the "placebo effect." It is impossible to be an informed consumer of health care without it. If you work on knowing the fundamentals of the scientific method and comprehend the essentials of the placebo effect, you are a long way down the road of being a thinking and open-minded and discriminating consumer of health information. So here goes.

Google Dictionary defines the placebo effect as a beneficial effect, produced by a placebo drug or treatment, that cannot be attributed to the properties of the placebo itself and must, therefore, be due to the patient's belief in that treatment. In other words, it is a remarkable phenomenon in which a placebo—a fake treatment, an inactive substance like sugar, distilled water, or saline solution—can sometimes improve a patient's condition simply because the person *has the expectation* that it will be helpful.[45]

It has long been known to medicinal science that substitution of sham or inert medications or treatments has been beneficial to healing and favorable outcomes. This seemingly favorable, however illogical, result has been labeled the placebo effect. *Placebo* is a Latin verb meaning "to please." I have found the term confusing, not knowing whether it is the physician who wishes to please the patient or the patient in response to the treatment wishing to please himself and/or the physician. In any event, no one can understand the outcomes of various forms of treatment including pharmacology without knowing that the placebo effect happens and to what extent with each modality of therapy, be it a drug or a device.

An early study by Henry Beecher in 1955 cited by science historian Anne Harrington[46] attributes 30–40 percent of any treated group as placebo responders and up to 55 percent placebo responders when treated for *pain relief*. This has been documented and is quite astounding. Why? Well, as anyone can see, the placebo effect complicates the interpretation of *any* treatment results and for two reasons: (1) how do we determine the variables in the placebo effect, and (2) how do we measure them in order to get at the true degree of efficacy for a medication or treatment? This is the great challenge of science and certainly draws us to the inevitable conclusion that we cannot see prescience as anything but incomplete and speculative.

Native Americans may have had tremendous faith in shamans' healing power, points out Porter Shimer in *Healing Secrets of the Native Americans.*[47] He goes on to quote an eighteenth-century observer, "The Indians had faith in the medicine, and so the medicine worked." So in prescience, generalities are made, but details are lacking, but it is fair to say that any good results were due to the placebo effect. Writing on pain, Melanie Thernstrom[48] observed:

> It is difficult to imagine what the history of medicine would have been like without the placebo effect: in a sense, there might not have been a history of medicine before modern times without the placebo effect, because it would have been obvious that most treatments made no difference.

Looking at the variables of the placebo effect, there are essentially four:

1. The patient: Factors in the patient are degree of suggestibility, the level of expectation the patient has in the proposed treatment, which is further influenced by cultural conditioning, personal experiences, and references researched prior to the treatment encounter.
2. The problem: The reason the patient may have for seeking treatment ranges from the trite and minor to the impossible or hopeless.
3. The physician: Factors include the personality, skill, experience, and training, plus the reputation in the community. Of paramount importance is the personal relationship that evolves between the physician and the patient.
4. The situation: This includes the environment and atmosphere prevailing at the site of treatment.

After the variables is the challenge of interpretation of the results. The methods of measurement must be determined and the percentage of the result due to the treatment must be separated from that due to the placebo. So the placebo effect has been recognized in the literature for what it is——a complex of many forces. If you explore the current medical literature, it is obvious that an enormous amount of research is being done on attempting to understand the science of it. Just google "Google scholar" for a sample. The placebo effect has been around a long time. Medical author Dr. Paul Offit[49] cites the Ebers Papyrus of 1500 BC, which contains more than seven hundred drugs of mineral, vegetable, and animal origin.

> Treatment included dirt and flyspecks scraped off walls; blood from lizards and cats; fat from geese, oxen, snakes, mice, hippopotamuses, and eunuchs; dung from pigs, dogs, sheep, gazelles, pelicans and flies (this couldn't have been easy); and ram's hair, tortoise shells, swine's teeth, donkey's hooves, and grated human skull. Again, just because pelican poop doesn't contain real medicine doesn't mean it didn't work to treat pain, fatigue, and heartburn 3,500 years ago. The placebo response is a powerful thing. And back then it was all they had. Now, because we have medicines that are much better than placebos, we often ignore placebo response.

The practitioners of alternative medicine, however, do not ignore the placebo effect but employ it as their fundamental process usually without any reference to it at all. Confidence in the physician was always significant as Galen noted, "He cures most successfully in whom the people have the most confidence."[50]

Looking at the history of the placebo effect may be helpful to further understanding. It was not until 1785 that the word *placebo* first appeared in the first medical dictionary, *Motherby's New Medical Dictionary*, as reported by Lemoine,[7] defined as "a commonplace medication or method," which was rather a poor definition. In was not until 1958 that the word *placebo* appeared in France in the seventeenth edition of *Garnier and Delamarre's Dictionary of Technical Terms in Medicine*. It required the introduction of double-blind controlled trials with random assignment that placebos attained scientific respect. A 1955 classic article by Beecher[51] of fifteen studies on 1,082 patients showed that a placebo analgesic is effective, on average in 35 percent of cases. Since then, there has accumulated a large literature on placebo effects for several diseases, some very sophisticated. For example, PET scan imaging[52] can visualize the anterior cingulate cortex of the brain, rich in opioid receptors, and placebo analgesia activates the prefrontal cortex, which can be interpreted as the expression of subjects' expectations, themselves correlated with doctors' expectations in anticipation of healing.[53] As reported in the *New York Times*, some are even advocating a placebo protocol for treading the epidemic of painkiller (Vicodin and OxyContin) addiction sweeping the country.[54]

The placebo response will be referenced in the several chapters to come. It must be understood in the context of an examination of quackery (the use of an agent to treat a symptom or disease with the intent to defraud). To start, we must agree on some fundamental concepts notably that a certain percentage of the population does not care about this differentiation. Their bottom line is, "I don't care. If it works, what's the beef: Why should I care whether it is science or not? I feel better, and what's more I think my insurance company will pay for it."

This attitude or conclusion is understandable but not responsible. It is not responsible because of the following:

1. It contributes to perpetuated dishonesty of the practitioner treating the patient. The attribution of a favorable result to the agent being used rather than the placebo response is dishonest.
2. It tends to legitimize propagation of misinformation.
3. It fosters an uncritical and sloppy thinking process in the diagnosis and treatment of illness.
4. It costs the entire health system unnecessarily.
5. It contaminates the licensing process with nonscience.

6.   It confuses the public and contributes to poor judgment by degrading critical judgment in health-care matters.

So one clear goal in evaluating the status of quackonomics in the chapters ahead will be the fair and scientific evaluation of what is a proven modality of treatment and what part is placebo masquerading as science.

Reporting of Results

One of the most frustrating experiences in modern America is picking up a newspaper and reading that such and such a study just recently reported, shows such and such—an interesting and surprising conclusion regarding your health. It may even refer to the university where the study was done, but try to track it down. It is most often impossible even with some of our most sophisticated search engines.

Thomas Lin., in 2012, on the occasion of the two hundredth anniversary of the *New England Journal of Medicine*, noted that for centuries, medical science was done in private (the stethoscope in 1816, ether anesthesia in 1846, and aseptic surgery in 1867) and then submitted for publication in medical journals, but it was always a maddeningly slow process.[55] He traces some efforts to simplify access to what is often restrictive access to journals. For example, the Public Library of Science (PLOS), founded in 2001 as a nonprofit open-access publisher, innovator, and advocacy organization with a mission to accelerate progress in science and medicine by leading a transformation in research communication.[56] It is not peer-reviewed and is more of a browsing site of seven different branches of science. It is somewhat of an open search engine and not helpful in following up on a specific article one might find from a newspaper. ResearchGate is a social networking site for scientists and researchers to share papers, ask and answer questions, and find collaborators.[57] It requires an affiliation with an institution and again is not a direct searcher for the public.

The great need is for the established peer-reviewed journals to publish "abstracts" for the public as part of any published article and for an open-sourced search engine that would allow any reader to find a follow-up of any published research. This would allow a consumer access that would have meaning and allow some critical thinking and informed consumer advocacy. If we did, perhaps we would not have a third of Americans believing that humans have existed in their present form since time began.[58]

That is not to say that there is not a plethora of web sources for medical information. There are. Wendy Boswell cites "The Top Four Medical Information Sites Online,"[59] and Google has more scores of pages of sites. As enormous as this literature is, it is still near impossible for a reader to search and find a specific citation. If space is a problem, the press should at least put the original reference on their website. In the name of access and translucency, it is imperative that this situation be corrected.

Endnotes

Chapter 3

Knowledge and Trust
How Good Is the American Consumer in Judging Science from Bunk?

[1]   Ian O'Neill, "1 in 4 Americans Don't Know Earth Orbits the Sun," last modified February 14, 2014, http://news.discovery.com.

[2]   Chris Kirk, "Map: Publicly Funded Schools that Are Allowed to Teach Creationism," last modified January 26, 2014, www.slate.com.

[3]   J. D. Miller, "Civic Scientific Literacy: A Necessity in the 21st Century," *Federation of American Scientists Public Interest Report* 55, no. 1 (January/February 2002).

[4]   John Timmer, "Ohio Lawmakers Want to Limit the Teaching of the Scientific Process," Ars Technia, accessed August 26, 2014, www.ArsTechnica.com.

[5]   Pearson: Instructional Resources K–12 Education Solutions, www.Pearsonschool.com.

Loss of Trust in Authority
[6]   http://www.people-press.org/2017/12/14/public-trust-in-government-1958-2017/.

7   www.Medpagetoday.com. Sangjay Gupta, MD, ed., "US Physician Leaders Suffer Loss of Public Trust—but Patients Still Like Their Own Doctors," MedPage Today. Primary ref.: Robert J. Blendon et al., *New England Journal of Medicine* 371 (October 23, 2014):1570–1572.

8   R. J. Blendon et al., "Public Trust in Physicians—US Medicine in International Perspective," *New England Journal of Medicine* 371 (2014): 1570–1572.

9   "Scientists Seen as Competent but Not Trusted by Americans," Woodrow Wilson School, last modified September 22, 2014, www.princeton/edu/news-and-events.

10 "The Vaccine Mess," http://www.pewinternet.org/interactives/public-scientists-opinion-gap/.

11 Wikipedia, org/wiki/Andrew Wakefield.

12 K. M. Madsen, A. Hviid, M. Vestergaard, et al., "A Population-Based Study of Measles, Mumps, and Rubella Vaccination and Autism," *The New England Journal of Medicine* 347, no. 19 (November 2002): 1477–82.

13 Brian Deer, "Revealed: MMR Research Scandal," *The Sunday Times* (February 22, 2004), retrieved December 12, 2012.

14 Margaret Talbot, "Not Immune," *The New Yorker*, February 16, 2013, 19.

15 Ibid., 20.

16 Jon Campbell, "In Albany, RFK Jr. Bashes Vaccine Bill," *Democrat and Chronicle*, June 3, 2015.

17 Ibid.

18 *Time*, February 9, 2015, 14.

19 Frank Bruni, "The Vaccine Lunacy," *The New York Times*, February 1, 2015.

20 "Who's Politicizing Kids' Vaccines?" 2015, A15.

21 Ibid.

22 Joel Achenbach, "The Age of Disbelief," *National Geographic* (March 2015): 47.

23 Wikipedia, ref. no. 137, Saerom Yoo, "Vaccine Researcher Wakefield to Testify in Oregon," *Statesman Journal* (February 24, 2015), retrieved March 3, 2015.

24 Eric W. Boyle, "Quack Medicine: A History of Combating Health Fraud in Twentieth-Century America," https://en.wikipedia.org/wiki/Alternative_medicine#cite_note-QMHCHF-132.

The Evolution of Alternative or Complementary Medicine

25 Eric W. Boyle, "Quack Medicine: A History of Combating Health Fraud in Twentieth-Century America" (Santa Barbara, California: Praeger, 2013), 162.

26 https://www.google.com/?gws_rd=ssl#q=a+history+of+alternative+medicine+-frontline.

27 http://www.pbs.org/wgbh/pages/frontline/shows/altmed/snake/evidence.html.

28 Ibid.

Oprah and the Rise of Celebrity Medicine—Dr. Oz

[29] http://www.biographyonline.net/humanitarian/oprah-winfrey.html.

[30] http://healthjournalism.org/blog/tag/oprah-winfrey/.

[31] Ibid.

[32] http://www.thedailybeast.com/articles/2016/02/26/does-the-oprah-winfrey-brand-still-sell.html.

[33] www.medscape.com/viewarticle/843389_print.

[34] https://www.washingtonpost.com/news/morning-mix/wp/2014/12/19/half-of-dr-ozs-medical-advice-is-baseless.

[35] Bill Gifford, "Dr. Oz Is No Wizard, but No Quack Either," New York Times, April 26, 2015.

The Effect of the Internet

[36] John Oro, MD, "The Dawning of e-healthcare: The Impact of the Internet on Medical Practice," *Bulletin of the American Association of Neurological Surgeons* 9, no. 3, https://www.aans.org/bulletin/pdfs/fall00.pdf.

[37] http://medicaleconomics.modernmedicine.com/medical-economics/news/modernmedicine/modern-medicine-feature-articles/5-tech-trends-will-affect-way.

[38] http://www.eplabdigest.com/articles/Social-Media-and-Medicine-2014-Update-and-Future-Impacts-Healthcare.

[39] http://www.pewinternet.org/fact-sheet/mobile/.

[40] Ibid., 1.

[41] Ibid., paragraph 4.

[42] http://www.beckershospitalreview.com/healthcare-information-technology/40-healthcare-apps-for-clinicians-and-consumers-to-know.html.

[43] https://www.teladoc.com/.

[44] http://www.beckershospitalreview.com/healthcare-information-technology/are-epic-and-cerner-healthcare-s-apple-and-android-7-core-thoughts.html.

Understanding the Placebo Effect

[45] http://www.medicinenet.com/script/main/art.asp?articlekey=31481.

[46] Anne Harrington, ed., "The Placebo Effect: An Interdisciplinary Exploration" (Cambridge: Harvard UP, 1997).

[47] Robert Shimer, "Healing Secrets of the Native Americans," *The Tess Press* (China: The Tess Press, 2004), 25.

[48] Melanie Thernstrom, "The Pain Chronicles" (New York: Farrar, Straus and Giroux, 2010), 100.

[49] Paul A. Offit, MD, *Do You Believe in Magic? The Sense and Nonsense of Alternative Medicine* (New York: Harper Collins, 2013).

[50] Anne Harrington, ed., "The Placebo Effect in Interdisciplinary Exploration," 13.

51 Patrick Lemoine, MD, PhD, "The Placebo Effect: History, Biology, and Ethics," October 9, 2015, www.medscape.com/view article/852144_print, 1–6.

52 P. Petrovic, E. Kelso, K. M. Petersson, M. Ingvar, "Placebo and Opioid Analgesia Imaging a Shared Neuronal Network," *Science* 295 (2002):1737–1790.

53 Lemoine, ibid., 5.

54 Jo Marchant, "A Placebo Treatment for Pain," *New York Times*, January 10, 2016.

Reporting Results
55 Thomas Lin, "Cracking Open the Scientific Process," *New York Times*, January 16, 2012.

56 https://www.plos.org/who-we-are.

57 https://en.wikipedia.org/wiki/ResearchGate.

58 Joel Achenbach, "The Age of Disbelief," *National Geographic*, March 2015, 41.

59 https://www.lifewire.com/medical-information-sites-3482069.

PART II

The Gamut of
Unscientific Therapies

1. Acupuncture

The history of medicine is the history of the placebo effect.

— *Melanie Thernstrom*

ACCORDING TO THE National Institutes of Health, "Costs of Complementary and Alternative Medicine (CAM) and Frequency of Visits to CAM Practitioners: United States, 2007,"[1] adults in the United States in 2007 spent $33.9 billion in out-of-pocket expenses on visits to CAM practitioners (11.2 percent of total out-of-pocket expenditures on health care). This 2007 study further concluded:

> Despite the overall decrease in visits to CAM providers in 2007 compared with 1997, visits to acupuncturists, a progressively more regulated and professionalized CAM provider group, increased over this same time period, with 17.6 million visits estimated for 2007 (79.2 visits per 1,000 adults), or three times that observed in 1997 (27.2 visits per 1,000 adults). The increase for acupuncture may in part be due to the greater number of states that license this practice and a corresponding increase in the number of

licensed practitioners in 2007 compared with
1997, as well as increased insurance coverage
for these therapies. Large numbers of articles in
the lay press about the benefits of acupuncture
were published during this period, increasing
awareness in the general population. Together,
greater opportunity and increased awareness may
explain much of the observed increase in adult
use of acupuncture.

From the same source, the best estimate of total cost (out-of-pocket plus insurance coverage) for acupuncture visits in 2007 was
$1.41 billion (17,630,000 visits × $80 per visit). State requirements
for licensure vary in the United States. Currently, forty-three states
plus the District of Columbia require the passage of the NCCAOM
(National Certification Commission for Acupuncture and Oriental
Medicine) examinations or NCCAOM certification as a prerequisite
for licensure. Some states require NCCAOM examinations, some
NCCAOM certification; in four states, there is no Acupuncture
Practice Act, and California has its own licensing protocol but will
use NCCAOM certification starting sometime in 2017.[2] There are
approximately *eighteen thousand licensed acupuncturists* in the US.
Out of that number, it is estimated that about twelve thousand are
actively in practice and that over 50 percent of those practices in the
coastal states of California and New York.[3] Some states that include
Chinese herbs in the scope of practice for acupuncturists, and others
add an exam. Five states have no practice act in Chinese herbs.

That is the broad picture. There are probably as many acupuncture practices as there are pizza parlors, but the question to be
answered is this: Is there any evidence that acupuncture is anything
more than the placebo effect? Here, from the medical literature, is a
sampling of different points of view in the use of acupuncture to treat
chronic knee pain for example.

A randomized clinical study of 282 patients over fifty years
of age from Victoria, Australia,[4] evaluated at twelve weeks and one
year, showed that needle acupuncture did not confer benefit over

sham for pain or function. Their conclusion: "Our findings do not support acupuncture for these patients." In contrast, a study out of Germany,[5] a randomized, controlled trial conducted in 255 general practices, 489 patients with chronic pain due to osteoarthritis of the knee or hip were evaluated for both quality of life and costs. The abstract states, "Patients receiving acupuncture had an improved QOL (Quality of Life) associated with significantly higher costs over the 3 months' treatment period compared to routine care alone." In conclusion, acupuncture was a cost-effective treatment strategy in patients with chronic osteoarthritis pain. And here is a third take from the Department of Family Medicine, University of North Carolina—Chapel Hill, North Carolina, published in the *Journal of Alternative and Complementary Medicine*.[6] They studied the entire population of consecutive patients seen in an acupuncture clinic from April 2002 through October 2006 (4,953 visits) and evaluated the utilization, financial costs, and benefits of incorporating acupuncture into university-based family medicine center. Their conclusion: "Our findings suggest that incorporating acupuncture into existing medical practices may benefit patients, providers, the clinic as a whole, and the larger community, but the profit margin associated with providing acupuncture in these settings is likely to be negative or slim."

The National Center for Complementary and Integrative Health, National Institutes of Health, Bethesda, MD, hosts a publication from the Mayo Clinic[7] that comprehensively examines the clinical trial evidence for the efficacy and safety of several specific approaches—acupuncture, manipulation, massage therapy, relaxation techniques, including meditation, selected natural product supplements (chondroitin, glucosamine, methylsulfonylmethane, S-adenosylmethionine), tai chi, and yoga—as used to manage chronic pain and related disability associated with back pain, fibromyalgia, osteoarthritis, neck pain, and severe headaches or migraines. The study results are mixed for acupuncture: 1+ and 2- for back pain, 1+ and 3- for fibromyalgia, and 1+ and 3- for osteoarthritis of the knee. The bottom line seems to be that government-sponsored studies at reputable institutions yield a mixed bag as far as acupuncture is concerned. Nine studies are currently still being conducted.

Let's look at an historical perspective to gain further understanding of acupuncture. While on my first visit to China in October of 1980, I had the opportunity to visit a barefoot doctor clinic in rural China and observe not only acupuncture but the close association to their herbal pharmacies. These barefoot doctors were Mao's answer to the need for spreading primary care to the countryside, and they admitted that modern Western medicine was increasingly preferred by the younger patients but that the older patients still demanded acupuncture for most conditions.

Reference to acupuncture can be traced back to the Shang Dynasty,[8] wherein began the first recorded history in China, between the eighteenth and sixteenth centuries BCE. Dr. Paul Offit noted that Chinese healers "reasoned that diseases were caused by an imbalance of energies" and "treated this imbalance by placing a series of thin needles under the skin."[9] Further, "Because Chinese physicians were prohibited from dissecting human bodies, they didn't know that nerves originated in the spinal cord…or even what nerves were." Dr. Offit writes that

> Chinese physicians believed that energy flowed through a series of twelve meridians that ran in longitudinal arcs from head to toe, choosing the number twelve because there are twelve great rivers in China. To release vital energy, which they called *chi*, and restore normal balance between competing energies, which they called *yin* and yang, needles were placed under the skin along these meridian lines. The number of acupuncture points—about 360—was determined by the number of days in the year. Depending on the practitioner, needles were inserted up to four inches deep and left in place from a few seconds to a few hours.[10]

The question of interest is, how did acupuncture, which came out of an ancient culture long before science of any kind, become a twenty-first-century method of treatment for such a wide variety of medical diagnoses? The answer, I believe, is the placebo effect and the phenomenon I call cultural hypnosis. If you can convince billions of people that it works, then you have preconditioned their expectations, and therefore, to some extent, it does.

So wherefore comes the question of deception and quackery? I recall the experience of a very close friend who was being treated for a metastatic malignant melanoma. Along with a chemotherapy program, he flew from Rochester, New York, to Boston every Friday to receive an acupuncture treatment. The acupuncturist told him that Western medicine "knew nothing about melanoma" and that he would cure him because of his expertise. That was pure fraud, deception, and a travesty. Art Caplan, professor of Bioethics at NYU Langone Medical Center, addressing the ethics of placebo medicine, is quoted by Dr. Paul Offit[11]:

> It's ethical to deceive the patient at low risk,
> at low cost, and at low burden.

I am afraid that I do not agree with this conclusion simply because it is not possible to draw the line and keep it there. I do agree with Caplan's further conclusion[12] that medicine should report accurately on the placebo effect and that certain things can induce it and that medical science should study it. The fact remains, however, I do not believe we should encourage and teach to our medical students deception in the name of the placebo effect.

The second reason to reject acupuncture use is that it carries some risk. Needles have transmitted HIV, hepatitis B and C plus, as reported from the Pacific College of Oriental Medicine, tuberculosis, mycobacterium, and methicillin-resistant staphylococcus aureus (MRSA) infection.[13] There are reports from the Mayo Clinic of puncture of organs such as lungs and liver.[14] From the Bulletin of the World Health Organization,[15] studies exclusively from China have shown an incidence of mild, transient, acupuncture-related adverse events that range from 6.71 percent to 15 percent. Quoted in the same abstract, another large-scale observational study showed a rate of adverse events requiring specific treatment of 2.2 percent (4,963 incidents among 229,230 subjects), admittedly low, but nonetheless real. In 2013 Acuwatch.org reported that during a twelve-year period, 117 reports of 308 adverse events from twenty-five countries and regions were associated with acupuncture (294 cases).[16] Details of this report showed 239 infections, thirteen incidents of pneumothorax, nine central nerve system injuries including five spinal cord injuries, five cases of heart injury including two with cardiac tamponade and seven other various injuries. There were three deaths in the same reference. Supporting the incidence of complications is the advertising of lawyers who specialize in malpractice defense of acupuncture untoward results.[17] An estimate of incidence of acupuncture malpractice could not be found.

The third argument against acupuncture is the expense. Fees for an initial visit range from *seventy-five dollars* to *ninety-five dollars* for an acupuncture session and medical consultation. Routine visits cost *fifty dollars* to *seventy dollars*.[18] Many practitioners recommend patients take specialized Chinese herbs, such as ginseng and gui pi wan, that are designed to supplement the acupuncture by treating chronic ailments like anxiety or insomnia, which also adds to the expense. There is now a national movement to reduce cost called community acupuncture.[19] They use points on the scalp and below the elbows and knees to treat the entire body, so there's no need to undress—just remove your shoes and roll up your pants and sleeves. And yes, we can even address your back pain by treating your wrists, visits costing from twenty dollars to fifty dollars.

In summary, Robert Todd Carroll, writing in his *Skeptics Dictionary*[20]:

> I can see no reason to consult an acupuncturist for any ailment I might have. I understand, however, why practitioners and patients alike are convinced that the benefits of acupuncture are due to sticking needles into people. I'm not

expecting these folks to change their minds about acupuncture on the basis of the evidence, which they will probably interpret differently. After all, there are plenty of opportunities for confirmation bias on both sides of this issue. Skeptics will continue to note any case where acupuncture doesn't help someone or causes harm, and we will continue to identify high caliber studies that support the hypothesis that acupuncture works by conditioning and placebo effects. Believers will continue to point to their successes and to the scientific studies that seem to support their viewpoint, while ignoring or misinterpreting the occasional high-caliber study that is published. Believers have the additional advantage of having on their side popular celebrities like "Deepak" Oprah and her celebrity doctor friend Mehmet Oz. A single celebrity endorsement carries more weight with many people than a thousand high-caliber scientific studies, especially with people who have a low opinion of scientific medicine. People who have had bad experiences with conventional medicine, or who are believers in the Big Pharma/AMA conspiracy to keep us sick, so they can make money, can easily find examples of experiences that support favoring acupuncture or other forms of alternative treatment over scientific medicine. To them I say: I hope all your ailments are minor ones, but if you have a heart attack or a stroke, I hope others will make sure you get the best treatment that scientific medicine has to offer.

The danger from acupuncture is that it is being promoted as superior to scientific medicine, when in fact it is clearly inferior. Acupuncture is touted as appropriate for almost any disorder or disease in man or beast, when the evidence clearly shows that such a belief is a dangerous delusion.

There are variations of acupuncture such as Ayurvedic (India) called marmapuncture,[21] based on the ancient principles which were established more than 2,500 years ago. The difference between traditional acupuncture and marmapuncture is that the former is based on the principles of Chinese medicine and the concept of qi, yin, and yang, and the latter is based on the principles of Ayurveda, chakras, and dosha. The points are very similar to one another, although marmapuncture can involve several extra points which correlate to specific chakras of the body.

There is also a Tibetan form of acupuncture. Tibetan acupuncture differs from the Chinese acupuncture predominantly in the use of different points and meridians.[22] Acupuncture is a part of the Tibetan medical system based upon Indian Buddhist literature (for example, Abhidharma and Vajrayana tantras) and Ayurveda. It continues to be practiced in Tibet, India, Nepal, Bhutan, Ladakh, Siberia, China, and Mongolia, as well as more recently in parts of Europe and North America. It embraces the traditional Buddhist belief that all illness ultimately results from the three poisons: ignorance, attachment, and aversion.[23]

There are also subsets of forms of acupuncture simply too numerous to classify. One commonality remains, however, and that is that those seeking help believe, to some degree, that it will help. Louis Lasagna, MD, one of the earlier researchers on the placebo effect, hypothesized:

> There is a certain psychologic set which *predisposes to anticipation of pain relief* and thus to a positive placebo response.[24]

Cost factors: An estimate from 2009 data estimated that the practice generates $3.5 billion per year. And the out-of-pocket expenses were near $0.9 billion.[25] In 2012, 8.5 percent of those getting acupuncture treatments were completely covered by insurance, and 16.5 percent by partial.[26] It is not unreasonable to assume that these figures have grown, but by how much, we do not know.

2. Chiropractic

*There is a name for alternative medicine
that works. It's called medicine.*
          —*Joe Schwarcz, professor of
Chemistry at McGill University*

Chiropractic was founded in 1895 by Daniel David (DD) Palmer in Davenport, Iowa.[1] Palmer was described as a "magnetic healer" saying he received it "from the other world." In this same reference, it is further noted:

> Early chiropractors believed that all disease was caused by interruptions in the flow of innate intelligence, a vitalistic nervous energy or life force that represented God's presence in man; chiropractic leaders often invoked religious imagery and moral traditions. D.D. and B.J., his son, both seriously considered declaring chiropractic a religion, which might have provided legal protection under the U.S. constitution, but decided against it partly to avoid confusion with Christian Science. Early chiropractors also tapped into the Populist movement, emphasizing craft, hard work, competition, and advertisement, aligning themselves with the common man against intellectuals and trusts, among which they included the American Medical Association (AMA).
>
> Palmer claimed, "I have received chiropractic from the other world, similar as did Mrs. (Mary Baker) Eddy." He thought that if he established chiropractic as a religion, it would further his chances of being allowed to practice.

"But we must have a religious head, one who is
the founder, as did Christ, Mohamed, Jo.Smith,
Mrs. Eddy, Martin Luther and others who have
founded religions. I am the fountain head. I am
the founder of chiropractic in its science, in its
art, in its philosophy and in its religious phase.
Now, if chiropractors desire to claim me as their
head, their leader, the way is clear. My writings
have been gradually steering in that direction
until now it is time to assume that we have the
same right to as has Christian Scientists."[2]

It is important to examine the origins of chiropractic and note
that, although Palmer mentions "science," there is not a single shred
of evidence that he understood what it was or, more importantly,
what the scientific method was all about. The fact that he considered
making chiropractic a religion is more absurd. Absurd or not, Palmer
and his son founded the first school of chiropractic and propagated
the practice, which survives to this day. However, much effort has
been exerted to make chiropractic a science it never was in its original
form, nor is there evidence that it is today or ever will be. It is best to
describe it as pseudoscience. That is not to say that it has not resulted
in satisfied customers, as was noted in the discussion of the placebo
effect. It is well to note in any balanced discussion that had there not
been science and only chiropractic, we would be essentially stuck
back in the nineteenth century for only the scientific method has
and will provide for progress in medicine. No spinal manipulation
would cure polio.

Dr. Paul Offit's account of the origins of chiropractic provides a
double denial of science:

In 1895 when a man who had been deaf
for seventeen years walked into his office, Palmer
tried something else. Believing that deafness was
caused by misaligned spinal column, which he
called "subluxation," Palmer pushed down on

the back of the man's neck, hoping to realign his spine. It worked; the man recovered his hearing immediately. (the event was often referred to as "the crack heard around the world"). Most miraculous about Palmer's cure is that the eighth cranial nerve, which conducts nerve impulses from the ear to the brain, doesn't travel through the neck. Palmer then took the next illogical step, arguing that *all* diseases were caused by misaligned spines. Because this isn't true, it shouldn't be surprising that studies have shown that chiropractic manipulations don't treat many of the diseases they claimed to, such as headaches, menstrual pain, colic asthma and allergies.[3]

The basis of chiropractic is the theory of subluxation.[4] All disease, he argued, results from disruption in the flow of "innate intelligence." Disruption in flow is caused by spinal subluxations, which are small misalignments in the spine that compress the spinal nerves. The term "subluxation" is used by doctors of chiropractic to depict the altered position of the vertebra and subsequent functional loss.[5] "Subluxation" has been defined medically as "a partial abnormal separation of the articular surfaces of a joint."[6] It is well to remember that this is propagated in the chiropractic literature as a theory or sometimes referred to as vertebral subluxation complex.[7] In a 2005 article by Keating et al. entitled "Subluxation: Dogma or Science?" the conclusion in the abstract reads:

> Subluxation syndrome is a legitimate, potentially testable, theoretical construct for which there is little experimental evidence. Acceptable as hypothesis, the widespread assertion of the clinical meaningfulness of this notion brings ridicule from the scientific and health care communities and confusion within the chiropractic profession. We believe that an evidence-orienta-

tion among chiropractors requires that we distinguish between subluxation dogma vs. subluxation as the potential focus of clinical research. We lament efforts to generate unity within the profession through consensus statements concerning subluxation dogma and believe that cultural authority will continue to elude us so long as we assert dogma as though it were validated clinical theory.[8]

The paper's summary conclusion: "The chiropractic subluxation stands pretty much today as it did at the dawn of the 20th century: an interesting notion without validation." As a Beth Israel Deaconess Medical Center article describes the mainstream understanding of vertebral subluxation theory,

No real evidence has ever been presented showing that a given chiropractic treatment alters the position of any vertebrae. In addition, there is as yet *no real evidence* that impairment of nerve outflow is a major contributor to common illnesses, or that spinal manipulation changes nerve outflow in such a way as to affect organ function.[9]

Who utilizes the services of chiropractors in the United States? A 2002 study concluded that more than 70 percent of patients specified back and neck problems as their health problem for which they sought chiropractic care. In other words, data support the theory that patients seek chiropractic care almost exclusively for musculoskeletal symptoms and that chiropractors and their patients share a similar belief system,[10] and what is it costing our health-care system? As a rough estimate, the number of chiropractors (40,500) × average income ($80,306 = $3,252,393).[11] From Health Services Research,[12] the chiropractic profession experienced significant growth in national utilization and expenditures over the decade from 1997 to 2006. From 1997 to 2006, the estimated total inflation-adjusted expenditures on US adult (≥18 years) chiropractic care increased from US $3.8 billion (95 percent CI: 2.9–4.7) to US $5.91 billion (95 percent CI: 5.0–6.8): a net increase of 55 percent. It can be reasonably assumed that it has increased significantly since that time and is at least $6 billion or more.

There are two schools of thought within the chiropractic community that cause confusion and detract from justice when chiropractic malpractice occurs. Peter J. Modde, DC, writing in 1979,[13] asked the simple question, "Are chiropractors trained to accurately diagnosis and refer?" His answer was "no." The reason he asserts is that schools of chiropractic are divided in education principles and practice into "straight" and "mixers." The straight branch insists on the emphasis on finding and treating the ever-elusive subluxation, while the mixer branch represents the vast majority of chiropractors who can use blood tests as an example. Modde points to a legal memorandum published in the journal of the American Chiropractic Association[14] concluding:

> The legal duty of the chiropractor, as with any other doctor, is to: first, diagnose the patient's problem; second, if the problem can be treated by spinal manipulation, then he may proceed; third, if he determines that the form of treatment required is outside the scope of his practice, then he must refer the patient to another doctor.

Two cases from my own practice as a vascular surgeon for thirty years illustrate the problems. The first case was personal as it involved my landlord, who, according to his wife, visited a chiropractor for back pain. He was treated with a manipulation and was sent home, only to be rushed by ambulance in the middle of the night with a ruptured abdominal aortic aneurysm, and died before he could reach the operating room. The other was of a thirty-five-year-old otherwise-healthy woman who, presenting with headache, underwent, according to her husband, "a rather vigorous manipulation of her neck and shoulder" and presented in the ER with an enormously swollen left arm caused by a thrombosis of the venous system or the arm requiring emergency surgery and prolonged anticoagulation. They sought to sue for malpractice. The attorney would not take the case, stating, "There was no money in it," and the reason was that it is impossible to establish "*a standard of care for chiropractic in a court of law.*" Both cases illustrate the variance in chiropractic education and the conflicts within the chiropractic profession to establish standards of diagnosis and treatment.

How much of a problem is chiropractic malpractice?[15]

According to statistics from the National Practitioner Data Bank ("NPDB") for the period from September 1, 1990 through January 29, 2012, there were a total of 5,796 medical malpractice reports involving chiropractors filed with the NPDB; 7,535 licensure, clinical privileges, professional society membership, and peer review organization reports filed with the NPDB involving chiropractors; and, 4,147 Medicare/Medicaid Exclusions Reports filed with the NPDB with regard to chiropractors throughout the United States.

California chiropractors had the most reports filed against them, with 990 medical malpractice reports, 904 licensure (etc.) reports, and 978 Medicare/Medicaid exclusions reports filed with the NPDB. The next closest U.S. states to California were Florida, with 425, 550, and 318 reports, respectively, and Texas, with 245, 653, and 313 reports, respectively.

The states with the lowest number of reports regarding chiropractors filed with the NPDA (excluding U.S. territories and other non-states) were Delaware (7, 5, 0 reports, respectively), Wyoming (13, 4, 2 reports, respectively), South

Dakota (22, 7, 5 reports, respectively), and
Vermont (16, 11, 9 reports, respectively).

For further reference on neck manipulation and strokes, see reference by Stephen Barrett, MD.[16]

Since the turn of the millennium, the practice of chiropractic has changed. *The Milbank Quarterly*, a multidisciplinary journal of population health and health policy, has reported comprehensively on these changes.[17] They are as follows:

1. In increasing numbers, chiropractors have expanded into the vanguard of complementary and alternative medicine (CAM), while CAM is receiving even greater proportions of expenditures.
2. While experiencing greater competition from acupuncturists and massage therapists, they are increasingly incorporating these modalities into their practices.
3. The boundary between chiropractic and primary medical care is being eroded.
4. Chiropractic has experienced continued conflict in finding a legitimate place in the age of evidence-based medicine. That is to say, there is a "widened schism" between the "straights and the mixers," with the mixers generally willing to examine their outcomes, whereas straights do not consider chiropractic a testable science but rather a *belief system*.
5. Patients with low back and neck pain are the majority of patients seeking chiropractic services, and reported studies of the efficacy of spinal manipulative therapy (SMT) remain mixed, perhaps because of variable quality within the studies themselves. The Office of Alternative Medicine (OAM) at NIH reporting most recently on their research on spinal manipulation for back pain[18]

       have shown that spinal manipulation can provide mild-to-moderate relief from low-back pain and appears to be as effective as conventional medical treatments. Results from one trial that examined long-term effects in more than 600 people with low-back pain suggest that chiropractic care involving spinal manipulation is at least as effective as conventional medical care for up to 18 months.

Various guidelines include the Agency for Health Care Policy and Research (AHCPR) and the Veterans Administration (VA), "while they do not preclude the possibility that SMT (Spinal Manipulative Therapy) has value in certain subgroups of patients, they offer only weak support for what is a mainstay of practice in chiropractic."

6. Chiropractors have extended services within the CAM umbrella to nutrition, nutrition products, herbal medicine, and various controversial modalities such as deep tissue laser therapy.

7. As a final observation, chiropractors, "having crossed the chasm into the reimbursed world of health care, they must now prove their quality, effectiveness, and value. Chiropractic is buttressed by satisfied patients and sympathetic politicians and by the general longing for someone who will listen and be supportive. But as our aging nation struggles to define the health care system that it can afford, it is uncertain whether this will be enough."

Although it is difficult to obtain current expenditures on chiropractic services alone, there is information (National Health Statistics Reports) published in 2016[19] on aggregate expenditures on complementary health services in the United States based on surveys done in 2012. This report showed that an estimated fifty-nine million persons aged four years and over had at least one expenditure for some type of complementary health service, resulting in total out-of-pocket expenditures of $30.2 billion. The complementary health approaches analyzed for this report included acupuncture, Ayurveda, biofeedback, chelation therapy, chiropractic and osteopathic manipulation, energy healing therapy, diet-based therapies, guided imagery, homeopathic treatment, hypnosis, massage therapy, meditation, naturopathy, natural product supplements, progressive relaxation, qigong, tai chi, yoga, movement therapies, craniosacral therapy, and "traditional healers." For individuals aged four and over, the mean annual per user out-or-pocket expenditure for all complementary health approaches was $510.[20] This analysis also showed that out-of-pocket expenditures on complementary health approaches also increased as family income increased. One can only assume that a certain portion of services, however small, were funded by insurance, so all figures for total expenditures are more than recorded here.

Cost factors: another way to estimate expenditures for chiropractic services is to multiply the number of chiropractic physicians by the average income. This calculation from the Federation of Chiropractic Licensing Boards reveals that the number of licenses to practice chiropractic in the United States is 92,943[21] times the average income $66,720 equals over $6.2 billion. Out-of-pocket cost was reported in 2007 to be about $4 billion.[22]

3. Herbal Medicine

> *Even though I believe we should promote Chinese medicine, I personally do not believe in it.*
> —*Mao Zedong*

Chinese herbal medicine. Included in the 2016 National Health Statistics Reports of complementary health approaches are *naturopathy* and *natural product supplements*. *Naturopathy* is defined as "an alternative medical system based on the belief that there is a healing power in the body that establishes, maintains and restores health. Practitioners work with the patient with a goal of supporting this power through treatments such as nutrition, lifestyle counseling, dietary supplements, medicinal plants, exercise, homeopathy and treatments from traditional Chinese medicine."[1] *Natural product supplements* also include herbs or herbal medicine.

For Chinese herbal medicine, the foremost reference is the modern edition of a classic sixteenth-century manual *Chinese Medicinal Herbs* by Li Shih-Chen, a translation of Li Shih-Chen's *Herbal Pen Ts'ao* of 1578.[2] According to the preface of this reference, the original book contained 1,892 species of drugs, animal, vegetable, and mineral and included 8,160 prescriptions. The current 1973 edition, over five hundred pages, makes fascinating reading. How many of the citations in the text are used today? I do not know. The back cover of the 1973 edition refers to the book as "a landmark treatise, a treasury of tried-and-true wisdom from centuries of practical experience." Again from 2016 publication of 2012 data, $32.1 million was the annual amount spent by adults out of pocket for natural product supplements and $2.3 million for children in the same category all part of the estimated $34 billion out of pocket expenses for complementary health approaches in the aggregate, representing 1.5 percent of total health expenditures and 11 percent of out-of-pocket cost.[3]

Currently, six fields of CAM practices are subject to licensure requirements and, therefore, some form of educational accreditation. They are osteopathic manipulation, chiropractic, acupuncture and traditional Asian medicine, massage therapy, naturopathy, and homeopathy.[4] It is difficult to imagine the extent of knowledge that pharmacology of Chinese herbal literature (Asian medicine) is demanded in these accreditations. That is not to say there is absolutely no way of determining evidence-based results for CAM.

There are reference databases that are searchable—for example, the Cochran Library, the webpage of which describes its purpose as follows:

> The Cochrane Library[5] is a collection of databases that contain high-quality, independent evidence to inform healthcare decision making. Cochrane Reviews represent the highest level of evidence on which to base clinical treatment decisions. The Cochrane Library consists of seven databases and is used by a broad range of people interested in evidence-based health care,

including consumers, clinicians, policy-makers, researchers, educators, students and others.

Support for the Cochran Library has come from several sources, including the publishing house John Wiley and Sons and Wikipedia. According to the Wiley website[6]:

> John Wiley & Sons (Wiley) has been Cochrane's principal publishing partner since 2003, working closely with Cochrane contributors and staff to support publication of the Cochrane Library on Wiley's internationally recognized electronic publishing platform. Over the course of the Cochrane-Wiley partnership, more than half the world's population has secured one-click access to Cochrane content through licenses or free access programmes. Wiley is a global provider of content-enabled solutions that improve outcomes in research, education, and professional practice. Our core businesses produce scientific, technical, medical, and scholarly journals, reference works, books, database services, and advertising; professional books, subscription products, certification and training services and online applications; and education content and services including integrated online teaching and learning resources for undergraduate and graduate students and lifelong learners.

When I searched "Chinese herbal medicine" in "Title, Abstract, Keywords" in Cochrane Reviews, the yield was 102 results from 9,784 records. The results were diverse and eclectic. Here are a few examples:

1. Chinese herbal medicines for hypercholesterolemia. Zhao Lan Liu, Jian Ping Liu, Anthony Lin Zhang,

Qiong Wu, Yao Ruan, George Lewith and Denise Visconte
   Online Publication Date: July 2011.
2. Chinese herbal medicine for chronic neck pain due to cervical degenerative disc disease, Xuejun Cui, Kien Trinh and Yong-Jun Wang
   Online Publication Date: January 2010.
3. Chinese herbal medicine for oesophageal cancer. Xi Chen, Linyu Deng, Xuehua Jiang and Taixiang Wu
   Online Publication Date: January 2016.
4. Chinese herbal medicine in the treatment of ectopic pregnancy. Hai Bo Qu, Wang Dengfeng, Taixiang Wu, Jane Marjoribanks, Sun Ying, Jia Haijun, Jing Zhang and Lina H
   Online Publication Date: July 2011.
5. Interventions for treating gas gangrene. Zhirong Yang, Jing Hu, Yanji Qu, Feng Sun, Xisheng Leng, Hang Li and Siyan Zhan
   Online Publication Date: December 2015.

In the long review of the last reference above (interventions for treating gas gangrene), the following statement is made:

Chinese herbal medicine consists of complex prescriptions of a combination of several herbal components. The mechanism of action of the herbal medicines is reported to involve haemostasis (prevention of bleeding), detumescence (subsidence of swelling; Appendix 1) and antibacterial activity (Hou 2010).

There was a notation of what constituted the makeup of the herbal medicine for one study of forty-six patients.

The herbal medicine was prepared locally with *Cirsium setosum* (field thistle / *Herba cirsii*), *Portulaca oleracea* (purslane/verdolaga), and *Sedum lineare* (carpet sedum / needle stonecrop). Information about who prepared and administered the herbal medicine was not available.

The cure rate defined in the trial for this group was 80.8 percent (21/26), but it must be pointed out that this group also received antibiotics by the same protocol as the group not receiving Chinese herbal medicine. It must be further pointed out that the herbs used as cited above do not appear in the 1973 edition of Li Shih-Chen's *Chinese Medicinal Herbs.*

A proper conclusion is that the Corcoran Library is a commendable effort, on the part of Wiley and all concerned, but the science of Chinese herbal medicine, as noted on this website, is questionable beyond saying that it might, in some cases, be "complementary."

Searching for information on the website National Center for Complementary and Integrative Health[7] is of interest. Under "All Health Topics from A–Z" is the heading "Chinese Herbal Medicine." Clicking on that brings up a page of the same heading on which is a featured topic: "Traditional Chinese Medicine: In Depth." Under the heading "Key Points" is the statement

> For most conditions, there is not enough rigorous scientific evidence to know whether TCM methods work for the conditions for which they are used.

Under "Side Effects and Risks," the same website page goes on to further explanation, which is rather disturbing:

> Herbal medicines used in TCM are sometimes marketed in the United States as dietary supplements. The U.S. Food and Drug Administration (FDA) regulations for dietary supplements are not the same as those for prescription or over-the-counter drugs; in general, the regulations for dietary supplements are less stringent. For example, manufacturers don't have to prove to the FDA that most claims made for

dietary supplements are valid; if the product were a drug, they would have to provide proof.

Chinese herbal products may be safe, but others may not be. There have been reports of products being contaminated with drugs, toxins, or heavy metals or not containing the listed ingredients. Some of the herbs used in Chinese medicine can interact with drugs, can have serious side effects, or may be unsafe for people with certain medical conditions. For example, the Chinese herb ephedra (ma huang) has been linked to serious health complications, including heart attack and stroke. In 2004, the FDA banned the sale of ephedra-containing dietary supplements, but *the ban does not apply to TCM remedies.*

In fairness, there is one positive note in the quagmire that is Chinese herbal medicine. It is the fact that in 2015, China celebrated their first Nobel Prize in a scientific discipline. It was awarded to a retired member of the China Academy of Chinese Medical Sciences, Tu Youyou.[8] The Nobel committee clearly stated that it was not honoring Chinese medicine but for specific scientific procedures she used to extract the active ingredient and create a chemical drug. Dr. Tu cited the original reference for the drug, used effectively by a secret Chinese project she conducted during the Vietnam War, was *The Handbook of Prescriptions for Emergencies*, written in 340 BC by Ge Hong.[9] In the same reference, *The New York Times* further reported that Chinese journalists established the fact that Dr. Tu, in the forty years since her discovery, had tried to find other (effective) herbs but had not succeeded.

Herbalism is not confined to the Chinese variety alone. R. Barker Bausell, PhD, former research director of the NIH Complementary and Alternative Medicine Specialized Research Center, in his book *Snake Oil Science*,[10] notes that herbs are a major component of several medical systems. He wrote:

There are CAM practitioners who label themselves as "herbalists" and prescribe (and often sell) a bewildering array of botanical products and compounds that can be (and are) tailored to treat just about every imaginable human illness.

Given the number of these products on the market, no one can categorically say that none has any utility or efficacious chemical action. No one can say with certainty that some aren't actually dangerous for certain conditions or that they don't interact adversely with other drugs. More than likely a substantial number of the myriad herbs prescribed in a day's work by an herbalist have no positive or negative effects at all, other than the enrichment of the prescribing herbalist (and of course the corporations that package the herbs themselves).

There may be a "miracle" cure or two residing on an herbalist's shelf somewhere. How it could ever be differentiated from the welter of surrounding compounds that do nothing at all, however, is not at all clear.

The NIH Office of Alternative Medicine was launched in 1995 with legislation sponsored by Senator Tom Harkin (D) Iowa, a populist elected to the Senate for five terms, who, unless he took a course in college, had no credentials in science. The legislation was accompanied by press conference at which a copy of a thick document, *Alternative Medicine: Expanding Medical Horizons*, was distributed, "covering everything from herbal medicine and acupuncture to faith healing and Lakota medicine wheels" all beyond the confines of mainstream Western scientific medicine.[11] According to Robert L. Park's account,[12] Harkin claimed to have been cured of his allergies by "swallowing vast quantities of bee pollen capsules" sold to him by a man who had settled a claim of $200,000 with the Federal Trade

Commission for making false claims in an infomercial, claiming that "the risen Jesus Christ on his return to earth consumed bee pollen."

This document cited in the above paragraph contained but a portion of the vast gamut that is herbal medicine which the government was sanctioned to perform scientific studies to establish effectiveness. As of 2009,[13] after spending $2.5 billion, the results were disappointing, as NBC News reported.

> Echinacea for colds. Ginkgo biloba for memory. Glucosamine and chondroitin for arthritis. Black cohosh for menopausal hot flashes. Saw palmetto for prostate problems. Shark cartilage for cancer. All proved no better than dummy pills in big studies funded by the National Center for Complementary and Alternative Medicine. The lone exception: ginger capsules may help chemotherapy nausea.
>
> Yoga, meditation and massage may relieve pain, anxiety and fatigue, but distance healing and prayer have little plausibility of scientific evidence.
>
> The government is also funding studies of purported energy fields, distance healing and prayer that have little if any plausibility of scientific evidence.
>
> Funding figures show that the National Center for Complementary and Integrative Health (NCCIH) as it is now called for fiscal year 2014 spent $100,093,000*. They also funded 28 other branches and subsections of NIH to the tune of over $250,000,000 making the total $363,000,000. These included the National Cancer Institute and the National Institute on Aging to name a few. This infiltration across numerous specialties about the country amounts to a plague of questionable science funded by our

tax dollars and detracting from the spending on the most promising science. True, the NCCIH budget is 7.3% of the 2015 budget for the National Cancer Institute which is rounded to $5 billion[13] but does not warrant that spending based upon these results after twenty-two years of effort. *The 2019 figure is $146,500,000.

Cost factors: Government surveys[14] do not break out costs of Chinese medical products, but the report of 2012[15] notes that $12.8 billion out of pocket was spent on "natural products" and $54.1 billion on "prescription drugs." A low estimate based upon Asian population statistics would be about $1.5 billion.

4. Vitamins and Supplements

If you were wise, you wouldn't be taking any of the thousands of herbal products on the market.
—Simeon Margolis,
MD, Johns Hopkins Medicine

Vitamins are a group of organic compounds that are essential for normal growth and nutrition required in small quantities in the diet because they cannot be synthesized by the body. The vitamins include vitamin D, vitamin E, vitamin A, and vitamin K, or the fat-soluble vitamins, and folate (folic acid), vitamin B_{12}, biotin, vitamin B_6, niacin, thiamin, riboflavin, pantothenic acid, and vitamin C (ascorbic acid), or the water-soluble vitamins. Vitamins, thirteen in all, are required in the diet in only tiny amounts, in contrast to the energy components of the diet. The energy components of the diet are sugars, starches, fats, and oils, and these occur in relatively large amounts in the diet.[1] There are three reasons to treat people with vitamins[2]:

1. The primary reason is to relieve a vitamin deficiency, when one has been detected. Chemical

tests suitable for the detection of all vitamin deficiencies are available.

2. A second reason for vitamin treatment is to prevent the development of an expected deficiency. Here, vitamins are administered even with no test for possible deficiency. For example, Vitamin D for subjects who do not get adequate sunlight.

3. The third reason is to prevent certain specific disease. For example, folic acid for the prevention of certain birth defects.

So what are the consequences of ignoring these three reasons and taking extra vitamins for whatever reason? It seems that there are now an accumulating avalanche of reports demonstrating the serious problems from doing so. A study published in the *Archives of Medicine* and quoted in the Johns Hopkins "Health After 50" report[3] suggests a link between multivitamins and increased risk of death for older women. The reference is to the Iowa Women's Health Study started in 1986 on thirty-nine thousand women from fifty-five to sixty-nine followed over nineteen years. The study discovered that women who took multivitamins, iron, copper, magnesium, zinc, vitamin B_6, and folic acid had a greater risk of dying earlier than those who did not take supplements. The Hopkins report noted:

> Most supplements accounted for a 2.4% (multivitamins) to a 5.9% (folic acid) greater risk of dying over the almost 2 decades. An exception was copper, accounting for an 18% increase. Iron, in particular, concerned the researchers: The higher the dose taken, the higher the death risk. Only calcium was associated with lower death rates.

In the same Johns Hopkins report was research results on men taking vitamin E and selenium to test prevention of prostate cancer.[4] More than thirty-five thousand men ages fifty and older were recruited for the study called the Selenium and Vitamin E Cancer Prevention Trial (SELECT). The trial was stopped in 2008 ahead of schedule because it was apparent that neither supplement was beneficial. When the data was reviewed in 2011, they found that men who took only vitamin E supplement were developing prostate cancer at a significantly higher rate than men who took either selenium only, a combination of the two or a placebo. Scientists have not been able to pinpoint how vitamin E increases prostate cancer risk.

The New York Times in 2013 summarized in an opinion article by Dr. Paul Offit, a series of like studies.[5] They quoted a study published in The New England Journal of Medicine in 1994 in which twenty-nine thousand Finnish men, all smokers, had been given daily vitamin E, beta-carotene, or both or a placebo. The study found that those who had taken beta-carotene for five to eight years were more likely to die from lung cancer or heart disease. (The human body converts beta-carotene into vitamin A [retinol]—beta-carotene is a precursor of vitamin A. We need vitamin A for healthy skin and mucus membranes, our immune system, and good eye health and vision. Beta-carotene in itself is not an essential nutrient, but vitamin A is.) Dr. Offit went on to note a study two years later from the same journal, reporting that eighteen thousand people who were at an increased risk of lung cancer because of asbestos exposure or smoking received a combination of vitamin A and beta-carotene or a placebo. Investigators stopped the study when they found that the risk of death from lung cancer for those who took the vitamins was 46 percent higher. There have been other studies as well backing the conclusion that beta-carotene and vitamins E and A increased mortality.

What is the explanation for supplemental vitamins causing increased rates of cancer? Dr. Offit's says the key is the antioxidant paradox.[6] In the contest between free-radical production by oxidation and free-radical destruction the balance can be disrupted by large amounts of antioxidants caused by taking supplemental vitamins. This is the paradox. More is less healthy. Dr. Offit concludes, because studies of large doses of supplemental antioxidants haven't clearly supported their use; respected organizations responsible for the public's health do not recommend them for otherwise healthy people.

You may ask, "Why has the FDA allowed this without doing something?" The answer is that they are unable to do so by law[7].

> On April 22, 1976, Congress passes the Vitamin-Mineral Amendment to the Federal Food, Drug, and Cosmetic Act. Also known as the Proxmire amendment (after Sen. William Proxmire, D-Wisc., its principal sponsor), the legislation prohibited the FDA from establishing standards to limit the potency of vitamins and minerals in food supplements or regulating them as drugs based solely on their potency.

The bill's cosponsors were Bob Dole, William Fulbright, Barry Goldwater, Hubert Humphrey, George McGovern, and Sam Nunn and were backed by one of the largest and most expensive lobbying efforts in the history of the Congress.[8]

Add to the vitamin market a large sector called "supplements." The FDA defines a dietary supplement[9] as a product intended for ingestion that contains a "dietary ingredient" intended to add further nutritional value to (supplement) the diet. A "dietary ingredient" may be one, or any combination, of the following substances: (a) vitamin, (b) mineral, (c) an herb or other botanical, (d) an amino acid, and (e) a dietary substance for use by people to supplement the diet by increasing the total dietary intake. It may be in the form of concentrate, metabolite, constituent, or extract.

FDA regulates dietary supplements under a different set of regulations than those covering "conventional" foods and drug products.[10] Under the Dietary Supplement Health and Education Act of 1994 (DSHEA), FDA is responsible for taking action against any adulterated or misbranded dietary supplement product after it reaches the market. David Kessler, commissioner of the FDA when DSHEA was approved, has stated that

The 1994 Dietary Supplement Act does not require that dietary supplements (defined broadly to include many substances, such as herbs and amino acids, that have no nutritive value) be shown to be safe or effective before they are marketed. The FDA does not scrutinize a dietary supplement before it enters the market-place. The agency is permitted to restrict a substance if it poses a "significant and unreasonable risk" under the conditions of use on the label or as commonly consumed... Congress has shown little interest in protecting consumers from the hazards of dietary supplements, let alone from the fraudulent claims that are made, since its members apparently believe that few of these products place people in real danger. Nor does the public understand how potentially dangerous these products can be.[11]

These lax rules have allowed the introduction of supplements known as "medical foods" or "nutraceuticals" as reported by *the Wall Street Journal*.[12] As this article notes, "To avoid the pricey process of getting a product approved as a drug, sometimes companies brand products as medical foods or supplements to speed them to the market." The failure to provide protection in the supplement market has resulted in fraudulent labeling of content. *USA Today* in 2015 reported on a suit brought by the AG of the state of Oregon, Ellen Rosenblum, against GNC, one of the largest retailers of vitamins and supplements accusing the company of knowingly selling products "spiked with two synthetic drugs."[13] The suit accuses GNC of selling workout and fat-burner supplement products that contained picamilon, a prescription drug in Russia used to treat neurological conditions. The article goes on to point out that a 2003 *USA Today* exposé had prompted GNC to remove a synthetic amphetamine-like chemical known as BMPEA from workout and weight-loss supplements indicating previous mislabeling fraud.

In April of 2015, *USA Today* reported,[14] "A handful of weight-loss and sports supplements contain a never-before-tested ingredient that's closely related to amphetamines—not the plant extract indicated on their label, according to a Harvard-led study published on line by the journal *Drug Testing and Analysis*." The products made by Hi-Tech Pharmaceuticals Inc. of Norcross, Georgia, were sold under the names JetFuel T-300, Fastin-XR, and Black Widow. According to Dr. Pieter Cohen, an assistant professor at the Harvard Medical School, such faulty labeling can trigger stroke, heart attack, and even death. The article cites the FDA for being unable to stop this contamination of supplements, but so far, only the testing labs and attorneys general have stood up to the fraud in labeling of supplements.

The *Journal Drug Testing and Analysis* above referenced is used for reporting testing for illegal and suspected substances in supplements used by athletes all around the world. One recent example from 2015 abstract:

Anti-doping laboratories test for substance listed by the WADA (World Anti-Doping Agency).

> Recently[15] a new designer stimulant, NN-DMPPA was found in the urine of four athletes on a routine screen. This chemical was detected in a nutritional supplement labeled NOXPUMP sourced from a store in Poland. The investigating lab further found that NN-DMPPA was not listed or otherwise noted on the label of the supplement.
>
> Many athletes are unaware of what is not unusual in this marketplace. There is certainly need for more legislation to protect athletes at all levels from such dangerous practices.

In 2013, *The New York Times* reported that "dietary supplements account for nearly 20 percent of drug-related liver injuries that turn up in hospitals, up from 7% a decade ago."[16] Many recover after discontinuing the supplement, but some require liver transplants and some die. The article again mentions the Dietary Supplement Health and Education Act of 1994, which "prevents the Food and Drug Administration from approving or evaluating most supplements before they are sold. Usually the agency must wait until consumers are harmed before officials can remove products from stores. Because the supplement industry operates on the honor system, studies show, the market has been flooded with products that are adulterated, mislabeled or packaged in dosages that have not been studied for safety." The same article quotes Dr. Herbert J. Bonkovsky, the director of liver, digestive, and metabolic disorders laboratory at Carolinas HealthCare System in Charlotte, North Carolina.

> "When people buy these dietary supplements, it's anybody's guess as to what they are getting." In fairness, a spokesman for the Council for Responsible Nutrition, a trade group is quoted as saying, "More popular supplements like vitamins, minerals, probiotics and fish oil had not been linked to 'patterns of adverse effects.'" Dr. Bonkovsky concluded that it was not always clear what exactly caused the liver injury, in part because "patients frequently combined multiple supplements and use products with up to 30 ingredients." One product of concern was green tea extract, which contains catechins, a group of potent antioxidants that reputedly increase metabolism. These extracts are marketed as fat burners, and are often added to weight-loss products and energy boosters and since most green tea pills contain many times the amount of catechins found in a single cup of green tea, they can be toxic to the liver. Many people are gullible and believe that if something is labeled "natural" than it must be safe.

The former attorney general of the state of New York, Eric Schneiderman unmasked fraud in the supplement market directed at arthritis treatment.[17] In 2015, he sent cease-and-desist orders to thirteen manufacturers of a supplement used to treat arthritis after a report found it contained the wrong ingredient. Testing showed that the supplement in question did not contain "devil's claw," a plant native to Africa, but "zeyheri," a plant with no benefits for bones or joints. The defense given by one spokesperson from the American Botanical Council was that the two ingredients in question were similar chemically and biologically. No mention was made as to whether they were claimed effective.

More extensive questions of fraud were raised by *The New York Times* in 2015.[18] The editorial reported that the New York State attorney general's office investigated store brands of well-known herbal products sold by four prominent national retailers: GNC, Target, Walgreens, and Walmart; among the popular products studied were ginkgo biloba, Saint-John's-wort, and ginseng pills.

> Four out of five of the products tested did not include any of the herbs listed on their labels. Even worse, hidden ingredients and contaminants could be dangerous to people with allergies to those substances. That such well-known brands should be found to be fraudulent suggests that the problem infects the entire industry.

The editorial goes on to report that the four companies selling the supplements in question stopped selling in New York State, but Walmart and GNC were continuing to sell their products outside New York State. Adding to the problem, cites the editorial, is the testing mechanism. The AG's office claims that the standards of testing include DNA barcoding and is highly reliable noting lab sources, whereas the United States Pharmacopeial Convention claims its testing is more accurate. The controversies surrounding the field of DNA barcoding as a method of identification is beyond the scope of this discussion, but the evidence seems to be that it is highly accurate for identification purposes.[19]

An article appearing in 2013 in the *Journal BMC*, an online open peer-reviewed journal, reported on contaminated supplements.[20] The article entitled "DNA Barcoding Detects Contamination and Substitution in North American Herbal Products" prints the abstract as follows:

Background

Herbal products available to consumers in the marketplace may be contaminated or substituted with alternative plant species and fillers that are not listed on the labels. According to the World Health Organization, the adulteration of herbal products is a threat to consumer safety. Our research aimed to investigate herbal product integrity and authenticity with the goal of protecting consumers from health risks associated with product substitution and contamination.

Methods

We used DNA barcoding to conduct a blind test of the authenticity for (i) 44 herbal products representing 12 companies and 30 different species of herbs, and (ii) 50 leaf samples collected from 42 herbal species. Our laboratory also assembled the first standard reference material (SRM) herbal barcode library from 100 herbal species of known provenance that were used to identify the unknown herbal products and leaf samples.

Results

We recovered DNA barcodes from most herbal products (91%) and all leaf samples (100%), with 95% species resolution using a tiered approach (rbcL + ITS2). Most (59%) of the products tested contained DNA barcodes from plant species not listed on the labels. Although we were able to authenticate almost half (48%) of the products, one-third of these also contained contaminants and or fillers not listed on the label. Product substitution occurred in 30/44 of the products tested and only 2/12 companies had products without any substitution, contamination or fillers. Some of the contaminants we found pose serious health risks to consumers.

Conclusions

Most of the herbal products tested were of poor quality, including considerable product substitution, contamination and use of fillers. These activities dilute the effectiveness of otherwise useful remedies, lowering the perceived value of all related products because of a lack of consumer confidence in them. We suggest that the herbal industry should embrace DNA barcoding for authenticating herbal products through testing of raw materials used in manufacturing products. The use of an SRM DNA herbal barcode library for testing bulk materials could provide a method for "best practices" in the manufacturing of herbal products. This would provide consumers with safe, high quality herbal products.

This article was cited by *The New York Times* in late 2013[21] summing up the widespread problem. The article noted that Americans spend billions a year on unproven herbal supplements. They concluded that DNA tests show, "Many pills labeled as healing herbs are little more than powdered rice and weeds." Two bottles labeled as Saint-John's-wort, which is used to treat mild depression, contained none of the medicinal herb. Instead, the pills in one bottle were made of nothing but rice, and another bottle contained only Alexandrian senna, a yellow Egyptian shrub that is a powerful laxative. Gingko biloba supplements, promoted as memory enhancers, were mixed with fillers and black walnut, a potentially deadly hazard for people with a nut allergy.

It is not hard imagining how difficult the problem of ensuring quality and effectiveness when there are an estimated twenty-nine thousand herbal products (one estimate) and substances sold throughout North America. The best estimate from government sources in November 2016 is that "Americans spend $30 billion a year on dietary supplements that do little."[22] The facts are that one in five Americans takes supplements, that the FDA only spot tests about 1 percent of the sixty-five thousand dietary supplements on the market, and that there's really no way for consumers to know what they're buying.[23]

In spite of the evidence supporting the view that we should stop wasting money on vitamin and mineral supplements,[24] the US supplement industry continues to grow. It is not only a huge business but is politically an enormous political force. The market is essentially divided into Big Pharma and Little Pharma.[25] This reference made the following observations:

> The Pharma giant Wyeth, for example, makes Centrum and other supplements, and Bayer HealthCare of aspirin fame makes the One-A-Day line. Unilever, Novartis, GlaxoSmithKline and other big pharmaceutical firms also make or sell supplements. "They're moving into more and more of these products," said Steven Mister, president of the trade group, Council for Responsible Nutrition. Big companies may be more likely to make a product that is pure and contains what it claims because "they have more to lose" by selling something that's inferior, said Dr. Tod Cooperman, president of ConsumerLab.com, a testing service. However, size does not guarantee quality. Big companies are more likely to seek out bulk ingredient suppliers in less developed

countries, said Jana Hildreth of the Analytical Research Collective, a group of scientists advocating better supplement testing. "They're going to demand lower prices, and with the prices they demand comes lower quality. You basically get what you pay for," she said.

Another way to get an idea of the size of this market is to see a list of the publicly traded nutritional supplement, vitamin and sports nutrition companies listed on the major US exchanges.[26] They range from large cap companies such as Mead Johnson (MJN) through Herbalife Ltd. (HLF) and Nu Skin Enterprises (NUS), GNC Holdings (GNC), and Vitamin Shoppe (VSI), to name a few, plus a group of micro caps of various evaluations. In April of 2017, Zion Market Research, the market research group, announced the analysis report titled "Dietary Supplements Market by Ingredients (Botanicals, Vitamins, Minerals, Amino Acids, Enzymes) for Additional Supplements, Medicinal Supplements, and Sports Nutrition Applications—Global Industry Perspective, Comprehensive Analysis and Forecast, 2016–2022."[27] The global market revenue of $132.8 billion in 2016 is expected to grow up to *$220.3 billion by 2022*. North America accounted for around 28 percent of the total market in 2016 and is projected to witness growth, owing to increasing consumption of products with reduced calorie level and high nutritional content. Another source, the *Nutritional Business Journal*, says the US supplement market is $37 billion.[28] The bottom line here is that enormous resources are available to prevent any further regulation in ensuring quality of product, keeping the door open for fraud, the criminal element and quackery.

A further problem with interpreting the value of supplements is that when science bends in the opposite direction from original claims, it is most difficult to alter human behavior. An example offered is the long controversy concerning the value of omega-3 fatty acids and prevention of cardiovascular disease. According to pediatricians William and James Sears,[29] the father of omega-3 research was Dr. Jorn Dyerberg, a Danish doctor who, in the 1970s, tried to figure out why Inuits who ate a high-fat, high-cholesterol diet had a low incidence of cardiovascular disease. Drs. Sears state, "He concluded that the Inuits' platelets contained a much higher proportion of omega-3s compared to the Danes', that this resulted in a slower to clot state and that the difference could help explain why the Inuits suffered fewer heart attacks." From this starting point exploded a massive literature on the value of omega-3 supplements with claims that involved every part of the human body, nearly every specialty of medicine, and was a driver in developing the supplement market in general. I am a surgeon and not a laboratory scientist, so I am not able to definitively evaluate these myriad claims. What does seem apparent is that of late, the pendulum is swinging in the opposite direction challenging the "omega-e effect." For example, a 2013 study quoted from *Lancet*[30] involving more than twelve thousand patients at high risk of a heart attack who were randomized to receive either 1,000 mg of fish oil per day or a placebo, after five years, there was no reduction in cardiovascular mortality and morbidity.

In a September 2012 *JAMA* study of 3,635 citations retrieved, 20 studies of 68,680 patients were included, reporting 7,044 deaths, 3,993 cardiac deaths, 1,150 sudden deaths, 1,837 myocardial infarctions, and 1,490 strokes; overall, omega-3 supplementation was not associated with a lower risk of all-cause mortality, cardiac death, sudden death, myocardial infarction, or stroke based on relative and absolute measures of association.[31] There are several other references that could be cited with similar conclusions. So what is the answer to opposite findings? Linda Antinoro, a dietician writing in *Today's Dietician*, offers this explanation:

> A possible reason for the seemingly contradictory results between the earlier and more recent studies on omega-3 supplementation, according to researchers, is that most of the later trials involve people with established heart disease who already are being treated with various medications, such as antihypertensives, antiarrhythmics, and statins. For example, in the GISSI trial,

only 5% of patients received statins at baseline. Patients already using cardioprotective agents may not experience further benefits when given omega-3 supplements since drug therapy can mimic or mask the actions of omega-3 supplements by lowering blood pressure, blood lipid levels, or inflammation.

The sad reality is that the original research by Dr. Jorn Dyerberg on the Inuits may be quackery. Dr. George Fodor, a Canadian cardiologist and head of research for the Prevention and Rehabilitation Centre at the University of Ottawa Heart Institute, published[32] in 2014, says,

It turns out that the Danish researchers relied on faulty public health records and hearsay about heart disease being rare among the Inuit in the 1970's. In fact, he found the opposite—a death rate from cardiovascular disease of between 8.5% and 11.8%, "excessive mortality due to cerebrovascular strokes" with an overall mortality rate of twice the non-Inuit population and a life expectancy that is about ten years shorter than the Danish population.

Quoted in the Ottawa News[33]:

"So, this is a sick population," says Dr. Fodor, "and if I were to draw any conclusion, I would say they eat a very dangerous diet."

Fodor says even more frustrating is that his colleagues blindly accepted this study as fact for more than 40 years.

"There were 5000 papers or more published, and probably hundreds of millions of dollars on research spent that could have been used for better purpose," he says.

In a large recent randomized trial called the VITAL Study conducted by Dr. JoAnn Manson and team (January 2019) from the Department of Medicine, Brigham and Women's Hospital and the Harvard Medical School, in 25,871 adults usual-risk participants during a median follow-up of 5.3 years, supplementation with omega-3 fatty acids did not result in a lower incidence of major cardiovascular events or cancer than a placebo.[34] The second part of the study, in the same research group, reported that supplementation with a high dose of vitamin D (at a dose of 2,000 IU per day) did not result in a lower incidence of cardiovascular events or risk of cancer (except for African Americans) than a placebo.[35]

In concluding this segment, it should be noted that there is the question of safety and effectiveness in the supplement arena. Dr. Simeon Margolis[36] in JohnsHopkinsHealthAlerts.com warns that,

> Many supplements contain herbs that are biologically active agents that can have powerful and sometimes unforeseen effects on the body. Herbal supplements can affect bleeding and coagulation, dangerous if you are taking an anticoagulant, have a bleeding disorder or are scheduled for surgery. Herbs can lower or raise your blood sugar, even if you don't have diabetes. Herbs can affect the production of liver enzymes interfering with the liver's ability to process medication. Subsequent interactions or adverse effects can range from ineffectiveness to toxicity. Several herbal supplements can make your blood pressure dangerously high or low. Some herbal supplements have hormone-like actions and affect hormone levels. Hormone-sensitive conditions like breast, uterine or ovarian cancers can be

made worse by exposure to supplement that act like estrogen or other hormones.

The New York Times magazine section regularly presents medical puzzles—difficult to diagnose even by professionals. A recent case[37] was of a man who had suffered two strokes and was on anti-coagulation to prevent another but decided to add supplements cinnamon and Coenzyme Q10 and turmeric he had gotten online ("They are from India and completely natural," he told his family). He presented with a third stroke, a hemorrhage into his brain seen on CAT scan. His hospital doctors researched the fact that turmeric is a blood thinner. The offending supplement was discontinued, and he promptly improved and was discharged.

His case reminds us again that "botanicals are only loosely regulated and not subject to the same rigorous testing as traditional medications."

Cost factors: Americans spent $21 billion on vitamins and herbal supplements in 2015. If protein powders are included, supplements are as big a market as all organic foods combined.[38] We can assume that the out-of-pocket expenses for vitamins and herbal supplements for 2018 are closer to twenty-five billion, and based on the 2012 data, about half is vitamin and half supplement expenditures.[39] The 2016 estimate is that Americans spend in the aggregate $30 billion on vitamins and supplements.[40]

5. Homeopathy

Should we keep an open mind about astrology, perpetual motion, alchemy, alien abduction, and sighting Elvis Presley? No, and we are happy to confess that our minds have closed down on homeopathy the same way. There is no scientific case for homeopathy: the debate is over.

—Edzard Ernst, academic physician and researcher

To herbalism must be added homeopathy as a major component of alternative medicine (CAM). Homeopathy was founded by Christian Friedrich Samuel Hahnemann, born in Germany in 1755.[1] He studied medicine in Leipzig and practiced there and in Vienna. From his study of cinchona bark, the source of quinine, he concluded that drugs produce symptoms similar to the sickness being treated (in this case malaria) and was the origin of his famous dictum, *similia similibus curantur* ("like cures like"). How he reached this conclusion is uncertain. What is certain is that it is not science or derived in any way from the scientific method. He held another corollary principle[2] that homeopathic remedies become stronger as they are diluted, as long as this dilution is accompanied by succession (a carefully prescribed, vigorous shaking of the mixture in a special manner).[3] The final prescription is often diluted to the point that it cannot be detected, but the remainder is said to possess the "memory" of the original ingredient that started out. It is said that Hahnemann's "own infinitesimal doses of medicine provoked the apothecaries of his day, who refused to dispense them; accordingly, he illegally gave his medicines to his patients, free of charge, and was prosecuted in every town in which he tried to settle from 1798 to 1810." He then spent his time testing, and he devised the *Homeopathic Pharmacopoeia*, a compendium of herbs and remedies, the name of which survives to this day. The regulation of the *Homeopathic Pharmacopoeia* has come under strong criticism: Stephen Barrett MD[4] notes on the website Quackwatch:

> Homeopathic "remedies" enjoy a unique status in the health marketplace: They are the only category of quack products legally marketable as drugs. This situation is the result of two circumstances. First, the 1938 Federal Food, Drug, and Cosmetic Act, which was shepherded through Congress by a homeopathic physician who was a senator, recognizes as drugs all substances included in the Homeopathic Pharmacopeia of the United States. Second, the FDA has not held

homeopathic products to the same standards as other drugs. Today they are marketed in health-food stores, in pharmacies, in practitioner offices, by multilevel distributors, through the mail, and on the Internet.

Regulation of homeopathic drugs is essentially a closed process.[5] Official homeopathic drugs are those that have monographs, which are official listings of drug data, in the *Homeopathic Pharmacopoeia of the United States* (HPUS). The HPUS is prepared by a *nongovernmental organization*, the Homeopathic Pharmacopoeia Convention of the United States (HPCUS), which is composed of scientists and clinicians trained in the medical specialty of homeopathic medicine. Since most homeopathic drugs are sold on a nonprescription basis, very few are subject to reimbursement by insurance. Industry estimates[6] suggest sales of homeopathic drugs in the United States in 2003 between $300 million and $450 million, with a compound average growth rate of approximately 8 percent per year.

To clarify further, it doesn't matter who or how homeopathic drugs are regulated since the dilution process, as advocated by the very principal that homeopathy dictates, leaves no trace of the medication in the final product. As Robert Park notes in his book, *Voodoo Science*,[7] a dilution of 30X, which is standard, would leave one part in 1,000,000,000,000,000,000,000,000,000,000 parts of water. The concept of "smart water" or the notion that a medication can leave some kind of an imprint on a molecule of water, which provides curative power, is wildly absurd and hardly worth discussing.

Although Hahnemann Medical School, which was established in 1848, did not survive the 1920s, Drexel University College of Medicine carries the legacy.[8] Through a series of transitions, the medical school became Drexel University College of Medicine in 2002, a now most respected medical educational institution.

Despite its unscientific basis, homeopathy training lives on today and is a part of the CAM movement. Homeopathic medicine is not licensed as an individual medical profession in the United States, but practitioners of the various medical disciplines often receive homeopathy training for use within their licensed practices.[9] One can even obtain a Certificate in Homeopathy Consulting Online (CHC)[10] and put a CHC after your name, indicating that there are few limits to the degree in which the scientific method may be abrogated, and CAM has put a smoke screen over the science of medicine.

The worrisome fact is that all these unsubstantiated therapies have contributed to a rejection of science as a path to truth, not only in the United States, but the trend is throughout the west. As pointed out by W. Sampson,[11] "This movement embraces the postmodernist doctrine that science is not necessarily more valid than pseudoscience." As Stephen Barrett[12] has summarized:

> In line with this philosophy, proponents of alternative approaches assert that scientific medicine (which they mislabel as allopathic, conventional, or traditional medicine) is but one of a vast array of health care options. Instead of subjecting their work to scientific standards, they would like to change the rules by which they are judged and regulated.

Indeed, with the election of Donald Trump as president, we have ushered in an entire administration and a Congress that is anti-science; the consequences of this will undermine any concerted effort to make America great again, forgetting their history that the first age of greatness was made possible by our dedication to an investment in science.

Cost factors: As of 2015, Americans spent $3 billion on homeopathy,[13] of which $2.9 billion was out of pocket[14]; and the market appears to be growing steadily,[15] even with packaging disclaimers by the government that says they do not work.

6. Naturopathy

Life expectancy would grow by leaps and bounds if green vegetables smelled as good as bacon.
—*Doug Larson*

127

As quoted from Wikipedia[1] and the *Journal of Complementary and Alternative Medicine*[2]:

> Naturopathy or naturopathic medicine is a form of pseudoscientific, alternative medicine that employs an array of practices branded as "natural," "non-invasive," and as promoting "self-healing." The ideology and methods of naturopathy are based on vitalism and self-healing, rather than evidence-based medicine.

Wikipedia, with abundant references, goes on to state:

> Naturopathic practitioners generally recommend against modern medical practices, including but not limited to medical testing, drugs, vaccinations, and surgery. Instead, study and practice are focused on unscientific notions, often leading naturopathic doctors to diagnoses and treatments that have no factual merit.
>
> Naturopathic medicine is considered by the medical profession to be ineffective and possibly harmful, raising ethical issues about its practice. In addition to accusations from the medical community, such as the American Cancer Society, naturopaths and naturopathic doctors have repeatedly been accused of being charlatans and practicing quackery. Over the years, many practitioners of naturopathic medicine have been found criminally liable in the courts of law around the world. In some countries, it is a criminal offense for naturopaths and naturopathic doctors to label themselves as medical professionals.

Dr. James C. Whorton, a scholar of the history of medicine, details the founder of naturopathy, Benedict Lust,[3] with this account:

Naturopathy, as Lust defined it, was an approach to healing that utilized "the beneficent agency of Nature's forces." Those forces could be administered in every form from water and herbs to electricity and sunlight, but in every case operated the same way, by assisting nature to remove the "Accumulation of Morbid Matter" in the body. As Lust defined it in 1903, naturopathy was a system of "Pathological Monism and Therapeutic Universalism"; it recognized only one disease—inhibition of the body's "natural power"—but a virtual infinity of healing agents—all of nature's benevolent forces. Grand as it already sounds, Therapeutic Universalism nevertheless, extended far beyond the utilization of all the natural modalities in the universe. Indeed, the final goal of natural treatments, as Lust saw it, was not the elimination of physical disease, but the restoration of human beings' appreciation of their proper place in the natural order of the cosmos. The "principal object" of naturopathy, he asserted, was "to re-establish the union of man's body, brain, heart and all bodily functions—with nature." Advocating what a later generation would call holistic healing and ecological medicine, Lust required matriculants at his American School of Naturopathy to study not only herbalism and hydrotherapy, but also such subjects as Self-Culture, Mental Regeneration, Pure Love, Soul-Marriage, Mental and Divine Healing, Spirit-Unfoldment, and God-Consciousness.

Whorton emphasizes the religious sources in early naturopathy—that the laws of health were "divine commandments," and the fall of Adam and Eve severed the "connection with the earth." He concludes that Lust placed the importance of naturopathy in historical perspective when Lust observed that "great spiritual upheavals" occurred every 500 years in Western Civilization marked first by Christ, then Muhammad, the Crusades, the Reformation followed by Naturopathy.

I can only conclude that the course of medical science since the Reformation has been uneven, but the progress that has been made is attributable to the scientific method rather than naturopathy.

According to the University of Maryland Medical Center,[4] in the mid-1920s to 1940, the use of naturopathic medicine declined. It was not until the 1960s that naturopathic-style, holistic medicine became popular again. Today, naturopaths are licensed care providers in many states. They offer a variety of natural therapies, including homeopathy, vitamin and mineral supplements, traditional Chinese medicine, relaxation techniques, and herbal remedies. As of 2009, fifteen states, the District of Columbia, and the US territories of Puerto Rico and the US Virgin Islands have licensing laws for naturopathic doctors. In these states, naturopathic doctors are required to graduate from a four-year, residential, naturopathic medical school and pass a postdoctoral board examination (NPLEX) to become licensed. Licensed naturopathic physicians must fulfill state-mandated continuing education requirements each year and have a specific scope of practice identified by state law. The fifteen states include Alaska, Arizona, California, Connecticut, District of Columbia, Hawaii, Idaho, Kansas, Maine, Minnesota, Montana, New Hampshire, Oregon, Utah, Vermont, Washington, United States Territories of Puerto Rico, and Virgin Islands.

Apparently, the District of Columbia (DC) is quite lax.[5] The requirement for a naturopathic doctor's certificate from the district is simple: The applicant's $176 check for a two-year registration must clear the bank. No licensing board reviews applicants, enforces the few city regulations on naturopathy, or disciplines anyone for misconduct. Registrants are required to tell clients they are not medical doctors, but no one enforces the rule.

Note that the DC Department of Health website notes that the requirements are the application package and a criminal background check.[6]

The cost of neuropathic practitioner treatments is not insignificant. According to RealizeHealth.org,[7] naturopathic doctor fees will vary, based on geographic location, experience, and time spent with each patient. On average, a first office visit ranges from $150 to $300. The sixty- to ninety-minute consultation usually involves a full medical history, review of prior lab tests and scans that you have brought with you, evaluation of current medications and supplements, answers to your questions, a physical exam, and a fully explained treatment plan. Specialized tests can cost anywhere from $50 to $500, averaging between $100 and $250.

The Deloitte Center for Health Solutions in Washington, DC, reported in 2011 on the hidden costs of US health care for consumers.[8] For purposes of accounting, the National Center for Complementary and Alternative Medicine suggests that

> defining CAM is difficult, because the field is very broad and constantly changing. CAM is generally thought to encompass a broad range of activities including natural products such as diet supplements; mind-body medicine such as yoga, acupuncture; manipulative and body-based practices including spinal manipulation and massage; and other CAM practices including movement therapies, traditional healers, manipulation of energy fields and traditional medicine systems including traditional Chinese medicine and Ayurvedic medicine.

The Deloitte report extracts from the National Health Expenditure Accounts that a total of $87 billion was spent as defined above, broken down to $55 billion on nutrition/supplements, $28 billion on CAM practitioners (which includes naturopaths), $2 billion on CAM products, and $2 billion on weight-reducing products.

Higher-income families spent more on supplements and alternative practitioners. Since these numbers are from 2011, we can assume a considerable increase since.

What is happening now, according to the Federation of Naturopathic Medicine Regulatory Authorities, is the lobbying to increase the number of states allowing licensure to practice naturopathy is at twenty-two, with Massachusetts being the most recent.[9]

A report from Australia in 2008 on registration of naturopaths[10] pointed out some serious risks to the health of the public.

- Removal from appropriate medical therapy
- Failure to refer
- Misdiagnosis
- Incorrect prescribing
- Prescribing preparations not suitable for the consumer's condition
- Failing to consider contraindications
- Prescribing medication in inappropriate dosages
- Prescribing medication for an inappropriate length of time
- Failing to consider and avoid known interactions with pharmaceuticals
- Failure to explain precaution

Cost factors: Annual costs of naturopathy included in the $28 billion spent on CAM practitioners as noted above. Out-of-pocket costs, according to Davis and Weeks 2012 report,[11] was $271 million.

7. Osteopathic Medicine

An osteopath is only a human engineer, who should understand all the laws governing his engine and thereby master disease.
—A. T. Still, MD, DO, Autobiography

Defining osteopathic medicine is best done by understanding the origins. According to the American Association of Colleges of Osteopathic Medicine (AACOM),[1]

> Osteopathic medicine is a distinctive form of medical care founded on the philosophy that all body systems interrelated and dependent upon one another for good health. This philosophy was developed in 1874 by Andrew Taylor Still, MD, who pioneered the concept of "wellness" and recognized the importance of treating illness within the context of the whole body.
>
> These beliefs formed the basis of a new medical approach, osteopathic medicine. Using this philosophy, Dr. Still opened the first school of osteopathic medicine in Kirksville, MO in 1892.

Dr. Still was born in Virginia in 1828. He served an apprenticeship under his physician father, studied at the College of Physicians and Surgeons in Kansas City, Missouri, and was a surgeon in the Union Army during the Civil War.

After the Civil War and after losing three of his children to "spinal meningitis,"

> His research and clinical observations led him to believe that the musculoskeletal system played a vital role in health and disease. He concluded that the body contained all of the elements needed to maintain health, if properly stimulated. Dr. Still believed that by correcting problems in the body's structure, through the use of manual techniques now known as osteopathic manipulative medicine (OMM), the body's ability to function and to heal itself could be greatly improved. He also promoted the idea of preven-

tive medicine and endorsed the philosophy that physicians should focus on treating the whole patient, rather than just the disease.[2]

It is of interest to note the similarities in the origins of chiropractic, homeopathy, naturopathy, and osteopathy, with emphasis on reliance on the body's own healing potential, the emphasis on natural ways rather than bloodletting, and further, how their origins were developed before the birth of modern medicine following the Flexner Report as referenced previously.

There is one key difference, however. Osteopathic medicine has "merged" to a large extent with traditional modern medicine[3]:

Osteopathic physicians use all of the tools available through modern medicine including prescription medicine and surgery. They also may use OMM (Osteopathic Manipulative Medicine) techniques to diagnose illness and injury, relieve pain, restore range of motion, and enhance the body's capacity to heal.

Reflective of the osteopathic philosophy of treating the whole person, many DOs serve in the primary care fields: family medicine, general internal medicine, and pediatrics. (And I might add Obstetrics).

In the 21st century, the training of osteopathic medical physicians in the United States is equivalent to the training of Doctors of Medicine (M.D.s).[3] Osteopathic medical physicians attend four years of medical school followed by an internship and a minimum two years of residency. They use all conventional methods of diagnosis and treatment.

In brief, osteopathy has gone mainstream in many communities throughout the fifty states. Although lumped in the category of

CAM organizations, this distinction should be made. Many have hospital privileges, and so quality assurance is monitored, but for those who do not, it will be up to state certification and rules to ensure compliance with standards, particularly when mixed with any CAM delivery system. It is at this point that the public should be most aware of possible deviation from standards.

This is not the only point of criticism. The use of OMM, which includes cranial and craniosacral manipulation, has come under attack.[4] Another area of criticism has been the relative lack of research and lesser emphasis on scientific inquiry at DO schools in comparison with MD schools.[5]

In summary, "there is currently a debate within the osteopathic community over the feasibility of maintaining osteopathic medicine as a distinct entity within U.S. health care."[6] J. D. Howell wrote in the *New England Journal of Medicine*[7]:

> If osteopathy has become the functional equivalent of allopathy [meaning the MD profession], what is the justification for its continued existence? And if there is value in therapy that is uniquely osteopathic, why should its use be limited to osteopaths?

In conclusion, until osteopathy can detach completely from chiropractic elements and CAM associations, one can only assume some cost factors must be attributable to unscientific and unnecessary treatments even though it is quite impossible without further data to determine the number of dollars involved.

Cost factors: No good estimate can be made for any unscientific portion that may be practiced, without more critical surveys.

8. Spiritual Healing

Religion is part of the human make-up. It's also part of our cultural and intellectual history. Religion was our first attempt at literature, the texts, our first attempt at cosmology, making sense of where we are in the universe, our first attempt at health care, believing in faith healing, our first attempt at philosophy.

—*Christopher Hitchens*

Spiritual healing is defined[1] as the activity of making a person healthy without using medicines or other physical methods, sometimes as part of a religious ceremony. As R. Barker Bausell points out,[2] the physician Daniel Benor[3] argues that spiritual healing is probably the oldest recognized therapy, used in some form in every known culture from time uncharted. There are various forms of prayer in every religion about the world. In pagan times, various objects or replicas of gods were used to try to effect a cure. As Christianity emerged, the potential for healing became the work of an increasing number of saints. Dr. Seymour Schwartz, eminent surgeon, and Christopher Hoolihan, in their book *Holystic Medicine*,[4] record that,

> In the first four centuries of the Common Era, martyrdom was the result of Roman persecution of Christians. The Memorial Day for each saint was established by the date of death, because it was believed that the saint was reborn at death into life everlasting and continued to carry out miracles of intercession as "a friend of God." Sometime around the fourth century, the list of saints was expanded to include individuals who were categorized as "confessors," namely those who evidenced their faith by exceptional words and deeds, and who died peacefully after a life of virtue and holiness. They were missionaries, pastors, caretakers of the poor and the sick, and defenders of the faith.

With respect to patronage,

> Among the large cadre of universally and locally recognized saints is a group that has been formally considered for their patronage of various illnesses. Some of these saints have been associated with more than one illness. Many illnesses and infirmities have the patronage of several saints.
>
> Among the patron saints of medicine, particularly those for whom an association between their lives and specific patronage is apparent, fascinating legends have appeared. In some instances, the purported events have been very dramatic. The tales of Saints Agatha, Anthony of Padua, Blasé, Cosmas and Damian, Edward the Confessor, Fiacre, Leodegar, Lucy, Peregrine and Sebastian are examples of intriguing legends that formed the bases for patronage.

In the Eastern Orthodox Church, the equivalent of canonization is called *Glorification* and may be performed by a bishop and the name of the saint inscribed in the calendar of saints.[5] Anglicans have a calendar of saints, but since the Reformation, only King Charles I has been canonized in the Church of England.[6] Some Lutherans have a calendar of saints, but most Protestants reject canonization and prayer requests of the dead.[7]

Perhaps the quintessential example "distance healing" is found in the Christian Bible[8] (Matthew 8:5–13) citing the faith of the centurion:

> When Jesus had entered Capernaum, a centurion came to him, asking for help. "Lord," he said, my servant lies at home paralyzed, suffering terribly Jesus said to him, "Shall I come and heal him?" The centurion replied, "Lord, I do not

deserve to have you come under my roof. But just say the word, and my servant will be healed. For I myself am a man under authority, with soldiers under me. I tell this one, 'Go,' and he goes; and that one, 'Come,' and he comes. I say to my servant, 'Do this,' and he does it."

When Jesus heard this, he was amazed and said to those following him, "Truly I tell you, I have not found anyone in Israel with such great faith. I say to you that many will come from the east and the west, and will take their places at the feast with Abraham, Isaac and Jacob in the kingdom of heaven. But the subjects of the kingdom will be thrown outside, into the darkness, where there will be weeping and gnashing of teeth." Then Jesus said to the centurion, "Go! Let it be done just as you believed it would." And his servant was healed at that moment.

The Christian tradition and faith have imparted such expectations to prayer and intercession directly to their God and through the saints of the church. Indeed, before the modern era, there was little else to seek in time of a health crisis.

Muhammad was born about AD 570 and, in addition to preaching, introduced ritual prayer after his first revelations.[9] Eschatological piety, ethical nobility, and prayer formed the basis of early Islam, according to Lapidas in his *A History of Islamic Societies.*[10] I think it not impossible to postulate that insofar as his tribe had been involved in commerce and the caravan trade and that he himself had been a caravaner that early Islam might have generated a basic set of rules to command law and order along these early essential caravan transport routes. The result was the creation of a community that transcended families, clans, and tribes into a new Arabian Society[11] with the five pillars of faith: *zagat* (almsgiving), *hajj* (pilgrimage), *fasting* (Ramadan), *shahada* (the obligation to bear witness to the one God and prophethood of Muhammad), and *salat* (ritual prayer). Whether safer arteries of trade were an objective or a by-product, the fact is that Islam became a military force, and the prophet the only military leader of a major religion.

In the process, prayer was more ritual than intercessional. The prophet was not into miracles. According to historian Denis Gril, the Quran does not overtly describe Muhammad performing miracles.[12]

> The supreme miracle of Muhammad is finally identified with the Quran itself. However, Muslim tradition credits Muhammad with several supernatural events.

There are two sura in the Koran that have been cited as praying for the sick.[13]

> *O mankind, there has come unto you a direction from your Lord and a healing for the heart and for those who believe in guidance and mercy.* (Quran 10:57)
> *We have sent down in the Quran that which is healing and a mercy to those who believe.* (Quran 17:82)

The same reference cites the use of meditation and personal prayer and the fact that the Sufi tradition of Islam has focused on prayer and healing.

The historian Albert Hourani traces the origin of sainthood in Islam[14]:

> The idea of a path of approach to God implied that man was not only the creature and servant of God, but could also become His friend. Such a belief could find its justification in passages of the Quran: "O thou, Creator of heavens and the earth, thou art my Friend in this world and the next." Gradually a theory of saint-

hood (wilaya) emerged. The friend of God was the one who always stood near Him... A woman as well as a man could be a saint. In time this idea as given formal expression... The friends of God could intercede with Him on behalf of others, and their intercession could have visible results in this world. It could lead to cures for sickness or sterility, or relief from misfortunes, and these signs of grace were also proofs of the sanctity of the friend of God. It came to be widely accepted that the supernatural power by which a saint called down graces into the world could survive his or her death, and requests for intercession could be made at his or her tomb. Visits to the tombs of saints, to touch them or pray in front of them, came to be a supplementary practice of devotion, although some Muslim thinkers regarded this as a dangerous innovation, because it interposed a human intermediary between God and each individual believer. The tomb of the saint, quadrangular, with a vaulted dome, whitewashed inside, standing by itself or in a mosque was a familiar feature of the Islamic landscape and townscape.

Some of the tombs of saints had become "National" or universal shrines such as Mawlay Idris (d.791), reputed founder of the city of Fez and Sidi Mahraz, patron saint of sailors in Tunis.

Prayer is very much a part of Jewish practice and tradition[15]:

Jewish prayers are the prayer recitations and Jewish meditation traditions that form part of the observance of Rabbinic Judaism. These prayers, often with instructions and commentary, are found in the siddur, the traditional Jewish prayer book.

Prayer—as a "service of the heart"—is in principle a Torah-based commandment. It is not time-dependent and is mandatory for both Jewish men and women. However, in general, today, Jewish men are obligated to conduct prayer three times a day, while, according to some, women are only required to engage in prayer once a day, others say at least twice a day.

In reform Judaism, in addition to specific psalms said to aid healing, there is a short prayer for healing called "Mi Shebeirach."[16]

A "mi sheberach" is a public prayer or blessing for an individual or group, most often recited in synagogue when the Torah is being read. Because it is not an officially mandated prayer, there is a lot of room for creativity regarding whom to bless or how they can be blessed. Thus, there are mi sheberachs for just about any person in need of some divine goodness—most notably those requiring healing.[17]

Hinduism, as an ancient religion, has no founder or known date of origin. The term "Hinduism" simply derives from the word "India" and refers to a wide variety of religious traditions and philosophies that have developed in India over thousands of years. Most Hindus worship one or more deities, believe in reincarnation, value the practice of meditation, and observe festive holidays.[18] In the Hindu religion is a mantra for healing:

The Mrityunjaya (mrit-yoon-jaya) Mantra is a secret mantra that was only passed along verbally for generations. It is widely known now, as a healing mantra to ward off illness, improve health (mental and physical), and even untimely death;

Om Trayambakam Yajamahe Sugandhim Pushti Vardhanam

Urvarukam Iva Bandhanan Mrityor Mukshiya Mamritat

Simple Translation: I implore you, the Source of the cycle of birth, life and death, to free me from its bondage, make me fearless, and lead me to the absolute truth and bliss.[19]

Buddhism is a tradition that focuses on personal spiritual development. Buddhists strive for a deep insight into the true nature of life and do not worship gods or deities.[20]

There is no belief in a personal god. Buddhists believe that nothing is fixed or permanent and that change is always possible. The path to Enlightenment is through the practice and development of morality, meditation and wisdom.

Buddhists believe that life is both endless and subject to impermanence, suffering and uncertainty. These states are called the *tilakhana*, or the three signs of existence. Existence is endless because individuals are reincarnated over and over again, experiencing suffering throughout many lives.

In Tibetan Buddhism, Guru Rinpoche taught, "Compared to any medical treatment or cure, the Six Syllables [*Om Mani Padme Hum*] are the strongest remedy against sickness and evil."[21] The mantras most often used for healing are those associated with the enlightened beings: the Medicine Buddha, Green or White Tara, and Chenrezig, the Bodhisattva of Compassion. Influenced by Tibetan Buddhism, Lama Zopa Rinpoche said, "Just touching and turning a prayer wheel brings incredible purification and accumulates unbelievable merit." Thus, the prayer wheel with the imprinted mantra spun into motion is a healing instrument. His Holiness, the Dalai Lama, has said that having the mantra on your computer works the same as a traditional *mani* wheel, as the digital form of the mantra spins around on your hard drive.[22] The Buddhist Centers also practice distance healing.

> Many Tibetan lamas of all traditions will perform special spiritual practices (pujas) for the benefit of individuals who are ill or recently deceased. A donation is appropriate to cover the cost of the materials (incense, etc.) used in the practice.[23]

It is apparent from the foregoing that prayer is a ubiquitous element of spiritual healing across many belief systems. The question is, as in all forms of therapy, can it be subjected to the scientific method? The answer is that it is being studied with the assumption that, if scientifically proven valid, the treatment being tested will be included in the science of medicine and that insurance companies will then be urged to pay for it. We recall that the origins of the NIH branch called the National Center for Complementary and Alternative Medicine (NCCAM)—the agency responsible for the research and testing.[24]

> The driving force behind the creation of NCCAM was Tom Harkin, a popular senator from Iowa who believed his allergies had been cured by eating bee pollen. Harkin figured that the only reason alternative remedies hadn't been brought into the mainstream was that they hadn't been properly tested. Once they were tested and everyone could see that they really worked, alternative medicine would be embraced by modern science and paid for by insurance companies.

Since its birth in 1999, NCCAM officials have spent about $1.6 billion studying alternative therapies (of which 1.8 million was spent to find out that prayer doesn't cure AIDS or brain tumors or improve healing after breast reconstruction surgery).

What are the results of studies on the effectiveness of spiritual healing or prayer? The source for an answer is Pub Med Central (PMC).[25] It is a "free archive of biomedical and life sciences journal literature at the U.S. National Institutes of Health's National Library of Medicine (NIH/NLM). In keeping with NLM's legislative mandate to collect and preserve the biomedical literature, PMC serves as a digital counterpart to NLM's extensive print journal collection. Launched in February 2000, PMC was developed and is managed by NLM's National Center for Biotechnology Information (NCBI)." At the top of the website page is a search box. Enter <spiritual healing> and you will find 7,769 citations—quite an astounding number by itself. Here is a sample:

> "A pragmatic, three-arm randomized controlled trial of spiritual healing for asthma in primary care," an article from the British Journal of General Practice. This study assessed the effectiveness of spiritual healing for asthma.
>
> The conclusion was, "This randomized controlled trial of spiritual healing for asthma did not find any evidence for effectiveness, indicating that this particular CAM should not be currently recommended."

Another fascinating publication was:

> "The effect of spiritual healing on in vitro tumour cell proliferation and viability—an experimental study," a study from the British Journal

of Cancer. The aim of this study was to test the hypothesis that spiritual healing will reduce proliferation and viability of two cancer cell lines *in vitro*.

The conclusion: While agreeing that psychological aspects are a part of healing in the human setting, proponents of spiritual healing stress that effects are due to mechanisms beyond conventional pharmacological, physiological and psychological factors, and that healing can be performed "at a distance" without conscious awareness on the part of the recipient, which can be any living being (person, animal, plant, cell, or other living system). However, in the present tightly controlled study there was no evidence of such an effect for the cell lines investigated. The theory of spiritual healing is highly controversial and in conflict with the generally agreed upon laws of science.

I could spend hours summarizing the thousands of papers, but I recommend that any reader search that site and make up their own mind. Suffice it to say, I was unable to find any consensus that spiritual healing had any scientific validity in this maze of literature.

Before tallying up the costs of spiritual healing to the consumer, we must add Christian Science as a category of alternative medicine. Mary Baker Eddy (1821–1910), founder of the movement, published her best-selling *Science and Health* in 1875. Her system of self-healing was based upon the notion that all creation is entirely spiritual—and that matter was an illusion. Spiritual healing was simply a matter of mind control.[26]

Mary Baker Eddy went on to establish the Church of Christ, Scientist, as a Christian denomination and worldwide movement of spiritual healers. She published 15 more books and

started several weekly and monthly magazines—
the Christian Science Sentinel, The Christian
Science Journal, and The Herald of Christian
Science—that feature articles on Christian
Science practice and verified testimonies of healing. In 1908, at the age of 87, she founded The
Christian Science Monitor, a global newspaper
that provides balanced, humane coverage of
world news, and that is as alert to progress and
promise as to humanity's need to address suffering and conflict. It was established to "injure no
man, but to bless all mankind" (*The First Church
of Christ, Scientist, and Miscellany*, p. 353). Today,
the Monitor is available via its website, weekly
digital and print editions, and through a Daily
News Briefing.[27]

Cost factors: The cost of spiritual healing in the US can only
be estimated. The total number of out-of-pocket expenditures for
CAM practitioners of all kinds is $33 billion in 2012 (5 percent of
142 billion).[28] The percentage of the US population using spiritual
healing in 1999 was 13.7 percent[29] so we can extrapolate a cost of
$4.5 billion as a low-end estimate and certainly much more by 2018.

On a broader scale and of even further interest was to bring
up PMC website searching <cost of CAM>.[30] This yielded 10,537
publications indicating that there is an avalanche of effort to utilize
CAM or CIM (Complementary Integrative Medicine) as an addition
or replacement for mainstream medical science. An example is:

*"Are complementary therapies and integrative
care cost-effective? A systematic review of economic
evaluations."*

The results: A total of 338 economic evaluations of CIM were identified, of which 204,
covering a wide variety of CIM for different populations, were published 2001–2010. A total of

114 of these were full economic evaluations. And 90% of these articles covered studies of single CIM therapies and only one compared usual care to usual care plus access to multiple licensed CIM practitioners. Of the recent full evaluations, 31 (27%) met five study-quality criteria, and 22 of these also met the minimum criterion for study transferability ("generalizability"). Of the 56 comparisons made in the higher-quality studies, 16 (29%) show a health improvement with cost savings for the CIM therapy versus usual care. Study quality of the cost-utility analyses (CUAs) of CIM was generally comparable to that seen in CUAs across all medicine according to several measures, and the quality of the cost-saving studies was slightly, but not significantly, lower than those showing cost increases (85% vs 88%, p=0.460).

The future here is clearly written. There will be a huge effort to prove that CAM or CIM will replace standard medicine in the *name of cost saving*, with possible disregard for the science involved.

9.   Energy Healing—Reiki

> *There is no medicine in the medicine.*
> —*Robert L. Park,*
> *author,* Voodoo Science

At a recent CAM conference I attended (2015), the speaker, who was designated as a Reiki master, began her presentation by sending several of her Reiki agents into the audience to place a hand over an audience subject's head for about a minute. She then asked if anyone felt anything or noted any change. Some said they did. I did not. Without asking further questions, she went on to note that Reiki was about balance and physical, mental, emotional, and spiritual spheres.

She stressed that industrialization of medicine has robbed doctors of time with patients. I noted the usual effort to discredit current medical care. She defined integrative medicine as combining conventional medicine by which I assume she met science-based medicine plus traditional or what she termed cultural-based medicine. Expanding on the notion of a spiritual aspect, she noted that you don't need spirituality, that Reiki is not about dogma, that there is a certain refuge and uncertainty, but that it involves personal responsibility, that it is solitary and neutral on religion of any kind. She went on to make further points, namely, that no diagnosis is necessary, that a treatment plan is optional but it is not goal-driven, and that Reiki touch generates response from the patient within.

In defining what she termed Reiki practice, it was noted that there was no trademark in that the practice is not trademarked, that there are no standards for treatment. But the concept and the idea of Reiki practice came from Japan, and there was a good deal of diversity in navigating the practice of Reiki. The presenter ended her presentation by stating, "Science has not yet identified a mechanism and that the mechanism for meditation, a fundamental of Reiki, is unknown."

Reiki is just one form of energy healing.[1] It is "a branch of CAM based on the belief that healers can channel healing energy into a patient and effect positive results. This idea itself contains several methods: hands-on, hands-off, and distant (or absent) where the patient and healer are in different locations." One can learn Reiki on YouTube,[2] where the several levels at explained from level I to level 3c, a Reiki grand master.

Many schools of energy healing exist[3] using many names—for example, biofield energy healing, spiritual healing, contact healing, distant healing, Qi Do, therapeutic touch, and Reiki or Qigong. This idea of influencing the balance of energies in a human body is an ancient one. Yin and yang energy forces were basic to the Chinese. As Paul Offit[4] reminds us,

> Because Chinese physicians were prohibited
> from dissecting human bodies, they didn't know

that nerves originated in the spinal cord. In fact,
they didn't know what nerves were. Rather they
interpreted events inside the body based on what
they could see outside, like rivers and sunsets.

So energy healers of today base their work on pseudoscience,
from ancient ideas discredited simply because they were never science—they were offered before there was any knowledge of anatomy.

Yet you can find, in the Wikipedia review cited above, CAM
articles on the use of energy healing for a variety of conditions, most
of which show no positive results. Note one summary of reviews[5]:

> Eight non-randomized and nine random-
> ized clinical trials were located. The majority of
> the rigorous trials do not support the hypothe-
> sis that distant healing has specific therapeutic
> effects. The results of two studies furthermore
> suggest that distant healing can be associated
> with adverse effects.
>
> Conclusion: Since the publication of our
> previous systematic review in 2000, several rigor-
> ous new studies have emerged. Collectively they
> shift the weight of the evidence against the notion
> that distant healing is more than a placebo.

To be balanced in this analysis, there is one advocate who might
be quoted, Edzart Ernst, MD, PhD,[6] from the *Annals of Internal
Medicine*: A total of 23 trials involving 2,774 patients met the inclusion criteria and were analyzed. Heterogeneity of the studies pre-
cluded a formal meta-analysis. Of the trials, five examined prayers
as the distant healing intervention, eleven assessed noncontact therapeutic touch, and seven examined other forms of distant healing.
Of the twenty-three studies, thirteen (57 percent) yielded statisti-
cally significant treatment effects, nine showed no effect over control
interventions, and one showed a negative effect. The conclusion was:

> The methodologic limitations of several studies make it difficult to draw definitive conclusions about the efficacy of distant healing. However, given that approximately 57% of trials showed a positive treatment effect, the evidence thus far merits further study.

This was published in 2000. Since that time, Dr. Ernst has been quoted as saying, "Scientific medicine has many failings, but alternative medicine offers no way forward in resolving them."[7]

Cost factors: With respect to cost of energy healing to the consumers in the United States, it is difficult to get solid data. The Department of Labor Statistics does not track Reiki salaries.[8] A 1999 government survey cited by Bausell[9] estimated that 2,142,000 adults used Reiki therapies over a year period. Multiplying this figure by $95 (average per session), we get a rounded estimate of $2.4 million. (This doesn't include the use of Reiki for horses and pets.[9]) I suspect that this market is much larger. According to the results of a survey released by Health Forum, a subsidiary of the American Hospital Association (AHA) and Samueli Institute, a nonprofit research organization that investigates healing-oriented practices, more than 42 percent of responding hospitals indicated they offer one or more CAM therapies, up from 37 percent in 2007.[10] If we multiply our estimated annual cost in the aggregate of Reiki therapy by 37 percent, we estimate the annual cost at $3.3 million, which doesn't include the other forms of energy healing.

10. Yoga

Yoga is my favorite way to pretend to work out.
—Internet Picture Quotes

Although no consistent definition of CAM exists,[1] the following list is presented in an appendix A of a publication by the Institute of Medicine of the National Academies entitled "Complementary and Alternative Medicine in the United States,"[2] a report, commissioned in September 2002, when sixteen NIH institutes, centers, and offices plus the Agency for Healthcare Research and Quality asked the Institute of Medicine to convene a study committee to explore scientific, policy, and practice questions that arise from the significant and increasing use of CAM therapies by the American public.

(Practitioners provided the individual therapy definitions cited below.)

Acupressure
Applying pressure to certain meridian points, similar to acupuncture, but without the use of needles.

Acupuncture
The Chinese art of stimulating the pathways of energy (14 main meridians plus branches) by puncturing, pressing, heating, using electrical current, or using herbal medicines.

Alexander Technique
Originally a technique used for respiratory re-education, now a comprehensive technique of psychophysical re-education to improve physical functioning.

Anthroposophy
A health care system defined by Rudolf Steiner. The study of the wisdom of the human being, inner development, and careful observation to more accurately reflect the patient as a whole and unique human being.

Apitherapy (Bee Venom)
The use of bee products from the European honey bee to promote health and healing.

Applied Biomechanics

The use of biomechanical principals of human motion and structure of the human body as well as the laws of mechanics to prevent and treat injuries. Most commonly used in sports medicines.

Applied Kinesiology

A form of patient biofeedback. A muscle is tested to discover allergies, weaknesses in the body. Any muscle in the body may be used to test when the patient is exposed to a substance or a thought.

Aromatherapy

The skilled and controlled use of essential oils, volatile liquids distilled from plants, shrubs, trees, flowers, roots and seeds. They contain oxygenating molecules that transport the nutrients to cells of the body.

Art Therapy

Increase awareness of self; cope with symptoms, stress, and traumatic experiences; and enhance cognitive abilities through the practice of creating art. Includes talking about it with a trained art therapist.

Autogenic Therapy

The practice of "passive concentration," a state of alert but detached awareness which allows the trainee to break through whatever excess stress is present. Western form of meditation.

Aversion Therapy

Exposure to an unpleasant stimulus while engaged in the targeted behavior. Usually associated with alcoholism and smoking.

Ayurvedic Medicine

A traditional health care system practiced in India. The "Science of Life." People are categorized into three basic constitutional types, Pitta, Kapha, Vata, with many different subdivisions. Treatment of the same illness will be different based on the type determined by the physician.

Bach Flower Remedies

Restoration of balance to disrupted states of mind, addresses the underlying emotional causes of disease using flowering plants.

Balneotherapy

Practice of healing using bath preparations. Essential oils in a preparation that will dilute in water.

Biofeedback

A treatment technique in which people train their bodies to respond to specific signals in their body. Used often to lower blood pressure and to slow heart rates.

Body Electronics

Preparing a client nutritionally and then using a specialized form of sustained acupressure.

Bowen Therapy

Gentle moves on the skin or through light clothing designed to result in overall relaxation, allowing the body to recharge, and cleanse itself.

Breathwork
Holotropic

Experiential method combining deep relaxation, expanded breathing, music, art and focused energy work.

Transformational

Directed breathing exercises to massage internal organs and tone diaphragm and abdominal muscles. The high volume of oxygen absorbed by the lungs cleanses and revitalizes the organ systems.

Cell Therapy (not done in U.S.)

Injection of healthy cellular material into the body to assist the body in its natural ability to heal.

Cheirology (Palmistry)

The art of hand analysis. A combination of the ancient Chinese Buddhist hand analysis and the best of traditional Western palmistry. A dialogue and touch therapy.

Chelation Therapy

A slow drip IV injection of a synthetic amino acid used for the purpose of removing plaque and calcium deposits from arteries.

Chiropractic

Based on a procedure that evaluates caus-ative factors in the biomechanical and structural derangements of the spine that may affect the nervous system and organs.

Chromatotherapy (See Color Therapy)
Cognitive Therapy

Short-term, focused psychotherapy. Used in treatment of depression, anxiety, anger, marital conflict, loneliness, and panic, among others.

Colon Hydrotherapy

The cleansing of the entire large intestine with a gentle enema-type system using filtered water and gentle abdominal massage.

Color Therapy

Known also as chromatotherapy, based on the concept that colors vibrate at different fre-quencies and can stimulate different responses in a person and the use of specific colors in a person's environment may promote balance and healing.

Contact Reflex Analysis (CRA)

A natural system for analyzing the body's structural, physical, and nutritional needs. Most commonly used by chiropractors.

Craniosacral Therapy

This therapy focuses on the eight bones of the cranial vault in conjunction with the spine and sacrum, and the cerebrospinal fluid. Light touch creates relaxation and a sense of energy moving within your body.

Crystal Therapy (Gemstone Therapy)

The practice of using crystals of different minerals to treat various disharmonies in the body.

Cupping (Moxibustion)

The placement of burning mugwort, a plant containing complex volatile oils such as camphor, at acupuncture points to stimulate qi and healing.

Detoxification Therapy

The various processes used to rid the body of toxins absorbed from the atmosphere, food, soil, and water.

Didjeridoo

A form of sound therapy, this aboriginal wind instrument has been used for healing for 40,000 years. Circular breathing supported by the sound frequency reaches deep into the subconscious.

Dream Therapy

The interpretation of dreams to assist in addressing problems and support resolution.

Ear Candling

Ear candles or cones of unbleached cotton or linen strips dipped in paraffin, beeswax, or herbs are burned, sending smoke and warmth inside the ear creating a vacuum effect to loosen buildup of wax and other debris.

Electrotherapy (TENS)

Transcutaneous Electrical Nerve Stimulation. Any form of medical treatment that uses electricity as a cure or relief. For example, as a way of stimulating nerves and connected muscles.

Emotional Freedom Technique (Tapping)

Also called Thought Field Therapy. A brief, effective psychotherapy for the rapid resolution of negative emotions; tapping with your fingertips on the acupuncture meridian points while repeating some specific phrases.

Energy Field Medicine

Seven major Chakras, vortexes of energy within the human body, serve as a network of mind-body-spiritual energies.

Enzyme Therapy

Diet supplemented with plant-derived enzymes and pancreatic enzymes either independent of each other or in combinations determined by the prescriber.

Essences Therapy

Similar to Bach flower remedies. Water-based infusion activated by natural sunlight, stabilized usually with brandy.

Eye Movement Desensitization and Reprocessing (EMDR)

The treatment of patients using guided eye movement while mentally focused on whatever mental image, negative thought, or body sensation the client wishes to address.

Fasting (Cleansing)

The complete abstinence from all substances except purified water in an environment of total rest. Benefits include the promotion of detoxification and it gives the digestive system a rest.

Feldenkrais Method

A blend of science and aesthetics, uses two approaches to healing. "Awareness Through Movement," directing students to move in specific ways related to early basic movements, and "Functional Integration," movement custom tailored to the unique needs of each student.

Gerson Therapy

Combination of vigorous detoxification with nutrition aimed at restoring the body's natural immunity and healing power.

Gestalt Therapy

Challenging a client with questions that increase awareness of feelings and so develop a stronger ability to face day-to-day situations and problems.

Guided Imagery

The use of relaxation and mental visualization to improve mood and or physical well-being.

Healing Touch

An energy based therapeutic approach to healing. Using hands-on and energy-based techniques to balance and align the human energy field.

Hellerwork

Similar to Rolfing. Stress-reducing body realignment, which adds verbal dialogue and emotional release to connective tissue bodywork and body movement education.

Herbal Medicine

The use of any plants, seeds, berries, roots, leaves, bark, or flowers for medicinal purposes.

Homeopathy

A philosophy of treatment "That which is similar ends suffering." Toxic remedies from raw materials and plants are administered in a highly diluted form to stimulate the body's own healing mechanisms.

Humor Therapy

Using laughter to release endorphins, increasing the body's ability to heal itself.

Huna

The exploration of body, mind, and spirit through shamanism and ancient Hawaiian healing. Increasing your own spirituality and healing powers.

Hydrogen Peroxide Therapy

Based on the theory, when injected into the vein, hydrogen peroxide is converted to water and singlet oxygen, an oxidizing agent, which inhibits growth of bacteria and viruses and enhances enzymatic metabolism.

Hydrotherapy

The placement of alternating heat and cold water to the skin in order to redirect the flow of blood.

Hyperbaric Oxygen Therapy

The delivery of pure oxygen at two to three times that of sea level(pressure). Among its uses is the treatment of leg ulcers that do not respond to other therapies.

Hyperthermia

Heat treatment to selectively destroy cancer cells using heating rods, microwaves, ultra sound, thermal blankets lasers, or pyrogens to induce fever.

Hypnotherapy

Intense focused concentration with partial or complete exclusion of awareness of peripheral phenomenon. Among its clinical uses are the treatment of pain, habit disorders, nausea, relaxation, and anxiety.

Iridology

The iris of the eye reveals abnormal conditions of the tissues, organs, and glands of the body. Diagnosis of disease is not made, but conditions of various parts of the body are revealed.

Jaffe-Mellor Technique (JMT)

A bioenergetic technique utilizing kinesiology and acupressure to relieve pain and symptoms associated with osteoarthritis, RA, and other complex health disorders.

Jin Shin Jyutsu

A gentle oriental art practiced by placing fingertips (over clothing) on (26) designated "safety energy locks" to harmonize and restore balance.

Juice Therapy

The use of raw vegetables and fruits turned into juice to make it easier to assimilate. Taken on an empty stomach, it is absorbed within 15 minutes.

Kegel Exercises

A form of biofeedback exercise. Pelvic floor exercises focus on women's abdominal organs and muscles.

Kirlian Photography

Photography of the body's auras and energy flow.

Light Therapy

Use of light, from natural sun exposure to high-tech sophisticated forms of light-assisted psychotherapy to treat physical and psychological disorders.

Macrobiotics

Changing or managing your diet for spiritual and healthful ends. Diet excludes meats and emphasizes whole grains.

Magnet Therapy

Use of natural and manmade magnets to enhance energy fields around and within the body to enhance healing.

Manual Lymphatic Drainage (MLD)

A highly systematic method of stimulating lymph flow through the entire body using a range of specialized and gentle rhythmic pumping techniques. This stimulates the lymphatic vessels that carry substances vital to the defense of the body and removes waste products.

Marma Therapy

A form of healing massage focusing on 108 points on the body where vein, artery, tendon, bone, and flesh meet.

Medical Intuitive

The utilization of a focused, intuitive instinct to "diagnose" or "read" energetic and frequency information in and around the human body.

Meditation

Relaxation and transformation therapy focusing mind on specific healing thoughts.

Transcendental Meditation™

A program specifically designed by Maharishi Mahesh Yogi.

Mind-Body Medicine

A philosophy and a system of health practices that is based on the concept that the mind and the body work together for healing.

Music Therapy

The prescribed use of music by a qualified person to effect positive changes in the psychological, physical, cognitive, or social functioning of individuals with health or educational problems.

NAET (Nambudripad's Allergy Elimination Therapy)

A combination of disciplines including kinesiology and acupressure designed to identify and eliminate allergies. The treatment stimulates acupuncture points along the spine while patient holds an allergen.

Naprapathy

Manipulation, mobilization, and soft tissue methods similar in some ways to chiropractic, but specializes in health problems that originate in the muscles, tendons, and ligaments.

Nasal Irrigation

Saline solution (nonionized salt, baking soda, and water) inhaled through nostril to clear mucus and reduce cough caused by post nasal drip.

Naturopathic Medicine

A system of primary health care which uses a holistic natural approach to health and healing, emphasizing the treatment of disease through stimulation, enhancement, and support of the inherent healing capacity of the person.

Naturopathy

The basic philosophy of Naturopathic Medicine, practiced by both licensed Naturopathic Doctors and other CAM practitioners.

Neuro-Linguistic Programming (NLP)

The study of the structure of subjective experience and what can be calculated from that, predicated upon the belief that all behavior has structure.

Neuromuscular Therapy (Trigger Point Myotherapy)

Consists of alternating levels of concentrated pressure on the areas of muscle spasm using fingers, knuckles, or elbows.

Nutritional Therapy

Use of food and supplements to encourage the body's own natural healing.

Orthomolecular Medicine

The prescription of large doses of vitamins and minerals, based on the philosophy that each individual is biochemically unique and therefore nutritional deficiencies affect certain people more than others.

Ozone-Oxygen Therapy (Bio-oxidative Therapy)

Small amounts of hydrogen peroxide and ozone are administered into the body as medicine.

Panchakarma Therapy

Ayurvedic herbal remedies designed to balance and cleanse, restore harmony.

Past Life Therapy

Treatment and release of phobias and emotional blockages through a regression process which explores past life traumas.

Pet Therapy

Animals of all sizes and breeds respond well to CAM therapies that stimulate their own natural powers; sometimes they are more responsive than human beings.

Pilates

Systematic practice of specific exercises coupled with focused breathing patterns.

Polarity

A system based on the belief that the flow and balance of energy in the body is the underlying foundation of health. The body's own electrical flow to muscles and organs is opened through a process of bodywork, diet, exercise and self-awareness.

Pranic Healing

Comprehensive system of subtle energy healing that utilized "prana" in balancing, harmonizing, and transforming the body's energy process.

Prayer

Some cultures and religions believe that prayer is the most powerful medicine.

Prolotherapy

Nonsurgical ligament reconstruction, treatment for chronic pain. Dextrose solution is injected into ligament or tendon where it attaches to the bone; inflammation increases blood supply and stimulates body's natural healing ability.

Qigong

Literally means "energy cultivation"; refers to exercises aimed at bringing about harmony, as well as improving health and longevity. Healing methods involve breathing, movement, the mind, and the eyes.

Radiance Technique (TRT)

7-degree transcendental energy system similar to Reiki.

Rapid Eye Technology

A transformational technology that facilitates healing on all levels. The client follows a lighted wand with their eyes, while the therapist gives verbal clues designed to release physical, emotional, or mental stress.

Reflexology

Noninvasive acupressure of the hands and feet. Points on the feet and hands correspond to various zones and organs throughout the body. Precise pressure on these reflex points stimulates energy and releases blockages to the specific area of pain or illness.

Reiki

An ancient Tibetan tradition, hand symbols and breathing draw in and manipulate energy forces to affect a balance. Power source energy travels through the Reiki practitioner into the client's body.

Relaxation Therapy
A variety of physical, mental, spiritual, and recreational methods of relaxing the body and the mind.

Rolfing (Somatic Ontology, Structural Integration)
The Rolfer slowly stretches and repositions the body's supportive wrappings, called fascia, with firm and gently directed pressure, to restore normal length and elasticity to the network of deep connective fibers.

Rosen Method
Mind, bodywork, and movement; combines emotional psychotherapy with physical awareness.

Rubenfeld Synergy
A holistic therapy that integrates body, mind, spirit and emotions using gentle touch, along with verbal dialogue, active listening, Gestalt Process, imagery, metaphor, movement, and humor.

Shamanism
Traditional native healing systems practiced throughout the world. Archaic magico-religious phenomenon in which the shaman may use fire, wind, or magical flight as part of a healing ceremony.

Shiatsu
A type of bodywork from Japan that uses acupuncture energy meridians to activate and balance the body's energy (chi).

Spiritual Healing

A healing philosophy incorporating the concept of spiritual energy as a healing force; using prayer, meditation, individual, or group spiritual resources and other methods of focusing thought energy.

Stress Management

Based on the belief that stress creates a "dis-ease" climate within the body, by reducing stress, the body's own natural healing resources are enhanced, such as the immune system.

Tai Chi

Balanced gentle movements, incorporating a combination of meditation and breathing, are designed to dissolve physical and karmic layers of tension in both the physical body and the energy body, and to open up the spiritual space inside.

TAO

A philosophy often related to CAM practices. The definition of Tao is "the way," "the law"; the rule of Tao is living in total harmony with the natural world.

Therapeutic Touch

Hands do not touch body, but perform smoothing and soothing movements above the body, "massaging" the human energy field surrounding body; involving mind, body, emotion, and spirit.

Traditional Chinese Medicine (Oriental Medicine)

The ancient (and modern) theory of medicine with unique diagnostic methods and systematic approach includes medication, pharmacology, herbology, acupuncture, massage, and QiGong.

Transsage

The use of therapeutic massage, deep relaxation (hypnosis), guided imagery, metaphors, and affirmations with the goal of increasing mental focus.

Trager Method

Based on the theory that patterns of stiffness and aging exist more in the unconscious mind than in the tissues, this method reeducates the body/mind to release old holding patterns that limit us physically and mentally. Rhythmic movement and soothing rocking are used.

Transpersonal Psychology

The extension of psychological studies into consciousness studies, spiritual inquiry, body-mind relationships, and transformations.

Trepanation

A small hole is drilled in the skull (solely in the bone, not entering the brain), to allow an expansion window in the brain to permanently regain its youth.

Tuina

2000-year-old Chinese massage, like acupuncture (without needles) Tuina works with the Qi (chi) energy of patients.

Urani Medicine

Traditional herbal healing system of ancient Persia and modern India, Australia, and other countries.

Urine Therapy

Using (your own) urine externally and internally to provide nutrients, purify blood and tissue, and signal what is out of balance.

Visualization

Similar to Guided Imagery. Creative visualization is the art of sending an image to your subconscious mind, and your subconscious mind will begin to create what it "sees."

Visceral Manipulation

Based on the specific placement of soft manual force to encourage normal mobility, tone, and inherent tissue motion of the viscera and their connective tissues.

Vitamin Therapy

Use of vitamins, minerals, enzymes, amino acids, fatty acids, and other nutritional support.

Watsu

A creative blend of meridian stretches, Indian chakra work, acupressure, Zen Sciatsu, and yoga movements performed in warm water.

Wave Work

A psycho-spiritual process for integration, based on deeper teachings of Yoga. Using breath and awareness of sensation to allow an organic shift in consciousness.

Yoga

A general term for a wide range of body-mind exercise practices, traditionally referred to as the art of "yoking" or hooking up the lower consciousness with the higher consciousness. Combines breathing, movement, meditation, and a sequence of sound to align, purify, and promote a healthy flexible body.

Zero Balancing

Hands-on body-mind system to align body energy with body's physical structure.

As noted, yoga is on this list, and according to the 2007 National Health Interview Survey,[3] yoga is the sixth most commonly used complementary health practice among American adults. According to the NCCIH website, yoga is defined as follows:

Yoga is a mind and body practice with origins in ancient Indian philosophy. The various styles of yoga typically combine physical postures, breathing techniques, and meditation or relaxation. There are numerous schools of yoga. Hatha yoga, the most commonly practiced in the United States and Europe, emphasizes postures *(asanas)* and breathing exercises *(pranayama)*. Some of the major styles of hatha yoga are Iyengar, Ashtanga, Vini, Kundalini, and Bikram yoga.

The terminology originates in the Sanskrit language. For example, a Yogi is one committed to the path yoga. The number of American yoga practitioners (Yogi) has increased to over 36 million in 2016, up from 20.4 million in 2012.[4] Yoga practitioners report spending over $16 billion on yoga clothing, equipment, classes, and accessories in the last year, up from $10 billion in 2012.[5]

The practice of yoga has created controversies. The controversies are not the growing popularity of yoga, or that people who practice it are not proclaiming helpful benefits, but whether there is science behind it. If there is science behind yoga, it is therefore part of medicine, and should it be reimbursed by health insurance? So let us look at the science behind yoga.

The first observation is the astounding number and variety of medical conditions that are reported as being improved by yoga. In his book *Yoga as Medicine*, Timothy McCall, MD,[6] records a list of conditions from alcoholism to hemorrhoids and from heart disease to menstrual problems that can be treated. Systematic reviews and meta-analyses (170 citations) and randomized controlled trials (207 citations) published by PubMed[7] further emphasize the variety of conditions and the mix of certitude in their conclusions. For example, in a paper entitled "Effects of a Yoga Intervention on Lipid Profiles of Diabetes (Type 2) Patients with Dyslipidemia," from the *Indian Heart Journal* (2013), the results showed a decrease in cholesterol, triglycerides, and LDL with an improvement in HDL. Note that there are no qualifications. Another example, "Pilot Study of Integral Yoga for Menopausal Hot Flashes" from a journal called *Menopause*, stated, "Results suggest that yoga can serve as a behavioral option for reducing hot flashes but may not offer any advantage over other types of interventions." Note the less certain aspect. Other studies noted "promising" results or "needs standardization" or characterized by "methodological weakness." There is also a mix of yoga systems used like Bikram[8] and Hatha.[9]

A further observation is that other therapies are added to the yoga regimen, and it is difficult to sort out the true amount complemented by yoga. In presenting the scientific evidence, Dr. McCall[10] cites Dr. Dean Ornish's studies:

Published in such leading medical journals as JAMA and *The Lancet* beginning in 1983 tell us more about the health benefits of a comprehensive program of yoga and lifestyle changes. The yoga portion of the Lifestyle Heart Trial, which was designed by Nischala—a modification of the standard Integral yoga class as taught by her guru Swami Satchidananda—included asana, pranayama, visualization, meditation, and deep relaxation. The rest of the program consisted of a low-fat vegetarian diet, smoking cessation, group support sessions, and aerobic exercise. Following the weeklong intensive training, patients attended regular meetings in their communities and were asked to continue the diet, yoga, and exercise in on their own. One year after starting the program, LDL, cholesterol levels dropped from an average of 144 to 87 in people who were not taking medication to lower their levels. Patients who followed Ornish's program had 91 percent reduction in the frequency of their angina, as well as a significant reduction in severity of attacks.

What was not considered or measured in this study was the well-known contribution of collateral circulation the heart makes in people with coronary heart disease. In this same reference, Dr. McCall goes on to claim reversal of the heart disease, which remains a questionable process.

In the face of the many problems of the science of yoga, there is evidence that the support of yoga grows, and reimbursement may yet happen. A 2014 article in the *American Journal of Managed Care*,[11] author Mary K. Caffrey tells the story of Aetna's interests in yoga. She notes, "Aetna funded the study after its chief executive took up yoga following a skiing accident and transferred the findings to an employee wellness program that the company touts to other employers as a way to improve employee heath and increase productivity."

She quotes an Aetna executive as saying, "While there is no timetable for reimbursement, we are moving in that direction." "We are making sure the results we have are evidence-based."

The search for "evidence-based results" goes on. A comprehensive article entitled "Overview of Systematic Reviews: Yoga as a Therapeutic Intervention for Adults with Acute and Chronic Health Conditions"[12] can best be summarized by reading the abstract published in 2013:

Objectives: Overview the quality, direction, and characteristics of yoga interventions for treatment of acute and chronic health conditions in adult populations.

Methods: We searched for systematic reviews in 10 online databases, bibliographic references, and hand-searches in yoga-related journals.

Results: We identified 2202 titles, of which 41 full-text articles were assessed for eligibility and 26 systematic reviews satisfied inclusion criteria. Thirteen systematic reviews include quantitative data and six papers include meta-analysis. The quality of evidence is generally low. Sixteen different types of health conditions are included. Eleven reviews show tendency towards positive effects of yoga intervention, 15 reviews report unclear results, and no reviews report adverse effects of yoga. Yoga appears most effective for reducing symptoms in anxiety, depression, and pain. Conclusion. Although the quality of systematic reviews is high, the quality of supporting evidence is low. Significant heterogeneity and variability in reporting interventions by type of yoga, settings, and population characteristics limit the generalizability of results.

The discussion of this huge review concludes, "The quality and quantity of evidence is a limitation to this overview." The favorable reviews tended to be for treatment of chronic pain, and the unclear results were for anxiety, arthritis, asthma, body mass index, diabetes management, muscular strength, epilepsy, hypertension, and pain for the elderly population. There is hardly an article in this, and the entire yoga literature that does not conclude that more research is necessary. Two other observations:

1. Once yoga gets involved with the politics of reimbursement, it may be very difficult to generate valid and objective science.
2. The need for science to study just a yoga system separately from extraneous other complementary systems may prove an unsurmountable challenge.

Cost factors:

The best estimates of cost of yoga to the American public are gathered by *Yoga Journal* and *Yoga Alliance*,[13] reported in 2016. It shows, "The number of US yoga practitioners has increased to more than 36 million, up from 20.4 million in 2012, while annual practitioner spending on yoga classes, clothing, equipment, and accessories rose to $16 billion, up from $10 billion over the past four years." Further details are on the referenced website, such as that 49 percent of Yogi take it up for improving physical fitness, which raises the question that has not been answered, and that is, is yoga comparable to exercise programs in general? So until science and time provide the critical answers, yoga remains uneasily in the unproven category of CAM, and $16 billion is a conservative figure for 2018.

11. Chelation Therapy

> *It is a capital mistake to theorize before one has data, insensibly one begins to twist facts to suit theories, instead of theories to suit facts.*
> —*Arthur Conan Doyle*

Chelation therapy is a chemical process in which a synthetic solution—EDTA (ethylenediaminetetraacetic acid), or a related agent, is injected into the bloodstream to remove heavy metals and/or minerals from the body.[1] From the same website, we learn that *chelation* means "to grab" or "to bind." When EDTA is injected into the veins, it "grabs" heavy metals and minerals such as lead, mercury, copper, iron, arsenic, aluminum, and calcium and removes them from the body. Except as a treatment for lead poisoning, chelation therapy is controversial and unproved. Chelation ("kee-lay'-shuh-n") therapy is the preferred medical treatment for metal poisoning, including acute mercury, iron (including cases of thalassemia), arsenic, lead, uranium, plutonium, and other forms of toxic metal poisoning. The chelating agent may be administered intravenously, intramuscularly, or orally, depending on the agent and the type of poisoning.[2]

There are many chelating agents used in special situations, and not all are approved by the FDA.[3] Dimercaptosuccinic acid (DMSA) has been recommended for the treatment of lead poisoning in children by poison control centers around the world.[4] The controversy regarding chelation focuses on removing not heavy metals but the treatment of coronary artery disease. The hypothesis is that since there is prevalence of calcium in significant coronary artery disease, indeed other arteries as well, chelation therapy aimed at "grabbing up" the calcium from these plaques would result in decrease of incidence of blockage and therefore be a valid treatment for coronary artery disease. To answer the question, the Trial to Assess Chelation Therapy (TACT) was done. According to NIH[5]:

> TACT was the first large-scale, multi-center study designed to determine the safety and efficacy of EDTA chelation therapy (specifically disodium EDTA) for individuals with prior heart attacks. The National Institutes of Health's (NIH) National Heart, Lung, and Blood Institute (NHLBI) and National Center for Complementary and Integrative Health (NCCIH) cosponsored TACT. This study was

more than 20 times larger than any previous study of chelation therapy. It was designed to be large enough to detect if there are any moderate benefits or risks associated with the therapy.

The study was a placebo-controlled, double-blind design that included 1,708 participants aged 50 years and older with a prior heart attack. Its purpose was to test whether EDTA chelation therapy and/or high-dose vitamin therapy is effective for the treatment of CHD. The addition of vitamin therapy in the mix is explained as follows.

EDTA chelation therapy, as practiced in the community, often includes administration of high doses of antioxidant vitamin and mineral supplements. To test whether some of the therapy's effect may be attributable to vitamin/mineral supplements or to the EDTA solution itself, the investigators randomly assigned participants to receive either EDTA chelation solution or placebo. Then, the patients in these two groups were again randomly selected to receive either low-dose or high-dose vitamin/mineral supplements.

The EDTA chelation therapy or placebo solution was delivered through 40 intravenous (into the veins) infusions that were administered over a 28-month course of treatment. The first 30 infusions were delivered on a weekly basis and the last 10 were delivered during a maintenance phase every two to eight weeks. Following the infusion phase, participants had contact with study staff at 3-month intervals until the study was complete (5–7 years).

The results were mixed. "Those receiving chelation had an 18% reduced risk of subsequent cardiac events such as heart attack, stroke, hospitalization for angina, or coronary revascularization. But, a cardiac event occurred in 222 (26%) of the chelation group and 261 (30%) of the placebo group. The conclusion was. These results are not, by themselves, sufficient to support the routine use of chelation as post-heart attack therapy."

There has been stout criticism of TACT.[6]

> "The reason why we're so uncertain about what to conclude is this chelation mixture had many components to it. It wasn't just chelating agents," says Dr. Elliott Antman, professor of medicine and Associate Dean for Clinical/Translational Research at Harvard Medical School. In addition to the main chelating chemical, EDTA, the infused solution contained vitamins, magnesium chloride, potassium chloride, and a cocktail of other ingredients. "We don't know which of these components is contributing to the results," he says.

Also unclear is why the benefit from chelation therapy was almost exclusively confined to people with diabetes. The combined uncertainties surrounding this trial make it too tenuous to use for making heart disease treatment recommendations. "On the basis of this trial, we do not feel that chelation therapy is ready for clinical use," Dr. Antman adds. A second study is underway to study the apparent better result in patients with diabetes.

As a retired vascular surgeon, I find it difficult to believe that an agent circulating in the blood aimed at extracting calcium from the plaque or reducing blood level of calcium would have much effect on either the formation or dissolution of plaque that has encased calcium to the extent that it can even be seen on x-ray. A study on the calcification of coronary arteries[7] has pointed out,

> Atherosclerotic plaques typically consist of a central necrotic core containing various amor-

phous material such as cholesterol crystals and calcific deposits bounded on the lumen side by a fibrous cap made of different cell types.

I do not think that chelation fluids can get through that fibrous cap and therefore predict that the second study will be no more determinative than the first.

Information on national spending on chelation therapy for heart disease is not readily available. A study form 2002 published in JAMA[8] concluded that there is no evidence to support a beneficial effect of chelation therapy in patients with ischemic heart disease, stable angina, and a positive treadmill test for ischemia. Quoting the same study:

> Estimating a cost of $4000 for the usual series of treatment sums to an annual expenditure of approximately $400 million. The actual amount is likely higher because these estimates do not include all the cardiac patients who do not undergo catheterization and all other noncardiac patients who seek chelation therapy.

We can only hope and trust that the NCCIH, NIH study currently underway will further clarify what is clearly an unproven treatment to date.

Cost factors: The last year information is available is 2005, and $3 billion was spent on this therapy in the US in that year.[9] For 2018, we must leave the amount as unknown.

12. Massage

We have nothing to fear but missing
our massage appointment time.
—Franklin D. Roosevelt

Complementary and Alternative Medicine in the United States[1] defines *massage therapy* as "a general term for a wide range of therapeutic techniques involving the manipulation of muscles and soft tissues, including kneading, rubbing, tapping, friction, vigorous or relaxing, deep or superficial." The same reference also mentions marma therapy, which is defined as "a form of healing massage focusing on 108 points on the body where, vein, artery, tendon, bone and flesh meet." From the home webpage of the American Massage Therapy Association,[2] research estimates that massage therapy is a $12.1 billion industry in 2015, and the profession boasts up to 375,000 massage therapists and massage school students in the United States. In the year 2015–2016, surveys indicate that roughly 43.8–57.6 million adult Americans (19–25 percent) had a massage at least once.

From the same website reference:

> Recent research has shown the effectiveness of massage for the following conditions:

- Cancer-related fatigue
- Low back pain
- Osteoarthritis of the knee
- Reducing postoperative pain
- Boosting the body's immune system functioning
- Decreasing the symptoms of carpal tunnel syndrome
- Lowering blood pressure
- Reducing headache frequency
- Easing alcohol withdrawal symptoms
- Decreasing pain in cancer patients
- Fibromyalgia

Let's look at an example of this research. R. Parker Bausell, in his critic of CAM,[3] argues that there are four criteria that should be used to determine whether a CAM trial should be considered credible scientific evidence. They are as follows:

1. The trial involves the random assignment of participants to both a CAM therapy and a credible placebo control group that is indistinguishable from the real thing.
2. The trial employs at least fifty participants per group. Small trials are simply not valid.
3. The trial doesn't lose 25% or more of its participants over the course of the study. Drop-outs often figure they are not being helped or think they have been assigned to the placebo group.
4. The trial is published in a high-quality, prestigious, peer-reviewed journal. The publishing journal takes on special importance in CAM research, since there are literally hundreds of CAM journals.

Since chronic low back pain is one of the most common conditions for which patients seek massage treatment, Bausell gave as an example a paper entitled "Randomized Trial Comparing Traditional Chinese Medical Acupuncture, Therapeutic Massage, and Self-Care Education for Chronic Low Back Pain" published in the *Archives of Internal Medicine*, a well-respected journal. His simple conclusion was that the study was invalid because of the absence of a credible placebo group (criterion number 1).

Bausell's overall criticism of CAM research is the prevalence of bias in CAM research and notes several areas of concern[4]:

1. Drug research paid for by pharmaceutical companies produces more positive studies—that is, greater benefits and fewer side effects—than does drug research paid for by public funds. He notes that whenever people study something that can be sold for a profit, there is the very real possibility of bias creeping into their research.

2. One source of bias is cultural in nature, as witnessed by the fact that some countries and even whole continents tend to produce almost nothing but positive results. In 252 papers on acupuncture trials, non-US/non-UK English speaking countries (Canada, Australia, New Zealand) reported 30% positive results where-as Asia (China, Hong Kong, Taiwan, Japan, Sri Lanka, Vietnam) reported 98% positive results, with others in between.

3. Publication bias refers to a well-documented tendency for research journals to favor positive results when deciding which articles, they will publish. Over time, this phenomenon means that positive studies tend to accumulate in research record, a fact that naturally builds in a strong negative incentive for investigators to even try to publish a negative study.

4. A facet of quality relatively unique to CAM involves Cam research published in therapy-specific Cam journals, which are more prone to publish positive results that reflect well on their specialties (whether acupuncture, traditional Chinese medicine, or homeopathy) than they are to publish negative ones.

(I suggest that these are the journals that are spread about the waiting rooms of these practitioners.)

There is evidence that massage relieves *acute* back pain. From my own experience, I injured my back some years ago playing tennis and found that a single massage relieved the accompanying spasm and pain, although some soreness lingered; I could function quite well. I mention this as acute back pain is seldom referenced in the CAM literature.

Finally, there are costs associated with practice of massage. Some forty-three states require licensure,[5] and some require renewal on a regular basis. Massage schools that teach around the national average of five hundred to six hundred hours tend to have tuition that costs on average $6,000 to $10,000, including the cost of textbooks and supplies.[6]

The medical science of the value of massage is mixed and filled with terms such as "positive," "mixed," "promising," and "more work needs to be done." A recent review[7] from the NCCIH on clinical trials for five common causes of pain shows

> that a variety of complementary health approaches hold promise for helping to manage pain. The researchers found that the following complementary approaches had more positive than negative results and thus may help some patients manage certain painful health conditions.
>
> - Acupuncture and yoga for back pain.
> - Acupuncture and tai chi for osteoarthritis of the knee.
> - Massage therapy for neck pain—short-term benefit.
> - Relaxation techniques for severe headaches and migraine.

At the end, they noted some methodological limitations to their review, including small trial sizes, uncertain clinical relevance even if statistical superiority was present, or differences in the interventions provided in each study.

Checking the Cochrane Library Review of low back pain,[8] reported randomized controlled trials from the broad literature,

In total we included 25 RCTs (Random Controlled Trials) and 3096 participants in this review update. Only one trial included patients with acute LBP (pain duration less than four weeks), while all the others included patients with sub-acute (four to 12 weeks) or chronic LBP (12 weeks or longer). Seven studies did not report the sources of funding, and sixteen studies were funded by not-for-profit organizations. One study reported not receiving any funding, and one study was funded by a College of Massage Therapists. The quality of the evidence for all comparisons was graded "low" or "very low" which means that we have very little confidence in these results. This is because most of the included studies were small and had methodological flaws. The conclusion was, we have very little confidence that massage is an effective treatment for LBP. Acute, sub-acute and chronic LBP had improvements in pain outcomes with massage only in the short-term follow-up. Functional improvement was observed in participants with sub-acute and chronic LBP when compared with inactive controls, but only for the short-term follow-up. There were only minor adverse effects with massage.

In summary, you can look at literature with rose-colored glasses or with a sceptic eye, but the truth is most likely that massage benefits are most likely from the placebo effect, except for the limited group treated for acute low back pain.

Cost factors: Research estimates that massage therapy was a $12.1 billion industry in the country in 2015.[9] Probable 2018 best estimate is over $13 billion.

13. Biofeedback Therapy

Life is like riding a bicycle, to keep your
balance, you must keep moving.

—*Anon*

To understand the concept of biofeedback, a brief review of the autonomic nervous system is helpful. As we know, the nervous system in humans is viewed as central (brain) and peripheral (nerves). Steven A. Goldman, MD, PhD, distinguished professor of Neuroscience and Neurology, professor of Neuroscience and Neurology, University of Rochester Medical Center, defines the peripheral nervous system[1]:

> The peripheral nervous system consists of more than 100 billion nerve cells that run throughout the body like strings, making connections with the brain, other parts of the body, and often with each other. Peripheral nerves consist of bundles of nerve fibers. These fibers are wrapped with many layers of tissue composed of a fatty substance called myelin. These layers form the myelin sheath, which speeds the conduction of nerve impulses along the nerve fiber. Nerves conduct impulses at different speeds depending on their diameter and on the amount of myelin around them. The peripheral nervous system has two parts, the somatic nervous system and the autonomic nervous system.

The somatic system consists of nerves that connect the brain and spinal cord with muscles controlled by conscious effort (voluntary or skeletal muscles) and with sensory receptors in the skin. (Sensory receptors are specialized endings of nerve fibers that detect information in and around the body.)

The autonomic system connects the brain stem and spinal cord with internal organs and regulates internal body processes that require no conscious effort and that people are thus usually unaware of. Examples are the rate of heart contractions, blood pressure, the rate of breathing, the amount of stomach acid secreted, and the speed at which food passes through the digestive tract.

The autonomic system is further separated into the sympathetic and the parasympathetic divisions. Sympathetic division's main function is to prepare the body for stressful or emergency situations—for "fight or flight." Parasympathetic division's main function is to maintain normal body functions during ordinary situations.

These divisions of the autonomic system work together, usually with one activating and the other inhibiting the actions of internal organs. For example, the sympathetic division increases pulse, blood pressure, and breathing rates, and the parasympathetic system decreases each of them.

The somatic (of the body) system pertains to parts that we can consciously control such as raising an arm or chewing our food. The autonomic (independent or self-governing) system works without our conscious control, such as our heart rate or peristalsis, the contraction in the alimentary canal which moves our digestive contents.

A consensus definition of biofeedback therapy is provided by the three professional biofeedback organizations[2]:

> is a process that enables an individual to learn how to change physiological activity for the purposes of improving health and performance. Precise instruments measure physiological activity such as brainwaves, heart function, breathing, muscle activity, and skin temperature. These instruments rapidly and accurately "feedback" information to the user. The presentation of this information—often in conjunction with changes in thinking, emotions, and behavior—supports desired physiological changes. Over time, these changes can endure without continued use of an instrument.

The first point to notice in this definition is that the purpose of "improving health and performance" is an extraordinarily wide agenda which seems to have no limits. I read it as meaning anything from controlling hypertension to improving your golf swing. If anything, it raises a level of skepticism. The second aspect of the definition to notice is that it can be accomplished "by learning." This assumes a capacity to learn and by implication to retain after the learning process. The third point to note is what measurables the subject learns to control—mentioned are brain waves, heart function, breathing, muscle activity, and skin temperature. The fourth point to note is that the conscious altering of measurements "supports" an objective. Apparently "often" is added conscious changes in thinking, emotions, and behavior. In other words, in a suggestive environment ("supportive"), the manipulation of certain body parameters which are not designed to be manipulated but controlled automatically can gain some designated goal with an enduring result.

With the definition in mind, let's look at the instrumentation that is currently used.[3] According to the Mayo Clinic, the following instruments are used for biofeedback therapy: (1) EEG (electroencephalograph) is used to present brain waves, (2) chest and abdominal bands are used to measure breathing, (3) ECG (electrocardiograph) is used to measure heart rate, (4) EMG (electromyograph) to measure skeletal muscle activity, (5) EDG (electrodermograph) to measure sweat gland activity, (6) temperature monitor on hands or feet to indirectly measure blood flow. In addition, there are also interactive computer devices and various wearables on the market of late.

According to the Cleveland Clinic,[4] the Association for Applied Psychophysiology and Biofeedback and the Society for Neuronal Regulation published criteria for evaluating the effectiveness of biofeedback. These criteria range from levels 1 to 5, with level 3 being "probably efficacious"; level 4, "efficacious"; and level 5, "efficacious and specific." Under level 5 was urinary incontinence in females—the only entry. Under level 4 was anxiety, attention deficit disorder, headache, hypertension, temporomandibular disorders, and urinary incontinence in males. Under level 3 was alcoholism and substance abuse, arthritis, chronic pain, epilepsy, fecal elimination disorders, pediatric migraine, insomnia, traumatic brain injury, and vulvar vestibulitis.

More recent literature (2010) details other points that proponents of biofeedback emphasize.[5] The term "biofeedback training" is preferred over "biofeedback therapy," and further, that in addition to improving health and wellness, the training can improve academic, athletic, and corporate performance. Quite a list!

There is nothing in the definition that tells us how feedback works. An overview of biofeedback on webMD states, "Researchers aren't exactly sure how or why biofeedback works. They do know that biofeedback promotes relaxation, which can help relieve a number of conditions that are related to stress." This raises the simple question as to whether the mechanism is but a form of relaxation through suggestion and conditioning, and the results are but a manifestation of the placebo effect.

Essentially, what we are dealing with is a form of relaxation applied as a medical therapy.[6] Others mentioned in this same reference by Bausell are transcendental meditation, concentrating on a single thought (mantra) and "mindfulness" meditation (of Buddhist origin), and focus on breathing without restricting the mind's attention. Bausell makes another distinction here:

> Sometimes these procedures are advocated as a lifestyle or stress reduction technique in which case they do not qualify as CAM and sometimes they are prescribed for specific medical problems in which they are classified as CAM.

Still other forms are progressive muscle relaxation, deep breathing therapy alone or with yoga or meditation, and finally, what is termed guided imagery.

Biofeedback uses instrumentation measuring various components of the autonomic nervous system to show how conscious effort to attain relaxation can be observed, often on a computer screen. Science recognizes that a human can consciously calm down from an excited state and measurable parameters can be used to document the transition and that the same can be accomplished by training to do so. Pavlov and his dogs[7] showed how it is manifest in other species. The bell is a neutral stimulus until the dog learns to associate the bell with food. Then the bell becomes a conditioned stimulus (CS) which produces the conditioned response (CR) of salivation after repeated pairings between the bell and food. The problem comes in proving that in the medical conditions selected for treatment, the result is other than the placebo effect—in other words, the training (conditioning) produces the anticipated or desired result rather than a direct cause-and-effect relationship. I suspect that is the reason the literature on the subject shows such great variation in results. In other words, there is a wide spectrum in the functions of the autonomic nervous system which are amenable to control. Witness the difference in the literature of ADHD and alleviation of pain of labor in women (see Cochran Library database system reviews). Since biofeedback is considered by advocates to be efficacious in ADHD,[8] it is of interest to cite a reference from *The Lancet*[9] entitled "Neurofeedback, Sham Neurofeedback, and Cognitive-Behavioral Group Therapy in Adults with Attention-Deficit Hyperactivity Disorder: A Triple-Blind, Randomized, Controlled Trial."

> All three groups showed improvements in symptoms. The neurofeedback group showed no greater improvements than the other groups.

Dr. Michael Schönenberg and coauthors provide this usual summary of the implications of all the available evidence concerning neurofeedback therapy for ADHD to date:

> Our results suggest that although neuro-feedback training is effective in reducing ADHD symptoms it neither outperforms sham neu-rofeedback nor group psychotherapy. As such, neurofeedback cannot be recommended as an *efficient* approach in the treatment of adults with

ADHD. Finally, owing to its comparative simplicity, meta-cognitive therapy should be viewed as viable and efficient treatment option for adults with ADHD.

In fairness, the best summary is to say that claims are stretched (see ref. 8) and more research might be of value. This is an area where it is difficult to control the placebo effect.[10] In the meantime, biofeedback remains on the experimental side of mainstream medicine.

Cost factors: The cost of biofeedback therapy to the consumer in the United States is difficult to estimate. Davis and Weeks from the Dartmouth Institute for Health Police document out-of-pocket expenses from 2012 report[11] at $ 84 million, so the 2018 number could be $100 million.

14. Magnet Therapy

> *The real purpose of the scientific method is to make sure nature doesn't mislead you into thinking you know something you actually don't know.*
> —*Robert Pirsig, Zen and the Art of Motorcycle Maintenance*

Magnets are advertised to alleviate pain and treat other health concerns. It is incorporated into the list of complementary and alternative (or integrative) medicine.[1] It is an astounding fact that worldwide magnet therapy industry sales total over a billion dollars per year,[2] including $300 million per year in the United States alone[3] when it is supported by little or no scientific evidence. In the United States, the Food and Drug Administration regulations prohibit marketing any magnet therapy product using medical claims, as such claims are unfounded.[4]

One of the largest studies reviewing randomized trials was published in the *Canadian Medical Journal*[5] in 2007. The study's methods are noted:

Systematic literature searches were conducted from inception to March 2007 for the following data sources: MEDLINE, EMBASE, AMED (Allied and Complementary Medicine Database), CINAHL, Scopus, the Cochrane Library and the UK National Research Register. All randomized clinical trials of static magnets for treating pain from any cause were considered. Trials were included only if they involved a placebo control or a weak magnet as the control, with pain as an outcome measure. The mean change in pain, as measured on a 100-mm visual analogue scale, was defined as the primary outcome and was used to assess the difference between static magnets and placebo.

Twenty-nine potentially relevant trials were identified. The interpretation by the authors was:

The evidence does not support the use of static magnets for pain relief, and therefore magnets cannot be recommended as an effective treatment.

The paper went on to explain that:

In this systematic review and meta-analysis, we assessed the clinical evidence from randomized controlled trials of static magnets for treating pain.

Magnets produce energy in the form of magnetic fields. Two main types of magnets exist: static or permanent magnets, in which the magnetic field is generated by the spin of electrons within the material itself, and electromagnets, in which a magnetic field is generated when an electric current is applied. Most magnets that are marketed to consumers for health purposes are static magnets of various strengths, typically between 30 and 500 mT. Magnets have been incorporated into arm and leg wraps, mattress pads, necklaces, shoe inserts and bracelets.

Cited as an excellent example of obvious flummery, James Randi,[6] well-known Canadian sceptic, tells the story of the Florsheim Shoe Company which introduced the "MagneForce" shoe in 1998—advertising that it was the first shoe with its own power supply, which had magnets embedded in the soles and sold for an extra twenty-five dollars a pair. He goes on:

> Florsheim—through Gary Null, their resident PhD, (whose degree had been questioned[7])—claimed that such a magnetic field applied to the body would stimulate blood circulation and had been shown to reduce pain and to increase "natural" healing. They touted the "rapid healing and relief" produced, and "reduction in foot, leg and back fatigue, an increase in the range of motion, reduced leg, hip and back pain, and resulting greater energy levels" from the MagneForce product. They claimed that "numerous clinical tests conducted at such institutions as Vanderbilt University, New York University and Baylor University have documented" these advantages, and that diabetics could thereby benefit, as well.
>
> Another howler by Null was published in the small book that accompanied the Florsheim wonder-shoes: "The earth is a giant magnet, with north and south poles and a hot liquid core. The hot liquid core creates a magnetic field which at the earth's surface is relatively weak but serves to

keep humans attached to the earth. Without this magnetic field, we would spin into outer space."

The absurdity of all this pseudoscience is exceeded only by the residual still driving the marketplace well after the debunking of magnets for health conditions.[8] You can go online at Amazon.com and buy a Deep Magnetic Therapy Spot Magnet Kit for $34.80 or Magnetic Foam Insoles for $12.59 or a VIKI LYNN Hematite Powerful Magnetic Bracelet for arthritis pain relief or for sports-related therapy for only $5.99—all being touted by "satisfied customers." You can even splurge on a Magnetico super sleep mattress/pad for between $1,910 and 3,650.[9] On their website is posted their interpretation of research:

> Dr. Kyoichi Nakagawa is considered the founder of modern magnetic research and the value of magnetism in enhancing health. He published a study in 1956, which claimed that the Earth's natural magnetic field had declined by at least 50%. He then went on to study the effects of magnetism on health. He coined the term Magnetic Field Deficiency Syndrome; this is where a lack of magnetic field causes aches and pains.

Medico sleep pads[10] also claim that

> Detoxification is among the multiple benefits associated with Magnetico Sleep Pads. Through our years of research and experience, we have found that the increased negative magnetic field produced by a Magnetico Sleep Pad assists your body in expelling environmental toxins. You will be amazed at the renewed energy and symptom relief you will experience once your body is free of this environmental "sludge."

Most toxins have a Positive (+) charge. The increased Negative (-) energy from the Magnetico Sleep Pad (which supplements the Earth's depleted field) passes through all the cells of your body, thereby assisting the release of toxins and waste products.

In order for your body to expel most of these toxins, they must be filtered through your lymphatic system, passed through your liver and kidneys, and finally excreted in your urine. Fatigue, brain fog, and sciatic nerve sensitivity often accompany detoxification. The presence of these symptoms will vary due to the health condition and toxicity of each individual. Most detoxification is accomplished in the first two weeks as the toxic load is lightened. It is important to note that a large percentage of people may not notice any significant detoxification symptoms, although some detoxification is occurring.

I can find no valid scientific literature to back up any of these claims of detoxification. It is to be noted, however, how often one form of unproven health claims is joined or complemented with another—in other words, how often quackery begets quackery.

One final point regarding the frequent claim of pseudoscience that iron magnetic fields influence iron in the blood, the basis of so many claims of products on the market: Iron in the human body is mostly in blood, in hemoglobin molecules, where it binds to oxygen molecule,[11] according to Ed Caruthers, a retired physicist, who goes on to explain that "oxyhemoglobin (Hb-O2), by experimental measurement, is diamagnetic (no net unpaired electrons)." Without unpaired electrons, the molecule does not move in or by a magnetic field. For a more detailed scientific explanation, see Wikipedia.[12]

Cost factors: Of the billion dollars spent globally, Americans spend over $500,000 as noted in 2006.[13] Estimates for 2018 are near $1 billion.

15. Aromatherapy

Of all smells, bread; of all tastes, salt.
—*George Herbert*

Aromatherapy is included in the 2005 list of CAM therapies in the United States,[1] but not in the 2008 NIH National Center for Complementary and Integrative Health report,[2] which interestingly made the distinction between "complementary medicine" (used together with conventional medicine) and "alternative medicine" (used in place of conventional medicine). It went on to introduce the term "integrative," explaining, "Integrative medicine combines conventional and CAM treatments for which there is evidence of safety and effectiveness," which is a very confusing distinction because it fails to designate between conventional and CAM as to the measure of safety and effectiveness each component has. Although not clearly noted, the conclusion seems to be that aromatherapy was not as popular at that time as it apparently is today, ten years later, as writer Rachel Monroe writing an exposé in *The New Yorker*[3] states:

> Essential oils' rising popularity is part of the contemporary appetite for wellness, an embrace of holistic healthy-living practices ranging from the low key (meditation) to the wacky (Brain Dust, a forty-dollar jar of adaptogenic herbs and mushrooms that promises to align you with the cosmic flow for great achievement).
>
> Much of the oils sold in the United States comes from two companies based in Utah, "Young Living" and "do Terra." The two companies have more than three million customers apiece, and a billion dollars in annual sales.

A definition of aromatherapy is given on the website[4] as:

> Aromatherapy is the practice of using the natural oils extracted from flowers, bark, stems, leaves, roots or other parts of a plant to enhance psychological and physical well-being.

Then come the claims:

> The inhaled aroma from these "essential" oils is widely believed to stimulate brain function. Essential oils can also be absorbed through the skin, where they travel through the bloodstream and can promote whole-body healing.

A form of alternative medicine, aromatherapy is gaining momentum. It is used for a variety of applications, including pain relief, mood enhancement, and increased cognitive function. There are a wide number of essential oils available, each with its own healing properties.

The science behind the many claims is thin at best. The search of the Cochran literature[5] found the following summary testing subjects sleep and behavioral problems seen in dementia:

> Aromatherapy is the use of pure essential oils from fragrant plants (such as peppermint, sweet marjoram, and rose) to help relieve health problems and improve the quality of life in general. The healing properties of aromatherapy are claimed to include promotion of relaxation and sleep, relief of pain, and reduction of depressive symptoms. Hence, aromatherapy has been used to reduce disturbed behavior, to promote sleep, and to stimulate motivational behavior of people with dementia. Of the seven randomized controlled trials that we found, only two trials including 186 people had useable data. The analysis of these two small trials showed inconsistent effects

of aromatherapy on measures of agitation, behavioral symptoms and quality of life. More large-scale randomized controlled trials are needed before firm conclusions can be reached about the effectiveness of aromatherapy for dementia.

A systemic review of the literature reported in the *British Journal of General Practice*[6] summarized as follows:

Aromatherapy is becoming increasingly popular; however, there are few clear indications for its use. To systematically review the literature on aromatherapy to discover whether any clinical indication may be recommended for its use, computerized literature searches were performed to retrieve all randomized controlled trials of aromatherapy from the following databases: MEDLINE, EMBASE, British Nursing Index, CISCOM, and AMED... All trials were evaluated independently by both authors and data were extracted in a pre-defined, standardized fashion. Twelve trials were located: six of them had no independent replication; six related to the relaxing effects of aromatherapy combined with massage. These studies suggest that aromatherapy massage has a mild, transient anxiolytic effect. Based on a critical assessment of the six studies relating to relaxation, the effects of aromatherapy are probably not strong enough for it to be considered for the treatment of anxiety. The hypothesis that it is effective for any other indication is not supported by the findings of rigorous clinical trials.

A website from the University of Minnesota[7] notes that

> A significant body of research on essential oils has been conducted by the food, flavoring, cosmetics, and tobacco industries. They are most interested in the flavor, mood alteration, and preservative qualities of essential oils. Some of these companies have also conducted extensive research on the toxicity and safety of essential oils.
>
> Although much of this research is proprietary and not generally available to consumers, some of it has made its way into cosmetic and plant product journals. These journals are important sources of information as we accumulate a growing body of knowledge on essential oils.
>
> Most of the studies that have been published in the English language scientific literature have been conducted in laboratories and they have *not been tested on humans*, but this is changing.

They also note that there are some issues in conducting research on essential oils: (1) essential oils are not standardized, (2) it is difficult to conduct blinded studies on aromatic substances, and (3) it is difficult to tell what caused the outcome.

One study from the *Journal of Alternative and Complementary Medicine*[8] concluded that

> Readily available aromatherapy treatments appear to be effective and promote sleep, but guidelines needed to be developed, presumably to differentiate inhalation from massage techniques.

Although the literature supporting the claims is extensive, the science seems to be unconvincing. The claims[9] are wildly extensive and include "helps the body detox," "good for getting the mind clear by activating the electrical properties in the oil, and aligns your DNA," "keeping your skin young," "evokes different physical or spiritual states," "kills microorganisms in the air," "antiviral," and "essential oils have a divine intelligence and discernment that allows them to heal without harming, to provide our cells with exactly what we need and nothing we don't."

Regarding research in aromatherapy, it should be pointed out that a bibliometric study[10] presented the results of publication on the topic of aromatherapy published between 1995 and 2014.

> Over half of the 549 articles originated from authors from non-English speaking regions of the world, (95% of the articles were written in English, however). Of the 1888 authors, the two most prolific authors in aromatherapy revealed by this study, Edzard Ernst and Myeong Soo Lee were also highly productive in other subfields of complementary medicine. As anticipated by the power law, most articles were concentrated in several journals. In fact, almost a quarter of the articles were published in only three journals, namely, *Journal of Alternative and Complementary Medicine, Complementary Therapies in Medicine,* and *Evidence-Based Complementary and Alternative Medicine.* Hence, these journals can be considered as the core journals for knowledge dissemination of aromatherapy research.

As prolific as these journals may seem, they are not mainline scientific journals. The idea that more publications mean more science seems to be a tactic of the CAM movement, perhaps a legacy of its origins in the congress of the United States. In hearings before the Committee on Health, Education, Labor, and Pensions[11] February 26, 2009, entitled "Examining Integrative Care: A Pathway to a Healthier Nation," Senator Harkin states in an opening statement:

I set up this Office of Alternative Medicine through the Appropriations Committee. In 1998, working with then-Senator Frist, we sponsored legislation to elevate the office to what is today the National Center for Complementary and Alternative Medicine. Now, again, I must say that one of the purposes—when we drafted that legislation back in 1992 and continuing in 1998—of this center was to investigate and validate alternative approaches. Quite frankly, I must say publicly it has fallen short. The focus—I think, quite frankly, in this center and previously the office before it—most of its focus has been on disproving things rather than seeking out and approving things.

I wonder if it occurred to Senator Harkin that the key reason they "focused on disapproving things" was that they were *not scientifically valid.*

A few final points brought out by Monroe[12] are that the marketing of these oils is by multilevel-marketing companies on the model of Amway and Mary Kay and that only a few people at the top of the pyramid make any money. Also, that if anything could give a bad name to alternative medicine, it is the fact that the founder of Young Living, D. Gary Young, had been arrested for practicing medicine without a license and that in 2014, the FDA admonished both do Terra and Young Living for distributors' claims about oils for cancer, brain injury, autism, Alzheimer's disease, and ADHD.

All this makes one wonder why these oils are called "essential."

Cost factors: Based upon global figures,[13] US spending on aromatherapy in 2018 is estimated at $4 billion.

16. Hydrotherapy (Aquatic Therapy) or Balneotherapy

The sea cures all ailments of man.

—*Plato*

Hippocrates, the Father of Medicine, was a proponent of hydrotherapy, as were Roman and Byzantine physicians Herophilus, Orebasius, and Paul of Aegina.[1] They believed in the curative effect of mineral and thermal springs. Plato remarked, "*The sea cures all ailments of man.*" Euripides said, "*The sea washes away all men's illnesses,*" and Cato the Elder mixed wine with seawater, a drink he served his slaves to maintain their energy. Water may be our oldest therapeutic agent.

The term *hydrotherapy* applies to use of water, and the term *balneotherapy* applies to the use of therapeutic bathing in medicinal and thermal springs. In today's world, Medicare billing sets codes for aquatic therapy and balneotherapy. A host of medical conditions are treated under these headings—for example, rheumatoid arthritis. A reference from PubMed.gov[2] concludes that,

> Overall evidence is insufficient to show that balneotherapy is more effective than no treatment, that one type of bath is more effective than another or that one type of bath is more effective than mudpacks, exercise or relaxation therapy.

Other claims are that hydrotherapy increases range of motion, relieves symptoms of fibromyalgia and low back pain, decreases anxiety, and provides for better sleep, all claims made by hot-tub manufacturers.[3] A 2006 meta-analysis reference on hydrotherapy and low back pain is from the British Society of Rheumatology.[4] The conclusion was

> Even though the data are scarce, there is encouraging evidence suggesting that spa therapy

and balneotherapy may be effective for treating patients with low back pain. These data are not compelling but warrant rigorous large-scale trials.

In the discussion, this study further states,

> The paucity of evidence is in stark contrast to the popularity of these treatments among patient populations and to the expenditure by health insurers on such interventions.

This clearly is referring to the fact some health insurance covers the cost of home hot tubs, which introduces another area of possible conflict of interest on the part of physicians and insurance companies. This was also addressed to some extent in the same reference:

> In some countries, such as Germany, the spa sector has suffered through political decisions to cut back on reimbursement for such treatments through the national health insurance system. The move was motivated by financial considerations but the paucity of compelling data on specific effectiveness and cost-effectiveness has also played a crucial role. Considering the potential role of balneotherapy and spa therapy, as shown in this meta-analysis, it is disappointing that more clinical trials have not been initiated. As always, the burden of demonstrating the worth of a medical intervention lies on the shoulders of those who claim that it works.

With respect to the claim that hydrotherapy provides better sleep, NIHNCCIH reports,

> There is some qualitative evidence that suggests that balneotherapy (hydrotherapy) may pro-

vide small improvement in pain and health-related quality of life for patients with fibromyalgia syndrome.

And with respect to pain in general, the website reports,

A 2014 qualitative systematic review and meta-analysis found moderate-to-strong evidence for a small reduction in pain (from eight randomized controlled trials involving 462 participants and three low-risk studies involving 223 participants) and moderate-to-strong evidence for a small improvement in health-related quality of life (from seven randomized controlled trials involving 398 participants, and three low-risk studies involving 223 participants). However, the study authors concluded that high-quality studies with larger sample sizes are needed to confirm the therapeutic benefits of balneotherapy or hydrotherapy for patients with fibromyalgia syndrome.

Note the language: "moderate-to-strong evidence for small reduction." The conclusion that more studies are needed seems to be a recurring theme throughout *all* the CAM literature.

It is near impossible to get a handle on the out-of-pocket expenses for hydrotherapy for health in the United States. It comes under so many headings as part of alternative medicine, such as naturopathy, occupational therapy, physiotherapy and various forms for treating pain in general and techniques such as underwater massage, balneotherapy, Kneipp treatments, Scotch hose, Swiss shower, thalassotherapy, whirlpool baths, hot Roman baths, hot tub, Jacuzzi, and mineral baths, to name a few. In sampling areas by simply googling "hydrotherapy near me," a figure of 3,800 facilities per million people yields a total expenditure of $3.8 billion as an estimate, assuming $100,000 gross income per facility. It is not clear what part of this is included in government figures for expenditures for alternative medicine. This estimate does not include YMCA aquatic exercise programs or so-called floating therapy pools.

Cost factors: About $3.8 billion, as noted above, is an annual estimate.

17. Iridology

I looked into his eyes and read his soul.
—President George W.
Bush on meeting Vladimir Putin

A definition of iridology as provided by Wikipedia[1] states:

> Iridology (also known as iridodiagnosis or iridiagnosis) is an alternative medicine technique whose proponents claim that patterns, colors, and other characteristics of the iris can be examined to determine information about a patient's systemic health. Practitioners match their observations to iris charts, which divide the iris into zones that correspond to specific parts of the human body. Iridologists see the eyes as "windows" into the body's state of health.
>
> Iridologists claim they can use the charts to distinguish between healthy systems and organs in the body and those that are overactive, inflamed, or distressed. Iridologists claim this information demonstrates a patient's susceptibility towards certain illnesses, reflects past medical problems, or predicts later health problems.

This same reference immediately cites evidence that all claims are not supported by science:

> As opposed to evidence-based medicine, iridology is not supported by quality research studies and is widely considered pseudoscience. The features of the iris are one of the most stable features on the human body throughout life. The stability of iris structures is the foundation of the biometric technology which uses iris recognition for identification purposes.

This is a critical fact that, were it not true, certainly iris patterns would be quite useless for personal ID biometric technology.[2, 3] The Wikipedia reference adds:

> In 1979, Bernard Jensen, a leading American iridologist, and two other iridology proponents failed to establish the basis of their practice when they examined photographs of the eyes of 143 patients in an attempt to determine which ones had kidney impairments. Of the patients, forty-eight had been diagnosed with kidney disease, and the rest had normal kidney function. Based on their analysis of the patients' irises, the three iridologists could not detect which patients had kidney disease and which did not.
>
> In Canada and the United States, iridology is not regulated or licensed by any governmental agency. Numerous organizations offer certification courses.

Yet the beat goes on, and iridology plunges deeper into not only pseudoscience but the plain fraud of quackery. Various examples can be reviewed on YouTube. One video shows the use of iris charts, which are "maps" of every organ in the body superimposed on the iris with different anatomic designations in each eye, and can be supposedly read by experts.[4] There are individual lessons on this video, the second of which purports to diagnose the need for detoxification of which we will examine and expose in a separate section. Another video concentrates on "reading the lymph system."[5] After reviewing a cross section of these so-called education videos, I could not find a single instance of before and after treatment views, and I would assume, after reading the disclaimer, that they do not exist.

The reader may use YouTube and also use Google to try to find the presence of iridology practitioners in their area. They are often part of a chiropractic office or detox facility. I found one that was associated with a massage program.

China remains a source of technical equipment such as cameras,[6] iriscopes, iris maps, and technical training and support through a company called Maikong Industries. Among their products is the iridology machine,[7] which the company claims to have:

1. The ability to see all body systems and organs at once
2. The ability (called Advanced Prognostics) to detect conditions that lead to disease

From the website, the cost appears to be upward of $5,000 USD, which brings to the bottom-line question, What does this alternative medicine fraud cost the consumer? What is the quackonomics of this? We might start with the International Iridology Practitioners Association (IIPA), a registered nonprofit organization founded in 1982.[8] From this site, it is not possible to gain information on the number of practitioners, only membership requirements and that there are members worldwide. Finding a practitioner is available at findiridologist.com.[9] From this site, an astounding list of "what iridology reveals" is listed:

IRIDOLOGY REVEALS
Many Signs
Inherently weak organs, glands and tissues.
Inherently strong organs, glands and tissues.

Constitutional strength or weakness.
What organ is in greatest need of repair and rebuilding.
Relative amounts of toxic settlements in organs, glands and tissues.
Stages of tissue inflammation and activity.
Where inflammation is located in the body.
Under activity or sluggishness of the bowel.
Spastic conditions or ballooned conditions of the bowel.
The need for acidophilus in the bowel.
Prolapsus (?) of the transverse colon.
Nervous condition or inflammation of the bowel.
High-risk tissue areas in the body that may be leading to a disease.
Pressure on the heart.
Circulation level in various organs
Nerve force and nerve depletion.
Hyperactivity or hypo activity of organs, glands or tissues.
Influence of one organ on another, contribution of one organ to a condition elsewhere in the body.
Lymphatic system congestion.
Poor assimilation of nutrients.
Depletion of minerals in any organ, gland or tissue.
Relative ability of an organ, gland or tissue to hold nutrients.
Results of physical or mental fatigue on the body.
Need for rest to build up immunity.
Tissue areas contributing to suppressed or buried symptoms.
High or low sex drive.
A genetic pattern of inherent weaknesses and their influence on other organs, glands and tissues.

Pre-clinical stages of potential diabetes, cardio-vascular conditions and other diseases.

Miasms.

Recuperative ability and the health level of the body.

Buildup of toxic material before the materialization of disease.

Genetic weaknesses affecting the nerves, blood supply and mineralization of bones.

Genetic influence on any symptoms present.

Healing signs indicating an increase in strength in an organ, gland or tissue.

Bone marrow problems.

Potential for varicose veins in legs as shown by inherent weakness.

Positive and negative nutritional needs of the body.

Probably allergy to wheat.

Sources of infection.

Acidity of the body or catarrh development, as indicated by acute signs in the iris.

Suppression of catarrh, as indicated by subacute or chronic signs in the iris.

Condition of the tissue in any part of the body or all parts of the body at one time.

Climate and altitude best for patient.

Potential contributions to sterility.

Effects of polluted environment.

Adrenal suppression, which may indicate low blood pressure, lack of energy, slowed tissue repair, deficiencies of vitamin C and adrenaline.

Resistance to disease, as shown by amount of toxic settlements in the body.

Relationship or unity of symptoms with conditions in organs, glands and tissues.

The difference between a healing crisis and a disease crisis.
The workings of Hering's Law of Cure.
Whether a particular program or therapy is working or not.
The quality of nerve force in the body.
Response to treatment; how well the body is healing itself and at what rate.
The "whole" overall health level of the body as a unified structure.

It is well to notice that there is extensive overlap of various alternative medicine practitioners as a Holistic and Alternative Medicine Directory features.[10] Here is a list from such a center in New Port Richey, Florida:

Therapies: Acupressure, Addiction Treatments, Akashic Records, Allergy Treatments, Angel Readings, Animal Health, Aromatherapy, Art Therapy, Astrological Counseling, Biofeedback, Channeling, Color Therapy, Craniosacral Therapy, Crystal Therapy, Distance Healing, EFT/TFT, Energy Clearing, Energy Healing, Flower Essences, Healing Touch, Herbology, Homeopathy, Iridology, Kinesiology, Laser Therapy, Light Therapy, Life Coaching, Magnetic Therapy, Matrix Energetics, Medical Intuitive, Meditation, Metaphysics, Microcurrent, Naturopathy, Neuro-Linguistic Programming, Neurofeedback, Nutrition, Polarity Therapy, Pranic Healing, Raindrop Therapy, Rapid Eye Technology, Reconnective Healing, Reiki, Remote Healing, Sclerology, Shamanic Healing, Sound Therapy, Spiritual Counseling, The Healing Codes, Therapeutic Touch, Theta Healing, Tibetan Medicine,

Wellness Centers, DNA Recalibration, Light Body Activation, Deeksha Oneness Blessings, Flowering Heart Blessings. PTSD Treatments and Healing for Veterans.

From an abstract cited on NIH PubMed in the Archives of Ophthalmology in 2000,[11] it is possible to extrapolate consumer spending in this area:

More than 1,000 licensed naturopathic physicians practice in the United States, and iridology is being described as "the most valuable diagnostic tool of the naturopath." Some therapists are using iridology as a basis for recommending dietary supplements and/or herbs.

Cost factors: Assuming 1,300 naturopathic physicians gross $2,000 per month from iridology × 12 months = $31.2 million annual expenditure in the United States, which is not including other alternative medicine centers with various mix of herbal and nutritional practices.

18. Reflexology

One estimate is that a third of the good done by modern medicine is attributable to placebo effect.
—David Wooton, Science Historian.

Reflexology[1] is an alternative medicine involving application of pressure to the feet and hands with specific thumb, finger, and hand techniques without the use of oil or lotion. It is based on a pseudoscientific system of zones and reflex areas that purportedly reflect an image of the body on the feet and hands, with the premise that such work effects a physical change to the body. *Complementary and Alternative Medicine*[2] defines reflexology as

Noninvasive acupressure of the hands and feet. Points on the feet and hands correspond to various zones and organs throughout the body. Precise pressure on these reflex points stimulates energy and releases blockages to the specific area of pain or illness.

The practice has much in common with iridology, in that like iridology, there is no scientific basis.[3, 4] Like iridology, it is self-governing with associations like the Reflexology Association of America[5] and the non-for-profit American Reflexology Certification Board[6] and, like iridology, is based upon charts showing anatomical connectivity that does not exist[7] and, like iridology, has adapted the terminology of legitimate mainstream medicine using terms like "board certification" and the Ontario "College" of Reflexology[8] in an attempt to appear scientific and legitimate in the eyes of the consumer. On a webpage[9] with sponsorship from the International Institute of Reflexology, the opening statement is that

Reflexology is a science which deals with the principle that there are reflex areas in the feet and hands which correspond to all of the glands, organs and parts of the body. Stimulating these reflexes properly can help many health problems in a natural way, a type of preventative maintenance. Reflexology is a serious advance in the health field and should not be confused with massage.

The concluding statement is a disclaimer:

The International Institute of Reflexology® wishes to make it perfectly clear that it does not purport to teach medical practice in any form. Reflexology is a unique modality in the health field. Its purpose is not to treat or diagnose for any specific medical disorder, but to promote better health and wellbeing in the same way as an exercise or diet program. Its practice should not be compared to massage or any other kind of manipulative procedure.

Excuse the pun, but legal requirements for the practice of reflexology by cities and states are all over the map.[10] Most states have no requirements such as Arizona and Michigan. Nebraska and New York are states that require a license in massage therapy. Tennessee is a state that requires registration as a reflexologist. According to the current Occupational Outlook Handbook of the US Bureau of Labor Statistics, the median national annual salary for massage therapists is $39,860.[11] Tuition for a reflexology education program costs approximately $1,500 to $3,500. Schools for reflexology vary from online programs to degree programs in massage therapy.[12]

Cost factors: If 10 reflexologists per 1 million people is a conservative estimate, then for our country of 323,000,000, there are 3,230 practitioners averaging $20,000 per year as a minimum to keep their businesses open, then a round estimate is that US consumers spend some $64.5 million out of pocket yearly on reflexology.

19. Tai Chi

It does not matter how slowly you
go as long as you do not stop.
—Confucius

Tai Chi, as practiced in the West, is best described as a moving form of yoga with a measure of meditation added. The history of Tai Chi is of interest[1]:

Many historians believe that Tai Chi originated with the ninth-century Taoist philosopher Li Daotzu (or Li Tao-Tzu), who defined the first 37 moves in a book called The Earlier Heaven

Movements. Two (or three or more) centuries later, according to legend, Zhang San Feng (or Cheung San-Feng), another priest in a Shaolin Temple in China, transformed the earlier philosophy into a system of self-defense, Tai Chi Chuan. It has been said that San Feng was inspired by a battle between a crane and a snake. The snake won the fight thanks to its slowness, its flexibility and its rounded movements that gave its opponent little control.

Interestingly, the "chi" of "tai chi" is not the same "chi" as the word meaning "life energy." The term "t'ai chi ch'uan"—later shortened to "tai chi"—translates as "supreme ultimate fist," "boundless fist," or "great extremes boxing."

Of the many martial arts practiced in China, there are two systems: the internal and the external.[2] Tai Chai belongs to the internal group emphasizing stability and limited major movements.

Initially, Tai Chi was practiced as a fighting form, emphasizing strength, balance, flexibility, and speed. Through time it has evolved into a soft, slow, and gentle form of exercise which can be practiced by people of all ages.

I was first introduced to Tai Chi on my first trip to China shortly after it opened to the West in October of 1980. I woke before dawn and, looking out of my hotel window, saw a formation of perhaps one hundred people, all in the Mao-style blue work uniforms, performing their morning ritual, led by a man holding a long sword. I dressed and quickly ran out to joint them and have been intrigued ever since.

Like yoga, Tai Chi literature claims value as an exercise, as a form of relaxation, and a form of mental fitness developing a balanced attitude which "carries over into the activities of daily life."[3]

These are quite commonsense benefits. What raises the red flag are medical claims that have not been substantiated. For example, from the same literature and website[4] are listed benefits:

> Assists in digestive function, helpful for arthritis and diabetes, promotes the elimination of toxins, and oxygenates cells and muscles.

Like nearly all the complementary literature, references can be easily accessed from the NIH (National Institutes of Health) National Center for Complementary and Integrative Health.[5] Review of this literature does not support the claim of effectiveness for type II diabetes or elimination of toxins. With respect to rheumatoid arthritis, reviews from the Cochrane Library[6] concluded:

> Four trials including 206 participants, were included in this review. Tai Chi-based exercise programs had no clinically important or statistically significant effect on most outcomes of disease activity, which included activities of daily living, tender and swollen joints and patient global overall rating.

What the review of the Tai Chi literature does show is that there are conditions in which studies conclude that there "might be benefit" and that "more vigorous randomized controlled trials" need to be done. Those conditions include fibromyalgia, Parkinson's disease, essential hypertension, fall prevention, and psychological health. "Cannot completely discount the possible influence of the placebo effect" is the common reason given that studies cannot be more certain. Conditions reported that show no benefit from Tai Chi are male infertility and chronic low back pain in seniors. A 2015 study from the Annals of Community Medicine and Practice[7] concluded that the "study may not provide sufficient evidence to launch a public health campaign to promote Tai Chi."

Cost factors: Statistics show that 3.71 million Americans participated in Tai Chi in 2016[8] (the same year 25.7 million practiced yoga and 59.1 were on treadmills). The best estimate on aggregate cost per year is $9.3 million. How much, if any, is covered by any health insurance is not readily available.

20. Hydrotherapy of the Colon—Detoxification

Everyone in New York and L.A., from celebrities to editors, is getting colonics—they're just not talking about it.

—*A detox website*

Colonic irrigation, high colonic, colonic detoxification therapy, coffee enemas, enema irrigation, hydrocolon therapy, high enema are the common other terms of hydrotherapy of the colon noted by the American Cancer Society.[1] This term should not be confused with routine colon preparation prior to colonoscopy or x-ray studies of the colon. The same citation notes:

> Available scientific evidence does not support claims that colon therapy is effective in treating cancer or any other disease. Rare cases of infection and death have been reported.
>
> As far back as the ancient Egyptians, enemas and other "cleansing rituals" were commonly used to rid the body of waste products believed to cause disease and death. In the 19th century, proponents described the large intestine as a sewage system and claimed stagnation caused toxins to form and be absorbed by the body, which led to the theory of "autointoxication." Laxatives, purges, and enemas were routinely recommended to prevent the accumulation of waste.
>
> Proponents of colon therapy consider it to be a method of detoxifying the body through the

removal of accumulated waste from the colon. Because they claim detoxification increases the efficiency of the body's natural healing abilities, it is sometimes promoted as a treatment for illness. It is often promoted as a general preventive health measure or as part of a routine internal hygiene regimen.

"Detoxes" and "cleanses" have become big business. According to the NIH Complementary and Integrative Health website[2]:

> A variety of "detoxification" ("detox") diets and regimens—also called "cleanses" or "flushes"—have been suggested as a means of removing toxins from your body or losing weight. Detoxification may be promoted in many settings and may also be used in naturopathic treatment.
>
> Detox programs may involve a variety of approaches, such as: fasting, consuming only juices or other liquids for several days, eating a very restricted selection of foods, using various dietary supplements or other commercial products, cleansing the colon (lower intestinal tract) with enemas, laxatives, or colon hydrotherapy (also called "colonic irrigation" or "colonics"), and combining some of these or other approaches.
> Bottom Line:
> There isn't any convincing evidence that detox or cleansing programs remove toxins from your body or improve your health. Weight loss on a detox diet may be because these diets are often very low in calories.

This same website, as a reference, should be read *very carefully* as it adds some important safety warnings.

The U.S. Food and Drug Administration (FDA) and Federal Trade Commission have taken action against several companies selling detox/cleansing products because they contained illegal, potentially harmful ingredients; were marketed using false claims that they could treat serious diseases; or (in the case of medical devices used for colon cleansing) were marketed for unapproved uses.

Juices that haven't been pasteurized or treated in other ways to kill harmful bacteria can make people sick. The illnesses can be serious in children, elderly people, and those with weakened immune systems.

Drinking large quantities of juice may be risky for people with kidney disease because some juices are high in oxalate, which can worsen kidney problems.

People with diabetes should follow the eating plan recommended by their health care team. If you have diabetes, consult your health care provider before making major changes in your eating habits, such as going on a detox diet.

Diets that severely restrict calories or the types of food you eat usually don't lead to lasting weight loss and may not provide all the nutrients you need.

Colon cleansing procedures may have side effects, some of which can be serious. Harmful effects are more likely in people with a history of gastrointestinal disease, colon surgery, kidney disease, or heart disease.

Detoxification programs often include laxatives, which can cause diarrhea severe enough to lead to dehydration and electrolyte imbalances

Fasting can cause headaches, fainting, weakness, and dehydration.

The term "detoxification" itself is questionable. The alternative medicine literature does not specify what a toxin actually is. They are often described as "unspecified"[3] as noted by Wikipedia:

Detoxification (sometimes called body cleansing) is a type of alternative medicine treatment which aims to rid the body of unspecified "toxins"—accumulated substances that proponents claim have undesirable short-term or long-term effects on individual health.

The concept has received criticism from scientists and health organizations for its unsound scientific basis and lack of evidence for the claims they make[4] the "toxins" usually remain undefined, with little to no evidence of toxic accumulation in the patient. The British organization Sense About Science has described some detox diets and commercial products as "a waste of time and money,"[5] while the British Dietetic Association called the idea "nonsense" and a "marketing myth."[6]

Huffington Post in 2014 published an article entitled "5 Reasons to Think Twice about Colon Cleansing,"[7] one of which was a warning about the effect on gut bacteria or the microbiome. The microbiome is a complex array of bacteria that reside normally in our intestinal tract.[8]

Absence of intestinal bacteria is associated with reductions in mucosal cell turnover, vascularity, muscle wall thickness, motility, baseline cytokine production, and digestive enzyme activity and with defective cell-mediated immunity.

Furthermore, the intestinal microflora makes important metabolic contributions to vitamin K, folate, and short-chain fatty acids, such as butyrate, a major energy source for enterocytes, and also mediates the breakdown of dietary carcinogens. The bacterial flora of the gastrointestinal tract varies longitudinally; the oral cavity contains about 200 different species, the stomach is almost sterile, and the bacterial content increases distally, with approximately 108 bacteria per g (dry weight) of ileal contents and up to 1012 bacteria per g (dry weight) of colonic contents. The conclusions of studies on the bacterial flora carried out some decades ago are still thought to be true. The large intestine contains organisms belonging to over 30 identified genera and as many as 500 separate species or phenotypes. The main types of bacteria in the colon are obligate anaerobes, and the most abundant bacteria are members of the genus Bacteroides, anaerobic gram-positive cocci, such as Peptostreptococcus sp., Eubacterium sp., Lactobacillus sp., and Clostridium sp. More recent studies of large bowel biopsies confirmed that Bacteroides was a dominant genus in the specimens examined.

The bacteria likewise play a protective role.[9]

The microflora of the intestinal microenvironment as a unit has important protective, metabolic, and trophic functions. Resident bacteria serve a central line of resistance to colonization by exogenous microbes and thus assist in preventing the potential invasion of the intestinal mucosa by an incoming pathogen. This protective function is known as the barrier effect or colonization resistance, and the bacteria have a number of important roles.

The Mayo Clinic Consumer website[10] notes complications from colonic detox practice.

> In fact, coffee enemas sometimes used in colon cleansing have been linked to several deaths. Colon cleansing can also cause less serious side effects, such as cramping, bloating, nausea and vomiting.

It is worth noting that the NIH National Center for Complementary and Integrative Health webpage[11] fails to cite *any* complications for colonic cleansing.

Further, colonic detox is not to be confused with "detox" originally meant to define medical regimens used in hospitals and clinics to rid the body of alcohol, drugs, and poisons—generally referred to as medical detox.[12] This same Harvard Health reference[13] warns against intestinal cleansing kits:

> Numerous kits are marketed for this purpose, most of which include a high-fiber supplement, a "support" supplement containing herbs or enzymes, and a laxative tea, each to be used daily. Manufacturers of the herbal detox kits recommend continuing the regimen for several weeks. Such regimens may be accompanied by frequent enemas. The aim is to eradicate parasites and expel fecal matter that allegedly accumulates and adheres to the intestinal walls. Several studies suggest that milk thistle, which is often included as a supportive supplement, may improve liver function with few side effects. But there's no medical evidence for the cleansing procedure. Promotional materials often include

photographs of snake-like gelatinous substances expelled during cleansing. When these pictures are not faked, they are probably showing stool generated by large doses of the regimen's fiber supplement. More important, the rationale for intestinal cleansing—to dislodge material adhering to the colon walls—is fundamentally mistaken. When fecal matter accumulates, it compacts into firm masses in the open interior of the colon; it does not adhere to the intestinal walls as the "sludge" depicted in the advertisements. Like fasting, colonic cleansing carries a risk of dehydration, electrolyte imbalance, impaired bowel function, and disruption of intestinal flora.

It is the disruption of the intestinal flora that may be the most damaging complication and, as of this date, has not been extensively studied scientifically. The diversity of human intestinal microbial flora[14] is reason enough not to disrupt it with colonic hydrotherapy. This article from *Nature* refers to the "immensely diverse ecosystem."

The human endogenous intestinal microflora is an essential "organ" in providing nourishment, regulating epithelial development, and instructing innate immunity; yet, surprisingly, basic features remain poorly described. We examined 13,355 prokaryotic ribosomal RNA gene sequences from multiple colonic mucosal sites and feces of healthy subjects to improve our understanding of gut microbial diversity. A majority of the bacterial sequences corresponded to uncultivated species and novel microorganisms. We discovered significant intersubject variability and differences between stool and mucosa community composition. Characterization of

this immensely diverse ecosystem is the first step
in elucidating its role in health and disease.

We know that a single bowel prep prior to routine colonoscopy
results in changes in intestinal microbiota of variable extent, some
long-lasting[15] and.[16] With this information, the argument for avoiding habitual colonic detox therapy is well-founded. An August 2011
article in the *Journal of Family Practice*[17] from Georgetown School
of Medicine provides an excellent review of the dangers of colon
cleansing.

> Even though colon cleansing is touted as a
> commonly used form of holistic, complementary
> and alternative medicine, the Natural Standard
> Professional Database concluded in a monograph
> that there is "limited clinical evidence validating
> colon therapy as a health promotion practice"
> and noted a "lack of sufficient evidence" for most
> of its prescribed uses.

Cost factors: How much are Americans spending on colonics? According to the Colon Therapists Network, prices for colon
irrigation range between $55 to $95 per treatment.[18] We know that
Americans spend $400 million per year on laxatives.[19] A 30-day
Detox & Weight loss package from one site lists at $1,250.[20] From
population extrapolations on cities with more than population of
500,000,$50 million is a very conservative estimate at wellness cen-
ters and spas, and another $20 million for equipment and products.

21. Weight Loss Fraud

Extraordinary claims require
extraordinary evidence.
—*Carl Sagan*

According to 2013 data by Marketdata Enterprises, a market research firm that specializes in tracking niche industries, Americans spend north of $60 billion annually to try to lose pounds, on everything from paying for gym memberships and joining weight-loss programs to drinking diet soda.[1] Marketdata estimates that the total US weight-loss market grew 2.2 percent in 2016, from $64.9 billion to $66.3 billion.[2] Here are some further numbers from Marketdata Enterprises:

> Commercial chains are posting a strong turnaround, boosted by an 18% sales gain at Nutrisystem and moderate growth at Weight Watchers in 2016, plus a strong Q1 2017. This segment of the market was worth $2.77 billion in 2016 and is forecast to grow 9.4% to $3.03 billion this year.
>
> Meal replacements (shakes, nutrition bars) are posting strong growth and are still popular with dieters. Sales of these products will outpace the growth of OTC diet pills to 2022 (7.2% per year vs. 4.8%). This market segment is worth a combined $4.16 billion in 2016. Multi-level marketing companies such as Herbalife, Shaklee, Isagenix and more provide a significant distribution channel for these products, since they are safe, portable and inexpensive.
>
> Prescription obesity drugs is a $615 million market that has been flat for years. Sales of the newest medications (Contrave, Belviq, Qsymia) have not gained traction due to cost, insurance coverage and very moderate weight loss. Drug company R&D has yet to produce an anti-obesity drug with blockbuster potential, constrained by slow FDA approval and side effects.
>
> Weight loss surgeries—An estimated 201,000 were performed in the U.S. in 2016,

up just 2.6%. Reimbursement for this typical $25,000 surgery remains a problem.

Medical weight loss clinics and franchises have grown in number as MDs seek to replace income lost to managed care. However, hospitals are still taking a wait and see attitude, trying to make sense of an uncertain healthcare environment and how to make a profit.

Low-calorie (diet) frozen entrée sales have been declining for years, as consumers avoid highly processed foods with artificial ingredients. However, producers such as Stouffer's (Lean Cuisine) have turned declines into growth via new items, more natural ingredients and attractive packaging.

Diet and fitness apps—Contrary to popular belief, free diet apps such as MyFitnessPal were NOT the main reason for recent diet company woes. Usage is waning, and research shows that they don't produce lasting weight loss. Rather, the problem has been a lack of compelling programs and management/structural problems at some companies.

Diet Websites… Online dieting is worth at least $990 million, by our estimates, and WeightWatchers.com is the leader with 2016 revenue of $349 million.

Evidence indicates that we clearly have an obesity epidemic in the United States and that it is growing on an annual basis. Key findings from data from the National Health and Nutrition Examination Survey,[3] a part of CDC, were:

- In 2011–2014, the prevalence of obesity was just over 36% in adults and 17% in youth.

- The prevalence of obesity was higher in women (38.3%) than in men (34.3%). Among all youth, no difference was seen by sex.
- The prevalence of obesity was higher among middle-aged (40.2%) and older (37.0%) adults than younger (32.3%).

Figures released by CNN in October of 2017[4] indicate that nearly 40 percent of adults and 19 percent of youth are obese, the highest rate the country has ever seen in all adults, according to research released by the National Center for Health Statistics.

What is *very striking* about this information is that there has been a 30% increase in adult obesity and 33% increase in youth obesity from 1999–2000 data to 2015–16, despite government-focused efforts to address the issue, according to Michael W. Long, assistant professor at the Milken Institute School of Public Health at George Washington University.[5]

Another perspective is to look at the cost of obesity to US business. A 1996 study[6] published in *The American Journal of Health Promotion* estimated the cost of obesity to US business at that time was $12.7 billion or 5 percent of total medical care costs. The nationwide real economic costs affect all of us, as reported by the National League of Cities.[7]

The estimated annual health care costs of obesity-related illness are a staggering $190.2 billion or nearly 21% of annual medical spending in the United States. Childhood obesity alone is responsible for $14 billion in direct medical costs. Obesity-related medical costs in general are expected to rise significantly, especially because today's obese children are likely to become tomorrow's obese adults. If obesity rates were to remain at 2010 levels, the projected savings for medical expenditures would be $549.5 billion over the next two decades.

The direct and additional hidden costs of obesity are stifling businesses and organizations that stimulate jobs and growth in U.S. cities. In the 10 cities with the highest obesity rates, the direct costs connected with obesity and obesity-related diseases are roughly $50 million per 100,000 residents. If these 10 cities cut their obesity rates down to the national average, the combined savings to their communities would be $500 million in health care costs each year.

A chart (2003–2013) from the Bureau of Labor Statistics shows that the annual increase in obesity follows the same slope as the increase in mean age in the United States.[8] So the bottom line is a depressing conclusion: We are obese, and it is costing us a lot of money, it is stifling business, and it is *getting worse at an alarming rate*. Even more depressing is the second conclusion: All the efforts at solving the problem of obesity at a national level have been obvious failures.

So where is the blame to be placed? Let's start with some fundamentals. What is obesity?

Obesity has been more precisely defined by the National Institutes of Health (the NIH) as a BMI (Body Mass Index) of 30 and above. (A BMI of 30 is about 30 pounds overweight.) The BMI, a key index for relating body weight to height, is a person's weight in kilograms (kg) divided by their height in meters (m) squared. Since the BMI describes the body weight relative to height, it correlates strongly (in adults) with the total body fat content. Some very muscular people may have a high BMI without undue health risks.[9]

An abstract from *Lancet*[10] sums it up:

> Excess bodyweight is the sixth most important risk factor contributing to the overall burden of disease worldwide. 1.1 billion adults and 10% of children are now classified as overweight or obese. Average life expectancy is already diminished; the main adverse consequences are cardiovascular disease, type 2 diabetes, and several cancers. The complex pathological processes reflect environmental and genetic interactions, and individuals from disadvantaged communities seem to have greater risks than more affluent individuals partly because of fetal and postnatal imprinting. Obesity, with its array of comorbidities, necessitates careful clinical assessment to identify underlying factors and to allow coherent management. The epidemic reflects progressive secular and age-related decreases in physical activity, together with substantial dietary changes with passive over-consumption of energy despite the neurobiological processes controlling food intake. Effective long-term weight loss depends on permanent changes in dietary quality, energy intake, and activity. Neither the medical management nor the societal preventive challenges are currently being met.

Setting aside genetic susceptibility and endocrine disorders, the fundamental equation is controlling the balance between calories in and calories out. If an individual takes in more calories than they burn, then weight gain occurs. The opposite case results in weight loss. Weight fraud involves the deception that this equation is not true or that it can be easily manipulated. The deceptions and disregard of science are (1) medications or nutritional supplements, (2) fad diets, (3) diets that are part of detox plans, (4) diets based upon starvation—extreme restriction of food, and finally, (5) self-deception that science is not a source of information or that obesity cannot be prevented or controlled, and (6) obesogens—early-life (in utero) exposure to traces of chemicals in the environment.

1.) Starting with medications, there are drugs that cause weight gain.[11] These include:

Drugs for diabetes, such as insulin, thiazolidinediones, and sulfonylureas.
Antipsychotic drugs such as haloperidol, clozapine, and lithium.
Antidepressant drugs like amitriptyline, paroxetine, and sertraline.
Drugs for epilepsy like valproate and carbamazepine.

There are drugs that cause weight loss[12]:

Anorexic medications
Appetite suppressing medications can be divided into several categories such as anti-infective drugs, antineoplastics, bronchodilators, cardiovascular drugs, stimulants and other medicines.

Anti-infective drugs:
Antibacterial—Metronidazole
Antifungals—Amphotericin B
Antimalarials—Atovaquone, Pyrimethamine
Antiretrovirals—Didanosine, Zalcitabine
Anti-TB—Ethionamide

Antineoplastic or anticancer drugs, also used to treat HIV and conditions such as psoriasis:
Aldesleukin and interleukin-2, Capecitabine, Carboplatin, Cytarabine, Dacarbazine, Fluorouracil, Hydroxyurea, Imatinib, Irinotecan, Methotrexate, Vinblastine sulphate, Vinorelbine tartrate.

Bronchodilators used to treat asthma, broncho-spasm, bronchitis, emphysema:
Salbutamol sulphate
Theophylline

Cardiovascular drugs:
Amiodarone, Acetazolamide, Hydralazine HCl, Quinidine

Stimulants:
Methylphenidate HCl—used to treat Attention Deficit Hyperactivity Disorder (ADHD) or narcolepsy
Phentermine—used in the appetite suppressant Duromine for slimming

Other medications:
Fluoxetine—antidepressant
Galantamine and Rivastigmine—used to treat dementia in conditions such as Alzheimer's disease
Sibutramine—used in slimming pills such as Ciplatrim
Sulphasalazine—used to treat ulcerative colitis and Crohn's disease
Topiramate—anti-epileptic medication

Precautions:

While some of the above listed medications such as sibutramine and phentermine are specifically used to suppress the appetite to induce weight loss in overweight patients, the weight loss caused by the other drugs is usually regarded as a negative side-effect.

As can be observed from this list of medications that can affect the "calories in / calories out" equation, no one should embark upon a drug-induced weight-loss program without consulting their physician or dedicated nutritionist. The same warning goes for people who have used dietary supplements such as hydroxycut. Hydroxycut is a popular weight-loss supplement which has been linked to hepatotoxicity reported in 2008 in the *World Journal of Gastroenterology*.[13] Within the discussion of this paper was a reference to the fact that hydroxycut contains chromium and that there have been case reports of chromium toxicity causing acute hepatitis, thrombocytopenia, and renal failure due to both environmental and dietary supplements. Each hydroxycut serving contains 133 mg of chromium, which, if taken three times daily, resuls in a cumulative daily consumption greater than twice the NAS (National Academy of Sciences) safe maximum dose. I again emphasize the fact that the FDA does not verify contents of nutritional supplements.

2.) Fad diets are fraudulent because they concentrate on the consumption of one type of food and although they may produce good initial results are most often not sustained.[14] The Academy of Nutrition and Dietetics has some sound advice[15]:

With all the focus on weight in our society, it isn't surprising that millions of people fall prey to fad diets and bogus weight-loss products. Conflicting claims, testimonials and hype by so-called "experts" can confuse even the most informed consumers. The bottom line is simple: If a diet or product sounds too good to be true, it probably is.

There are no foods or pills that magically burn fat. No super foods will alter your genetic code. No products will miraculously melt fat while you watch TV or sleep. Some ingredients in supplements and herbal products can be dangerous and even deadly for some people.

Steer clear of any diet plans, pills and products that make the following claims:

1. Rapid Weight Loss

Slow, steady weight loss is more likely to last than dramatic weight changes. Healthy plans aim for a loss of no more than 1 to 2 pounds per week. If you lose weight quickly, you'll lose muscle, bone and water. You also will be more likely to regain the pounds quickly.

2. Quantities and Limitations

Ditch diets that allow unlimited quantities of any food, such as grapefruit and cabbage soup. It's boring to eat the same thing over and over and hard to stick with monotonous plans. Avoid any diet that eliminates or severely restricts entire food groups, such as carbohydrates. Even if you take a multivitamin, you'll still miss some critical nutrients.

3. Specific Food Combinations

There is no evidence that combining certain foods or eating foods at specific times of day will help with weight loss. Eating the "wrong" combinations of food doesn't cause them to turn to fat immediately or to produce toxins in your intestines, as some plans claim.

4. Rigid Menus
5. Life is already complicated enough. Limiting food choices or following rigid meal plans can be an overwhelming, distasteful task. With any new diet, always ask yourself: "Can I eat this way for the rest of my life?" If the answer is no, the plan is not for you.
6. No Need to Exercise

Regular physical activity is essential for good health and healthy weight management. The key to success is to find physical activities that you enjoy and then aim for 30 to 60 minutes of activity on most days of the week.

Another instructive website is titled "14 Fad Diets You Shouldn't Try."[16]

The raw food diets

Any weight-loss expert would agree that boosting your veggie and fruit intake while reducing the amount of junk you eat is a safe and effective way to lose weight, but this diet bans foods that have been cooked or processed in any way. Why? Raw foodies say cooking destroys nutrients. Though it's true that cooking produce can sometimes reduce nutrient levels, cooked veggies still pack plenty of fiber, vitamins, and minerals, and in some instances cooking actually enhances nutrients while also killing bacteria. The biggest issue with this extreme form of veganism? Food prep—it's totally impractical, says Christopher N. Ochner, PhD, director of research development and administration at the Mount Sinai

Adolescent Health Center. Raw foodies spend hours upon hours juicing, blending, dehydrating, sprouting, germinating, cutting, chopping, and rehydrating.

Alkaline diets

The alkaline diet—also known as the alkaline ash diet and the alkaline acid diet—requires you cut out meat, dairy, sweets, caffeine, alcohol, artificial and processed foods, and consume more fresh fruits and veggies, nuts, and seeds. The diet certainly has positive points; it's heavy on fresh produce and other healthy, satisfying foods while eliminating processed fare, which in itself may spur weight loss. But your body is incredibly efficient at keeping your pH levels where they need to be, so cutting out these foods really won't affect your body's pH, says Ochner. Not to mention there's no research proving that pH affects your weight in the first place. The bottom line: the diet is strict, complicated, and bans foods that can have a place in a healthy eating plan, such as meat, dairy, and alcohol.

The Blood-Type Diet

Developed by naturopathic physician Peter D'Adamo, the Blood Type Diet is based on the notion that the foods you eat react chemically with your blood type. For example, on the diet, those with type O blood are to eat lean meats, vegetables, and fruits, and avoid wheat and dairy. Meanwhile, type A dieters go vegetarian, and those with type B blood are supposed to avoid chicken, corn, wheat, tomatoes, peanuts, and sesame seeds. However, there's no scientific proof that your blood type affects weight loss. And depending on your blood type, the diet can be extremely restrictive.

The werewolf diet

Also called the lunar diet, this one is simply fasting according to the lunar calendar. Its quick-fix version involves a day of fasting allowing only water and juice during a full or new moon—and supposedly losing up to six pounds in water weight in a single day. The extended version starts with that daylong fast and continues with specific eating plans for each phase of the moon. While you'll lose some weight from not eating, it has nothing to do with the moon, and it will come right back, Ochner says.

Cookie diets

Dr. Siegal's Cookie Diet, The Hollywood Cookie Diet, and the Smart for Life Cookie Diet all promise that eating cookies will help you drop pounds. Of course, you don't get to chow down chocolate-chip cookies—you eat about 500 to 600 calories a day from high-protein and high-fiber weight-loss cookies (one cookie company even makes the cookies from egg and milk protein) for breakfast, lunch, and any snacks. Then you eat a normal dinner, for a total of 1,000 to 1,200 calories a day. If you stick to the diet, you will likely lose some weight, but by depriving yourself all day, you set yourself up for bingeing come dinnertime, Ochner says.

The Five-Bite Diet

Eat whatever you want—but only five bites of it. On this diet, developed by obesity doctor Alwin Lewis, MD, you skip breakfast and eat only five bites of food for lunch and five more for dinner. "I'm OK with the idea of eating whatever you want in smaller portions, but you need to round out the rest of your eating with nutrient-dense foods to give your body the fuel it needs," Alexandra Caspero, RD, a nutritionist based in Sacramento, Calif says. "On this diet, even if you take giant bites of heavily caloric food, you're still barely consuming 900 to 1,000 calories a day."

The Master Cleanse / lemonade diet

This diet has been around for decades, and there are a ton of variations. Pretty much all involve subsisting for days on only lemon juice, maple syrup, and cayenne pepper mixed in water. "You are essentially just drinking diuretics," Ochner says. "You'll shed mostly water weight." Once you start eating solid foods again, you will gain all the weight back. Common side effects include fatigue, nausea, dizziness, and dehydration. Plus, on an extremely low-calorie diet like this one, you are going to lose muscle, exactly the kind of weight you don't want to lose, Caspero says.

The baby food diet

If a baby can grow up eating the mushy stuff, eating some definitely won't hurt you, but guess what: You aren't a baby. Dieters replace breakfast and lunch with about 14 jars of baby food (most baby food jars contain 20 and 100 calories apiece), and then they eat a low-calorie dinner. It's easy to get too few calories for your body to run its best, Ochner says. Besides, who really wants to take jars of baby food to work each day?

The cabbage soup diet

The grandmother of all fad diets, the bulk of this plan is fat-free cabbage soup, eaten two to three times a day for a week along with other low-calorie foods such as bananas and skim milk. In the short term, it does yield weight loss. "It works because you are eating a low-calorie diet full of fiber and water to help aid in fullness," Caspero says. "But it's just a quick fix diet. It can also promote bloating and gas from all the cabbage, and is lacking in protein, which is needed to preserve lean body mass. While I am a fan of nutrient-dense, low calorie foods for weight loss, it should be balanced with other foods such as fruits, carbohydrates, healthy fats, and lean protein."

The grapefruit diet

We are all for including produce at every meal, but the various versions of this 80-year-old fad diet instruct dieters to focus all their meals on grapefruit or grapefruit juice, claiming that the fruit contains fat-busting enzymes that will help dieters lose 10-plus pounds in 12 days. "Any time you are following a very-low calorie diet you will lose weight," Caspero says. And this diet definitely hits that, limiting dieters to 800 to 1,000 calories a day. Some iterations also prohibit eating extremely hot or extremely cold foods, preparing foods in aluminum pans, and requires dieters to space "protein meals" and "starch meals" at least four hours apart.

The Sleeping Beauty diet

If you're asleep, you're not eating. Rumored to have been followed by Elvis Presley, this diet takes that simple fact to the extreme, encouraging people to use sedatives to stay asleep for days on end. But sleeping the days away not only starves the body and causes muscle deterioration from a lack of movement, but actually risks death: "Every time you go under, there's a risk," Ochner says. "Sure, you might wake up 2 pounds lighter, but you might not wake up at all."

The HCG diet

This edge-of-starvation diet limits you to about 500 calories a day while taking human chorionic gonadotropin (HCG), a hormone that proponents tout as a powerful appetite suppressant. However, there's no evidence that HCG does more than act as a placebo, Ochner says. Yes, you'll lose weight, but only due to the extreme calorie restriction. Though a health care provider may legally give you HCG injections, they're typically used to treat fertility issues in women and the FDA has not approved them for weight loss. As for over-the-counter homeopathic products that supposedly contain HCG? Those are illegal.

The tapeworm diet

"You don't need a doctor to tell you that ingesting a tapeworm is a bad idea," Ochner says. But apparently, some people do. This weight-loss tactic has been around for decades, preying on especially desperate dieters. Here's how it goes: Ingest tapeworm eggs, let the tapeworm eat the food you consume once it gets to your intestines, and then, when you lose enough weight, get a doctor to prescribe you an anti-worm medication. But some tapeworm eggs can migrate to various parts of your body or cause other potentially life-threatening problems. Freaked out yet? Good.

The cotton ball diet

Consuming cotton balls soaked in orange juice—a diet technique may have been born on YouTube, in chat rooms, and on Facebook—is an incredibly dangerous way to suppress your appetite. "This makes my eating-disorder therapy head spin," Caspero says. Not only does consuming cotton balls in place of food deprive the body of nutrients, eating anything that isn't actually food can cause blockages in your intestines. What's more, most cotton balls aren't even made of cotton—they're composed of bleached, synthetic fibers.

I had to include all of them, as several I could not believe myself.

3.) Diets that are part of a detox or cleansing plan are highly questionable. One example is Isagenix reviewed on the website, "Science-based Medicine[17]:

Isagenix is a wellness system sold by multilevel marketing. It consists of a suite of products to be used in various combinations for "nutritional cleansing," detoxification, and supplementation to aid in weight loss, improve energy and performance, and support healthy aging. It allegedly burns fat while supporting lean muscle, maintains healthy cholesterol levels, supports telomeres, improves resistance to illness, reduces cravings, improves body composition, and slows the aging process. And makes millions for distributors who got on the bandwagon early and are high on the pyramid.

I would recommend to anyone interested in starting this diet to read the content of this science-based medicine website in detail because the conclusion is as follows:

> The results are uninterpretable. This study does nothing to suggest that the Isagenix system has any advantage over other calorie-restricted diets. Neither does it tell us anything about the possible benefits of intermittent fasting. And the study is not "an important first step to understanding the underlying mechanisms that mediate the cardio-protective effects of this novel diet" since it has not been established that there are any cardio-protective effects to understand.

4.) Diets based upon starvation—extreme restriction of food have been studied to explore the limits of the human body. One of the most famous was the Minnesota Starvation Experiment,[18] conducted toward the end of WWII.

Thirty-six male conscientious objectors toward the end of WWII volunteered to participate in a thirteen-month starvation study conducted by the University of Minnesota under researcher Ancel Keys. The effects of food restriction on behavior were noted in the semistarvation state. For six months, the subjects were restricted to 1,600 calories per day, but not to the edge of death. They were observed to exhibit behavior to the "threshold of insanity," specifically depression, hysteria, hypochondriasis, and social withdrawal.

A twenty-week rehab period followed the experiment. The surprise finding was that as physical recovery progressed, the men showed a mental decline that took three months to stabilize. Some men said their eating was still not normal. Keys concluded that semistarvation closely resembled eating disorder, anorexia nervosa and bulimia, with recovery-needing nourishment and psychological treatment.

There is other science relating to severe caloric restriction. In the 1950s, the work of Rockefeller University's Jules Hirsch[19] showed that for obese people,

> Long-term weight loss is a lifelong struggle. Hirsch found that although obese subjects could shed a substantial amount of weight through drastic calorie restriction, their metabolic rates would dip in response to calorie restrictions. This effect meant, for example, that if an obese woman dropped down from 200 lb. to 130 lb., she would have to consume fewer calories to remain at 130lb. than would a 130-lb. counterpart whose weight had always held steady. The previously obese woman, then, required more "willpower" to maintain her reduced weight than someone who had never been obese. In 1995, Hirsch and his former Rockefeller colleagues Rudolph Leibel and Michael Rosenbaum observed that just as the metabolism of subjects who had lost 10% of their body weight decelerated, the metabolism of those who had gained 10% of their body weight revved up. These findings suggested that the body has built-in mechanisms that resist attempts to resize it for the long term.

I might further add that this work seems to be a strong argument against gaining excessive weight in the first place. This leads to the question of, "What might be ideal weight?" Perhaps the best reference here is the health results from the biosphere 2 in which eight people were sealed in the facility in the Arizona desert for two years. The conclusion from one report[20]:

Human beings can eat less. Out of necessity, gerontologist Roy Walford conducted the first reliable long-term experiment on caloric restriction in people. They got all the nutrition they needed but less chow, and each emerged with dramatic improvements in blood pressure, cholesterol level, and other health indicators.

The seminal scientific paper from this experiment can be summed up in the abstract published in 2002[21]:

Abstract

Four female and four male crew members, including two of the present authors (R. Walford and T. MacCallum)—seven of the crew being ages 27 to 42 years, and one aged 67 years—were sealed inside Biosphere 2 for two years. During seven eighths of that period they consumed a low-calorie (1750–2100 kcal/d) nutrient-dense diet of vegetables, fruits, nuts, grains, and legumes, with small amounts of dairy, eggs, and meat (approximately 12% calories from protein, approximately 11% from fat, and approximately 77% from complex carbohydrates). They experienced a marked and sustained weight loss of 17 +/- 5%, mostly in the first 8 months. Blood was drawn before entry into Biosphere 2, at many time-points inside it, and four times during the 30 months following exit from it and return to an ad libitum diet (eat what you want). Longitudinal studies of 50 variables on each crew member compared outside and inside values by means of a Bayesian statistical analysis. The data show that physiologic (e.g., body mass index, with a decrease of 19% for men and 13% for women; blood pressure, with a systolic decrease of 25%

and a diastolic decrease of 22%), hematologic (e.g., white blood cell count, decreased 31%), hormonal (e.g., insulin, decreased 42%; T3, decreased 19%), biochemical (e.g., blood sugar, decreased 21%; cholesterol, decreased 30%), and a number of additional changes, including values for rT3, cortisol, glycated hemoglobin, plus others, resembled those of rodents or monkeys maintained on a calorie-restricted regime. Significant variations in several substances not hitherto studied in calorie-restricted animals are also reported (e.g., androstenedione, thyroid binding globulin, renin, and transferrin). We conclude that healthy nonobese humans on a low-calorie, nutrient-dense diet show physiologic, hematologic, hormonal, and biochemical changes resembling those of rodents and monkeys on such diets. Regarding the health of humans on such a diet, we observed that despite the selective restriction in calories and marked weight loss, all crew members remained in excellent health and sustained a high level of physical and mental activity throughout the entire 2 years.

Ideal body weight may be considered that weight which is within normal range as determined by the World Health Organization and can be calculated with the aid of an ideal weight calculator available on the web at Calculator.net.[22] The recommended healthy BMI range of the World Health Organization (WHO) is 18.5–25 for both male and female. The ideal dietary intake, therefore, is simply that range or caloric intake that maintains you within the BMI range. Most people who are measured at "overweight" can probably reach their ideal BMI by moderate diet restrictions. Those measuring "obese" on the charts are best advised to seek professional help for a long-term program to meet their goals.

5.) Self-deception, believing that science is not a source of information or that obesity cannot be prevented or controlled. This might be termed cognitive deception, a subject evolutionary biologist Robert Trivers has spent thirty years trying to figure out.[23] In his book *The Folly of Fools: The Logic of Deceit and Self-Deception in Human Life*, he explores the causes of why we deny ourselves the truth. He points out that we do it both as individuals and as institutions.

Witness NASA's leaders persuaded themselves to ignore warnings issued by the scientists deep within the bowels of the place—self-deception with fatal consequences. Even decisions to go to war, which can cost tens of thousands of lives, are often made in a cloud of self-deception, he argues.

It might be concluded that people who are obese simply have convinced themselves that their health is not that important. In a 2008 medical journal,[24] researchers found that only 22.2 percent of obese women and 6.7 percent of obese men correctly classified themselves as obese. Finally, one could argue that it is not self-deception but just a case of poor education.

6.) Obesogens. One cause of the epidemic of obesity not yet mentioned may be the most troubling of all, and that is obesogens in our environment. An excellent history of the role obesogens play was published in *Newsweek* in 2009.[25] Here is my summary:

Obesity in infants under six months has increased since 1980 by 73%, a finding published by Harvard School of Public Health. After Various connecting of dots, scientists conclude that environmental chemicals acting before and after birth, account for a "good part" of the obesity epidemic and unfortunately beyond a person's control.

The idea of linkage between synthetic chemicals and obesity was slow to develop. Scientists in Japan discovered that low levels of bisphenol A, a component of plastic formed baby bottles affected cells in laboratory dishes—that fibroblasts cells could easily be turned into fat cells. The fact that diabetes drugs Actos and Avandia have obesity as side effects led to naming compounds that reprogram cells to be adipocytes to be called obesogens. It is safe to say that the more adipocytes you have, the more obese you become.

Newsweek concluded that traces of obesogens are found in every Americans tested, and that variations on weight are probably due to variations in timing of exposure. Needless-to-say, further research is eagerly anticipated not only for obesity, but for other conditions in utero-exposures of toxic chemicals might cause.

Wikipedia provides a list of obesogens in everyday life[26]:

- *Bisphenol-A* (BPA) is an industrial chemical and organic compound that has been used in the production of plastics and resins for over a half century.
- *High-fructose corn syrup* (HFCS) is found in many food products on grocery store shelves: by 2004, for example, it accounted for 40 percent of caloric sweeteners added to foods and beverages sold in the United States.
- *Nicotine* is the chemical found in tobacco products and certain insecticides. As an obesogen, nicotine mostly acts on prenatal development. A strong association has been made between maternal smoking and childhood overweight/obesity, with nicotine as the single causal agent.

- *Arsenic* is a metalloid (i.e., an element with some metallic properties) found in and on most naturally occurring substances on earth. It can be found in the soil, ground water, air, and small concentrations in food.

- *Pesticides* are substances used to prevent, destroy, repel, or mitigate pests, and they have been used throughout all recorded history. Several cross-sectional studies have shown pesticides as obesogens, linking them to obesity, diabetes, and other morbidities. Certain antidepressants, known as selectively serotonin reuptake inhibitors (SSRIs), are potentially adding to the almost one hundred million obese individuals in the US.

- *Organotins* such as tributyltin (TBT) and triphenyltin (TPT) are endocrine disruptors that have been shown to increase triglyceride storage in adipocytes. Although they have been widely used in the marine industry since the 1960s, other common sources of human exposure include contaminated seafood and shellfish, fungicides on crops and as antifungal agents used in wood treatments, industrial water systems, and textiles.

- *Perfluorooctanoic acid* (PFOA) is a surfactant used for reduction of friction, and it is also used in nonstick cookware. PFOA has been detected in the blood of more than 98 percent of the general US population. It is a potential endocrine disruptor. Animal studies have shown that prenatal exposure to PFOA is linked to obesity when reaching adulthood.

Cost factors: Assigning the out-of-pocket costs to this area of obesity, recognizing the complexity of the issues, must be a general estimate. The Marketplace Enterprise's 2016 number of $60 billion (quoted above) may be increasing annually but possibly offset by some diet consultation expenses covered by insurance. We all look forward to more research on the causes of obesity. The fact that trace chemicals in our environment can cause cells in early development period, destined for one function, to become fat cells indicates to me that there probably are other trace elements or chemicals that can cause derangement of brain cells that result in the various forms of autism. The cost of obesity may be way much more.

22. Cupping Therapy

> *What consumers think of as healthy*
> *is not always science-based.*
> —*Indras Nooyi, CEO of Pepsi*

If on your computer, you go to the National Center for Complementary and Integrative Health and search "all health topics from *A* to *Z*," you will easily find "cupping" under *C*.[1] There is a summary of cupping as a form of traditional Chinese medicine, that it involves placing a cup down on the skin and applying suction, that proponents claim that it increases blood flow and promotes healing, and that one medical journal (*PLoS One*) claims that it "could be effective" in treating neck pain and low back pain.[2] Under the next heading, "The Scientific Literature," you can select "Systematic Reviews" / "Reviews" / "Meta-analyses" (PubMed®), and when you do, you get search results from PubMed. Of these twenty listed, one is from the Chinese medical journal *PLoS One*, cited above, and another from the same *PLoS One*—named journal entitled "An Updated Review of the Efficacy of Cupping Therapy."[3] Clicking that will bring the following conclusions of the paper:

> Numerous RCTs (randomized controlled trials) on cupping therapy have been conducted and published during the past decades. This review showed that cupping has potential effect in the treatment of herpes zoster and other specific conditions. However, further rigorously designed trials on its use for other conditions are warranted.

Reading further on this list, the reader can observe that this reference is not the only one by the author Cho but that there are three others: one from BMC Complementary Alternative Medicine, one from Alternative Therapeutic Health Medicine, and J Alternative Complement Medicine. Note that there are no references in more creditable journals, and further note that the conclusions of these papers read like a mantra: "Further rigorously designed trials are warranted." This statement appears with great repetition. *This is not science. This is churning and a wasteful habit of spending US taxpayers' money.* A reference number 26 by J. I. Kim from the same list is entitled "Cupping for Treating Pain: A Systematic Review."[4] The conclusion of this paper is the following:

> Currently there are few RCTs testing the effectiveness of cupping in the management of pain. Most of the existing trials are of poor quality. Therefore, more rigorous studies are required before the effectiveness of cupping for the treatment of pain can be determined.

At least there is one researcher who will attest to the *poor equality* of most of the existing trials.

One final reference from the PubMed list is simply false.[5] The article entitled "History of Cupping (Hijama): A Narrative Review of Literature" appears in yet another alternative journal, *The Journal of Integrative Medicine*, authored by the Ministry of Health from Riydah, Saudi Arabia. The final line from the abstract that reviewed eighty-three references out of over six hundred dating from the Egyptians is as follows:

> Cupping therapy with a good safety profile has a checkered history and is a well-recognized traditional method for managing medical conditions. Currently, the scope of cupping therapy is expanding, and a growing body of research is providing additional evidence-based data for the

further advancement of cupping therapy in the treatment of a variety of diseases.

If there is a growing body of evidenced-based data, it was not given. It must be emphasized that cupping *is not a well-recognized traditional method of managing medical conditions.*

A subcategory of cupping is detox cupping, also of Chinese origin.[6] After a review of the literature on cupping, I cannot find a single creditable reference or scientific evidence of this process either defining what toxin is targeted or what mechanism is supposed to be at work. It remains simply an unfounded claim.

Cupping, because it is so clearly out of the mainstream of established scientific practice, is an excellent example of the problem of applying evidence-based practice (EBP) to complementary medicine (CM) because so much of CM is traditional Chinese medicine (TCM). This issue is confronted by Stephen Janz of Australia in an article entitled "Evidence-Based Practice: What Is It? Its Relevance and Consequences for Traditional Chinese Medicine and Complementary Medicine."[7] The argument centers on the key criticism of RCT's and EBP—that it shifts the focus of care to treating populations, not individuals:

> An RCT is not interested in what works for any one individual, only in statistically significant outcomes for a population.

I find this argument narrow and specious by inferring that EBP physicians do no treat their patients as individuals or that they are unaware of their preferences. It further deprecates the EBP physicians by failing to recognize that EBP physicians and nurses have a moral obligation to avoid deceiving a patient with a complementary treatment documented to be of no value or even harmful.

The British epidemiologist Archie Cochrane (1909–1988), for whom the international EBP research center, the Cochrane Collaboration, was named in 1993 argued that

As resources for health care are limited, they should be used effectively to provide care that has been shown, in valid evaluations, to result in desirable outcomes. He emphasized the importance of randomized controlled trials in providing reliable information on the effectiveness of medical interventions.

The final conclusion of this paper is that complementary therapists should not support RCT's until significant bodies of appropriate evidence using a suitable methodology have first been established.

The practice of cupping demonstrates another aspect of complementary medicine—the propagation of the idea that if a well-known sport person uses it, it must be valid. Michael Phelps in the 2016 summer Olympics is a case in point.[8] Photos of Phelps in the pool with circular welts over his back flashed around the world. The usual claims were made—that it relaxes tight muscles, brings improved blood flow, hydrates the body, and increases blood flow. The conclusion was that

Very little evidence has come up in scientific literature to support the practice, but it's important to note that little has been found to disprove it either. For some, it could just be the placebo effect at play.

Another source[9] concluded:
Cupping is pseudoscience.

Cupping is no different than acupuncture, bloodletting, phrenology, or any other medical pseudoscience. The treatment is based in pre-scientific superstitions, and has simply been rebranded to more effectively market the treatment to modern customers. It is now just another alternative treatment, lacking plausibility, lacking any compelling evidence for efficacy, and promoted for the usual array of subjective symptoms with the usual array of handwaving justifications. It is unfortunate that elite athletics, including the Olympics, is such a hot bed for pseudoscience. The Olympic Games are supposed to celebrate excellence, hard work, dedication, and friendly competition. Now it also represents gullibility and superstition, and spreads that gullibility to the viewing world.

Cost factors: How much Americans pay out-of-pocket for cupping therapy is difficult to even estimate. The website for the International Cupping Therapy Association[10] provides information on the number of licensees in each state of the United States, and from this, it can be estimated that there are about 5,800. We also know that a cupping session averages about $60 per session. Data on how many cupping sessions each therapist provides per year is not readily available. If they each do 10 per week or 50 per year, then that calculation means that each therapist is bringing in $30,000 per year. $30,000 per year × 5,800 therapists = $174 million annually. It is difficult to generate further estimations in that so many providers of this service are competing with chiropractic, naturopathic, and multiservice spas and now sports medicine clinics that also provide cupping as a listed available service. It would be reasonable to consider $200 million as conservative out-of-pocket annual figure.

23. Low "T" and the Medicalization of Natural Aging

Don't regret growing older. It's a
privilege denied to many.

—*Anon*

TV ads for testosterone therapies increased in the US between 2009 and 2013 and were associated with increased testosterone testing, new use of testosterone therapies, and use of testosterone without testing, according to a study from the University of North Carolina.[1]

> "This all occurred during a time when there was rapidly increasing use (of testosterone), but with unresolved safety concerns and little evidence of benefit for treating men with normal, age-related testosterone-reductions or non-specific symptoms," said Bradley Layton, lead researcher and an epidemiologist at UNC.

As of this writing, there has been a distinct reduction in TV advertising, and I suspect that it has resulted from the emergence of lawsuits. In November of 2014, it was reported by Bernstein Liebhard LLP, a New York law firm,[2] that:

> As testosterone lawsuits continue to be filed in U.S. courts on behalf of men who allegedly suffered serious heart problems due to their use of AndroGel and similar medications, Bernstein Liebhard LLP notes a new report suggesting that the safety concerns surrounding the drugs may be causing sales to slow. According to Bloomberg Businessweek, sales of AndroGel dropped 5% in the first half of 2014, while sales of the entire class of medications fell 6%.
>
> The decline followed the U.S. Food & Drug Administration's (FDA) announcement in January that it was looking into the cardiovascular side effects that may be associated with low testosterone therapy. Spending on advertising for low testosterone therapy is also down this year, which may reflect growing concerns over how the drugs are marketed, according to Bloomberg Businessweek.

Throughout 2017, there have been several multimillion-dollar jury awards to plaintiffs claiming heart attacks from testosterone treatments and one jury that failed to convict Auxilium, a maker of gel Testim. This is one of over six thousand cases pending against Auxilium, and trials will begin in earnest in 2018. (See NastLaw.com for updates.)

The science of testosterone is that in men, testosterone levels decline with age,[3] with the lowest levels seen in men over seventy years. This is *part of the aging process*, and therein lies the first element in the controversy over the need for treatment, asking, "Is natural aging a medical problem?" Critics like sociologist Peter Conrad have labeled this a prime example of "medicalization" or the making of a natural process into a medical disease.[4] His book *Medicalization of Society* is well worth reading. Argument is made that very low circulating levels of testosterone could be labeled "hypogonadism" and, if symptomatic, would warrant treatment.[5] From the same reference, a word about the symptoms of low testosterone in the aging male: most are very vague such as listlessness, lower libido, and moodiness.

> Testosterone replacement results in an improvement in muscle strength and bone mineral density, plus effects on the hematopoietic system (increase in red blood cells). Data on cognition and lipoprotein profiles are conflicting.
>
> The adverse effects can be deleterious in men with compromised cardiac reserve and prostate cancer remains an absolute contraindication to androgen therapy.

Clinical trials of testosterone therapy were reported in 2017 for the public in the *New York Times*.[6] The article confirmed improvement in anemia and bone density but

> A red flag warning of possible risks to the heart emerged from the studies: imaging tests found a greater build of plaque in the coronary

arteries of men treated with testosterone for a year, an indicator of cardiac risk, compared to those who were given a placebo gel.

Only about 15 percent of men 65 and over have low testosterone levels studied in recent trials. Most men experience only slight declines in testosterone as they age, *so the trial results are not necessarily applicable to the general population of older men.*

The researchers even noted that for erectile function, drugs like Viagra are more effective (acknowledging that previous studies showed "modest" improvement in libido). Testosterone didn't help older men walk farther, nor did it temper fatigue or increase men's sense of vitality, though it did improve mood slightly.

And here is another critical point:

Testosterone has been available as a drug for so long that it was never subjected to clinical trials of safety and efficacy as most new drugs are today.

But facts and science were not the focus of big Pharma when they realized they could "medicalize" a huge market and expand it from older men to all men, including young bodybuilders.

Testosterone prescriptions in the United States nearly doubled in recent years to 2.2 million in 2013 up from 1.2 million in years earlier.

The marketing of low T as a common medical condition helped propel sales of testosterone gels, patches, injections, and tablets to about $2 billion in the United States in 2012.[7]

Today the low T trend is global. From 2000 to 2001, there was a major increase in testosterone use in 37 countries, according to a study published in the Medical Journal of Australia.

Here is an example of how we contaminate the rest of the world with bad science and poor regulation. The medical profession in the US did not standby this troubling development without resistance.[8]

"The market for testosterone gels evolved because there is an appetite among men and because there is advertising," said Joel Finkelstein, an associate professor of Harvard Medical School who is studying male hormone changes with aging. "The problem is that no one has proved that it works, and we don't know the risks."

Finally, he added, no one has really defined what is a "normal" testosterone level, and yet, physicians often order tests for "low T." (Note, this reference is dated 2013.)

Dr. Eric Topol, a cardiologist and chief academic officer at Scripps Health in San Diego is alarmed by the high percentage of patients he sees who use the roll-on prescription products, achieving testosterone levels that he described as "ridiculously high." These medicines come with a risk of coronary artery disease.

So let's tally up the fraud: (1) pushing drugs by Pharma or physicians with unknown or suspected long-term consequences; (2) assuming, excepting several genetic endocrine conditions, that the gradual decrease in testosterone with aging is pathological; (3) not warning the public or physicians of the risks of prostate cancer and progressive cardiovascular disease; (4) Indiscriminate use of testosterone in bodybuilding; and (5) starting treatment without even bothering to get a blood test.[9]

I am not saying that there is not a legitimate place for testosterone in medicine today. There may be a place for testosterone supplementation therapy, for example, in men with prostate cancer on active surveillance.[10] Recent trials[11] reported that

> A total of 788 men took part in the Testosterone Trials, including controls who were given a placebo gel. On the positive side, testosterone therapy significantly increased bone density in 211 men and corrected anemia in 126 men by increasing hemoglobin levels. While the two studies in JAMA Internal Medicine hinted at health benefits, this remains to be demonstrated. For example, a larger and longer follow up trial to the bone density study will be needed to determine if the therapy decreases the risk of fractures.

Then there is the bizarre argument from the *Journal of Sexual Medicine* that TD is (notice the wording) "involved in the development of CVD, DM, and ORGs" and adds to costs if not treated.[12]

Endocrinology researcher David J. Handelsman of the University of Sydney wrote that[13]

> Beyond prescribing testosterone for its only valid indication, testosterone replacement therapy for pathological hypogonadism, there increasing prevalence of testosterone misuse and abuse in most countries. Testosterone misuse is when testosterone is prescribed for non-valid medical indications such as male infertility, sexual dysfunction (in men without pathological hypogonadism), but most commonly for anti-aging. Androgen abuse is the non-prescription use of testosterone or a synthetic androgen unrelated to medical indications but rather for doping,

body building, or other recreational, cosmetic, or occupational reasons.

The bottom line is, more research and more discriminating distribution based upon the science is necessary, not "feel-good TV ads." But that is a huge challenge. This ideal seems more of a lofty goal than a feasible objective. The FDA requires rigor and detailed follow-up to provide answers, but there are many challenges to bringing this about. Such studies are costly in both time and effort and beg the question, Who will finance and execute these endeavors? Will the pharmacy companies be trusted to do so?

Cost factors: The costs to the consumer are not only out-of-pocket, but add to this the enormous cost for the impending litigation that is now before us. The millions that might be rewarded from litigation could go a long way to learn the necessary science for best clinical practice.

Add to this the cost of prescriptions and testing/monitoring testosterone therapy. Annual testosterone drug revenue in the US in 2013 and 2018 (in billion US dollars) was $2.4 billion and projected $3.8 billion.[14]

24.   Cognitive Enhancement—the Brain

Science is the true theology.
—Thomas Paine

The fact that an estimated 5.5 million Americans are living with Alzheimer's dementia in 2017, that an estimated 5.3 million are age sixty-five and older and approximately two hundred thousand individuals are under age sixty-five and have younger-onset Alzheimer's can easily explain the anxious and desperate market for a medication that will improve memory.[1]

There is no cure for Alzheimer's, but there are five prescription drugs currently approved by the FDA to treat the symptoms, according to the website of the Alzheimer's Association.[2] A website called Drugs.com[3] lists thirty medications available for treatment of the disease, some over-the-counter (OTC), some off-label. It is obvious that all we are doing is managing symptoms according to the Mayo Clinic, with drugs approved for specific Alzheimer's stages, but are not approved for mild cognitive impairment (MCI).[4]

> This condition (MCI), which involves subtle changes in memory and thinking, can be a transitional stage between normal age-related memory changes and Alzheimer's disease. Many people with MCI—but not all—eventually develop Alzheimer's or another dementia.

It is this prevalence of the "senior moment" that sparks the fear of MCI and hence the market for any medication promising to combat MCI.

Prevagen® is the number 1 selling memory supplement in drugstores in the US. Prevagen.com[5] claims:

- Prevagen® improves memory.
- Prevagen is a dietary supplement that has been clinically shown to help with mild memory problems associated with aging.
- Prevagen contains apoaequorin, which is safe and uniquely supports brain function.

It comes in 10 mg and 20 mg capsules of the active ingredient apoaequorin (pron. "a-po-ah-kwor-in"), which the company Quincy Bioscience claims "improved certain aspects of cognitive function over a ninety-day period." Note the asterisk, referenced on all TV ads, and at the bottom of the webpage declaring,

> These statements have not been evaluated by the Food and Drug Administration. This product is not intended to diagnose, treat, cure or prevent any disease.

We are back to the old problem of the FDA jurisdiction over drugs but not supplements as mentioned before. That did not mean that Quincy Bioscience is off scot-free. The Federal Trade Commission and New York State Attorney General charged the marketers of the dietary supplement Prevagen with making false and unsubstantiated claims that the product improves memory, provides cognitive benefits, and is "clinically shown" to work.[6]

> "The marketing for Prevagen is a clear-cut fraud, from the label on the bottle to the ads airing across the country," said New York Attorney General Eric Schneiderman. "It's particularly unacceptable that this company has targeted vulnerable citizens like seniors in its advertising for a product that costs more than a week's groceries, but provides none of the health benefits that it claims."
>
> The FTC is a member of the National Prevention Council, which provides coordination and leadership at the federal level regarding prevention, wellness, and health promotion practices. This case advances the National Prevention Council's goal of increasing the number of Americans who are healthy at every stage of life.

That was January 2017. In October 2017, Federal district Judge Louis Stanton dismissed FTC lawsuit over Quincy Bioscience's memory supplement Prevagen.[7] In court, the Quincy Bioscience lawyers used the *clinical study done by the company*. So we have court-determined science, and beat goes on.

According to Truth in Advertising.org (TIAA),[8] the active ingredient never gets to the brain. TIAA notes:

> Prevagen cannot work as represented because apoaequorin, the only purported active ingredient in Prevagen, is completely destroyed

by the digestive system and transformed into common amino acids no different than those derived from other common food products such as chicken, cold cuts, hamburgers, etc.

The FDA sent Underwood (President of Quincy Bioscience) a warning letter in 2012 over the alleged illegal marketing of Prevagen as a drug without the agency's approval. The letter also noted that the product did not satisfy the definition of a dietary supplement because the only dietary ingredient on the label—"synthetically produced apoaequorin"—did not qualify as such.

Update: On Friday, February 8, 2019, I attended the appeal before the Second Circuit Court of Appeals at Foley Square, in New York City. The FTC lawyer opened by stating that Quincy Biosciences (maker of Prevagen) presented false advertising on TV. He documented that Quincy was guilty of "cherry-picking" the research and further documented that Quincy knew the active agent in their supplement did not survive digestion in the stomach and so could not enter the bloodstream. Next, the attorney for NYS Attorney General argued that Prevagen was a classic case of deception, since it could not be detected beyond the blood/brain barrier. The attorney for Quincy then responded by merely restating Judge Stanton's position but added that the actives ingredient did cross the blood/brain barrier because it does so in dogs. He gave no evidence or references to this statement. He then made what I viewed as a fatal mistake, stating that this whole case had been instigated by "Democrats at the end of the Obama Administration." He was allowed to finish but was properly admonished by one of the three judges for introducing politics into the proceedings.

My observations on this proceeding were:

1. This is what happens when courts are obliged to judge science.

2. This case is an indictment of the lax federal supplement policy. As a drug, Prevagen would never survive the scrutiny of the FDA with the information available.

3. This is a case of a good judge (Stanton) playing bad scientist—and the public paying the price.

4. Neither Judge Louis Stanton nor former NYAG Eric Schneiderman understood one of the first principals of the scientific method—that is, science that is not reproduced by an independent is not science.

5. Until congress decides to be on the side of protecting the people and bring the vitamin/supplement under FDA standards, rather than on the side pharmacology companies, matters will worsen!

As a follow-up, the Second Circuit Court of Appeals overturned the lower court's ruling and sent it back to lower court for retiral, a clear victory for those seeking the truth.

This is not the first such case. In 2015, a federal judge in New Jersey ruled in favor of Bayer Corporation in a years-long dispute with the federal government over advertising statements related to a probiotic supplement known as Phillips's Colon Health. The case reflected fundamental disagreements between the broader dietary supplement industry and FTC over the evidence required to adequately support—or "substantiate"—an advertising claim.[9] Apparently, all you need is an in-house "company study."

TIAA points out that Prevagen is but the top of the iceberg in the "brain supplement market." Here is a portion of the list that was or is in the courts:

- The CVS supplement, which it calls Algal-900 DHA, is manufactured by Martek Biosciences' successor, DSM Nutritional Products LLC, and is promoted as "Memory Support." Was cited by the FTC in 2016.

- October 2014: A class-action lawsuit was filed against Bayer Healthcare for allegedly falsely advertising Flintstone Healthy Brain Support, a dietary supplement containing Omega-3 DHA, as supporting healthy brain function without scientific evidence to support such claim. (Kaplan et al v. Bayer Healthcare, LLC, Case No. 14-cv-23789, S. D. FL.)

- In November 2017, a class-action lawsuit was filed against Biogenesis for allegedly falsely promoting its liquid vitamin B supplements as containing a specific amount of vitamin B12 per serving when, according to the complaint, the supplements do not provide the amount stated on the product labels because the supplements begin to degrade after they are opened resulting in the amount of vitamin B12 in the supplement becoming negligible and ineffective.

- December 2014: A class-action lawsuit was filed against Bayer for allegedly falsely advertising the Flintstones Healthy Brain Support supplement (a gummy, chewable supplement with DHA) as able to "Support Healthy Brain Function" without scientific evidence to support such claims. (Gershman et al v. Bayer Healthcare, LLC, Case No. 14-cv-05332, N. D. CA.)

  August 2016: This lawsuit was voluntarily dismissed because the parties entered a confidential settlement agreement.

- August 2017: A federal judge granted final approval of the settlement dating March 2016 when a federal judge preliminarily approved a settlement agreement in a false advertising class-action lawsuit against i-Health, Inc. The complaint, which was originally filed in 2012 and amended in 2014, alleges that the company markets BrainStrong dietary supplements with DHA algal oil—including BrainStrong Toddler, BrainStrong Kids, and BrainStrong Adult— as supporting brain health and function when such claims are not true and not supported by adequate scientific evidence.

I will end the list here because there is not enough room to include all the references on this subject. But wait! Then there are the Nootropic supplements—Healthline.com, one of the hundreds of nutrition-content sites on line,[10] lists,

Natural supplements or drugs that have a beneficial effect on brain function in healthy people.

Many of these (claim to) boost memory, motivation, creativity, alertness and general cognitive function. Nootropics may also reduce age-related declines in brain function. Here are the 10 best nootropic supplements to boost your brain function according to the wellness newsletter put out by healthline.com 1. Fish Oils, 2. Resveratrol, 3. Caffeine, 4. Phosphatidylserine, 5. Acetyl-L-Carnitine, 6. Ginkgo Biloba, 7. Creatine, 8. Bacopa Monnieri, 9. Rhodiola Rosea (Rhodiola rosea is a perennial flowering plant in the family Crassulaceae. It grows naturally in wild Arctic regions of Europe, Asia, and North America, and can be propagated as a groundcover), and 10. S-Adenosyl Methionine.

Note that most of these health websites have no scientific references at all.

With respect to what Americans are spending out-of-pocket on brain supplements, we might assume that is included in the $37 billion figure estimated in 2015.[11] But there is a better estimate. In December of 2017, a report by GAO reveals that US citizens are spending $643 million in 2015 on dietary supplements to improve their memory.[12] Growing at 10 percent per year calculates to an estimate of $778 million in 2018.

25. Marijuana and the Cannabinoids

Of all the things I've lost, I miss my mind the most.
—Found on a cocktail napkin

The first observation to be made is the jurisdictional dispute that the use of marijuana and cannabinoids (derivatives) presents. When we go to NIH's website, the National Center for Complementary and Integrative Health,[1] clearly a branch of the federal government, there is a listing for "Marijuana and the Cannabinoids," whereas marijuana is illegal under federal law even in states that legalize it. The federal government, through the DEA (Drug Enforcement Agency), under the Department of Justice, sorts drugs through a scheduling system and classifies marijuana as a schedule I, meaning it's perceived to have no medical value and a high potential for abuse. Marijuana[2] is in the same category as heroin—Schedule I. The difference between Schedule I and II is "medical value." DEA says Schedule II has, but Schedule I does not have medical value. The barrier to clarification is proper medical (pharmacological) studies just like any new drug. So, marijuana is in a Catch 22—no studies, no clarification. No clarification no rescheduling and remains by law illegal.

It seems to me that this is simply tangled law, which could be clarified if and when there are enough adults in Washington to act on a common sense fashion.

The next question is obvious. What about the cannabinoids? The answer[3] is as follows:

> Legal status of CBD. Cannabidiol is not listed separately in the Code of Federal Regulations (CFR); it is controlled in Schedule I by definition as a "derivative" or "component" of marijuana (21 USC 802). This is also true of other individual cannabinoids.

Before sorting this out further, let's review some fundamental pharmacology. It is a fact that in smoking marijuana, chemicals from the plant pass through the lungs into the bloodstream.[4]

> The person begins to experience effects almost immediately. Many people experience a pleasant euphoria and sense of relaxation. Other common effects, which may vary dramatically among different people, include heightened sensory perception (e.g., brighter colors), laughter, altered perception of time, and increased appetite.
>
> Pleasant experiences with marijuana are by no means universal. Instead of relaxation and euphoria, some people experience anxiety, fear, distrust, or panic.
>
> Although detectable amounts may remain in the body for days or even weeks after use, the noticeable effects of smoked marijuana generally last from 1 to 3 hours, and those of marijuana consumed in food or drink may last for many hours.

Physiological changes are notable[5]:

> Within a few minutes after inhaling marijuana smoke, a person's heart rate speeds up, the

breathing passages relax and become enlarged, and blood vessels in the eyes expand, making the eyes look bloodshot. The heart rate—normally 70 to 80 beats per minute—may increase by 20 to 50 beats per minute or may even double in some cases. Taking other drugs with marijuana can amplify this effect.

Marijuana use affects school, work, and social life.[6]

Research has shown that marijuana's negative effects on attention, memory, and learning can last for days or weeks after the acute effects of the drug wear off, depending on the person's history with the drug. Consequently, someone who smokes marijuana daily may be functioning at a reduced intellectual level most or all the time. Considerable evidence suggests that students who smoke marijuana have poorer educational outcomes than their nonsmoking peers. For example, a review of 48 relevant studies found marijuana use to be associated with reduced educational attainment (i.e., reduced chances of graduating). A recent analysis using data from three large studies in Australia and New Zealand found that adolescents who used marijuana regularly were significantly less likely than their non-using peers to finish high school or obtain a degree. They also had a much higher chance of developing dependence, using other drugs, and attempting suicide. Several studies have also linked heavy marijuana use to lower income, greater welfare dependence, unemployment, criminal behavior, and lower life satisfaction.

For more in-depth information, visit the National Institute on Drug Abuse site[7] for details on marijuana effect on driving, long-term effects on the brain, tendency toward addiction and on pregnancy, among many other issues. Finally, I emphasize the addiction risk[8]:

> Despite some contentious discussions regarding the addictiveness of marijuana, the evidence clearly indicates that long-term marijuana use can lead to addiction. Indeed, approximately 9% of those who experiment with marijuana will become addicted (according to the criteria for dependence in the Diagnostic and Statistical Manual of Mental Disorders, 4th edition [DSM-IV]).
>
> The number goes up to about 1 in 6 among those who start using marijuana as teenagers and to 25 to 50% among those who smoke marijuana daily.[9]

The clear conclusion is that marijuana is not good for you.

Next question. If marijuana and the cannabinoids (more than sixty) are listed as agents of alternative medicine, is there science to substantiate the claim? A summary of medical use of marijuana is found in *Goldfrank's Toxicologic Emergencies*[10]:

> In 2003, the Institute of Medicine undertook an extensive review of the evidence supporting the medical use of marijuana. It concluded that in some circumstances, cannabinoids show promise for use as therapeutics, but the quality of current studies necessitated further research specifically for the treatment of chronic pain. In addition, smoked marijuana is a crude and unpredictable delivery mechanism, and safer, more precise methods of administration are

needed. No data reviewed since that publication is sufficient to reverse that opinion.

Pharmaceutical cannabinoids are proposed for use in the management of many clinical conditions but have generally been approved only for the control of chemotherapy-related nausea and vomiting that are resistant to conventional antiemetics, for breakthrough postoperative nausea and vomiting, and for appetite stimulation in human immunodeficiency virus (HIV) patients with anorexia-cachexia syndrome. The claims of benefit in the other medical conditions (Anxiety, Asthma, Depression, Epilepsy, Glaucoma, Head Injury, Insomnia, Migraine headaches, Multiple sclerosis, Muscle spasticity, Neurologic disorders, Pain, Parkinson disease and Tourette syndrome) are not supported by evidence.

As of this writing, cannabinoid receptor agonists (a chemical capable of activating a receptor) like nabilone and dronabinol are used and FDA-approved for reducing chemotherapy induced vomiting.[11, 12] A scientific paper in the *Annals of Medicine* in 2016 states[13]:

Where medical cannabis is legal, patients typically see a physician who "certifies" that a benefit may result. Physicians must consider important patient selection criteria such as failure of standard medical treatment for a debilitating medical disorder. Medical cannabis patients must be informed about potential adverse effects, such as acute impairment of memory, coordination and judgment, and possible chronic effects, such as cannabis use disorder, cognitive impairment, and chronic bronchitis. In addition, social dysfunction may result at work/school, and there is increased possibility of motor vehicle accidents.

The utility of marijuana in specific medical conditions has been studied, but its effects on driving performance and risk of motor vehicle collision remain unclear.[14]

As of December 1, 2017, medical marijuana is legal in twenty-nine states and DC, and eight states have made both medical and recreational use legal.[15] The wording of state legislation for the removal of restrictions is of interest. An example is Alaska's Ballot approved in 1998[16]:

> Removed state-level criminal penalties on the use, possession and cultivation of marijuana by patients who possess written documentation from their physician advising that they "might benefit from the medical use of marijuana."
>
> Approved Conditions:
>
> Cancer, glaucoma, HIV or AIDS, any chronic or debilitating disease or treatment for such diseases, which produces conditions that may be alleviated by the medical use of the marijuana: cachexia; severe pain; severe nausea; seizures, including those that are characteristic of epilepsy; or persistent muscle spasms, including those that are characteristic or multiple sclerosis. Other conditions are subject to approval by the Alaska Department of Health and Social Services.

Note the phrases "might benefit from" and "may be alleviated by," hardly a convincing vocabulary. Connecticut's approval[17] in 2012 added "Parkinson's disease, multiple sclerosis, damage to the nervous tissue of the spinal cord with objective neurological indication of intractable spasticity, epilepsy, cachexia, wasting syndrome, Crohn's disease, post-traumatic stress disorder (PTSD), or…any medical condition, medical treatment or disease approved by the Department of Consumer Protection." In other words, states are naming some conditions but not going to worry about any fine points of science here. The emphasis is on legalizing!

The reason is simple. Criminalizing marijuana has not worked. We need no references here to make that point. Approval by the remaining states for both medical and recreational uses will probably depend upon the experiences of the "legal" states in the complex regulatory implications and the record of providing an additional flow of income from taxation in whatever form. The potential problem of laundering of money from recreational sales may be difficult to solve. In a Los Angeles Times commentary, "Your business is legal, but you can't use banks. Welcome to the cannabis all-cash nightmare."[18]

> This is the outrageous and untenable conflict imposed on legal businesses by the federal government's continuing obstinacy about cannabis.
>
> The federal government regards marijuana as an illegal drug; it is classified by the Drug Enforcement Administration as a controlled substance with no accepted medical use, on par with heroin. Banks are regulated by the feds; most will not touch cannabis cash. (Neither will most armored car companies.)
>
> As a result, an estimated 70% of cannabis businesses have no bank accounts.
>
> "We are talking about an industry expected to come short of $7 billion beginning in 2018, with expected tax revenues of approximately $1 billion," California Treasurer John Chiang told me Friday. "This is trouble waiting to happen."
>
> It's already begun.
>
> In 2012, an Orange County medical cannabis dispensary owner was kidnapped and sexually tortured by a quartet of thieves trying to find and steal his cash. Rife with gruesome details, that case drew worldwide attention.

But many cannabis growers have been ripped off in less spectacular fashion or are afraid they will be.

Last month in Sacramento, Chiang heard some of these horror stories during testimony at the first meeting of his Cannabis Banking Working Group.

The goal is to come up with recommendations—including potential federal legislation—to open up banking to this new burgeoning and legal industry. The next meeting is in Los Angeles on Feb. 10. (2018)

A number of banking institutions are beginning to service accounts for marijuana businesses.[19]

As of the end of September (2018), there were 375 banks and 111 credit unions maintaining financial services for cannabis businesses, according to a report published this month by the U.S. Treasury Department's Financial Crimes Enforcement Network (FinCEN).

So we will stand by for the next part of the story. Recently resigned Attorney General Jeff Sessions was reportedly planning to let federal prosecutors aggressively enforce federal antimarijuana laws in states where pot has been legalized, but that will await a future AG. Further complexity is noted on the website reason.com[20]:[*1]

What gives the federal government the authority to target legal state pot? The answer is not the Constitution. This federal power grab

---

[1] *Permission to publish granted by the Reason Foundation, Chris Mitchell, Director of Communications.

is the product of two awful Supreme Court precedents.

In 1942 the federal government brought sanctions against an Ohio farmer named Roscoe Filburn. His crime? He grew twice the amount of wheat that he was permitted to grow under the terms of the Agricultural Adjustment Act of 1938. That sweeping federal law, ostensibly passed as part of Congress's power to regulate interstate commerce, sought to raise agricultural prices by limiting the supply of crops.

Filburn defended himself from the feds by pointing out that his extra wheat never once entered the stream of interstate commerce. In fact, he noted, that extra wheat never even left his Ohio farm. He used it to feed his livestock and to make flour for use in his family's kitchen.

But the Supreme Court ruled against him on Commerce Clause grounds anyway. Filburn's extra wheat may not have crossed state lines, the Court conceded in Wickard v. Filburn, but it still had a "substantial economic effect" on the interstate wheat market. As a result, Congress had every right to regulate Filburn and other farmers in this manner.

Six decades later, in the case of Gonzales v. Raich (2005), the Supreme Court applied and extended the Filburn precedent by upholding the federal ban on marijuana, even as applied to plants that were cultivated and consumed by patients for their own doctor-prescribed use in states where medical cannabis was perfectly legal. "The [Controlled Substances Act] is a valid exercise of federal power," declared the majority opinion of Justice John Paul Stevens, "even as applied to the troubling facts of this case."

Which brings us back to (the Justice Department). If the attorney general follows through on threats to unleash the federal government against legal state marijuana, make sure you reserve a portion of your outrage for the lousy SCOTUS (Supreme Court of the US) decisions that empowered the feds in the first place.

A brief look at cost/benefit factors may prove of value. To begin, there is a monetary award that accrues to government at all levels with the legalization of marijuana. The *Huffington Post* in 2013 cited an economist[21] estimating that prohibition of marijuana costs federal and state governments $20 billion per year. A CNBC commentary counters that side of the ledger by arguing that legalizing marijuana is not worth the costs[22]:

> There are significant cost burdens that come along with increased marijuana use. For example, there will be a greater social cost from decline in worker productivity and school performance. Legalization will also lead to a greater need for drug education, rehabilitation and treatment. And there will be costs associated with selling the drug.
>
> The additional costs of drug education and rehabilitation combined with the increased social costs associated with increased marijuana use and sale are all greater than the potential revenue gained through legalization.

Are medical marijuana laws cutting Medicare drug spending? *US News* reported a study[23] published in the *Journal Health Affairs:*

> Doctors are prescribing medical marijuana in place of medications that have been typically used to treat patients for disorders like pain, sei-

zures, sleep disorders, depression and anxiety. The swap appears to have saved the Medicare program—whose patients include seniors and people with disabilities—$104.5 million in 2010 and $165.2 million by 2013, because doctors are prescribing other drugs less.

To conduct the study, researchers used data on prescriptions filled by Medicare Part D enrollees from 2010 to 2013. They looked at drugs for which medical marijuana was an alternative treatment, including drugs like antidepressants, muscle relaxants and sedatives, along with 17 other categories of medicines. They also included ailments that these medications treat other than those the FDA has tested them for, so called "off-label" prescribing.

If there were savings, they were a drop in the bucket, and the key question in this study is how legitimate is saving money with off-label alternative cannabinoids?

What do states that have legalized have to report? In Colorado, a billion-dollar-a-year legal industry has evolved since January 2014.[24] On the plus side:

- Legalization has ushered in thousands of new jobs in the burgeoning industry, brought $135 million into state coffers last year, and ended the prohibition of a widely used substance.
- State Representative Jonathan Singer, a leader on marijuana issues in the House, said what legalization has done is "allowed marijuana to pay its own way," with the cost of regulation paid for by dispensaries and consumers.

On the negative side:

- But police say they struggle to enforce a patchwork of laws covering marijuana, including drugged driving. Officials fret about the industry becoming like big tobacco, dodging regulation and luring users with slick advertising. And this state, long a leader in cannabis use, has the highest youth rate of marijuana use in the nation, according to the most recent data available from a federal drug-use survey.
- Yet law enforcement officials offer a more negative, chaotic view. They paint a picture of a quickly evolving array of laws, regulations, and ordinances that outpace their enforcement tools for related issues, such as drugged driving.
- Another problem with edible marijuana products, said Dr. Michael DiStefano, who directs emergency medicine clinical operations at Colorado's only top-level pediatric trauma center: the inability of kids to distinguish between normal products and those infused with THC.

Cost factors: Returning to the cost/benefit issue finally, all we can do is a rough estimate. If the national aggregate cost of prohibition is $20 billion and Colorado's experience is a revenue stream of $135 million in a year, and if we consider Colorado an average-sized state and multiply by 50, then the return is $6.75 billion for a year. Rounded to $7 billion, the nation could save ($20–$8 billion) $12 billion per year. That would allow a sizable source for funding the necessary education programs necessary to teach our children at all levels and avert the increase in usage that we have seen in Colorado.

Will that happen? Not if the experience from the 1998 Master Tobacco Settlement is any indication.[25] As a result of the settlement, tobacco companies have paid billions to state governments as part of a twenty-five-year $246 billion settlement. Though the money was meant to be spent on prevention and smoking-related programs, it didn't come with a mandate. Myron Levin, who covered the tobacco industry for the *Los Angeles Times* for many years, says talking states into spending settlement money on tobacco prevention is a tough sell.[26]

To show the settlement was not just a big money grab, Levin says, there was definitely a feeling that states had a moral obligation to spend at least a sizeable chunk of money on programs to help people quit smoking and to prevent kids from starting.

"So, it was understood without being codified into the agreement that states would make a big investment in this," he says. "They haven't."

To help guide state governments, in 2007 the Centers for Disease Control and Prevention recommended that states reinvest 14 percent of the money from the settlement and tobacco taxes in anti-smoking programs. But most state governments have decided to prioritize other things: Colorado has spent tens of millions of its share to support a literacy program, while Kentucky has invested half of its money in agricultural programs.

"What states have actually done has fluctuated year by year…but it's never come close to 14 percent," Levin says. "There are some fairly notorious cases of money being used for fixing potholes, for tax relief [and] for financial assistance for tobacco farmers."

Levin says some states don't have any money coming in anymore because they securitized their future payments with an investor in order to receive a lump sum. That lump sum often went into their state's general fund.

Do the marijuana legalization laws come with any mandate? The answer is debatable. An essay by Alia Wong in the *Atlantic* entitled "The False Promise of Marijuana Money in Education"[27] reported that

the law, stipulates that the first $40 million raised from taxes on the sale of recreational pot help pay for construction to improve Colorado's "crumbling" public-school buildings, a problem the state has long struggled to address because of limited funding.

There is no specific language that mandates marijuana revenue from either medical or recreational sources be used for education of youth about the true nature of marijuana usage. Returning to our cost/benefit analysis, it may be extrapolated from the CDC experience with the tobacco settlement that 14 percent recommended of the $8 billion national marijuana revenue will never be spent on marijuana education—an amount equal to $1.12 billion. The real fraud will be many times that because we have not factored in the damage done to the young brains. Dr. Marilyn Huestis, chief of the chemistry and drug metabolism section at the National Institute on Drug Abuse, lectures that the harmful effects of marijuana last longer than you may realize.[28]

The primary psychoactive chemical in marijuana, Δ-9-tetrahydrocannabinol (THC), is stored in the body after chronic, frequent marijuana use.

Studies reveal that marijuana negatively affects brain development and is associated with decreased IQ, especially in kids who start using pot when they're younger than 15. Huestis said persistent marijuana use from childhood to middle age can cause significant neurological decline.

How do we attach a dollar value to damaged IQ in the young? You can't, but I can proffer $5 billion per year as a good estimate making my evaluation of annual cost over $6.1 billion in 2018. It may eventually turn out that, indeed, the cost of legalizing recreational marijuana may be equal to or greater than the cost of prohibition.

As of this writing, Vermont is the most recent state to legalize recreational use, and the law has no provision for use of any revenue for education.[29] Of further confusion, Vermont's new law is silent on how people will purchase marijuana if they don't already have it.

Summary of the Gamut

Although we have covered twenty-five leading examples of questionable scientific treatments, this does not complete the gamut. There needs to be listed additional areas of quackonomics other than CIM therapies for which there is not enough space to cover in this book. Among these in no particular order are (1) the danger of sports drugs and energy drinks, (2) antiaging centers, (3) exorcism of disease-causing daemons, (4) immune system enhancement, (5) shark cartilage and rhino horn, (6) medical devices to treat depression (e.g., bracelets and lasers), (7) post-Lyme disease syndrome, (8) pseudo-nutrition, (9) overdiagnosis, and (10) gold treatments. (11) The mistaken notion that cholesterol causes atherosclerosis. (See books by Dr. Malcolm Hendrick in Additional Reading section at the end of this book)

Three observations remain painfully costly:

1. Even though a treatment be shown to be over 97 percent effective, some people refuse to vaccinate their chil-

dren using a "doctor's note" or claim religious conviction. Witness the recent emergence of measles on the west coast[30] and about the nation in 2019.

2. Once an unscientific statement is widely dispersed, it is essentially impossible to retract it. A considerable number of people will continue to believe it forever, no matter what.

3. As my artist daughter Ellen Granter has observed,

> US schools are obsessed with teaching to the state/national standards. They must do this by law. They cover scientific method in every grade. We produce amazing world class scientists, Nobel laureates, doctors, coders, researchers and millions of citizens who "get it." The question becomes why so many people choose non-science IN SPITE of being taught science.[31]

Endnotes

Part II
The Gamut
1. Acupuncture

[1] https://nccih.nih.gov/news/camstats/costs/costdatafs.htm.

[2] http://www.nccaom.org/regulatory-affairs/state-licensure-map/.

[3] https://mx.nccaom.org/StateLicensing.aspx.

[4] Rana S. Hinman et al., "Acupuncture for Chronic Knee Pain: A Randomized Clinical Trial," *JAMA* 312, no. 13 (2014): 1313–1322.

[5] Thomas Reinhold, Claudia M. Witt, Suzanne Jena, Benno Brinkhaus, Stefan N. Willich, "Quality of Life and Cost-Effectiveness of Acupuncture Treatment in Patients with Osteoarthritis Pain," *The European Journal of Health Economics* 9, no. 3 (August 2008): 209–19.

[6] Y. L. Loh, A. Reilly, W. Chen, R. R. Coeytaux, "Incorporating Acupuncture in a University-Based Family Medicine Center: Lessons Learned," *Journal of Alternative and Complementary Medicine* 15, no. 2 (February 2009): 115–20.

[7] Richard R. L. Nahin et al., "Evidence-Based Evaluation of Complementary Health Approaches for Pain Management in the United States," *Mayo Clinic Proceedings* 91, no. 9 (September 2016): 1292–1306.

[8] Ancient Civilizations, http://www.ushistory.org/civ/9b.asp.

9 Paul A. Offit, MD, *Do You Believe in Magic?* (New York: Harper Collins, 2013), 28.

10 Ibid., 29.

11 Ibid., 232.

12 http://www.mayoclinic.org/tests-procedures/acupuncture/basics/risks/prc-20020778.

13 http://www.pacificcollege.edu/news/blog/2015/04/27/science-acupuncture-safety-risks-harms-and-ancient-goodness.

14 http://www.mayoclinic.org/tests-procedures/acupuncture/basics/risks/prc-20020778.

15 Junhua Zhang, Hongcai Shang, Xiumei Gao, and Edzard Ernst, "Acupuncture-Related Adverse Events: A Systematic Review of the Chinese Literature," *Bulletin of the World Health Organization* 88 (2010): 915–921C, doi: 10.2471/BLT.10.076737, web reference: http://www.who.int/bulletin/volumes/88/12/10-076737/en/.

16 "Adverse Events of Acupuncture: A Systematic Review of Case Reports," https://www.acuwatch.org/reports/adverse_events.pdf.

17 https://alliedhealth.insureon.com/professions/acupuncturists/96.

18 http://health.costhelper.com/acupuncture.html.

19 http://www.weacupuncture.com/community_acupuncture.html.

20 http://skepdic.com/acupuncture.html.

21 https://pranajiacupuncture.com/acupuncture/.

22 http://www.iattm.net/uk/faculties/ttm-intro.htm.

23 https://en.wikipedia.org/wiki/Traditional_Tibetan_medicine.

24 L. Lasagna, F. Mosteller, J. M. Von Felsinger, H. K. Beecher, "A Study of the Placebo Response," *American Journal of Medicine* 16, no. 6 (June 1954): 770–9.

25 https://www.cdc.gov/nchs/data/nhsr/nhsr018.pdf.

26 https://nccih.nih.gov/research/results/spotlight/insurance-coverage-patterns.

2. Chiropractic

1 https://en.wikipedia.org/wiki/Chiropractic.

2 D. D. Palmer's letter in 1911 to P. W. Johnson in the archives of the David D. Palmer Health Sciences Library in Davenport, Iowa, http://chiro.org/Plus/History/Persons/PalmerDD/PalmerDD's_Religion-of-Chiro.pdf.

3 Ibid., 39–40.

4 https://sciencebasedmedicine.org/chiropractic-a-brief-overview-part-i/.

5 http://www.spine-health.com/treatment/chiropractic/subluxation-and-chiropractic.

6 *Mosby's Medical Dictionary*, version 1.5 (Mosby-Year Book Inc., 1995).

7 https://en.wikipedia.org/wiki/Vertebral_subluxation.

8 Joseph C. Keating Jr., corresponding authors: Keith H. Charlton, Jaroslaw P. Grod, Stephen M. Perle, David Sikorski, and James F. Winterstein, "Subluxation:

Dogma or Science," Chiropr Osteopat, 13 (2005): 17, https://www.ncbi.nlm.nih.gov/pmc/articles/PMC1208927/.

9 Robin Brett Parnes, MS, MPH, "Chiropractic Treatment: What You Should Know," Beth Israel Deaconess Medical Center.

10 Ian D. Coulter, PhD, et al., "Patients Using Chiropractors in North America: Who Are They and Why Are They in Chiropractic Care?" *Spine* 27, no. 3 (February 1, 2002): 291–298, https://datausa.io/profile/soc/291011/.

11 https://datausa.io/profile/soc/291011/.

12 Matthew A. Davis, Brenda E. Sirovich, and William B. Weeks, "Utilization and Expenditures on Chiropractic Care in the United States from 1997 to 2006," *Health Services Research* 45, no. 3 (June 2010): 748–761, https://www.ncbi.nlm.nih.gov/pmc/articles/PMC2875758/.

13 https://www.chirobase.org/01General/modde.html.

14 Evans, Hoemeker, Casey, "Legal Memorandum: Scope of Chiropractic Diagnosis," *ACA Journal of Chiropractic* (March 1972).

15 https://www.medicalmalpracticelawyers.com/blog/chiropractor-malpractice-statistics/.

16 http://www.quackwatch.org/01QuackeryRelatedTopics/chirostroke.html.

17 Richard A. Cooper and Heather J. McKee, "Chiropractic in the United States: Trends and Issue," *Milbank Q.* 81, no. 1 (March 2003): 107–138.

18 https://report.nih.gov/NIHfactsheets/ViewFactSheet.aspx?csid=85.

19 R. L. Nahin, P. M. Barnes, B. J. Stussman, "Expenditures on Complementary Health Approaches: United States, 2012," National Health Statistics Reports no. 95 (Hyattsville, Maryland: National Center for Health Statistics, 2016).

20 Ibid., 3.

21 http://directory.fclb.org/Statistics/RatioofLicensestoPopulation,US/RatioUS2013-2015.aspx.

22 https://www.cdc.gov/nchs/data/nhsr/nhsr018.pdf.

3. Chinese "Medicine"

1 R. L. Nahin, P. M. Barnes, B. J. Stussman, "Expenditures on Complementary Health Approaches: United States, 2012," National Health Statistics Reports no. 95 (Hyattsville, Maryland: National Center for Health Statistics, 2016), 10.

2 Li Shih-chen, F. Porter Smith and G. A. Stuart, translator and researcher, *Chinese Medicinal Herbs* (Mineola, New York: Dover Publications, 1973).

3 Nahin et al. (US Department of Health and Human Services), ibid., 1.

4 http://www.accessmedicinecom/popup.aspx?alD=9106843&print=yes.

5 Harrison's Principles of Internal Medicine, 18e, www.acceeessmedicine.com/content.aspx?alD=9106846.

6 http://www.wiley.com/WileyCDA/Brand/id-6.html?category=For+Working.

7 http://onlinelibrary.wiley.com/doi/10.1002/14651858.CD010577.pub2/full.

8 https://nccih.nih.gov/.

[9] Ian Johnson, "Nobel Renews Debate on Chinese Medicine," *New York Times*, October 11, 2015.

[10] Science and Technology, "Wisdom, Ancient and Modern," *The Economist*, October 10, 2015.

[11] R. Barker Bausell, *Snake Oil Science* (New York: Oxford University Press, 2007).

[12] Robert L. Park, *Voodoo Science: The Road from Foolishness to Fraud* (New York: Oxford, 2000), 64–67.

[13] http://www.nbcnews.com/id/31190909/ns/heallth-lternative_medicine/t/billlion-spent-on-alternative-cures-found/#.VXNtDixViko.

[14] https://www.google.com/search?rlz=1C1LOQA_enUS627US655&q=What+is+the+budget+for+the+National+Cancer+Institute%3F&oq.

[15] https://nccih.nih.gov/research/statistics/NHIS/2012/cost.

4. Vitamins and Supplements

[1] http://medical-dictionary.thefreedictionary.com/vitamins.

[2] Ibid.

[3] Margolis, Simeon, ed., "Health After 50," Johns Hopkins Health Alerts.com, February 2012.

[4] Ibid., 2.

[5] Paul A. Offit, "Don't Take Your Vitamins," *New York Times*, June 9, 2013.

[6] Paul A. Offit, *Do You Believe in Magic? The Sense and Nonsense of Alternative Medicine* (New York: Harper Collins, 2013).

[7] https://en.wikipedia.org/wiki/Federal_Food,_Drug,_and_Cosmetic_Act.

[8] Swann, John P. "History o Efforts to Regulate Dietary Supplements in the USA". On line library, Wiley.com/doi/full/10.1002/dta.1919 (First published 23 Nov 2015.)

[9] https://www.google.cm/search?q=FDA+defines+supplements&rlz=C1SQJL_enUS818US818&pq=FDA+defines+supplements&aqs=-chrome.69i57j0l2.14454j1j8&sourceid=chrome&ie=UTF-8.

[10] https://www.fda.gov/food/dietarysupplements/.

[11] https://en.wikipedia.org/wiki/Dietary_Supplement_Health_and_Education_Act_of_1994.

[12] Shirley S. Wang, "Medical Foods and Supplements," *Wall Street Journal*, July 24, 2012.

[13] Alison Young, "GNC Accused of Selling Spiked Products," *USA Today*, October 23, 2015.

[14] Karen Weintraub, "Untested Supplements Chemical Found," *USA Today*, April 7 2015, 3B.

[15] http://onlinelibrary.wiley.com/doi/10.1002/dta.1741/abstract.

[16] Anahad O'Connor, "Spike in Harm to Liver Is Tied to Dietary Aids," *New York Times*, December 22, 2013.

17 N. Muscavage, "NY Authorities Target Arthritis Supplement," *Democrat and Chronicle*, September 11 2015.

18 "Herbal Supplements without Herbs," *The New York Times*, February 7, 2015.

19 https://en.wikipedia.org/wiki/DNA_barcoding#Identifying_flowering_plants.

20 https://www.ncbi.lnlm.nig.gov/pmc/articles/PMC3851815/.

21 Anahad O'Connor, "Herbal Supplements Are Often Not What They Seem," *The New York Times*, November 3, 2013.

22 http://www.blacklistednews.com/Americans_Spend_$30_Billion_a_Year_on_Dietary_Supplements_that_Do_Little,_Says_Study/55299/0/38/38/Y/M.html.

23 http://www.healthline.com/health-news/americans-spend-billions-on-vitamins-and-herbs-that-dont-work-031915#1.

24 "Enough Is Enough: Stop Wasting Money on Vitamin and Mineral Supplements," *Annals of Internal Medicine* 159, no. 12: 850–851.

25 http://www.foxnews.com/story/2009/06/10/many-vitamins-supplements-made-by-big-pharmaceutical-companies.html.

26 http://investsnips.com/list-of-publicly-traded-nutritional-supplement-companies/.

27 http://www.econotimes.com/Dietary-Supplements-Market-size-expected-to-reach-2203-Billion-in-2022-Zion-Market-Research-660892.

28 http://www.nutraingredients-usa.com/Markets/NBJ-The-US-supplement-industry-is-37-billion-not-12-billion.

29 W. Sears and J. Sears, *The Omega-3 Effect* (New York: Little, Brown and Co., 2012).

30 http://www.todaysdietitian.com/newarchives/030314p52.shtml.

31 http://jamanetwork.com/journals/jama/article-abstract/1357266.

32 George J. Fodor, Eftyhia Helis, Narges Yazdekhasti, Branislav Vohnout, "'Fishing' for the Origins of the 'Eskimos and Heart Disease' Story. Facts or Wishful Thinking? A Review," *Canadian Journal of Cardiology* (April 2012).

33 http://ottawa.ctnews.ca/fish-oil-study-is-fishy-ottawa-cardiologist-says-1.1814923.

34 JoAnn E. Manson et al., "Marine n-3 Fatty Acids and Prevention of Cardiovascular Disease and Cancer," *New England Journal of Medicine* 9, no. 380 (January 2019): 23–32, https://www.vitalstudy.org/findings.html.

35 JoAnn E. Manson et al., "Vitamin D Supplements and Prevention of Cancer and Cardiovascular Disease," *New England Journal of Medicine* 9, no. 380 (January 2019): 33–44.

36 Simeon Margolis, ed., "Health After 50," Johns Hopkins Health Alerts.com, summer 2013.

37 Lisa Sanders, "Diagnosis," *New York Times*, May 14, 2017, 20–11.

38 https://www.google.com/search?q=what+do+americans+spend+on+vitamins+and+suplements%3F&rlz=1C1LOQA_enUS627US655&oq=what+do+American.

[39] https://www.cdc.gov/nchs/data/nhsr/nhsr095.pdf.

[40] https://www.google.com/search?q=How+much+is+spent+on+vitamins+and+supplemenets+in+the+US%3F&rlz=1C1LOQA_enUS627US655&oq=How+mu.

5. Homeopathy

[1] Roy Porter, ed., *The Cambridge Illustrated History of Medicine* (Cambridge: Cambridge University Press, 1996), 114.

[2] R. Barker Bausell, *Snake Oil Science: The Truth about Complementary and Alternative Medicine* (Oxford University Press, 2007).

[3] E. H. Chapman, "Homeopathy," in W. B. Jonas and J. S. Levin, eds., *Essentials of Complementary and Alternative Medicine* (New York: Lippincott Williams and Wilkins, 1999), 472–89.

[4] http://www.homeowatch.org/reg/fda_hearing_2015/comment.html.

[5] http://www.hylands.com/news/regulation.php.

[6] Ibid.

[7] Robert L. Park, *Voodoo Science: The Road from Foolishness to Fraud* (New York: Oxford University Press, 2000), 53.

[8] http://drexel.edu/medicine/about/history/.

[9] http://www.naturalhealers.com/alternative-medicine/homeopathy-training/.

[10] https://achs.edu/program/certificate-homeopathy-consulting-online-chc.

[11] W. Sampson, P. R. Gross, N. Levitt, M. W. Lewis, eds., *The Flight from Science and Reason* (New York: New York Academy of Sciences, 1996), 188–97.

[12] S. Barrett, "'Alternative' Nutrition Therapies," in *Modern Nutrition in Health and Disease*, 9th ed. (Williams & Wilkins).

[13] https://www.vox.com/2015/3/11/8190427/homeopathy.

[14] Richard L. Nahin et al., "Costs of Complementary and Alternative Medicine (CAM) and Frequency of Visits to CAM Practitioners: United States, 2007," National Health Statistics Reports, CDC, no. 18, July 30, 2009.

[15] http://www.slate.com/articles/health_and_science/medical_examiner/2016/11/the_ftc_s_new_homeopathic_medicine_rules_will_backfire.html.

6. Naturopathy

[1] https://en.wikipedia.org/wiki/Naturopathy.

[2] Tom Jagtenberg, Sue Evans, Airdre Grant, Ian Howden, et al., "Evidence-Based Medicine and Naturopathy," *Journal of Alternative and Complementary Medicine* (April 2006), 12.

[3] Whorton, James C. "Nature Cures: The History of Alternative Medicine in America."

[4] http://www.umm.edu/health/medical/altmed/treatment/naturopathy.

[5] https://www.washingtonpost.com/archive/local/2003/09/29/plan-could-cost-doctors-their-dc-credentials/06acea77-db38-42cd-99c5-21375ab2ef0b/.

6   https://doh.dc.gov/node/148942.
7   http://realizehealth.org/about-naturopathic-medicine/a-visit-to-a-naturopath-ic-doctor/treatment-cost/.
8   https://www.insightbenefits.com/research/Hidden_Costs_of_US_Health_Care_for_Consumers_032111_by_Deloitt.pdf.
9   http://www.fnmra.org/news/4700871.
10 https://www.academia.edu/714356/Safer_Care_National_Registration_of_Naturopaths_ and_Western_Herbalists
11 Matthew A. Davis and William B. Weeks, "Concentration of Out-of-Pocket Expenditures on Complementary and Alternative Medicine in the United States," *Alternative Therapies* 18, no. 5 (September/October 2012): 41.

7. Osteopathic Medicine

1   http://www.aacom.org/become-a-doctor/about-om/history.
2   Ibid.
3   Ibid.
4   Ward Robert, *Foundations for Osteopathic Medicine: The Research Status of Somatic Dysfunction*, 2nd ed. (Philadelphia: Lippincott Williams & Wilkins, 2002), 1188–1193, https://en.wikipedia.org/wiki/Osteopathic_medicine_in_the_United_States#Criticism_and_internal_debate.
5   N. Gevitz, "Researched and Demonstrated: Inquiry and Infrastructure at Osteopathic Institutions," *The Journal of the American Osteopathic Association* 101, no. 3 (March 2001): 174–179.
6   C. T. Meyer, A. Price, "Osteopathic Medicine: A Call for Reform," *The Journal of the American Osteopathic Association* 93, no. 4 (April 1, 1993): 473–485.
7   Howell, J.D. "The Paradox of Osteopathy." *New England Journal of Medicine* 4 Nov. 1999: 1415-1468.

8. Spiritual Healing

1   http://dictionary.cambridge.org/us/.
2   R. Barker Bausell, *Snake Oil Science: The Truth about Complementary and Alternative Medicine* (New York: Oxford University Press, 2007), 16.
3   D. J. Benor, "Spiritual Healing," in W. B. Jones and J. S. Levin, eds., *Essentials of Complementary and Alternative Medicine* (New York: Lippincott Williams and Wilkins, 1999), 369–92.
4   Seymour I Schwartz and Christopher Hoolihan, *Holystic Medicine, The Patron Saints of Medicine* (St. Louis: Quality Medical Publishing, 2012), xxv.
5   Ibid.
6   Ibid.
7   Ibid.
8   https://www.biblegateway.com/passage/?search=Matthew+8:5-13.
9   Ira M. Lapidus, *A History of Islamic Societies* (New York: Cambridge University Press, 1988), 24.

10 Ibid., 28.

11 Ibid., 28.

12 https://en.wikipedia.org/wiki/Islamic_view_of_miracles.

13 http://www.islam-usa.com/index.php?option=com_content&view=article&id=183:prayers-and-healing&catid=68:health%E2%80%94medicine&Itemid=137.

14 Albert Hourani, *A History of the Arab Peoples* (Cambridge, Massachusetts: Harvard Press, 1991), 155–157.

15 http://www.reformjudaism.org/practice/prayers-blessings/mi-shebeirach-prayer-healing.

16 http://www.reformjudaism.org/practice/prayers-blessings/mi-shebeirach-prayer-healing, http://www.beliefnet.com/faiths/hinduism/articles/mantras-for-peace-healing-and-ebkughtenment.aspx.

17 http://www.chabad.org/library/article_cdo/aid/2903187/jewish/Mi-Sheberach.htm.

18 http://www.worldhealingprayers.com/5.html.

19 http://www.beliefnet.com/faiths/hinduism/articles/mantras-for-peace-healing-and-enlightenment.aspx.

20 http://www.bbc.co.uk/religion/religions/buddhism/and-enlightenment.aspx.

21 http://www.dharma-haven.org/tibetan/meditation.htm#Mantra.

22 Ibid.

23 Ibid.

24 Paul A. Offit, *Do You Believe in Magic? The Sense and Nonsense of Alternative Medicine* (New York: Harper Collins, 2013), 97.

25 https://www.ncbi.nlm.nih.gov/pmc/?term=Spiritual+healing.

26 Roy Porter, ed., *The Cambridge Illustrated History of Medicine* (Cambridge: Cambridge University Press, 1996), 115.

27 http://www.christianscience.com/what-is-christian-science/mary-baker-eddy.

28 https://www2.deloitte.com/content/dam/Deloitte/us/Documents/life-sciences-health-care/us-lchs-dig-deep-hidden-costs-112414.pdf.

29 R. Barker Bausell, *Snake Oil Science: The Truth about Complementary and Alternative Medicine* (New York: Oxford Press, 2007), 5.

30 https://www.ncbi.nlm.nih.gov/pmc/?term=cost+of+cam.

9. Energy Healing-Reiki

1 https://en.wikipedia.org/wiki/Energy_medicine.

2 https://www.youtube.com/watch?v=HZpFm85UYIo.

3 Ibid., ref. 1.

4 Paul A. Offit, *Do You Believe in Magic? The Sense and Nonsense of Alternative Medicine* (New York: Harper Collins, 2013), 28.

5 https://link.springer.com/article/10.1007%2FBF03040322.

6 https://en.wikipedia.org/wiki/Energy_medicine.

7 https://sciencebasedmedicine.org/edzard-ernst-does-it-again/.

8   https://www.google.com/search?rlz=1C1LOQA_enUS627US655&bi-w=1257&bih=610&q=Reiki+salaries&oq=Reiki+salaries&gs_l=psy-ab.3.0i22i30k1l2.

9   R. Barker Bausell, *Snake Oil Science: The Truth about Complementary and Alternative Medicine* (New York: Oxford Press, 2007), 5.

10 https://iarp.org/reiki-for-horses-the-benefits-of-equine-reiki/.

11 https://iarp.org/reiki-and-medicine/.

10. Yoga

1   Committee on the Use of Complementary and Alternative Medicine by the American Public, *Complementary and Alternative Medicine in the United States* (Washington, DC: National Academies Press), 19.

2   Ibid., 283.

3   https://nccih.nih.gov/health/yoga/introduction.htm

4   https://www.yogaalliance.org/Portals/0/2016%20Yoga%20in%20America%20Study%20RESULTS.pdf.

5   https://www.yogaalliance.org/.../2016%20Yoga%20in%20America%20Study%20RESU.

6   Timothy McCall, *Yoga as Medicine* (New York: Bantam, 2007), 5.

7   https://www.ncbi.nlm.nih.gov/pubmed?term="Yoga"%5BMesh%5D%20AND%20"humans"[MeSH%20Terms]%20AND%20English[lang]%20AND%20Randomized%20C.

8   B. L. Tracy, C. E. Hart, "Bikram Yoga Training and Physical Fitness in Healthy Young Adults," *Journal of Strength and Conditioning Research* 3 (March 27, 2013): 822–30, doi: 10.1519/JSC.0b013e31825c340f, PMID: 22592178.

9   B. Taspinar, U. B. Aslan, B. Agbuga, F. Taspinar, "A Comparison of the Effects of Hatha Yoga and Resistance Exercise on Mental Health and Well-Being in Sedentary Adults: A Pilot Study," Complementary Therapies in Medicine 3 (June 22, 2014): 433–40, doi: 10.1016/j.ctim.2014.03.007.

10 McCall, ibid., 340.

11 C. Kusnick, G. Kraftsow, M. Hilliker, "Building Bridges for Yoga Therapy Research: The Aetna, Inc., Mind-Body Pilot Study on Chronic and High Stress," *International Journal of Yoga Therapy* 22 (2012): 91–91.

12 M. C. McCall, A. Ward, N. W. Roberts, C.Heneghan, *Evidence-Based Complementary Alternative Medicine* (2013), doi: 10.1155/2013/945895. https://www.ncbi.nlm.nih.gov/pmc/articles/PMC3670548/.

13 http://www.prnewswire.com/news-releases/2016-yoga-in-america-study-conducted-by-yoga-journal-and-yoga-alliance-reveals-growth-and-benefits-of-the-practice-300203418.html.

11. Chelation Therapy

1   http://www.webmd.com/balance/tc/chelation-therapy-topic-overview#1.

2   https://en.wikipedia.org/wiki/Chelation_therapy.

3   Ibid.

4   J. J. Chisolm Jr., "Safety and Efficacy of Meso-2, 3-Dimercaptosuccinic Acid (DMSA) in Children with Elevated Blood Lead Concentrations," *Journal of Toxicology: Clinical Toxicology* 38, no. 4 (2000): 365–75, PMID 10930052.

5   https://nccih.nih.gov/health/chelation/TACT-questions.

6   https://www.health.harvard.edu/blog/chelation-therapy-offers-small-if-any-benefit-for-heart-disease-201303266030.

7   http://www.sciencedirect.com/science/article/pii/S0735109797004439.

8   Merril L. Knudtson, D. George Wyse, P. Diane Galbraith et al., Rollin Brant, Kathy Hildebrand, Diana Paterson, Deborah Richardson, Connie Burkart, Ellen Burgess, "Program to Assess Alternative Treatment Strategies to Achieve Cardiac Health (PATCH) Investigators," *JAMA* 287, no. 4 (2002): 481–486, doi:10.1001/jama.287.4.481.

9   https://journals.lww.com/jaapa/Citation/2005/01000/Chelation_therapy_for_heart_disease.10.aspx.

12. Massage

1   Committee of the Use of Complementary and Alternative Medicine, *Complementary and Alternative Medicine in the United States* (Washington, DC, 2005), 288.

2   https://www.amtamassage.org/infocenter/economic_industry-fact-sheet.html.

3   R Barker. Bausell, *Snake Oil Science: The Truth about Complementary and Alternative Medicine* (Oxford University Press, 2007), 180.

4   Ibid., 167–174.

5   https://www.abmp.com/practitioners/state-requirements.

6   https://www.google.com/search?q=How+much+is+tuition+at+massage+-schools%3F&rlz=1C1LOQA_enUS627US655&oq=How+much+is+tu-ition+at+ma.

7   https://nccih.nih.gov/research/results/spotlight/five-painful-conditions.

8   http://www.cochrane.org/CD001929/BACK_massage-low-back-pain.

9   https://www.amtamassage.org/infocenter/economic_industry-fact-sheet.html.

13. Biofeedback Therapy

1   http://www.merckmanuals.com/home/brain,-spinal-cord,-and-nerve-disorders/biology-of-the-nervous-system/nerves#v733549.

2   https://en.wikipedia.org/wiki/Biofeedback.

3   http://www.mayoclinic.org/tests-procedures/biofeedback/home/ovc-20169724?p=1.

4   Michael G. McKee, "Biofeedback: An Overview in the Context of Heart-Brain Medicine," *Cleveland Clinic Journal of Medicine* 75, no. 2 (March 2008): S3 1–34.

5   https://www.ncbi.nlm.nih.gov/pmc/articles/PMC29394554/.

[6] R. Barker Bausell, *Snake Oil Science: The Truth about Complementary and Alternative Medicine* (Oxford University Press, 2007), 18.

[7] https://www.google.com/search?q=pavlov%27s+dog&rlz=1C1LOQA_enU-S627US655&oq=Pav%3Bov&aqs=chrome.5.69i57j0l5.8712j0j8&sourceid=-chrome&ie=UTF-8.

[8] *Mental Health in Family Medicine* 7, no. 2 (June 2010): 85–91.

Table 1

Efficacy Ratings for Biofeedback Training on Various Medical Conditions

Level 5—Efficacious and specific

Level 2—Possibly efficacious

Urinary incontinence (females)

Asthma

Autism

Level 4—Efficacious

Bell's palsy

Anxiety

Cerebral palsy

Attention deficit hyperactivity disorder

Chronic obstructive pulmonary disease

Chronic pain

Coronary artery disease

Constipation (adult)

Cystic fibrosis

Epilepsy

Depressive disorders

Headache (adult)

Erectile dysfunction

Hypertension

Fibromyalgia / chronic fatigue syndrome

Motion sickness

Hand dystonia

Raynaud's disease

Irritable bowel syndrome

Temporomandibular disorder

Post-traumatic stress disorder

Repetitive strain injury

Level 3—Probably efficacious

Respiratory failure: mechanical ventilation

Alcoholism/substance abuse

Stroke

Arthritis

Tinnitus

Diabetes mellitus

Urinary incontinence (children)
Fecal incontinence
Headache (pediatric)
Level 1—Not empirically supported
Insomnia
Eating disorders
Traumatic brain injury
Immune function
Urinary incontinence (males)
Spinal cord injury
Vulvar vestibulitis
Syncope

[9] Volume 4 (September 2017), 673, www.thelancet.com/psychiatry.

[10] Volume 4 (September 2017), 650, www.thelancet.com/psychiatry.

[11] Matthew A. Davis and William B. Weeks, "Concentration of Out-of-Pocket Expenditures on Complementary and Alternative Medicine in the United States," *Alternative Therapies* 18, no. 5 (September/October 2012): 41.

14. Magnetic Therapy

[1] Institute of Medicine, *Complementary and Alternatives Medicine in the United States* (New York: National Academies Press, 2005), 288.

[2] https://en.wikipedia.org/wiki/Magnet_therapy.

[3] L. Finegold, B. L. Flamm, "Magnet Therapy," *The BMJ* 332, no. 7532 (January 2006): 4.

[4] "Magnets," CDRH Consumer Information, Food and Drug Administration, 2000-03-01.

[5] Max H. Pittler, Elizabeth M. Brown, and Edzard Ernst, "Static Magnets for Reducing Pain: Systematic Review and Meta-Analysis of Randomized Trials," *Canadian Medical Association Journal* 177, no. 7 (September 25, 2007): 736–742, https://www.ncbi.nlm.nih.gov/pmc/articles/PMC1976658/.

[6] James Randi, Edzard Ernst, ed., "Healing, Hype, or Harm? A Critical Analysis of Complementary or Alternative Medicine," *An Amateur's View of CAM Science* (Charlottesville, Virginia: Societas Imprint Academic, 2008), 89–96.

[7] https://lee-phillips.org/null/phd.html.

[8] https://nccih.nih.gov/health/magnet/magnetsforpain.htm.

[9] https://magneticosleep.com/about-magnetism/origins-of-magnetism/.

[10] https://magneticosleep.com/about-magnetism/detoxification/.

[11] https://www.quora.com/Why-isnt-blood-attracted-to-a-magnet-since-it-contains-iron.

[12] https://en.wikipedia.org/wiki/Hemoglobin#Iron.27s_oxidation_state_in_oxyhemoglobin.

[13] https://www.csicop.org/si/show/magnet_therapy_a_billion-dollar_boondoggle.

15. Aromatherapy

[1] Committee of the Use of Complementary and Alternative Medicine, "Complementary and Alternative Medicine in the United States" (Washington, DC, 2005), 284.

[2] https://nccih.nih.gov/research/statistics/2007/camsurvey_fs1.htm.

[3] Rachel Monroe, "Something in the Air—Essential Oils Have Become Big Business—but Are They Medicine or Marketing?" *The New Yorker*, October 9, 2017, 32–37.

[4] http://www.aromatherapy.com/.

[5] http://www.cochrane.org/CD003150/DEMENTIA_aromatherapy-for-promotion-of-relaxation-and-sleep-relief-of-pain-and-reduction-of-depressive-symptoms-in-dementia.

[6] https://www.ncbi.nlm.nih.gov/pmc/articles/PMC1313734/.

[7] https://www.takingcharge.csh.umn.edu/explore-healing-practices/aromatherapy/what-does-research-say-about-essential-oils.

[8] https://www.ncbi.nlm.nih.gov/pubmed/25584799.

[9] Rachel Monroe, "Something in the Air," 32–37.

[10] https://bmcresnotes.biomedcentral.com/articles/10.1186/s13104-016-2371-1.

[11] Government Printing Office (US), https://www.gpo.gov/fdsys/pkg/CHRG-111shrg47852/html/CHRG-111shrg47852.htm.

[12] Rachel Monroe, "Something in the Air," 34.

[13] https://www.prnewswire.com/news-releases/essential-oil-market-size-to-reach-1167-billion-by-2022-grand-view-research-inc-531216151.html.

16. Hydrotherapy

[1] http://www.greekmedicine.net/therapies/The_Water_Cure.html.

[2] Cochrane Database of Systematic Review 4 (April 11, 2015), doi: 10.1002/14651858.CD000518.pub2, https://www.ncbi.nlm.nih.gov/pubmed/25862243.

[3] https://www.google.com/search?q=caldera+spas&rlz=1C1LOQA_enUS627US655&oq=Cdaldera+Spa&aqs=chrome.1.69i57j0l5.10514j0j8&sourceid=chrome&ie=UTF-8.

[4] https://academic.oup.com/rheumatology/article/45/7/880/1788686.

17. Iridology

[1] https://en.wikipedia.org/wiki/Iridology.

[2] Rama Chellappa, Tistarelli Massimo, Stan Z. Li, eds., *Handbook of Remote Biometrics: For Surveillance and Security* (New York: Springer, 2009), 27.

[3] Anil K. Jain and Ruud Bolle and Charath Pankanti, eds., *Biometrics: Personal Identification in Networked Society* (New York: Springer, 1996), 117.

[4] https://www.youtube.com/watch?v=k6jy-VGpUE8.

[5] https://www.youtube.com/watch?v=DDAo3o5FCfQ&t=7s.

[6] http://www.iriscope.org/.

7 http://www.iriscope.org/iridology-machine.htm.

8 https://www.iridologyassn.org/info/.

9 www. Findiridologist.com.

10 http://www.alternativesforhealing.com/business-directory/wpbdp_category/iridology-practitioners/.

11 https://www.ncbi.nlm.nih.gov/pubmed/10636425.

18. Reflexology

1 https://en.wikipedia.org/wiki/Reflexology.

2 Committee of the Use of Complementary and Alternative Medicine, "Complementary and Alternative Medicine in the United States" (Washington, DC, 2005), 290.

3 A. R. White et al., "A Blinded Investigation into the Accuracy of Reflexology Charts," *Complementary Therapies of Medicine* 8 (2000): 166–72.

4 https://www.ncbi.nlm.nih.gov/pubmed/21111551.

5 http://reflexology-usa.org/.

6 https://arcb.net/.

7 https://www.headtofeet.co.uk/content/treatments_chart/.

8 https://www.ocr.edu/.

9 http://www.reflexology-usa.net/facts.htm.

10 http://www.foot-reflexologist.com/LAWS_1.html.

11 https://www.naturalhealers.com/massage-therapy/reflexology-career/.

12 http://study.com/reflexology_schools.html.

19. Tai Chi

1 http://www.108taichimoves.com/history.html.

2 https://web.stanford.edu/group/taichi_wushu/taichi.history.html.

3 www.rtccc.com.

4 Ibid.

5 https://nccih.nih.gov/.

6 http://www.cochrane.org/CD004849/MUSKEL_tai-chi-for-rheumatoid-arthritis.

7 https://www.jscimedcentral.com/CommunityMedicine/communitymedicine-1-1005.pdf.

8 https://www.statista.com/statistics/191622/participants-in-tai-chi-in-the-us-since-2008/.

20. Hydrotherapy of the Colon

1 https://web.archive.org/web/20150424180208/http://www.cancer.org/Treatment/TreatmentsandSideEffects/ComplementaryandAlternativeMedicine/ManualHealingandPhysicalTouch/colon-therapy.

2 https://nccih.nih.gov/health/detoxes-cleanses.

3   https://en.wikipedia.org/wiki/Detoxification_(alternative_medicine).

4   http://onlinelibrary.wiley.com/doi/10.1111/jhn.12286/abstract.

5   https://web.archive.org/web/20130826124704/http://www.senseaboutscience.org/pages/debunking-detox.html.

6   https://www.bda.uk.com/foodfacts/detoxdiets.pdf.

7   https://www.huffingtonpost.com/2014/10/30/colon-cleansing_n_6077378.html.

8   http://iai.asm.org/content/76/8/3360.full.pdf.

9   Ibid.

10 https://www.mayoclinic.org/healthy-lifestyle/consumer-health/expert-answers/colon-cleansing/faq-20058435.

11 https://nccih.nih.gov/.

12 https://www.health.harvard.edu/staying-healthy/the-dubious-practice-of-detox.

13 Ibid.

14 https://www.ncbi.nlm.nih.gov/pubmed/15831718.

15 L. Drago, M. Toscano, R. DeGrandi, V. Casini, F. Pace, "Persisting Changes of Intestinal Microbiota after Bowel Lavage and Colonoscopy," *European Journal of Gastroenterology & Hepatology* 28, no. 5 (May 2016): 532–7.

16 "The Effects of Bowel Preparation on Microbiota-Related Metrics Differ in Health and in Inflammatory Bowel Disease and for the Mucosal and Luminal Microbiota Compartments," *Clinical and Translational Gastroenterology* 11, no. 7 (February 2016): e143.

17 http://www.mdedge.com/sites/default/files/Document/September-2017/6008JFP_Article1.pdf.

18 https://www.leaf.tv/articles/how-much-does-colonic-hydrotherapy-cost/.

19 http://www.seniorcitizensguide.com/articles/southjersey/colon-hydrotherapy.htm.

20 http://www.alivecolonhydrotherapy.com/shop/#!/30-Day-Detox-&-Weight-Loss-Package-vanilla/p/46572497/category=12073306.

21. Weight Loss Fraud

1   https://money.usnews.com/money/personal-finance/articles/2013/01/02/the-heavy-price-of-losing-weight.

2   https://www.webwire.com/ViewPressRel.asp?aId=209054.

3   https://www.cdc.gov/nchs/data/databriefs/db219.pdf.

4   http://www.cnn.com/2017/10/13/health/adult-obesity-increase-study/index.html.

5   Ibid.

6   http://journals.sagepub.com/doi/abs/10.4278/0890-1171-13.2.120.

7   http://www.healthycommunitieshealthyfuture.org/learn-the-facts/economic-costs-of-obesity/.

[8] https://www.bls.gov/opub/btn/volume-6/cost-of-care.htm.

[9] https://www.medicinenet.com/script/main/art.asp?articlekey=11760.

[10] D. W. Haslam, W. P. James, *Lancet* 1, no. 366 (October 2005): 1197–209, https://www.ncbi.nlm.nih.gov/pubmed/16198769.

[11] https://www.urmc.rochester.edu/encyclopedia/content.aspx?contenttypeid=56&contentid=DM300.

[12] http://www.health24.com/Medical/Meds-and-you/Using-medicines/Meds-that-cause-extreme-weight-loss-20120721.

[13] https://www.ncbi.nlm.nih.gov/pmc/articles/PMC2773866/.

[14] http://www.upmc.com/patients-visitors/education/nutrition/pages/fad-diets.aspx.

[15] http://www.eatright.org/resource/health/weight-loss/fad-diets/staying-away-from-fad-diets.

[16] http://www.health.com/health/gallery/0,20833428,00.html#dubious-diets-1.

[17] https://sciencebasedmedicine.org/isagenix-study-is-not-convincing/.

[18] http://www.refinery29.com/minnesota-starvation-experiment.

[19] Chin Jou, "The Biology of Genetics of Obesity—A Century of Inquiries," *The New England Journal of Medicine* 370, no. 20 (2014): 1874.

[20] https://www.wired.com/2004/12/biosphere/.

[21] https://www.ncbi.nlm.nih.gov/pubmed/12023257.

[22] http://www.calculator.net/ideal-weight-calculator.html.

[23] http://discovermagazine.com/2013/june/01-lying-to-yourself-helps-you-lie-to-others.

[24] https://www.ncbi.nlm.nih.gov/pmc/articles/PMC3234679/.

[25] http://www.newsweek.com/why-chemicals-called-obesogens-may-make-you-fat-79445.

[26] https://en.wikipedia.org/wiki/Obesogen.

22. Cupping Therapy

[1] https://nccih.nih.gov/.

[2] https://nccih.nih.gov/news/cupping.

[3] H. Cao, X. Li, J. Liu, "An Updated Review of the Efficacy of Cupping Therapy," *PLOS One* 7, no. 2 (2012): e31793, doi: 10.1371/journal.pone.0031793.

[4] J. I. Kim, M. S. Lee, D. H. Lee, K. Boddy, E. Ernst, "Cupping for Treating Pain: A Systematic Review," *Evidence-Based Complementary and Alternative Medicine* (2011), doi: 10.1093/ecam/nep035.

[5] https://www.ncbi.nlm.nih.gov/pubmed/28494847.

[6] http://cuppingforlife.blogspot.com/2011/01/detox-cupping-treatment-how-it-works.html.

[7] http://www.kenmorecentreforhealth.com.au/wp-content/uploads/2010/11/EBP_WFCMS_2006_Janz.pdf.

[8] https://www.newstatesman.com/politics/sport/2016/08/science-cupping-why-olympic-swimmer-michael-phelps-covered-purple-blotches.

9 https://sciencebasedmedicine.org/cupping-olympic-pseudoscience/.

10 https://www.cuppingtherapy.org/.

23. Low "T"

1 http://www.newsobserver.com/news/local/counties/orange-county/article139921073.html.

2 https://www.prnewswire.com/news-releases/testosterone-lawsuit-news-safety-concerns-slow-sales-of-androgel-other-testosterone-replacement-medications-bernstein-liebhard-llp-reports-282284001.html.

3 S. Basaira and A. S. Dobs, "Risks versus Benefits of Testosterone Therapy in Elderly Men," *Drugs and Aging* 2 (August 15, 1999): 131–142.

4 Peter Conrad, "The Medicalization of Society" (Baltimore: Johns Hopkins University Press, 2007), 4–5.

5 Ibid., Basaira and Dobs.

6 R. C. Rabin, "Mixed Results for Testosterone," *New York Times*, March 28, 2017, D4.

7 http://nytimes.com/2013/11/24/business/selling-that-new-man-feeling.html?ref=hea.

8 http://www.nytimes.com/2013/10/16/us/a-push-to-sell-testosterone-gels-troubles-doctors.

9 L. Shaffer, "Testosterone," Discovermagazine.com, June 2015.

10 http://www.sciencedirect.com/science/article/pii/S0039128X14001706.

11 https://jamanetwork.com/journals/jamainternalmedicine/article-abstract/2604138?redirect=true.

12 https://www.jsm.jsexmed.org/article/S1743-6095(15)30261-7/pdf.

13 D. J. Handelsman, "Irrational Exuberance in Testosterone Prescribing: When Will the Bubble Burst?" *Med Care* no. 53 (2015): 743–5.

14 https://www.statista.com/statistics/320301/predicted-annual-testosterone-drug-revenues-in-the-us/.

24. Target—the Brain

1 https://www.google.com/search?q=incidence+of+alzheimer%27s+disease&rlz=1C1LOQA_enUS627US655&oq=Incidences+of+Alzheimers&aqs=.

2 https://www.alz.org/dementia/downloads/topicsheet_treatments.pdf.

3 https://www.drugs.com/condition/alzheimer-s-disease.html.

4 https://www.mayoclinic.org/diseases-conditions/alzheimers-disease/in-depth/alzheimers/art-20048103.

5 http://www.prevagen.com/.

6 https://www.ftc.gov/news-events/press-releases/2017/01/ftc-new-york-state-charge-marketers-prevagen-making-deceptive.

7 https://www.naturalproductsinsider.com/blogs/insider-law/2017/10/judge-dismisses-ftc-lawsuit-over-quincy-bioscienc.aspx.

8 https://www.truthinadvertising.org/prevagen/.

9   Ibid., 7.

10 https://www.healthline.com/nutrition/best-nootropic-brain-supplements.

11 https://www.nutraingredients-usa.com/Article/2015/06/01/ NBJ-The-US-supplement-industry-is-37-billion-not-12-billion.

12 https://sputniknews.com/us/201706171054715954-americans-spend-money-memory/.

25. Marijuana and the Cannabinoids

1   https://nccih.nih.gov/.

2   https://www.vox.com/cards/marijuana-legalization/marijuana-schedule.

3   https://www.google.com/search?rlz=1C1LOQA_enUS627US655&ei=0QN-hWvPZL822sAXVwrGgCA&q=Are+cannabinoids+legal+under+federal+.

4   https://www.drugabuse.gov/publications/research-reports/marijuana/ what-are-marijuana-effects.

5   https://www.drugabuse.gov/publications/research-reports/marijuana/what-are-marijuana%E2%80%99s-effects-on-other-aspects-of-physical-health%3F.

6   https://www.drugabuse.gov/publications/research-reports/marijuana/ how-does-marijuana-use-affect-school-work-social-life.

7   https://www.drugabuse.gov/.

8   https://www.ncbi.nlm.nih.gov/pmc/articles/PMC4827335/.

9   W. Hall, L. Degenhardt, "Adverse Health Effects of Non-Medical Cannabis Use," *Lancet* 374 (2009): 1383–91.

10 Lewis R. Goldfrank, ed., *Goldfrank's Toxicologic Emergencies*, 10th ed. (New York: McGraw Hill, 2015).

11 https://www.ncbi.nlm.nih.gov/pubmed/27086601.

12 https://www.medicaljane.com/2017/05/01/ the-3-cannabis-based-medicines-approved-by-the-fda/.

13 https://www.ncbi.nlm.nih.gov/pubmed/26912385.

14 https://www.ncbi.nlm.nih.gov/pubmed/24648180.

15 https://medicalmarijuana.procon.org.

16 Ibid.

17 Ibid.

18 http://www.latimes.com/local/abcarian/la-me-abcarian-cannabis-cash-20170129-story.html.

19 https://www.marijuanamoment.net/more-banks-welcome-marijuana-business-accounts-new-federal-report-shows/.

20 http://reason.com/blog/2018/01/04/blame-scotus-for-allowing-the-feds-to-ta.

21 https://www.huffingtonpost.com/2013/04/20/marijuana-prohibition-costs_n_3123397.html.

22 https://www.cnbc.com/id/36267217.

23 https://www.usnews.com/news/articles/2016-07-07/ medical-marijuana-availability-saves-taxpayers-money.

[24] https://www.bostonglobe.com/metro/2016/02/21/from-colorado-glimpse-life-after-marijuana-legalization/rcccuzhMDWV74UC4IxXIYJ/story.html.

[25] https://en.wikipedia.org/wiki/Tobacco_Master_Settlement_Agreement.

[26] https://www.npr.org/2013/10/13/233449505/15-years-later-where-did-all-the-cigarette-money-go.

[27] https://www.theatlantic.com/education/archive/2015/05/the-false-promise-of-marijuana-money-in-education/392165/.

[28] https://nihrecord.nih.gov/newsletters/2014/08_15_2014/story1.htm.

[29] https://www.usatoday.com/story/news/nation-now/2018/01/23/vermont-legal-marijuana-law-what-know/1056869001/.

[30] https://www.cdc.gov/measles/cases-outbreaks.html

[31] Personal Communication

PART III

Fraud Found along the Way

*The common good depends on people
trusting that most others in society will also
adhere to the common good rather than lie
or otherwise take advantage of them.*
— *Robert Reich*

I N THE PROCESS of researching the cost of unscientific health care, I discovered several areas in which elements of fraud and quackery were seemingly embedded in the system. When looking at the cost factors, it is evident that quackonomics exits in the various systems that support the delivery of health care in the United States, so I have added them as they presented.

Corruption in the System

Fraud in the science literature. Although we admire and appreciate the advances in medical science derived from the scientific method, there has crept into the process a darker side. Scientists are not saints, and the scientific literature is not infallible. It is most disheartening to learn that in recent times, corners have been cut and standards have not been met in the conduct and reporting of important information from medical experimentation despite the wads of money spent.[1]

The NIH invests nearly $32.3 billion annually in medical research for the American people. More than 80% of the NIH's funding is awarded through almost 50,000 competitive grants to more than 300,000 researchers at more than 2,500 universities, medical schools, and other research institutions in every state and around the world. About 10% of the NIH's budget supports projects conducted by nearly 6,000 scientists in its own laboratories, most of which are on the NIH campus in Bethesda, Maryland.

Historical background from the Office of Research Integrity (a branch of the US Department of Health and Human Services) reveals the origins of the wrongdoing.[2]

Research misconduct became a public issue in the United States in 1981 when then Representative Albert Gore, Jr., chairman of the Investigations and Oversight Subcommittee of the House Science and Technology Committee, held the first hearing on the emerging problem. The hearing was prompted by the public disclosure of research misconduct cases at four major research centers in 1980. Some twelve cases of research misconduct were disclosed in this country between 1974–1981. Congressional attention to research misconduct was maintained throughout the 1980s by additional allegations of research misconduct and reports that the National Institutes of Health (NIH), universities, and other research institutions were inadequately responding to those allegations.

Congress took action in 1985 by passing the Health Research Extension Act. The Act, in part, added Section 493 to the Public Health Service

(PHS) Act. Section 493 required the Secretary of Health and Human Services to issue a regulation requiring applicant or awardee institutions to establish "an administrative process to review reports of scientific fraud" and "report to the Secretary any investigation of alleged scientific fraud which appears substantial."

Although fraud in scientific papers began to be noted in the 1970s, it was not until the 1980s that C. Glen Begley, the CEO of Amgen and Lee Ellis, an academic scientist from MD Anderson Cancer Center in Houston, brought the matter public in 2012 in the journal *Nature*. The story is well told in Richard Harris's book *Rigor Mortis: How Sloppy Science Creates Worthless Cures, Crushes Hope, and Wastes Billions*.[3] They documented the "Reproducibility Crisis"—the fact that scientific papers reported results that could not be duplicated, and what is worse, they were incredibly common. Harris points out that,

> Drug companies rely heavily on academic research for new insights into biology—and particularly for leads for new drugs to develop. If academia is pumping out dubious results, that means pharmaceutical companies will struggle to produce new drugs.

A nonprofit called Global Biological Standards Institute (GBSI) founded in 2013 is dedicated to enhancing the quality of biomedical research by advocating best practices and standards to accelerate the translation of research breakthroughs into lifesaving therapies.[4] The monetary costs stated by GBSI are truly astounding:

> Studies looking at the prevalence of irreproducibility estimate a rate of 50% ($28.2 B). Poor reference material and study design are among the largest contributing factors.

Janet Woodcock, MD, director of FDA's Center for Drug Evaluation and Research, says the clinical trials system is "broken" and there needs to be new ways to collect and utilize patient data, blaming the underlying science as not being rigorous.[5]

There are some scientists deeply concerned with the lack of rigor and reproducibility in biomedical research. Two such people,[6] Steve Goodman of Stanford University and John Ioannides (trained at Harvard and Tufts and now professor of medicine and of health research and policy at Stanford University School of Medicine and a professor of statistics at Stanford University School of Humanities and Sciences), founded METRICS, Meta-Research Innovation Center, at Stanford. Harris[7] quotes Ioannides on the shortcomings of research involving human subjects as saying:

> Most of the time what we would find out was that the data were horrible. The analysis had major problems. There were strong biases… And most of the time, if you had to be honest, you would conclude despite all this data, I really don't know what's going on here.
>
> In one classic study, Ioannidis looked at papers from major medical journals—a mark that they were having a major impact on the field. Of the forty-nine studies that met this criterion, seven had been flatly contradicted by further studies. Those included some famous mistakes in biomedicine, such as the claim that estrogen and progestin benefited women who had had hysterectomies, when in fact the drug combination increased the risk of heart disease and breast cancer. Another ballyhooed study, which found that vitamin E reduced heart disease risk, turned out not to be true either.

Scientists Ferric C. Fanga, R. Grant Steen, and Arturo Casadevall documented retractions of scientific papers in a study entitled "Misconduct Accounts for the Majority of Retracted Scientific Publications."[8] Quoting their abstract:

> A detailed review of all 2,047 biomedical and life-science research articles indexed by PubMed as retracted on May 3, 2012 revealed that only 21.3% of retractions were attributable to error. In contrast, 67.4% of retractions were attributable to misconduct, including fraud or suspected fraud (43.4%), duplicate publication (14.2%), and plagiarism (9.8%). Incomplete, uninformative or misleading retraction announcements have led to a previous underestimation of the role of fraud in the ongoing retraction epidemic. The percentage of scientific articles retracted because of fraud has increased ~10-fold since 1975. Retractions exhibit distinctive temporal and geographic patterns that may reveal underlying causes.

Not only are retractions and irreproducibility a problem, but the equality of journals themselves is a deteriorating study in fraud. The government website serving Contemporary and Integrative Medicine banks heavily on PubMed. But what is PubMed? According to the blog of the Society for Scholarly Publishing[9]:[2*]

> Twenty years ago, PubMed was a credentialing system, an online port of the MEDLINE index. This shift of medium quickly made it a search engine, but one built on a manual and highly curated index. If your journal was in MEDLINE/PubMed, it had gone through an

---

2 * Reproduced with permission from the author, Kent Anderson, "The Scholarly Kitchen," Sept. 7, 2017 at https:scholarlykitchen.sspnet.org/2017/09/07/confusion-journals-pubmed-now.

exhaustive evaluation, and had earned a badge of legitimacy. You were searching a credentialing system. You were getting filtered results based on MEDLINE inclusion criteria, which were well-accepted.

Part of the extension of PubMed's original purpose has come through brand extension via PubMed Central, which has been used to muddy the waters about what is PubMed and what is not. PubMed inclusion has been used, for example, as an incentive for journals to include themselves in PubMed Central, eroding the idea that PubMed is a neutral arbiter of quality.

If you wish to verify a questionable journal listing, refer to Beall's List of Predatory Journals and Publishers[10] or Fake Research Journal Publishers.[11]

Is it possible that leading medical researchers could believe in their hypothesis so much that they would alter their data to fit their obsession? Far-fetched you say, but here is an example. Gina Kolata reported in the *New York Times* in October of 2018,[12]

Harvard Medical School and Brigham and Women's, former employers of Dr. Pier Anversa, accused him and his laboratory of extensive scientific malpractice. Officials concluded that more than 30 research studies produced over more than a decade contain falsified or fabricated data and should be retracted. The hospital paid $10 million settlement to the federal government after the Department of Justice alleged that Dr. Anversa and two members of his team were responsible for fraudulently obtaining research funding from the NIH.

Dr. Anversa believed that stem cells could be used to regenerate heart muscle after a heart attack. Breakthrough science—no doubt! But fraudulent fixing of the data is not the way to go. Dr. Jil C. Tardiff, a professor of medicine at the University of Arizona and a heart-muscle cell researcher, had it right: "This was a perfect storm of ego, wishful thinking and a lack of accountability." Dr. Anversa was forced out of Harvard in 2015, said he was betrayed by a rogue colleague.

Conflict of Interest in Medical Journal Reporting— Top Doctors Ties to Health and Drug Industry

ProPublica, a nonprofit journalism organization in collaboration with the *New York Times* reported that leading medical figures were among dozens of doctors who failed in recent years to report their financial relationships with pharmaceutical and health-care companies.[13] The report notes,

> Calls for transparency stem from concerns that ties to the health and drug industries increase the odds that they will, consciously or not, skew results to favor the companies with whom they do business. Studies have found that industry-sponsored research tends to be more positive than research financed by other sources. And that in turn can sway which treatments become available to patients. As Dr. Jeffrey R. Botkin, an associate vice president for research at the University of Utah recently argued, "Money is a very powerful influencer, and people's opinions become subtly biased by that financial relationship."
>
> The issue has gained traction since September [2018], when Dr. José Baselga, who was chief medical offices at Memorial Sloan Kettering Cancer Center in New York, resigned after The Times and ProPublica reported that he

had not revealed his industry ties in dozens of journal articles.

In addition to the widespread lapses by doctors, the review found that journals themselves often gave confusing advice and did not routinely vet disclosures by researchers, although many relationships could have been easily detected on a federal database.

The message is clear. If you have now a skeptical mind, dial it up to *superskeptical.*

As consumers, we can only trust that the situation is being addressed and that integrity and trust can again dominate our biomedical research. Several medical schools have initiated offices to teach and monitor. Johns Hopkins Medicine, for example,[14] has an Office of Policy Coordination (OPC), which serves as the primary resource for school of medicine faculty, staff, and students to educate, evaluate, and interpret policies regarding research integrity and the ethical conduct of research.

In summary, what is "fake bioscience literature" costing us? We can start with the GSBI figure stated above of $28.2 billion in the United States, recognize that it was well researched with the aid of two economists and is five years old, but assume there has been improvement since that time and come up with an estimate of $22.6 billion, a 20 percent improvement, but still unacceptable.

Pharma and Associates Corruption

1. Reporting of Adverse Drug Events

The FDA has a system of reporting adverse drug events called the Federal Adverse Event Reporting System (FARES), a database designed to support the FDA's postmarketing safety surveillance program for drug and therapeutic biologic products, to which healthcare professionals, consumers, and manufacturers voluntarily submit reports.[1] From this website, you can launch the FARES "Dashboard,"[2] which presents, in brief, the annual number of reports. In 2017, there were *1,815,738* of which 951,656 were reports that contained at least one adverse event that is not currently described in the product labeling and for which the patient outcome is serious (in the jargon of the FDA called "expedited"). Some 803,516 were described as "nonexpedited" reports, which did not meet the criteria for expedited reports plus a further description which cannot be deciphered. The remaining reports, 60,566 were direct reports which were submitted directly to the FDA through the MedWatch program by professionals or consumers. The total number of reports since 1968 is 14,840,596 of which 8,434,750 were labeled serious and 1,491,711 were deaths. *Note the number and percentage (10%) of deaths*, which by itself seems incredible. A button on the upper task bar provides access to report a problem by health professional or consumer to MedWatch, but the page is the ultimate in confusion in what to and what not to report. For example, under what to report are cosmetics, medical devices, special nutritional products, and foods/beverages while under what not to report "mandatory reporting by regulated industry listing Drugs and Biologicals." Confusing enough, but to confirm that FARES has received a report, the submitter must file a freedom of information form to get an answer. How user-unfriendly can you be?

Backing up a bit and look at pre- and postmarketing. Premarketing trials are required by the FDA for approval[3]: some of the points made by Lana L Pauls, MPH, from Center for Drug Evaluation and Research, FDA, are pre-marketing trials:

- measure the risks vs benefits of the trial drug.
- are usually just large enough to support efficacy.
- findings are needed to develop labeling instructions on how to use the drug to obtain its benefits and reduce risks of harm.

But have limitations:

- Subjects have the disease being tested, usually nothing else.

- Limited sample size and observation periods.
- Limit reliable detection of side effects to those most common and having short latency periods.
- Enrollment exclusions limit generalizability.
- Significant underrepresentation of women and elderly.

From the same reference, regarding postmarketing surveillance,

- Postmarketing trials are often done to enhance sales or are inconclusive.

In 2009, the American College of Physicians submitted a monograph to the FDA with recommendations to improve the postmarketing reporting system.[4] The summary stated,

> Health care providers and patients expect that the medications they prescribe and use as indicated and directed will generally have beneficial effects and not cause them significant harm. The FDA plays a crucial role in ensuring that approved prescription drugs are both safe and effective. Unfortunately, over the years the Agency's ability to approve and monitor new drugs has been compromised by chronic underfunding, limited regulatory authority, and insufficient organizational structure. The College's recommendations are intended to support and strengthen the FDA's capacity to regulate prescription drugs.

The FARES Public Dashboard shows the chart of accelerating number of adverse reports and, therefore, the apparent failure of such efforts.[5]

A study from the *Journal of Pharmacology & Pharmacotherapeutics*[6] estimated the annual cost of adverse drug reactions in 2013 at $30.1 billion annually. The characteristics of adverse drug events that led to US emergency department (ED) visits were reported by a *JAMA* article in 2014[7]:

> Based on 2013–2014 nationally representative surveillance data, an estimated 4 ED visits for adverse drug events occurred per 1000 individuals annually. Among children (aged ≤5 years), antibiotics were most commonly implicated; among older children and adolescents (aged 6–19 years), antibiotics were most commonly implicated, followed by antipsychotics; and among older adults (aged ≥65 years), anticoagulants, diabetes agents, and opioid analgesics were implicated in approximately 60% of ED visits for adverse drug events.

There is evidence that more favorable bleeding profiles of the newer anticoagulants reduce the use of warfarin and may lower the ADRs in the elderly.[8] *This fact plus efforts to reduce the problem in most recent years would prompt me to adjust the annual cost downward to $25 billion.*

2. Price Gauging

> *The real reason we're not liked is because we have used price hikes to cover up the gaps in innovation.*
> —*Len Schleifer, Regeneron Founder*

According to an article in the Cornell Law Review[1] entitled "The Untold EpiPen Story: How Mylan Hiked Prices by Blocking Rivals":

> In the summer of 2016, Mylan found itself under fire for high EpiPen prices. Between 2009 and 2016, Mylan raised the price of this life-saving device, which delivers epinephrine to treat anaphylactic shock, 15 times, resulting in an

increase of more than 400%. The medicine in the EpiPen costs only pennies a dose.

Raising the price of a two-pak from $100 to $600 brought Mylan's CEO Heather Bresch to testify before the House Oversight Committee.[2] In defending the company, she said that Mylan had no plans to lower prices despite a public outcry and questions from skeptical lawmakers. As columnist Rex Nutting[3] noted,

> Mylan is getting a lot of criticism for its decision to jack up the price of its lifesaving EpiPen by nearly 500% over the past decade, which just shows how confused some people are about how capitalism works. Nothing Mylan did was unexpected or immoral. It just did what companies do when they can.
>
> Contrary to what some people seem to believe, Mylan isn't in the business of saving people from life-threatening allergic reactions; Mylan is in the business of maximizing its profits, so it can put as much money as possible into the pockets of its owners.

This point of view seems rather crass, but that is the behavior of a monopoly. As poet Ogden Nash jabbed, "In the land of mules, there are no rules." But monopolies do not last forever. In January of 2017, CVS Pharmacies introduced a generic version based on Impax Laboratories' Adrenaclick, for $110 for a two-pak[4] or $140 at Walmart and $205 at Rite-Aid.[5]

Mylan Pharmaceuticals is not the only culprit. Valeant Pharmaceuticals and Turing Pharmaceuticals AG (privately held) found themselves in court because they have exploited distortions in supply and demand,[6] according to Kenneth L. Davis writing in *Forbes* magazine:

Valeant and Turing bought monopoly positions in old drugs that faced no direct competition in the United States. But they are important medicines. Nitropress, used to treat patients whose blood pressure has risen to dangerous levels, jumped in price by more than three times to $805 per vial immediately after Valeant's purchase, while Isuprel, which addresses heart rhythm problems, soared more than six times to $1,346 per vial. Turing purchased a 63-year-old anti-parasite pill, Daraprim (pyrimethamine), and took the even more brazen step of inflating its price by more than 5,000 % to $750/tablet. The drug treats toxoplasmosis, an infection from a common parasite found in cats, which can be deadly for babies in utero and present serious symptoms, including seizures, lung complications and blurred vision for those with compromised immune systems. In the United States, the market is small enough that no company produces a generic alternative.

President Donald Trump, in his 2018 State of the Union address,[7] promised to bring down drug prices. He also took credit for removing more regulations in his first year as president than any other in history. We will all anxiously await the outcome of this tug-of-war in the three years ahead. The 2018 new year started with increases[8]:

Many drug makers rang in the new year with increases in list prices of dozens of drugs that will take effect in 2018. Early data suggest the increases generally remained within a 10% self-imposed limit that was popularized by Allergan's chief executive, Brent Saunders, in 2016, when he pledged to keep price rises below the 10% figure as part of what he called the company's "social contract with patients."

Saunders' pricing promise may have become something of a de facto price pledge for many companies, one that was made in response to Mylan's price hike on Epipen auto-injectors, which set off a public controversy. Pfizer has been a notable exception to the voluntary 10% price cap pledge. In 2017, Pfizer raised US prices on close to 100 of its drugs by an average of 20%.

The GAO[9] has tracked the increases in drug spending:

Pharmaceutical and biotechnology sales revenue increased from $534 billion to $775 billion between 2006 and 2015, according to a recent report from the U.S. Government Accountability Office. About two-thirds of drug companies saw their profit margins increase over that period, averaging 17.1%.

How much of the recent increase is not justified would take congressional hearings, which are unlikely, but one could speculate that Big Pharma was proactive in increasing prices this year, anticipating possible political pressure to hold or reduce the pricing structure.

One way to look at excessive pricing is to note the profit margins. Big Pharma has high profit margins,[10] comparable to communications equipment and information technology.[11]

The largest average profit margin is for major drug manufacturers at 18.4 percent. This group includes Pfizer, AstraZeneca and Bristol-Myers Squibb.[12]

A company's profit margin is calculated by dividing a company's net income by its total revenues and is expressed as a percentage.[13]

> Companies in the financial services indus-
> try have a strong history of consistency in return
> as well as steady dividend payments to investors.
> The average profit margin for the financial ser-
> vices industry is 14.71%.

According to Yardeni Research, S&P, 500 reported profit margin in 2018 was 9%,[14] half as much as the major drug manufacturers. Johnson & Johnson, ranking 35th on the *Fortune 500 list*, reports a profit margin of 23% on profits of 16.5 B.[15]

Looking at the big picture, what is a good estimate for how much Big Pharma is gouging the American consumer? For the year 2016, a dozen Big Pharma companies' gross revenue for the US and Canada was $515 billion. Subtracting $15 billion for Canada, $500 billion is the revenue from US.[16] If 18 percent is an estimate of profit margin for Big Pharma (18% × $500 billion) = $90 billion, twice what it would be for average S&P 500, then half of $90 billion or $45 billion would be the estimate of what we might call a gauging number. With the growth in the past two years, *$50 billion would be the best estimate for 2018*. We can assume that with the corporate tax cut, the figure is probably much higher.

3. Lack of Independence of the FDA

We begin with a brief history of the FDA. In June 1906, President Theodore Roosevelt signed into law the Food and Drug Act.[1] The act applied penalties to the interstate marketing of "adulterated" drugs in which the "standard of strength, quality, or purity" of the active ingredient was not either stated clearly on the label or listed in the United States Pharmacopoeia or the National Formulary. Funding of the FDA presents the obvious lack of independence, which critics like Sidney Wolf, MD, director of Public Citizen's Health Research Group, have pointed out.[2]

These critics have reminded us of the fact that for the first eighty-six years of the Federal Drug Administration, starting in 1906, funding was part of the annual budget. The Prescription Drug

User Fee Act of 1992 changed that arrangement. From that time, the FDA was paid for drug applications and review by the pharmaceutical industry itself.

Critic Sidney Wolf, MD, labels this a "very unhealthy relationship." Such an agreement on the surface is clearly a conflict of interest and has been the root cause of some significant safety concerns. The large contributions of congressional campaigns by lobbying are outrageous. The Pharmaceutical Research and Manufacturers of America, the lobbying group is one of the top spenders influencing elections and the legislative efforts. Dr. Wolf rightly concludes that "big pharma has a stranglehold on Washington."

A 2007 report "FDA Science and Mission at Risk" by the Subcommittee on Science and Technology[3] detailed how the FDA cannot fulfill its stated mission because:

- its scientific base has eroded, and its scientific organizational structure is weak,
- its scientific workforce does not have sufficient capacity and capability, and
- its information technology (IT) infrastructure is inadequate.

Let us hope that there have been corrective measures since that dated report.

In summary, this "pay to play" arrangement is a conflict of interest in that it jeopardizes the necessary vigilant attitude the FDA must have to carry out their responsibilities. We must remind ourselves that it is the Congress that has made these decisions and only Congress can correct it. To date, Congress has been on the side of industry and not on the side of the consumer. There are arguments on both sides of the pay-to-play question, but the fact remains that objectivity can be easily influenced by money. At the very least, the consumer must be aware of this enormous conflict of interest and keep a constant skeptical eye on the FDA and those sources quoting their pharmaceutical results.

The quackonomics angle here is impossible to estimate and must be considered an intangible. Problems with the control of dietary supplement market are a good example.[4]

4. Surrogate Endpoints

The National Cancer Institute explains the value of surrogate endpoints in testing drugs premarket.[1]

> In clinical trials, an indicator or sign used in place of another to tell if a treatment works. Surrogate endpoints include a shrinking tumor or lower biomarker levels. They may be used instead of stronger indicators, such as longer survival or improved quality of life, because the results of the trial can be measured sooner. The use of surrogate endpoints in clinical trials may allow earlier approval of new drugs to treat serious or life-threatening diseases, such as cancer. Surrogate endpoints are not always true indicators or signs of how well a treatment works.

The obvious benefits are to speed the process and reduce the cost.[2]

> However, it is important to note that misusing surrogate endpoints can mislead researchers to come up with wrong conclusions which could, in turn, place patients' lives at risk.

The FDA has been using surrogate endpoints to push new drugs into the postmarketing phase with the understanding that manufacturers will conduct postmarketing studies to determine the true clinical benefit and that the FDA will monitor closely and rescind approval if needed.[3] Reuters reported in 2016 that the FDA failed to rescind approval even when postmarketing studies show drugs to be inferior to other options or even worse than doing nothing.[4]

> Researchers evaluated studies done on 18 cancer drugs approved between 2008 and 2012 by the U.S. Food and Drug Administration (FDA). None of the drugs had been found to prolong life, and only one had enough evidence to say it improved quality of life. Yet, all but one retained its approval status.
>
> The problems associated with accelerated approval of drugs by the FDA have been prominent in the past two years.[5] The criticism is that accelerated approval policy by-passes the "gold-standard randomized controlled trials"[6] and that too many doctors are not familiar with the underlying clinical trials and simply "go with the flow."

In an article entitled, *"The Perils of Surrogate Endpoints,"*[7] the authors conclude:

> The use of surrogates is complex, and there is no single criterion or standard that can readily be applied. An understanding of causality and consideration of the relevant practical criteria is important, but the adoption of a surrogate must always be considered on a case by case basis. The place of surrogates in phase II trials may be reasonable as a guide to pivotal phase three trials. However, the uncertainty of surrogates must limit their use in phase III trials, where the unreliability of surrogates alone for registration is recognized, to avoid potential risk to public health.

With respect to cost when surrogates do not work out, we have again an intangible.

5. Generic Drugs and Biosimilars

Generic drugs are a further study in the complexity of the pharmaceutical market. Congress in 1984 passed the Waxman-Hatch Act providing for companies to manufacture drugs after patent monopolies had expired, also known as the Drug Price Competition and Patent Term Restoration Act.[1] The law allowed the FDA to develop a speedier and simpler way to turn out lower-priced copycat versions of established drugs, because it eliminated the need for costly clinical trials. This commonsense consumer-benefiting law was, by most measures, a success. By 2015, generic drugs accounted for 88 percent of all prescriptions, up from 20 percent in 1983.[2]

Though a "win-win" situation, the early story is marred by corruption. Jerome A. Greene, MD, a medical historian, tells the story in his erudite book *Generic: The Unbranding of Modern Medicine.*[3]

> In the summer of 1989, two FDA officials testified in front of Rep. John Dingell's House Energy and Commerce Subcommittee on Oversight and Investigations that they had accepted manila envelopes stuffed with several thousand dollars from the executive of the generic firm Superpharma. In exchange, regulators had orchestrated the slowing of reviews for competing generic products, burying key files in desk drawers while speeding others through the regulatory machinery.

The investigation did not stop there. Unlike brand-name drugs, generics were approved on the basis of proof of similarity.

Rep Dingell's committee further revealed outsourcing—that many of the tests of bioequivalence were conducted by private companies. One company Vitarine, rather than sending its own product, sent a sample of a popular diuretic called Dyazide to be tested for bioequivalence essentially testing Dyazide against itself. Fraud was discovered in at least four other companies. Bolar was found guilty of doing the same against a Sandoz pill. It was discovered that the Sandoz logo was incompletely scratched from the pill, a dead give-away of deceit.

Fortunately, justice was done, and regardless of leadership problems at FDA, the generic market evolved, and as expected, competition drove down prices, but as Donlan points out,[4] in time,

> consolidation of the generic producers ensued, and big inventive research-oriented pharmaceutical companies began to look like dinosaurs. They reduced their investments in research, closing labs and dismissing staff. Even monopolies couldn't create enough profit to pay for decades of research and decades of compliance with premarket regulations intended to guarantee efficiency and safety.

Enter the cavalry over the hill—bugles blaring, TV budgets bulging! Wall Street to the rescue to finance the emergence of speculative start-ups. Again, Donlon notes:

> The Big Pharma companies are now primarily marketing and advertising giants, reducing their risk of failure by buying the rights to new products from the successful start-ups.
>
> Equally unforeseen was the fewer and bigger generic-drug companies, and the market for generics began to look more like the brand name market. More than 50% of generic drugs are supplied by only one or two manufacturers, so generic prices now are often as firmly fixed and profitable as those of patented drugs.

If it oinks like a pig and squeals like a pig, then it must be a pig, and that pig is money. So thanks to greed, we have evolved another inefficient market with all its abusive consequences, including the price gauging noted.

Making the generic market more noncompetitive is the egregious practice by pharmaceutical companies refusing makers of generics drug samples needed to develop their products. To gain approval, FDA requires bioequivalence testing of samples to demonstrate that generics are the same as their branded counterparts. The FDA has listed manufacturers of over fifty drugs, who have refused to sell samples. A Kaiser Health News analysis[5]:

> Found that 47 of the drugs cost Medicare and Medicaid almost $12 billion in 2016. By delaying development of generics, drug makers can maintain their monopolies and keep prices high.

Senator Patrick Leahy, D-VT, and Senator Chuck Grassley, R-IO, are sponsoring the Creating and Restoring Equal Access to Equivalent Samples Act of 2019 (CREATES Act),[6] which would allow generics companies to sue brand-name drug manufacturers to compel them to provide adequate samples and end this anticompetitive tactic. This could be a classic turning point for the congress to decide whether it is on the side of Big Pharma or the people they represent. *The Hill* reported in April 2018 that the Pharmaceutical Research and Manufacturers of America, known as PhRMA, spent approximately $10 million in 2018 on lobbying efforts—including efforts to halt progress of the CREATES Act.[7] So the battle lines are formed.

Biosimilars[8] are different from generics. In generics, the active ingredient is identical to the reference brand-name drug. Biosimilars differ from generics in complexity, manufacturing processes and in the data needed to demonstrate similarity for approval.[9] Where generics have simple, well-defined molecules, biosimilars are derived from living cells and are complex with structural variations; generics have a low potential for adverse immune reaction, biosimilars have a higher potential; generics require clinical trials in healthy volunteers, biosimilars require large clinical trials in patients.

Humira, the best-selling prescription drug in the world, is a biosimilar. It is AbbVie's "life-changing" drug used to treat colitis, Crohn's disease and psoriasis widely viewed on TV.[10]

> The Humira play is to start at a high price and keep raising it even higher, but incrementally. Humira accounted for nearly two-thirds of AbbVie's $26 billion in revenue in 2016.
>
> The industry has argued that high American prices are needed to fund drug development, but a 2016 study published by the JAMA found "no evidence of an association between research and development costs and prices; rather, prescription drugs are priced in the United States primarily on the basis of what the market will bear."
>
> The price of Humira, dispensed in an injectable pen, has risen from about $19,000 a year in 2012 to more than $38,000 today per patient after rebates according to SSR Health, a research firm. That is an increase of 100%.
>
> Looking at the international picture tells its own story. A prefilled carton with two syringes cost $2,669 in the US, compared with $1,362 in Britain, $822 in Switzerland and $552 in South Africa, according to a 2015 report from International Federation of Health Plans.
>
> P.S.
> AbbVie joined a few of its rivals in saying it would limit price increases to single digits this year, and so only raised Humira by another 9.7% this January.

We should recall that this situation originated in the industry's lobbying of the George W. Bush administration in 2006 that bars Medicare from negotiating drug prices.[11] This is probably the largest obstacle to better market drug pricing in the US.

To further complicate the terminology and variable approval routes, we now have to add the term "biobetter."[12]

> The term biobetter refers to a recombinant protein drug that is in the same class as an existing biopharmaceutical but is not identical; it is improved over the original. Biobetters are being developed using protein or glyco-engineering which, experts say, reduces the risk of immunogenicity, makes the drug safer and more effective, and requires lower dosing. A biobetter has the same target as the original biological, but its effect on the target lasts for an extended period of time.
>
> Because a biobetter is a new drug, it will enjoy 12 years of market protection in the US and other markets, unlike a biosimilar. In addition, biobetters tend to have lower R and D costs.
>
> Many of the first-generation biologics are going off-patent and will face competition from biosimilars.
>
> It remains to be seen if biobetters will be competitive.

Cost factors: According Back Bay Life Science Advisors[13] to a White Paper,

> Although it is not clear who the winners and losers will be in the biologics and biosimilars market, what is certain is that the landscape is shifting.

Development of biosimilars (copycats), although in its infancy, is a major part of the Trump Administration's effort to lower drug costs in the United States.[14]

> Copycats of biotech products pose a threat to the industry, just as generics have challenged pharma firms.

So time will tell whether there will be increasing or decreasing costs, although the Humira story cited above is not encouraging. From the information that AbbVie's revenue from Humira is $17 billion and profit margin information,[15] *it is estimated that the gauging from this alone is 3.2 billion.*

6. Pharmacy Benefit Managers (PBMS)

A Pharmacy Benefit Manager is a third-party administrator (TPA) of prescription-drug programs for commercial health plans, self-insured employer plans, Medicare Part D plans, the Federal Employees Health Benefits Program, and state government employee plans.[1] The National Community Pharmacists Association (NCPA)[2] explains on their website:

> Pharmacy Benefit Managers are largely unrecognized by most employees—and even by many employers. But they have a tremendous impact on U.S. health care decision-making. Three large companies—Express Scripts, CVSHealth and OptumRx (United Health group)—cover more than 180 million lives, or roughly 78% of the market, and while their role is largely unnoticed, employers and government entities must be vigilant as the non-transparent nature of the traditional PBM business model can add hidden costs and lead to higher prices.

Since 1987, when Advance PCS/Caremark (now CVSHealth) became the last of the original "big 3" PBMs to incorporate, the others being Medco and Express Scripts which merged in 2012, total prescription drug expenditures have skyrocketed 1010% and per capita expenditures have increased 756%.

Large PBMs have evolved into behemoth corporations that affect nearly all aspects of the prescription drug marketplace. PBMs determine which pharmacies will be included in a prescription drug plan's network and how much said pharmacies will be paid for their services, entice plan sponsors to require plan beneficiaries to use a mail order pharmacy (often one owned/operated by the PBM) for certain medications, and determine which medications will be covered by the plan or the plan formulary. For access to the formulary, drug manufacturers often pay "rebates" to the PBM.

But the PBMS don't always pass on the rebates and discounts to the health-plan clients[3] and won't tell its clients how much the PBM is pocketing (the black-box aspect of the industry). In addition,

Most contracts allow the PBM to decide whether a drug is considered generic or brand— thereby changing a 78% discount to a 15% discount. Contracts also allow PBMS to relabel rebates, so they needn't be shared with health plans.

As one prominent industry attorney, Linda Cahn, summed it up.

> Health plans don't realize they are signing contracts that effectively say, "Charge me whatever you want."
>
> They need to realize they are being scalped.

PBMS have other impacts on the over 180 million patients covered by contracts with companies that claim a cost-containment mission.[4]

> In 1998, PBMS were under investigation by the federal Justice Department and their effectiveness in reducing prescription costs and saving client money, were questioned.
>
> A 2013 Centers for Medicare & Medicaid services study found negotiated prices at mail order pharmacy to be up to 83% higher than the negotiated prices at community pharmacies.
>
> In 2015 there were seven lawsuits against PBMs involving fraud, deception or antitrust claims.
>
> In 2017, the Los Angeles Times wrote that PBMs cause an inflation in drug costs, especially within the area of diabetes drugs.
>
> The Secretary of HHS, Alex Azar stated regarding PBMs, "Everybody wins when list prices rise, except for the patient. It's rather a startling and perverse system that has evolved over time."

The idea of using giant buying power, formulary alternatives, and management know-how to pass on drug cost savings to the consumer is a splendid one. Where did it go wrong? The story is that initially they were successful,[5] as the Laura and John Arnold Foundation point out.

The PBMs went wrong in three areas, consolidation, rebate revenue and transparency.

But market power (consolidation) has made a flawed business model sticky. Commercial insurers complain that PBMs are not passing through the rebate revenue. Which brings us to transparency. The drug pricing world is shrouded in secrecy.

On January 31, 2019, HHS (Health and Human Services) proposed new rules to eliminate drug rebates.[6]

HHS Secretary Alex Alzar stated,

"This proposal has the potential to be the most significant change in how Americans' drugs are priced at the pharmacy counter, ever, and finally ease the burden of the sticker shock that millions of Americans experience every month for the drugs they need." The Trump administration believes that eliminating the AKS discount safe harbor protection for rebates based on list prices of drugs will reduce incentives for drug manufacturers to increase list prices and result in out-of-pocket savings for federal beneficiaries. This approach assumes that the estimated 26 to 30 percent of drug list price attributed to rebates that are provided to Medicare Part D plans, Medicaid managed care plans and PBMs will be passed on directly to patients to alleviate their out-of-pocket costs.

We shall see.

What are all these shenanigans costing the American consumer? If we add the $100 billion per year of CVS's PBM business to $48 billion of Optum Rx's plus $102 billion in revenue by Express Scripts that equals $250 billion for the big three. If 10 percent could be saved by simply writing better contracts favoring the consumer, then *$25 billion is what the consumer is paying unnecessarily*. By my calculation, this comes out to an overcharge of $0.47 per prescription. (Express Scripts cash flow / RX = $5.43 and CVS's $3.98, the average of 10 percent cut in each.)[7]

7.   The Opioid Crisis

There were over sixty-four thousand drug-overdose deaths in the United States in 2016 compared to less than twenty thousand in 1999.[1] The *New York Times* in 2017 reminded us of the chilling facts[2]:

> It's the deadliest drug crisis in American history. Drug overdoses are the leading cause of death for Americans under 50, and deaths are rising faster than ever, primarily because of opioids. Overdoses killed more people last year than guns or car accidents and are doing so at a pace faster than the H.I.V. epidemic at its peak. In 2015, roughly 2 percent of deaths—one in 50—in the United States were drug-related.

The National Institute of Drug Abuse (NIDA) states that every day ninety Americans die from overdosing on opioids.[3] The Center for Disease and Prevention

> estimates that the total economic burden of prescription opioid misuse alone in the United States is $78.5 billion a year, including the costs of healthcare, lost productivity, addiction treatment, and criminal justice involvement.

To what extent can the makers of the opioid drugs, Big Pharma, be held responsible for this epidemic? Research from the NIDA[4] indicates that in the late 1990s, pharmaceutical companies reassured the medical community that patients would not become addicted to prescription opioid pain relievers, and healthcare providers began to prescribe them at greater rates. This subsequently led to widespread diversion and misuse of these medications before it became clear that these medications could indeed be highly addictive. Opioid overdose rates began to increase. In 2015, more than 33,000 Americans died because of an opioid overdose.

That same year, an estimated 2 million people in the United States suffered from substance use disorders related to prescription opioid pain relievers, and 591,000 suffered from a heroin use disorder (not mutually exclusive).

The NIDA website says, "Roughly 21% to 29% of patients prescribed opioids for chronic pain misuse them. Between 8% and 12% develop an opioid use disorder. An estimated 4% to 6% percent who misuse prescription opioids transition to heroin. About 80% of people who use heroin first misused prescription opioids."

If the drug companies misled the medical community as NIDA concludes, then what was the basis for the misleading? Multiple sources trace the origin to a letter to the editor in the New England Journal of Medicine, January 10, 1980[5], headed "Addiction Rare in Patients Treated with Narcotics."

It reads:

Recently, we examined our current files to determine the incidence of narcotic addiction in 9,946 hospitalized medical patients who were monitored consecutively. Although there were 11,882 patients who received at least one narcotic preparation, there were only four cases of reasonably well documented addiction in patients who had no history of addiction. The addiction was considered major in only one instance… We conclude that despite widespread use of narcotic drugs in hospitals, the development of addiction is rare in medical patients with no history of addiction.

Jane Porter
Hershel Jick, MD
Boston Collaborative Drug
Surveillance Program, Boston University.

Nearly forty years later, the controversy continues. NIDA contradicts the letter observing that for 2015 for example, more than thirty-three thousand Americans died because of opioid overdose of one kind or another.

The tragedy of the famous letter, sometimes called the "Big Bang" letter, was that it was cited more than 600 times in the literature and countless times by the opioid manufactures in selling campaigns. The very fact that it was sourced in the New England Journal of Medicine carried the heavy weight of veracity.

I include this rather long story with the only conclusion possible. A pox on both your houses—Big Pharma for using a "sloppy" interpretation of a single reference to flood the market, and the medical community for forgetting the principles they learned in their pharmacology class in medical school. More on the medical community later.

The New York Times[6] cited

a handful of influential journal articles that relaxed fears among doctors about prescribing opioids for chronic pain. "The pharmaceutical industry took note, and in the mid-1990s began aggressively marketing drugs like OxyContin.

This aggressive and at times fraudulent marketing, combined with a new focus on patient satisfaction and the elimination of pain, sharply increased the availability of pharmaceutical narcotics," the Times said.

The crisis has its roots in the over prescription of opioid painkillers, but since 2011 overdose deaths from prescription opioids have leveled off. Deaths from heroin and fentanyl, on the other hand, are rising fast. In several states where the drug crisis is particularly severe, including Rhode Island, Pennsylvania and Massachusetts, fentanyl is now involved in over half of all overdose fatalities.

Let us look at one example: Purdue Pharma of Stamford CN and, specifically, their OxyContin marketing plan of 1999.[7]

Purdue "aggressively" promoted the use of opioids for use in the "nonmalignant pain market." In 1998, a training video with this message was sent to thousands of physicians, targeting primary-care doctors and stating that the risk of addiction was much less than 1 percent.

The Industry mantra was:

- Opioids are safe and effective for chronic pain.
- Opioid addiction is rare in pain patients.
- Opioid therapy can be easily discontinued.
- Opiophobia: causes patients to needlessly suffer.

The next chapter in the Perdue Pharma story is that the US Senate investigation resulted in a guilty plea on May 10, 2007. The findings were that Perdue misled regulators, doctors, and patients about the enormous addiction and abuse potential of OxyContin and paid $600 million in fines.[8] In addition,

Also, in a rare move, three executives of Purdue Pharma, including its president and its top lawyer, pleaded guilty as individuals to misbranding, a criminal violation. They agreed to pay a total of $34.5 million in fines.

The latest (February 11, 2018) is that Purdue Pharma announced that it will no longer market its OxyContin to doctors.[9] All this means is that the company's salesforce is cut by more than 50 percent, to a total of about two hundred. Purdue also plans to send a letter to prescribers to announce its sales personnel will no longer come to their offices to discuss the company's opioids. It did not say that it plans on curtailing production or alternative marketing plans.

The opioid epidemic has cost the nation billions in dollars and human tragedy, but the greater threat is, the quackonomics is yet to come if response to the problem is not comprehensive and evidence-based and de-politicized. The objectives are clear: (1) treat current population of patients with opioid addiction (substance use disorder) using medical principals without stigmatization and (2) stop new addiction with a national program that includes decriminalization and a massive education program. Simple enough to state, but both branches of the plan require leadership and money. More than sixty-four thousand overdose deaths in 2016—this cannot go on! Where to start? The State of Vermont has taken a lead with a "hub and spoke model[10] that is certainly a start.[3] Pioneered by Dr. John Brooklyn, a family doctor and addiction specialist in Vermont, and former Gov. Peter Shumlin (D). In general, Dr. Brooklyn observes,

the system provides a referral point for providers who have complicated patients struggling with addiction.

---

[3] Permission to publish granted by author, German Lopez, german.lopez@vox.com. Title, "I looked for a state that's taken the opioid epidemic seriously. I found Vermont." 2017.

The model took shape in the real world after the legislature authorized it in 2012, with strong support from then-Gov. Peter Shumlin (D). Now there are six hubs in 10 locations and dozens of spokes spread out across the state.

The Affordable Care Act ("Obamacare"), passed in 2010, was crucial for all of this. The law included a special Medicaid waiver that Vermont obtained to help subsidize the hub and spoke model. In the ensuing years, Obamacare also shifted the costs of insurance to the federal government—as more Vermonters got on Obamacare's marketplaces and Medicaid expansion instead of the low-income health insurance plans that the state previously provided on its own. As a result, Medicaid alone now pays for most of the expenses incurred by the system's more than 8,000 opioid addiction patients, each of whom costs on average nearly $16,600 a year.

But challenges remain.

Part of the issue is that the hub and spoke system is still relatively new, so it has yet to reach its full impact. It was only in September of this year, after all, that the state eliminated lengthy waiting periods at hubs.

But there are problems, beyond the previous waiting periods, that came up time and time again as I talked to providers and patients within the system.

One is the lingering stigma around addiction. Despite some progress in Vermont, this still affects just about every aspect of addiction care: It makes some doctors and nurse practitioners reluctant to take on patients with drug use disorders. It makes some people with addiction too nervous to admit to their illness, and it might

even cause self-loathing. And it can make lawmakers and the public skeptical of dedicating too
many resources to the problem.

The second objective is to stop new addition.

"For 100-plus years as a society, we've punished and crimi-
nalized people who use drugs," said Sarah Wakeman, an addiction
medicine doctor and medical director at the Massachusetts General
Hospital Substance Use Disorder Initiative.[11]

She is absolutely right. Attacking the problem with more funding to police departments and law enforcement, as Senate Majority
Leader Mitch McConnell leader seems to think in commenting on
the $6 billion appropriated (February 2018), is not the way to go.[12]

> The research backs up Wakeman. Studies
> have found that "tough on crime" efforts have
> little impact on drug use; a 2014 review of the
> research by Peter Reuter at the University of
> Maryland and Harold Pollack at the University
> of Chicago, for example, concluded that pro-
> hibition does make drugs more expensive and
> therefore less accessible, but more stringent mea-
> sures—such as harsh police crackdowns or lon-
> ger prison sentences—have no significant effect
> beyond that of prohibition.

President Trump's declaring the opioid epidemic a National
Public Health Emergency in 2017 is doing little to solve the
problem.[13]

> The President directed acting Health
> Secretary Eric Hargan to declare a public health
> emergency under the Public Health Services
> Act—which directs federal agencies to provide
> more grant money to combat the epidemic—

not a national emergency through the Stafford Disaster Relief and Emergency Assistance Act.

In other words, this was not going all out—not an "all hands-on-deck" order!

A comprehensive public health approach is outlined by Andrew Kolodny and associates[14] in an annual review entitled "The Prescription Opioid and Heroin Crisis: A Public Health Approach to An Epidemic of Addiction." This review should be read by everyone interested in the details of prevention. I quote from key points on prevention.

> The aim of primary prevention is to reduce the incidence of a disease or condition. Opioid addiction is typically chronic, life-long, difficult to treat, and associated with high rates of morbidity and mortality. Thus, bringing the opioid addiction epidemic under control requires effort to prevent new cases from developing.
>
> Several states, including Iowa, Kentucky, Massachusetts, Ohio, Tennessee and Utah have passed mandatory prescriber education legislation. In addition, the FDA is requiring manufacturers of extended release and long acting Opioid Pain Relievers (OPRs)to sponsor educational programs for subscribers. Unfortunately, some of these educational programs, including those required by the FDA imply that OPRs are safe and effective for chronic non-cancer pain instead of offering prescribers accurate information about OPRs risks and benefits. It remains unclear whether or not educational programs such as these will reduce OPR prescribing for common conditions where risks of use are likely to outweigh benefits.

So it looks like we will have to add the FDA to the list of those needing education if such is true. The wider perspective, however, is the urgent need for in-depth education that must be part of our primary and secondary education, both public and private. I would envision a program starting at least in the fourth grade with a curriculum that is part of teaching the scientific method. Such a program would be evidence-based and, at the secondary level, include a course in the principles of pharmacology. We will need teachers with degrees specializing in health science. The education part of this solution must be at federal, state, and local school district levels. It will be akin to the Manhattan Project that produced our atomic bomb; otherwise, we must live with our own time bomb. If the president truly believes in "America First," then this is a prime place to start.

Although the economic burden for the opioid crisis cited above is 78.5 billion, the Council of Economic Advisers (CEA) argues from a 2017 report[15] that

> the economic cost of the opioid crisis was $504.0 billion, or 2.8 percent of GDP that year (2015). This is over six times larger than the most recently estimated economic cost of the epidemic. This is up from 11.5 billion in 2011.

The council said,[16]

> Previous studies focused exclusively on prescription opioids, while its study also factors in illicit opioids, including heroin.
> "Previous estimates of the economic cost of the opioid crisis greatly underestimate it by undervaluing the most important component of the loss—fatalities resulting from overdoses."

The aggregate national cost of the opioid crisis is the CEA figure of $504 billion, because it is a more inclusive number.

Medical Device Fraud

In January of 2016, a former owner and the former operator of a durable medical equipment supply company selling power wheelchairs based in Long Beach, California, were sentenced for their roles in a $1.5 million Medicare fraud scheme.[1]

> Evidence further showed that the defendants paid illegal kickbacks to patient recruiters in exchange for patient referrals and paid kickbacks to physicians for fraudulent prescriptions, primarily for expensive, medically unnecessary power wheelchairs—which the defendants then used to support fraudulent bills to Medicare. Between 2006 and 2013, the defendants submitted $1,520,727 in claims to Medicare and received $783,756 in reimbursement for those claims, according to evidence presented at trial.

Since its inception in March 2007, the Medicare Fraud Strike Force, now operating in nine cities across the country, has charged more than 2,300 defendants who have collectively billed the Medicare program for more than $7 billion.[2]

In March of 2016, Olympus Corporation of America agreed to pay the federal government $623 million to settle a whistleblower lawsuit accusing the device maker of systematically violating the US Anti-Kickback Statute (AKS) to gain market share dominance for its products.[3] The settlement was the largest ever for a medical device company and for AKS violations. Tavy Deming, an attorney representing the whistleblower, observed,

> This case is testament to the fact that without external fraud reporting avenues afforded by current whistleblower laws, corporate greed will go unchecked.

Other cases of note are[4]:

> 2012: Orthofix agreed to pay the government over $34 million to resolve allegations that the company engaged in a number of schemes to defraud the government, including waiving patient co-payments thereby causing the government to overpay, giving kickbacks to physicians to induce them to use the company's devices, and failing to advise patients of their right to rent devices rather than purchase them. The whistleblower received over $9 million as a result of the settlement.

And:

> 2011: Medtronic paid over $23 million to settle two False Claims Act lawsuits alleging that the company improperly used fees in post-market studies and device registries as a means of providing kickbacks to doctors to induce them to implant the company's pacemakers and defibrillators. The two whistleblowers shared in an award of nearly $4 million.

In 2014, *The Washington Post* reported[5] that since 1999, Medicare has spent $8.2 billion to procure power wheelchairs and "scooters" for 2.7 million people. The government could only guess at how much of that money was paid out to scammers.

In August of 2016, according to Kaiser Health News, the University of California regents agreed to pay nearly $8.5 million to settle two lawsuits alleging a well-known UCLA spine surgeon failed to disclose his conflicts of interest with a leading device maker before using the company's products in harmful surgeries.[6]

The cases shine a light on the controversial role industry money continues to play in research and patient care at academic medical centers. Nationwide, doctors and universities have come under increasing scrutiny over the money they receive from drug and device makers. Although the rules for accepting money vary widely among institutions, Congress in recent years has required all drug and device companies to publicly disclose their payments.

The total amount companies paid to doctors and teaching hospitals in 2015, according to the new federal data, was $6.5 billion.

The case represents, in its complexity, the need for total transparency when it comes to patients making treatment choices.

According to the Newsletter of the Medical Device and Diagnostic Industry,[7] *fraud and accounting problems*, taken together, were responsible for one-third of medical device firm defaults, causing a total of five defaults (2012–2014). In S&P's report, the consultancy notes that it did not expect to find that fraud would be a common cause of default for medical device companies. In the end, the prevalence of fraud in the sector is higher than in other industries because of the high prevalence of third-party payments in health care, according to S&P. The newsletter went on to elaborate:

Notable cases of fraud included Liberty Medical Supply, the direct-to-consumer diabetes supply company that used veteran actor Wilford Brimley in its TV commercials. U.S. Express Scripts acquired Liberty in 2012 through its $29 billion deal with Medco, then sold Liberty to its management team. The company was filing a chapter 11 bankruptcy within a year amid $160 million-worth of claims over alleged Medicare and Medicaid overpayments made to Liberty between 2008 and 2010, according to S&P.

Another case is that of IMG.

International Manufacturing Group Inc. (IMG), also known as Relyaid, meanwhile defaulted in 2014 after the West Sacramento, Ca-based dental supply manufacturer's owner Deepal Wannakuwatte was charged with running a Ponzi scheme with more than 100 victims who were fleeced out of $109 million that Wannakuwatte spend on himself and his family, as well as lulling payments to investors to keep the scheme alive. Wannakuwatte claimed to have more than $125 million in US Department of Veterans Affairs contracts, when his VA contract only amounted to up to $25,000 a year, according to federal prosecutors. Wannakuwatte, a former owner of the Sacramento Capitals tennis team, ended up pleading guilty to wire fraud in 2014 and was sentenced to 20 years in prison.

When googling for "medical device fraud," there is an extensive seemingly nonending list. This is not a scare tactic but certainly a reality check. Durable Medical Equipment (DME) fraud is rampant. The US Government Accountability Office (GAO)[8] reported that, in 2010, about 16 percent of all Medicare/Medicaid fraud cases—basically, one in six—involved DME suppliers. According to the US Office of Management and Budget, improper payments under Medicaid alone in fiscal year 2015 amounted to $29.15 billion. DME fraud certainly totals in the billions: it is estimated to range from $1.5 billion to $5 billion each year.[9]

One important aspect of the cases reviewed for DME fraud is that judges have added substantial prison terms in addition to monetary punishment, and that will hopefully decrease the incidence.[10]

If 16 percent of Medicare/Medicaid is DME fraud, and $60 billion is reported (2015) as annual aggregate fraud,[11] then DME annual estimate of fraud is $9.6 billion.

Elimination of the Office of Technology Assessment (OTA)

The OTA was established in 1972.[1]

> More specifically, it followed a decade of work by the Science Committee of the House of Representatives and the Labor and Human Resources Committee of the Senate with the help of the private academic and industrial sectors, in particular the National Academy of Sciences. During the ensuing 23 years, under the guidance of an equally bipartisan congressional board, OTA evolved a structure and a process which provided analysis, information, and options to Congress and a reputation for nonpartisan, accurate and complete reporting. Importantly, OTA also provided, through the intense use as advisers of experts and stakeholders from the nongovernmental sector, an open interface between many American communities and Congress.

It was abruptly abolished in the first session of the 104th Congress as part of the "Contract with America" as Newt Gingrich became Speaker of the House of Representatives.[2]

> The new congressional majority singled out OTA, by far the smallest of the support agencies, for elimination since its elimination was conveniently symbolic. That is, while OTA's budget was less than 1 percent of the Legislative Branch Appropriations Budget, its elimination allowed

the House Leadership to claim credit for abolishing an entire federal agency—the only such elimination that was ultimately sustained as part of the Contract with America proposals.

Ellis R. Mottur, a Public Policy scholar, in his book *Technology Assessment in the War on Terrorism and Homeland Security*, pointed out the unique qualities of the OTA[3] and contributions to national security. The move was criticized at the time, including Republican representative Amo Houghton (R. NY), who commented at the time of OTA's defunding, "We are cutting off one of the most important arms of Congress when we cut off unbiased knowledge about science and technology."[4]

Cost factor: This is another intangible. How do you measure an example of erosion of democracy or put a price tag on it?

Fraud by the States

On January 11, 1964, Luther L. Terry, MD, surgeon general of the US Public Health Service, released the first report of the Surgeon General's Advisory Committee on Smoking and Health.[1] After a two-year review of the scientific literature on the health effects of smoking, the committee concluded that cigarette smoking was,

- a cause of lung cancer and laryngeal cancer in men,
- a probable cause of lung cancer in women,
- the most important cause of chronic bronchitis.

Early on, the US Congress adopted the Federal Cigarette Labeling and Advertising Act of 1965 and the Public Health Cigarette Smoking Act of 1969. These laws

- required a health warning on cigarette packages,
- banned cigarette advertising in the broadcasting media,
- called for an annual report on the health consequences of smoking.

Over the next ten years, the public was quite aware of the hazards of smoking, an example of how evidenced-based science favorably impacted health policy. It did, however, miss one key point.[2]

On one issue the committee hedged: nicotine addiction. It insisted that the "tobacco habit should be characterized as a habituation rather than an addiction," in part because the addictive properties of nicotine were not yet fully understood, in part because of differences over the meaning of addiction.

As a practicing surgeon in those days (I was serving as a lieutenant commander in the US Public Health Service at the time), I might add one other observation. Whereas the concentration of findings was on cancers of the respiratory system, it was not until the second surgeon general's report was issued on the fiftieth anniversary of the first report that it was proven that the most devastating danger of smoking was not cancers but the great damage to the cardiovascular system. The recognition of the addictive qualities of nicotine and the cardiovascular damage was even more convincing reasons to curb smoking. Why it took fifty years to issue the second report is not clear to me, but I suspect efforts on the part of the tobacco lobby played a major role.

"In spite of hard-hitting media campaigns, smoke free air policies, optimal tobacco excise taxes, barrier-free cessation treatment, and comprehensive statewide tobacco control programs funded at CDC-recommended levels" the acting Surgeon General Boris D. Lushniak, M.D prefaced the 50th report noting that "smoking remains the leading preventable cause of premature disease and death in the United States."[3]

Enter the story of tobacco litigation. The first wave of litigation in the 1950s was brought by smokers who usually had developed lung cancer.[4] Plaintiffs used several legal theories including

- negligent manufacture—the tobacco companies failed to act with reasonable care in making and marketing cigarettes,
- product liability—the tobacco companies made and marketed a product that was unfit to use,
- negligent advertising—the tobacco companies failed to warn consumers of the risks of smoking cigarettes
- fraud, and
- violation of state consumer protection statutes (most of which prohibit unfair and deceptive business practices).

Tobacco manufacturers responded in full force, fighting each lawsuit and refusing to settle out of court.

The Tobacco companies won all these early suits.

In the 1980s, a second wave of litigation introduced the concept of addiction.[5]

In the landmark case of that time, Cipollone v. Liggett, the plaintiff and her family alleged that cigarette manufacturers knew—but did not warn consumers—that smoking caused lung cancer and that cigarettes were addictive. Although Rose Cipollone's husband was awarded $400,000, an appellate court reversed the decision. Other plaintiffs also sued, claiming that tobacco companies knew cigarettes were addictive and caused cancer.

In defending these lawsuits, the tobacco companies argued that smokers had knowingly assumed the risks of cancer and other health problems when they began smoking. The companies also argued that various state laws were preempted by federal laws. That is, that federal laws governing tobacco advertising superseded state laws regarding the same thing, and plaintiffs couldn't sue under the state law. For the most part, the tobacco industry was successful in these lawsuits.

In the 1990s, plaintiffs began having success, and many states joined in the action which characterized the third wave, and quackonomics by the states became the deplorable situation that needs to be understood.

Some cigarette company documents were leaked showing the companies were aware of the addictive nature of tobacco. The first big win for plaintiffs in a tobacco lawsuit occurred in February 2000, when a California jury ordered Philip Morris to pay $51.5 million to a California smoker with inoperable lung cancer.

The states began to realize the enormous cost to taxpayers that consequences and complications of smoking were inflicting on our public health systems, and so forty-six states sued the tobacco companies under state consumer protection and antitrust laws (the remaining four settled separately).[6]

In November 1998, the attorneys general of 46 states and four of the largest tobacco companies agreed to settle the state cases. Terms of the settlement are referred to as the (Tobacco) Master Settlement Agreement.

Big Tobacco saw a unique opportunity to buy off the states in return for ensuring protection from any liability from tobacco use in the future. According to the *New York Times* in 2014,[7]

> In return, the tobacco companies agreed to make annual payments, in perpetuity, to the states to fund anti-smoking campaigns and public health programs. The industry guaranteed a minimum of $206 billion over the first 25 years.
>
> While a requirement that the states use these funds as intended was not written into the agreement, it was anticipated that they would do so.
>
> The sad truth—THEY HAVEN'T.
>
> Only a fraction of the money has gone to the tobacco prevention. Instead, the states have used the windfall for various and unrelated expenditures. For example, Niagara County, N.Y. spent $700,000 for a public golf course's sprinkler system, and $24 million for a county jail and office building.
>
> Nine states—Alaska, California, Iowa, Michigan, New Jersey, New York, Ohio, Rhode Island and West Virginia and Washington, D.C., Puerto Rico and Guam decided to get as much of those annual payments as fast as they could by mortgaging any future payments as collateral and issuing bonds. They traded their future lifetime income for cash today—at only pennies on the dollar.

According to ProPublica,[8] here is how it worked. This handful of states promised to pay $64 billion on $3 billion advanced. Wall Street sold the idea that private investors—not the taxpayers—would take the hit if people smoked less and the tobacco money fell short.

A ProPublica analysis of more than 100 tobacco deals since the settlement found that they are creating new fiscal headaches for states, driving some into bailouts or threatening to increase the cost of borrowing in the future.

One source of the pain is a little-known feature found in many of the deals: high-risk debt that squeezed out a few extra dollars for the governments but promised massive balloon payments, some in the billions, down the road.

These securities, called capital appreciation bonds, or CABs, have since turned toxic. They amount to only a $3 billion sliver of the approximately $36 billion in tobacco bonds outstanding, according to a review of bond documents and Thomson Reuters data. But the nine states, three territories, District of Columbia and several counties that issued them have promised a whopping $64 billion to pay them off.

Under the deals, the debts must be repaid with settlement money and not tax dollars. Still, taxpayers lose out when tobacco income that could be spent on other government services is diverted to paying off CABs. And states can't simply walk away from the debt—bondholders have a right to further tobacco payments even after a default.

In several counties in New York (my own county of Monroe included), the quick money was used to balance the annual budgets. The politicians from these same counties ran for election on the record that they did not raise taxes. In my judgment, this is a form of "quackonomics squared"—bad leadership and bad government. Where you might ask, are the anti-smoking education programs? According to Tobacco-Free Kids Reports,[9]

In the current budget year, Fiscal Year 2018, the states will collect $27.5 billion from the settlement and taxes. But they will spend less than 3 percent of it—$721.6 million—on programs to prevent kids from smoking and help smokers quit.

There are several ways of viewing the costs to the system that the Master Settlement Agreement (MSA) presents. We as a country should be thankful that only nine states, three territories, and the District of Columbia decided on taking advances in exchange for issuing CABs. The other states had the good sense to avoid a major cost in the future as the bonds come due. The major cost that must be considered is that the states have missed a golden opportunity to aim for a smoke-free country. The fifty-year progress report stated,[10]

Despite significant progress since the first Surgeon General's report, issued 50 years ago, smoking remains the single largest cause of preventable disease and death in the United States.

Smoking rates among adults and teens are less than half what they were in 1964; however, 42 million American adults and about 3 million middle and high school students continue to smoke.

Nearly half a million Americans die prematurely from smoking each year.

More than 16 million Americans suffer from a disease caused by smoking.

On average, compared to people who have never smoked, smokers suffer more health problems and disability due to their smoking and ultimately lose more than a decade of life.

The estimated economic costs attributable to smoking and exposure to tobacco smoke continue to increase and now approach $300 billion

annually, with direct medical costs of at least
$130 billion and productivity losses of more than
$150 billion a year.

The major cost to the country is the missed opportunity cost—
the opportunity to educate our youth not only about smoking as a
health risk but, more importantly, on the nature and horrid consequences of *addiction*. This must be done at an early age. One obvious course is to harness this tobacco settlement money to the opioid
epidemic campaign. Because addiction is the common denominator,
this can best be done with federal leadership and additional funds to
ensure treatment and success. It can be best done in a nonpartisan
way. If we cannot agree on making ourselves healthy, what can we
agree on?

Cost factors: Aggregate cost of tobacco smoking in the US in
2018 is *$331 billion*.[11]

Tobacco kills more than 480,000 people
annually—more than AIDS, alcohol, car accidents, illegal drugs, murders and suicides combined. Tobacco costs the U.S. approximately
$170 billion in health care expenditures and
more than $150 billion in lost productivity each
year.

N.B.: Annual tobacco industry expenditures lobbying Congress in 2016: $20.1 million.

Continuous Pressures On The FDA

FDA is an agency of the United States Department of Health
and Human Services, part of the executive branch of our federal
government.[1]

The Food and Drug Administration is
responsible for protecting the public health
by ensuring the safety, efficacy, and security of

human and veterinary drugs, biological products, and medical devices; and by ensuring the safety of our nation's food supply, cosmetics, and products that emit radiation. Dec 29, 2017.

By any measure, this mission is an enormous responsibility. Wikipedia summarizes some of the criticisms the FDA has endured.[2] We can start with charges of over regulation:

- Alleged problems in the drug approval process.
  The economist Milton Friedman claimed that the regulatory process is inherently biased against approval of some worthy drugs, because the adverse effects of wrongfully banning a useful drug are undetectable, while the consequences of mistakenly approving a harmful drug are highly publicized and that therefore the FDA will take the action that will result in the least public condemnation of the FDA regardless of the health consequences.

Friedman may have been a Nobel Prize winner, but I give him a C- in science for his double talk.

The thalidomide birth defects crisis led to passage of the 1962 Kefauver Harris Amendment, which required proof of efficacy in addition to safety for approval of new drugs. Proving efficacy is much more expensive and time-consuming than proving safety. By requiring proof of efficacy in addition to safety, the Kefauver Harris Amendment added considerable cost and delay to the drug approval process—which critics say may well have cost many more lives than it was said to save. Prior to passage of the Kefauver Harris

Amendment, the average time from the filing of an investigational new drug application (IND) to approval was 7 months. By 1998, it took an average of 7.3 years from the date of filing to approval. Prior to the 1990s, the mean time for new drug approvals was shorter in Europe than in the United States, although that difference has since disappeared.

For those who continually harp on length of time it takes for proving safety *and* efficacy, a short reflection on the thalidomide crisis should be enough. Cutting corners is dangerous territory.

- Allegations that FDA regulation causes higher drug price.

  Studies published in 2003 by Joseph DiMasi and colleagues estimated an average cost of approximately $800 million to bring a new drug to market, while a 2006 study estimated the cost to be anywhere from $500 million to $2 billion. The consumer advocacy group Public Citizen, using a different methodology, estimated the average cost for development to be under $200 million, about 29% of which is spent on FDA-required clinical trials. DiMasi rejects the claim that high R&D costs alone are responsible for high drug prices. Instead, in a published letter, DiMasi writes, "Longer development times increase R&D costs and shorten the period during which drug companies can earn the returns they need to make investment financially viable. Other things being equal, longer development times reduce innovation incentives. Consequently, fewer new therapies might be developed."

This argument does not hold water, because we cannot use the profit motive to shorten scientifically determined testing time. Moreover, a proper testing time that extends the evidence of efficacy is a worthy objective for a pharmaceutical product and favors a more profitable product.

- Allegations of censorship in food and drug labeling.

The FDA has been criticized by advocates for the supplement industry for prohibiting dietary supplement manufacturers from making research supported claims of effectiveness on the labels of their products. Manufacturers of supplements, which are considered foods for regulatory purposes, are allowed to make only limited "structure/function claims" and are prohibited from claiming that the supplement can prevent, cure, or mitigate a disease or condition regardless of whether or not the supplement undergoes actual testing of its safety and efficacy. Ron Paul (R-TX) opined: "But the FDA and the drug companies are in bed together and they squeeze out competitions and build up their monopolies and they love government medicine because they make more money." Ron Paul also introduced a bill on November 10, 2005 titled the "Health Freedom Protection Act" (H.R. 4282) which proposed to stop "the FDA from censoring truthful claims about the curative, mitigative, or preventative effects of dietary supplements, and adopts the federal court's suggested use of disclaimers as an alternative to censorship."

The supplement industry has trouble differentiating a supplement from a drug, and it is an endless battle to educate the public and to prevent the supplement market from sneaking in a substance that has not been held to the highest standards of drug effectiveness and safety. Ron Paul does the public no service by trying to cut corners. As a physician, he should be held to higher standards and meet his obligation to "do no harm." One wonders how much the supplement market contributes to his campaigns.

Then, of course, there is the charge of under-regulation.[3]

In addition to those who see the FDA as a source of excessive regulation, other critics believe that the FDA does not regulate some products strictly enough. According to this view, the FDA allows unsafe drugs on the market because of pressure from pharmaceutical companies, fails to ensure safety in drug storage and labelling, and allows the use of dangerous agricultural chemicals, food additives, and food processing techniques.

A $1.8 million 2006 Institute of Medicine report on pharmaceutical regulation in the U.S. found major deficiencies in the current FDA system for ensuring the safety of drugs on the American market. Overall, the authors called for an increase in the regulatory powers, funding, and independence of the FDA.

In the case of Vioxx, a pre-approval study indicated that a group taking the drug had four times the risk of heart attacks when compared to another group of patients taking another anti-inflammatory, naproxen. The FDA approval board accepted the manufacturer's argument that this was due to a previously unknown cardio-protective effect of naproxen, rather than a risk of Vioxx, and the drug was approved. In 2005, the results of a randomized, placebo-controlled study showed that Vioxx users suffered a higher rate of heart attacks and other cardiovascular disorders than patients taking no medication at all. The manufacturer, Merck, withdrew the drug after disclosures that it had withheld information about its risks from doctors and patients for over five years, resulting in between 88,000 and 140,000 cases of serious heart disease of which roughly half died. David Graham, a scientist in the Office of Drug Safety within the CDER, testified to Congress that he was pressured by his supervisors not to warn the public about dangers of drugs like Vioxx. He argued that an inherent conflict of interest exists when the office responsible for post-approval monitoring of drug safety is controlled by the same organization which initially approved those same drugs as safe and effective. He said that after testifying against Vioxx, he was "marginalized by FDA management and not asked to participate in the evaluation of any new drug safety issues. It's a type of ostracism. In a 2006 survey sponsored by the Union of Concerned Scientists, almost one-fifth of FDA scientists said they "have been asked, for non-scientific reasons, to inappropriately exclude or alter technical information or their conclusions in a FDA scientific document."

The FDA has been criticized for allowing the use of recombinant bovine growth hormone (rBGH) in dairy cows. rBGH-treated cows secrete higher levels of insulin-like growth factor 1 (IGF-1) in their milk than do untreated cows. IGF-1 signaling is thought to play a role in sustaining the growth of some tumors, although there is little or no evidence that exogenously absorbed IGF could promote tumor growth. The FDA approved rBGH for use in dairy cows in 1993, after concluding that humans drinking such milk were unlikely to absorb biologically significant quantities of bovine IGF-1. A 1999 report of the European Commission Scientific Committee on Veterinary Measures relating to Public Health noted that scientific questions persist regarding the theoretical health risks of milk from rBGH-treated cows, particularly for feeding to infants. Since 1993, all EU countries have maintained a ban on rBGH use in dairy cattle.

The FDA has also been criticized for permitting the routine use of antibiotics in healthy domestic animals to promote their growth, a practice which allegedly contributes to the evolution of antibiotic-resistant strains of bacteria. The FDA has taken recent steps to limit the use of antibiotics in farm animals. In September 2005, the FDA withdrew approval for the use of the fluoroquinolone antibiotic enrofloxacin (trade name Baytril) in poultry, out of concern that this practice could promote bacterial resistance to important human antibiotics such as ciprofloxacin.

Finally, there is the unremitting pressure of Big Pharma lobbyists on the FDA, described by one former FDA director as "constant, tremendous, sometimes unmerciful pressure" from the drug industry and that the drug company lobbyists, combined with the politicians who worked on behalf of their patrons, could bring "tremendous pressure" to bear on him and his staff, to try preventing FDA restrictions on their drugs.[4]

A historical example of how the FDA seemingly favors the pharmaceutical industry either from clandestine direct money payments to FDA directors and scientific advisers or other undisclosed or unknown means was seen with the generic drug droperidol. Droperidol was a widely used antiemetic used perioperatively safely for over 30 years. During that time there had never been a case reported in peer-reviewed medical literature of cardiac arrhythmias or cardiac issues when given at doses typically used for post-operative nausea and vomiting. Nonetheless, and without warning, in 2001 the FDA issued a black box warning regarding QTc prolongation (a dangerous finding on an ECG [electrocardiogram] which can lead to cardiac arrest) with the use of droperidol. This effectively killed the common use of droperidol and made way for heavy usage of the much more expensive non-generic 5-HT3 serotonin receptor antagonists on the market even though these newer drugs had also been shown to prolong QTc as much, if not more than droperidol. In addition, each of the 5-HT3 antagonists available at that time had peer-reviewed reports of causing significant cardiac abnormalities, and in some cases, death. Despite an apparent discrepancy that deeply concerned the anesthesia community, the FDA persisted in keeping the black box warning, while at the same time did not place any restrictions on the more expensive 5-HT3 antagonists.

On April 14, 2017, House and Senate leaders announced a bipartisan agreement to extend the FDA's ability to collect high user fees from drug companies and medical device manufacturers. This law allowed and continues to allow the FDA to charge huge licensing fees to drug manufacturers, which has led to enormous increases in generic drug pricing. In 2013 and 2014, generic drug pricing for over two hundred drugs increased over 100 percent. Many of those drugs had price hikes over 100 percent. It has been reported that 75 percent of the FDA generic drug oversight budget comes directly from private drug companies. It is difficult to avoid a conflict of interest when you are obligated to regulate the people who are paying you. It is like the bond rating agencies that contributed to the Wall Street financial disaster of 2007–8.

How much is spent lobbying the FDA each year? The answer is, "A lot." According to the Union of Concerned Scientists between 2009 and 2011, prescription drug, biotechnology, and medical device companies spent more than $700 million lobbying Congress and the Obama administration.[5] There were 398 clients who were involved in lobbying the FDA in 2017, according to the Center for Responsive Politics.[6] This website has a spreadsheet showing the amount of money spent by each client. The bottom line here is not just the corruption per se but the destructive pressure on the scientific integrity of scientists within the FDA, an issue they have been struggling with for some time (see 2006 report also from the Union of Concerned Scientists).[7]

Dr. Scott Gottlieb was appointed commissioner of the FDA by President Trump. One positive note can be found in the fact that, according to the *New York Times*,[8] he beat out a contender, Jim O'Neill:

> a former official at the Health and Human Services Department who is an associate of the Silicon Valley billionaire and Trump supporter Peter Thiel. Mr. O'Neill has argued that companies should not have to prove that their drugs work in clinical trials before selling them to consumers.

To that, I can only say, "Wow!" PS: As of this writing, Dr. Gottlieb has resigned, and the position has not been filled.

Early evaluation by *The Times*[9] has given Dr. Gottlieb good marks for balancing the huge opposing forces that clash at the doors of the FDA. The Congress and the people will be watching in this new Trump era of cutting regulations. The FDA responses to the addiction crisis are likely to be the key point of focus. One critic, Dr. Andrew Kolodny,[10] argues,

> Had the FDA been doing its job properly with regard to opioids, we never would have had this epidemic. After Dr. Scott Gottlieb resigned as commissioner of the FDA, he joined the board of Pfizer, less than three months after he left the agency. Senator Elizabeth Warren[11], candidate for president, said that his decision to join "one country's leading pharmaceutical companies smacks of corruption." Senator Warren is supporting legislation that would prohibit this "revolving door" between government and industry.

Aside from the conflict of interest issues, the only quackonomics in pressuring the FDA is lobbying intended to cut corners, resulting in problems of quality. There is a cost, to be sure, but it is not possible to assign an annual amount.

Within the Medical Profession

*The first principal is that you must not fool
yourself—and you are the easiest one to fool.*
—Richard Feynman, physicist

1. Invasion of CIM into Scientific Medicine

Scientific medicine is confronted with the unproven alternative medicine forces more and more each day. Even such highly regarded institutions as the Cleveland Clinic[1] have reverted to questionable practices and use terms like "functional medicine" or "integrated" medicine to supposedly champion a "more personalized," "system-oriented" model that "empowers patients and practitioners to achieve the highest expression of health by working in collaboration to address the underlying causes of disease." This is the vocabulary of pure marketing and salesmanship! It is as if your doctor or home institution couldn't possibly be doing what they, the Cleveland Clinic, are, and at this advertised high level. And of course, like the museum, there is a gift shop. Step right up, folks! Only here it is called the Healthy Living Shop, where you can buy supplements and alternative medicine products.

David Gorski, a surgical oncologist and a member of the American College of Surgeons, on the website Science-Based Medicine, sums it up quite well.[2]

> Quackery has been steadily infiltrating academic medicine for at least two decades now in the form of what was once called "complementary and alternative medicine" but is now more commonly referred to as "integrative medicine." Of course, as I've written many times before, what "integrative medicine" really means is the "integration" of quackery with science-based and evidence-based medicine, to the detriment of Science-Based-Medicine. As my good bud Mark Crislip once put it, "integrating" cow pie with apple pie does not improve the apple pie. Yet that is what's going on in medical academia these days—with a vengeance. It's a phenomenon that I like to call quackademic medicine, something that's fast-turning medical academia into medical quackademia. It is not, as its proponents claim, the "best of both worlds."

The critique on this website is well worth reviewing in detail. He notes how George Washington University, in Washington, DC, has gone well beyond the Cleveland Clinic. Dr. Gorski goes on to say,

> From my vantage point it's depressingly true that the Cleveland Clinic has gotten very,

very bad indeed with respect to its promotion of medical pseudoscience. Besides its traditional Chinese medicine clinic and its Center for Functional Medicine, just take a look at its Center for Integrative Medicine, which offers chiropractic, acupuncture, and the magical faith healing that is reiki.

Then look at the Center for Integrative Medicine at the George Washington University Medical Center (GWCIM). Compared to the GWCIM, the Cleveland's integrative medicine program looks like a bastion of science-based medicine. GWCIM's list of services includes acupuncture, chiropractic, craniosacral therapy, infrared light therapies, glutathione infusions, Myers' Cocktail, naturopathy, reiki, intravenous high dose vitamin C, and genetic profile results that include "customized interpretation of 23andme.com genetic profile results with specific accent on methylation and detoxification profiles." It's a truly horrifying website to contemplate, given how little of it has any resemblance to science-based medicine and how much of it includes outright quackery like reiki.

The costs at the Cleveland Clinic for Functional Medicine visit is $1,500 for eighty minutes and $240 for a nutritionist.[3] The physicians do not accept insurance. It is difficult to get a handle on how much more quackademia is adding to the national cost of nonscience medicine, but it is certainly millions and growing. The growth in the nonscience component is partially due to joining with an organization called the Institute for Functional Medicine, which sponsors certification programs, which also add to the costs and are based upon many forms of unproven medicine.[4]

In 2016, the Cleveland Clinic announced the doubling of the size of the Functional Medicine Center.[5] And as you might have guessed, it has a lot to do with money. Medical director Dr. Patrick Hanaway states,

> While many people hold that functional medicine is incompatible with insurance, Dr. Paul Hanaway (Medical Director) believes that making it work within insurance settings is essential for the future, not only at major institutions like Cleveland Clinic but also in the trenches of solo and small group practice.
>
> "The out-of-pocket sector is limited. Finding ways to make this work within insurance-based medicine is essential for the future," he says. "There's a huge demand for this kind of care, but the reality is most people rely on their insurance plans, so we have to learn how to do this in that context."
>
> He added that the ultimate challenges for functional medicine as a movement are to bring the logic of functional medicine into tertiary care, and simultaneously to figure out ways to make it work for the Medicaid population.
>
> Though the Cleveland Clinic environment is clearly very different from medical life on Mainstreet USA, Dr. Hanaway believes that community-based functional medicine practitioners who deliver the clinical goods and who figure out the insurance equation, will meet the same robust response that his CFM (Cleveland Functional Medicine) team experienced.

In other words, he sees making insurance pay for unproven, unscientific medicine is the key to success in the private sector, and in so doing, it will be easy to get government programs such as Medicaid to swallow the costs. I am one of those who believe that "functional medicine is incompatible with insurance," as Dr.

Hanaway observed. Insurance companies should not be coerced into paying for complementary, integrated, functional, or whatever the nonscience pseudomedicine of the day is called. But the pressure is there. Look forward to big buyouts of insurance companies to meet these ends. Quackonomics will not stand still where greed is the goal.

The sad reality is that the medical profession may simply cave because of the pressure of large institutions, plus the pressure of lowered professional standards. For example, in my searching for a functional medicine practitioner online, of sixteen presenting in a 150-mile radius, nine of those were not MDs.[6]

Most recently, there have been signs of contraction of functional clinics.[7] The Continuum Center for Health and Healing on First Avenue in NYC, formerly a thirty-two-clinician integrative center, closed in 2016 after a merger between Continuum Health Partners and the now-dominant Mt. Sinai Medical Center. This was a showcase, with feng shui-designed office space, thirty-three practitioners, including homeopath, chiropractor, Chinese medicine, massage, acupuncture, and aromatherapy services plus five family physicians. Nationally, there is a tug-of-war.

> On the expanding side, we see significant expansion at Jefferson in Philadelphia, a new 17,000 square foot space for the Center for Functional Medicine at the Cleveland Clinic, and system-wide integrative health at Meridian Health plus the build-up of integrative health and research in the Veterans Administration.
>
> On the contracting side, the shutdown of the Banner/Center for Integrative Health in Phoenix which was intended as a proving ground for integrative care; the Allina/Penny George Institute shut its research department and limited its inpatient program; and while not a clinical site, the Samueli Institute, an engine of integrative health research, also announced that it is ending operations.

As Nutraceuticals World[4] website concludes,[8]

> Most insurance plans still do not cover holistic and functional medicine, and coverage is marginal in Medicare and Medicaid plans. Those hospitals that have embraced "integrative" medicine tend to silo it in distinct clinics rather than truly integrating its principles into routine patient care.
>
> As the sudden forced closures of the centers in Arizona and New York illustrate, hospital-based integrative centers dwell on precarious ground, and they can be dashed quickly if hospital administrators feel the numbers just aren't adding up.
>
> For all its successes—and the needle has moved a good bit in the last 20 years—the integrative medicine movement failed to scale.
>
> While most Americans have ready access to dietary supplements and a wealth of information about natural healthcare, only a small minority has routine access to affordable integrative medical services provided by fully trained and licensed healthcare professionals. Practitioner membership in the organizations committed to integrative medicine has hit a plateau in the last few years, as has attendance at conferences. While many organizations are solid and thriving, they are still small—both in numbers and in political clout—compared to the associations representing mainstream medical specialties.
>
> As was shown in an Institute for Functional Medicine survey last year, physicians often take

---

[4] Permission to publish granted by Rodman Media. First published in Nutraceuticals World.com, courtesy Sean Moloughney, Editor, 2017.

a significant income hit—sometimes as much as 30%—when they leave conventional drug-based, insurance-dominated practices and go full-time into alternative care models. This is a big reason why integrative medicine is more of a hobby than a full-time living for many of its would-be adherents in clinical practice.

On the hospital network side, where big-ticket procedures mean big revenue, integrative medicine's emphasis on preventing costly episodes looks like a questionable investment. Hospitals make money by doing invasive procedures, not preventing them.

For a list of medical institutions that have an official association with at least one form of complementary and alternative pseudo-medicine, see Society for Science-Based Medicine.[9]

The monetary cost of unscientific care was outlined in part II of this book, but it is worth emphasizing some intangible costs to the system by the medical profession. Besides blurring the line between science and nonscience and confusing the public, there is the issue of coercing insurance companies and thereby pandering to quackonomics. Finally, it deflects dollars away from legitimate research and contaminates the medical education system, all intangibles difficult to attach a price.

2.   Complicity in the Opioid Epidemic

Why do we have prescriptions? Why not simply sell all medications over-the-counter? The answer is obvious. Pharmacology is a science and a branch of medicine dealing with the discovery, preparation, uses, and effects of drugs and, as a result, requires specific knowledge and experience. Pharmacology is expanding, is complex, and requires constant education to keep up-to-date. That is why society designates physicians with this responsibility—the responsibility to prescribe—to prescribe for the right patient, the right medication, at the right time, for the right amount, and for the right length of time.

It is sad to comment that a sizable number of practicing physicians in many clinical fields failed in this responsibility regarding opioids. In my judgment, it was lapse in understanding the pharmacology of the medications being prescribed, a failure to be critical of pharmaceutical firms claiming their product was not addictive, a failure to follow patients closely to monitor the process, and finally, the failure to inform patients of the basic pharmacology of the drug they were taking for pain. This triad contributed to the perfect storm. In 2014, the guidelines from the American College of Physicians changed.[1]

It now recommends that patients should physically see the doctor to get a refill instead of just calling the office. Doctors are also encouraged to address acute pain with shorter prescriptions and no refills.

Liberal use of opioids for postsurgical recovery has led to drug dependence and addiction.[2]

Roughly 1 in every 16 surgical patients who were prescribed opioids were still getting the drugs three to six months later, University of Michigan researchers found. The larger the opioid prescription, the greater the chance of long-term use.

The Center for Disease Control (CDC) has proposed guidelines for prescribing opioids for chronic pain.[3]

The CDC's 2016 Guideline for Prescribing Opioids for Chronic Pain draft proposal, urges primary care doctors to try drug-free methods to relieve chronic pain, such as exercise, weight loss and physical therapy, as well as non-opioid pain relievers such as acetaminophen and ibuprofen, before resorting to powerful opioid pills. If opioids are needed, the guidelines recommend starting with the smallest effective dose of immediate-release opioids, avoiding more dangerous time-release formulations except when needed.

But this is not a simple issue anymore. The physicians must generate a more proactive stance.[4]

"Opioid abuse is a much more complicated issue than the CDC and lawmakers would have us believe," says Lynn Webster, MD, Vice President Scientific Affairs, PRA Health Sciences. "While it's true we are seeing a continual increase in opioid-related overdose deaths, this coincides with a significant drop in opioids prescribed. Reducing the supply side does not address the demand for opioids, nor does it help address the needs of people with addictions. Reducing the amount of prescribed opioids may in fact force many of those denied opioids for pain to seek illegal opioids such as heroin and synthetic fentanyl, which are far more dangerous. The unintended consequence could be even more fatal overdoses."

As of this writing, over a hundred people a day are dying from overdose, and the question at hand is, how do we manage the physician responsibility for pain management and at the same time the responsibility to respond to the presidential emergency declaration? Time will tell whether this administration can do the job.

I have little faith that it will, after witnessing the White House Conference on Opioid Addiction presented on TV on March 1, 2018. The conference started with presidential adviser Kellyanne Conway presenting the First Lady, Melania Trump, who read a brief statement of commitment to the crisis and then was promptly escorted out of the room by what appeared to be a security detail. She did not even stay to hear several cabinet-level officials detail possible solutions for the symposium to consider. Of the four of these, the Secretary of Veterans Affairs, Dr. David Shulkin, speaking without notes, gave the most cogent and logical set of solutions with pain practice guidelines, many of which had already been working well at the VA. It was with deep disgust that I learned that hardly ten days later, the president announced that he was replacing Dr. Shulkin with Rick Perry, Secretary of Energy (later changing his mind and naming his personal physician, Rear Admiral Ronny Jackson, who was forced to resign for complaints, including writing questionable opioid prescriptions). Nor did the First Lady stay to hear any of the other experts or the testimonials and experiences of many of the invited guests. Some leadership!

Witness President Trump's visit to New Hampshire on March 19, 2018,[5] where he declared, "If we don't get tougher on drug dealers, we are wasting our time. That toughness includes the death penalty."

> The president also called for repealing the Affordable Care Act, which expanded Medicaid to cover much of the addiction treatment provided around the United States over the past few years.
>
> (Note, New Hampshire is the only state in New England that still allows capital punishment, though it has not executed anyone since 1939.)

The first statement is a waste of time, and the second position would only worsen the crisis by depriving the patients with drug-addiction adequate care, recovery, and follow-up and drive them into the heroin/fentanyl death spiral.

We will wait and see what kind of leadership the medical profession can muster now that this epidemic has been declared a national emergency. It will not be just a question of better guidelines for pre-scription writing but leadership at the state and local levels in long-range follow-up and maintaining the health of this most unfortu-nate population. We will need research efforts in our pharmacology departments in our medical schools. We will need leadership from the medical community in the education effort that will be necessary in our public-school system and the educating of elected leaders to generate the necessary funding for a successful effort. We need our medical societies to be leaders in the various task forces being formed in every county of the country. A crisis requires everyone to take part.

As of this writing, six months after President Trump declared the opioid crisis a public health emergency,

> The White House Office charged with over-seeing his administration's response hasn't come up with a congressionally mandated strat-egy to address it.
>
> The office charged with coordinating the federal response to illegal drugs has been threat-ened with budget cuts and operating without a Senate-confirmed leader since Trump took office.[6]

It is difficult to place a cost figure on the medical professions' contribution to the opioid crisis, but it is certainly a notable part of the $504 billion cost. Until more clarity comes out of that figure, assigning $5 billion is probably a token amount.

3. Abusing Medicare/Medicaid Billing

Fraud, abuse, and waste in Medicaid cost states billions of dol-lars every year, diverting funds that could otherwise be used for legit-imate health-care services.[1]

Not only do fraudulent and abusive practices increase the cost of Medicaid without adding value—they increase risk and poten-tial harm to patients who are exposed to unnecessary procedures. In

2015, improper payments alone—which include things like payment for non-covered services or for services that were billed but not provided—totaled more than $29 billion according to the Government Accountability Office.

In addition to physician fraud, patient and insurance fraud was included in this amount. Wikipedia[2] reports that

> In June 2015, Federal officials charged 243 people including 46 doctors, nurses, and other medical professionals with Medicare fraud schemes. The government said the fraudulent schemes netted approximately $712 million in false billings in what is the largest crackdown undertaken by the Medicare Fraud Strike Force. The defendants were charged in the Southern District of Florida, Eastern District of Michigan, Eastern District of New York, Southern District of Texas, Central District of California, Eastern District of Louisiana, Northern District of Texas, Northern District of Illinois and the Middle District of Florida.

A report released in 2015 to Congress from the US Government Accountability Office (GAO) showed that the core of the problem was the 23,400 potentially fake or bad addresses on Medicare's list of health-care providers.[3]

> The report says that the Centers for Medicare and Medicaid Services (CMS), the federal agency that administers Medicare, estimates that last year some $60 billion of American taxpayer money, or more than 10 percent of Medicare's total budget, was lost to fraud, waste, abuse and improper payments.

In August of 2017, an Oklahoma physician was hit with $580,000 settlement to resolve false Medicare billing allegations. The government alleged that Dr. Gordon Laird caused false claims to be submitted to Medicare for service not provided.[4]

> The government alleged that Laird caused false claims to be submitted to Medicare that he neither provided nor supervised, including in 2011, when he allegedly allowed Prevention Plus to use his National Provider Identifier (NPI) numbers to bill Medicare for evaluation and management physical therapy services that he didn't provide or oversee. Additionally, allegations against Laird state that in December 2011, he separated from Prevention Plus, ceased services for Prevention Plus, and deactivated his NPIs connected to Prevention Plus.
>
> Then, in March 2012, the government claimed he reactivated those NPIs so Prevention Plus could use them to bill Medicare for services in January and February 2012. Those billings were for services Laird neither provided nor supervised, the DOJ said.

Also, from a running list of 2017 health-care fraud[5] is this story of a sixty-year-old Dallas, Texas, doctor who was convicted of Medicare/Medicaid fraud. Dr. Jacques Roy was sentenced to thirty-five years in prison plus payment of $238 million restitution penalty for conspiring with five other codefendants to defraud the government using several of their companies, including Medistat Group Associates, Apple of Your Eye Healthcare Services, Ultimate Care Home Services, and Home Care Services. Dr. Roy, who intended to flee to Canada, directed the recruiting of individuals from Dallas homeless shelters, billing for falsely documented homebound care plans. The DOJ uncovered eleven thousand cases of fraudulent claims. The home-wealth conspiracy had yielded $375 million in

Medicare/Medicaid billing. One US attorney on the case was quoted, saying, "This takes brazen to a whole new level."

South Florida is scene of a saga of medical fraud.[6] From the Christian Science Monitor, staff writer Warren Richey, on June 21, 2017, broke the saga of how a Miami psychiatrist cheated the system but finally collided with a determined health-care fraud investigator.[5*]

> It started with a letter from US Senator Charles Grassley. In December 2009, the Iowa Republican demanded to know how a Miami psychiatrist was writing more than 96,000 prescriptions for Medicaid patients. It was nearly twice the number of the second highest prescriber in Florida.
>
> The psychiatrist, Dr. Fernando Mendez-Villamil, responded with a tartly worded message of his own. "I never thought I would be faulted for working hard or for being very organized and efficient," he wrote the senator.
>
> Even after Dr. Mendez-Villamil was kicked out of Medicaid and barred from Medicare, he continued to operate an elaborate network of bribes, kickbacks, and payoffs that helped hundreds of fake patients fraudulently obtain Social Security disability payments.
>
> Among hard-boiled fraud investigators in Miami, the strange and circuitous case of Dr. Mendez-Villamil stands out as a monument to criminal innovation, brazen defiance, and greed. This is the story of how a Miami psychiatrist managed to beat the system year after year, but finally met his match in a health-care fraud investigator named Alberico Crespo.

---

[5] *From the *Christian Science Monitor.* © 2017 Christian Science Monitor. All rights reserved. Used under license.

For Crespo, the investigation began in mid-2010, a few weeks after he joined the Department of Health and Human Services as a special agent in the Inspector General's Office. That's when he was assigned the Mendez-Villamil case.

With the earlier letter from Senator Grassley and keen interest from HHS headquarters, the case of the defiant Miami psychiatrist had "trouble" written all over it. It was the kind of thankless, pain-in-the-neck case that almost always seems to find its way to the new guy's desk.

But Crespo had an advantage over many other investigators in the Inspector General's Miami Lakes office. He holds a master's degree in psychology, so he knew the language and understood the medical concepts. He also had years of prior law enforcement experience in South Florida as a police officer and as an agent with the Drug Enforcement Administration. According to his colleagues, Crespo has another advantage as well—the personality of a detective. Chief among those traits are patience and perseverance, they say.

At first Crespo focused on the unusually large volume of prescriptions the doctor was writing. "I go to the doctor's office and I am seeing just an extraordinary number of patients," Crespo says. "I thought they were handing out free items because they were lined up out the door."

Mendez-Villamil was seeing nearly 60 patients every day, six days a week. He allotted 10 to 15 minutes per patient and was writing 2 to 3 prescriptions for each patient. It amounted to 1,400 to 1,500 patients each month. At that rate, if he billed the standard $45 for each patient visit, he would receive between $63,000 and $67,000 each month under the Medicaid program. On an annual basis that could be as much as $800,000 a year in revenue just from patient visit fees.

Through a check of pharmaceutical records, Crespo discovered that the doctor was prescribing large amounts of quetiapine, a drug approved to treat psychiatric patients diagnosed with bipolar disorder. It is sold commercially under the name Seroquel. According to federal agents, there is a well-established black market in quetiapine, with street names including "jailhouse heroin," and "Susie Q."

The prescriptions Mendez-Villamil wrote were paid through Medicaid, so it didn't cost the patients anything. They could then either use the drugs as prescribed, abuse the drugs, or sell them to others on the street. "It was a free-for-all," Crespo says.

In October 2011, Crespo executed a search warrant at the doctor's office, seizing about 300 boxes of patient files and other medical records. Back at his office in Miami Lakes, the agent and other analysts randomly selected 30 of the boxes and began to compare the doctor's patient files.

The examination revealed something disturbing. "The clinical notes were all the same," Crespo says. "They could be a photocopy of each other." It suggested the psychiatrist was offering little, if any, individual attention to his patients.

There was more. Mendez-Villamil's patients never seemed to improve. "The way mental health works, you have peaks and valleys, but [his patients] tend to always get worse," Crespo says.

Rather than a medical practice set up to help patients, the office seemed to be organized as an assembly line to facilitate billing. What Crespo soon discovered is that Mendez-Villamil wasn't just collecting patient consultation fees and prescribing large amounts of drugs. There was more going on.

Crespo found that many of Mendez-Villamil's patients were receiving Social Security disability payments. The doctor had provided the medical assessments necessary to verify that his patients' mental conditions rendered them completely disabled. Acting on those medical assessments, the Social Security Administration had awarded a large number of his patients full disability benefits.

Crespo reached out to an agent with the Social Security Administration. Together they had several of Mendez-Villamil's patients re-evaluated to test whether they were truly disabled.

"Now the stars are starting to align," he says of the investigation. Crespo and the other agent watched as patients currently collecting government disability payments were brought into the office and interviewed one by one. Many who were clearly not mentally disabled nonetheless tried to act the way they thought someone with a mental disability might act.

"People would come in crying. One guy came in drooling and playing with a moth ball. I mean like ridiculous behavior," Crespo says.

At 6 a.m., the morning after one of these interviews, Crespo staked out that patient's home. During the interview the man had told Social Security officials he was barely able to function. But what Crespo saw at the patient's house was far different.

Confronting fraud face-to-face;

"Today, he is all shaved and clean and he has a $50,000 truck," Crespo says. "He's got a boat and a license to harvest lobsters. And by the way, his wife, she jumps in the vehicle—she's pregnant." (The day before he'd told the examiners that he had no relationship with his wife.) Crespo followed the husband and wife to a social services office where the wife applied for Medicaid to help pay expenses for the arriving baby.

The agent then confronted the "disabled" man.

"How are you," Crespo says he asked the man.

"What?"

"Nothing. I'm just making sure you are okay," Crespo said to the man. "You okay?"

"Yeah, I'm fine," the man said, apparently failing to recognize the agent.

Crespo adds of the encounter: "The same guy yesterday couldn't talk and couldn't function."

That's when the agent began to see the outline of a massive scam.

"It all became a joke," Crespo says, a very expensive joke on the US government and American tax payers. Crespo estimates that Mendez-Villamil helped 3,500 to 3,800 individuals fraudulently obtain Social Security disability payments. "At one point he was disabling up to 10 people a week," the agent says.

For $1,500 to $3,500 in cash, Mendez-Villamil would falsely diagnose anyone as having a severe mental disorder that would qualify him or her to receive Social Security disability payments.

Once the payment was received, the doctor's staff prepared a patient file that was typically back-dated a year or more to show the condition was chronic and to create a fake paper trail purporting to document a prolonged period of medical treatment, according to court documents.

"It was just straight back-dating, you come in today and I started treating you last year," the agent says. The scam would include decoy notes that would support the doctor's diagnosis of a prolonged psychological impairment so severe that the individual was unable to function effectively in any work environment.

The file would reflect regular visits and prescription drug maintenance. But it was all a ruse designed to convince officials at the Social Security office to award disability payments. That wasn't the only disability scam the doctor was running. For $200 in cash, Mendez-Villamil helped immigrants cheat on the US citizenship test, according to federal court documents.

The psychiatrist would falsely certify that an individual had a mental impairment that prevented that person from taking the English language test and/or the civics test which are part of the application to become a naturalized US citizen. The false disability certification helped them obtain a waiver from those requirements.

His "patients" also used the fake disability diagnosis to obtain waivers from paying fees charged to become a US citizen.

Further investigation revealed that all three members of Mendez-Villamil's own office staff had been diagnosed with severe psychological impairments. One staff member used the diagnosis to avoid having to take the civics test to become a US citizen. The two other employees were collecting Social Security disability payments.

One of the workers even had her then 13-year-old daughter falsely diagnosed with a severe disabling psychiatric condition. The mother then had herself designated as the representative payee for the teen's government disability checks.

"The girl was a typical socially active young Miami teenager. She tried out for the Miami Heat dancers," says Morales, the former prosecutor. "She was supposed to be so psychotic that she doesn't leave her room," he says. "This is egregious."

Mendez-Villamil paid his office workers off the books and in cash in part to prevent the government from discovering that each could, in fact, function and work despite their continuing receipt of Social Security disability payments, Crespo says.

One of the men working in the psychiatrist's office was simultaneously receiving $733 a month in fraudulent disability payments.

During his re-evaluation, the worker falsely told officials he had not worked since receiving disability, that he couldn't drive, and that his depression was so severe many days he could not leave his apartment, according to a signed statement filed as part of the worker's guilty plea in the Mendez-Villamil case.

"He goes to Cuba every other month for two to three weeks at a time," Crespo says of the "disabled" worker. "He doesn't drive, he doesn't get out of bed. He comes into Social Security and starts to cry. 'All I can do is get up and get a carton of milk and cry my way back to bed,'" the agent says quoting the man.

When asked how he arrived for his interview at the Social Security office since he was unable to drive, the worker told officials he had been dropped off. But moments after the interview, Crespo took several photos as the man got into his car and drove himself away.

Crespo wasn't the only government official concerned about Mendez-Villamil. "I had administrative law judges calling me and telling me this guy is a crook," the agent says.

After the media attention surrounding Senator Grassley's letter, Mendez-Villamil was dropped from the Medicaid program in June 2010. He was barred from billing under the Medicare program in September 2013. And the following month, the Florida Department of Health issued a $15,000 fine and reprimand against the doctor for maintaining sloppy and inconsistent medical files.

Crespo says he was forced to put his investigation on hold while the state pursued its own charges against the psychiatrist. Through it all, Mendez-Villamil kept his medical license and avoided any jail time.

Many doctors facing such intense scrutiny might be tempted to clean up their practice and stop violating the law, at least while federal and state investigators were actively examining their operations. Not Mendez-Villamil. "It made no difference to him. He was so brazen he reached the point where he was so far in the pit with snakes that he couldn't get out," Crespo says.

"He had a whole network of patient recruiters—people who were bringing him people—and he was just way too entangled," the agent says.

Instead of ending the fraud, the psychiatrist ramped up the Social Security disability scam as well as the citizenship test fraud, according to court records.

An FBI agent managed to locate an individual who knew one of the workers in the psychiatrist's office and was able to actually get an appointment to see the doctor.

The agents sent the confidential informant into the doctor's office with a hidden video camera. No undercover investigation ever goes completely as planned. The informant was forced to wait to see the doctor. During the wait, the camera's battery ran out.

"Who knew that it was going to take three hours to see him," Crespo says. Fortunately, a backup audio device kept recording.

Later, the agents nervously reviewed the audio tape until Crespo recognized the doctor's voice. "It was him," Crespo says. "I can identify his voice. I've talked to him."

The confidential informant was able to gain access to the doctor's office because 12 years earlier his friend had suggested he could help him obtain disability payments with a doctor's diagnosis even though he had no mental disability.

In mid-2015, the confidential informant reconnected with his friend and said he was now interested in receiving disability payments. The informant was told it would cost $1,500 and that his medical file would be backdated to January 2014. He was also told he would likely also be deemed eligible for Medicaid.

During his visit to the psychiatrist's office, the confidential informant was handed an envelope and told to put $1,500 inside. The informant was instructed that if he started receiving disability payments through Social Security that he could not be paid on the books for any employment. They told him any pay for work would have to be received under the table and in cash.

In the meeting with the doctor, the informant mentioned that he was also applying for US citizenship. He was told a diagnosis that would exempt him from the US government's citizenship test would cost $300—$150 up front and $150 later.

Nothing during his meeting with the psychiatrist resembled an authentic psychiatric examination, Crespo says. An office worker instructed the confidential source how to behave in any interview with Social Security officials, so his actions would appear consistent with the diagnosis they were about to write in his file, the agent says.

During the meeting, the psychiatrist wrote a prescription for medication that the confidential source could purchase cheaply, but the doctor warned him not to actually take the medication, according to court documents. The psychiatrist also told the confidential source that he did not have to see him every month, but that the doctor would update the patient file as if he had come into the office every month for a face-to-face consultation, court files show.

After a request for supporting documents from the Social Security Administration, Mendez-Villamil's office faxed 35 pages of false, back-dated medical records for the informant to the Social Security office. Some of the files included the patient's signature, which the informant discovered had been forged.

The fake medical records included a false diagnosis that said the informant was having "auditory hallucinations," was "disheveled," and was suffering from "bipolar" disorder, "depression with psychosis" and that his prognosis was "poor." None of it was true.

The sending of those false documents by the doctor's office to the Social Security Administration, combined with the audio tape of the doctor and his staff explaining how the fraud would be conducted, were the last two pieces of evidence necessary to make the case against Mendez-Villamil.

A guilty plea and $50.7 million

Confronted with the fruit of Crespo's detailed investigation, Mendez-Villamil pleaded guilty to health-care fraud in May 2016. He agreed to pay the government $50.7 million in restitution. He is serving a 12-½ year sentence in federal prison and has surrendered his medical license. According to a statement signed by Mendez-Villamil as part of his guilty plea, the psychiatrist's false diagnoses caused Social Security to make $20.3 million in undeserved disability payments to various "patients" between 2002 and January 2016.

In addition, the Medicaid program was billed $25.9 million in false claims, of which $16.7 million was paid for office visits that never occurred and for medications that were never needed or taken, according to the signed statement.

Mendez-Villamil also admitted that he submitted $15.8 million in false claims under the Medicare program, of which nearly $12.9 million was paid for office visits that never occurred and for medications that were never taken or needed.

The psychiatrist also said that from 2001 to 2016 he provided false diagnoses to help immigrants bypass portions of the US citizenship test. His disability certifications helped scores of individuals obtain waivers of immigration fees. Court papers show the waived fees cost the US government more than $814,000.

With Mendez-Villamil behind bars, the question remains: What about all those patients fraudulently receiving Social Security disability payments?

"A lot of them are now off the rolls and are starting to pay the government back," Crespo says. The fraud wasn't just about receiving disability payments. Someone who qualifies for disability under Social Security also qualifies for Medicaid and may also qualify for Medicare. Among beneficiaries it is called "Medi-Medi" and it is considered the gold standard for government-funded health-care insurance.

"That's like an unlimited American Express card in Miami. The sky is the limit," Crespo says.

"Every [doctor's office] will see you and you get put to the front of the line for Section 8 subsidized housing, you get subsidies on your electricity, your cable, and food stamps," he says.

"It is crazy the way the ripple effect extends across many, many social programs," he adds.

With so much fraud in South Florida, Crespo is asked whether he ever feels he's waging a hopeless battle against health-care crooks.

"It has become socially acceptable," he says of fraud against insurance companies, Medicaid, and Medicare. During jury selection, prospective jurors in South Florida are frequently asked if they have heard of health-care fraud. The jurors laugh, Crespo says.

"There is a perception that there are no repercussions for Medicare beneficiaries who defraud the system. I've had people tell me you can't do anything to me—straight to my face," Crespo says.

There seems to be no end to Florida fraud. This is the case of a physician being involved in health-care facility fraud.

In July of 2016, three Florida residents were charged in the "largest single criminal health-care fraud case ever brought against individuals" by the US Justice Department[6]—an alleged Medicare fraud and money laundering scheme that netted participants a whopping $1 billion since 2009, prosecutors revealed Friday.[7]

The owner of more than 30 Miami-area skilled nursing and assisted living facilities, as well as a hospital administrator and a physician's assistant were charged in an indictment with conspiracy, money laundering and health-care fraud, the U.S. Attorney's office in Miami said.

An explosive indictment and other court documents filed Friday claim that the massive alleged scam helped wealthy health-care operator Philip Esformes, 47, fund a lifestyle that included private jets, a $600,000 watch, meetings with escorts in hotel rooms, and a private basketball coach for his son.

---

[6] Permission to publish from CNBC. © 2016 CNBC, All Rights Reserved. Used under license.

The indictment claims that Esformes, 47, with his co-conspirators, cycled thousands of Medicare and Medicaid beneficiaries through his Esformes Network facilities despite the fact they didn't qualify for such care.

At those facilities, prosecutors said, they also "received medically unnecessary services that were billed to Medicare and Medicaid," the huge government-run health programs that cover primarily senior citizens and the poor, respectively.

"Furthermore, Defendant [Esformes] and his co-conspirators preyed upon his beneficiaries' addictions by providing them with narcotics so that the beneficiaries would remain in Esformes Network facilities, allowing the cycle of fraud [to] continue," prosecutors said in a court filing.

"Esformes is alleged to have been at the top of a complex and profitable health-care fraud scheme that resulted in staggering losses—in excess of $1 billion," said FBI Special Agent in Charge George Piro. Prosecutors say that Esformes operated the Esformes Network for "more than 14 years…to enrich himself through false and fraudulent billings."

Assistant Attorney General Leslie Caldwell of the Justice Department said: "This is the largest single criminal health-care fraud case ever brought against individuals by the Department of Justice, and this is further evidence of how successful data-driven law enforcement has been as a tool in the ongoing fight against health-care fraud."

South Florida is a hot spot for health-care billing fraud schemes that target the huge federal Medicare program, and the giant joint federal-state Medicaid program. As a result, the region has received special scrutiny from federal health regulators and prosecutors.

Miami U.S. Attorney Wifredo Ferrer said, "Medicare fraud has infected every facet of our health-care system."

Prosecutors said Esformes faces a potential prison term of life imprisonment under federal sentencing guidelines.

In addition to Esformes, 49-year-old Odette Barcha, who had been director of outreach programs at Larkin Community Hospital, and physician's assistant Arnaldo Carmouze, 56, also were charged in the case and arrested early Friday morning. After being presented in federal court Friday afternoon, they were ordered held in jail pending detention hearings, with Carmouze's scheduled for next Wednesday.

Esformes and Barcha, who are scheduled to appear at an Aug. 1 detention hearing, were also charged with obstructing justice

"According to the indictment, following the 2014 arrest of co-conspirators Guillermo and Gabriel Delgado"—in a prior case involving their alleged sale of the names of Medicare patients to a corrupt pharmacist—"Esformes attempted to fund Guillermo Delgado's flight from the United States to avoid trial in Miami," the U.S. Attorney's office said.

"The indictment further alleges that Barcha created sham medical director contracts following receipt of a grand jury subpoena in June 20, 2016, in order to conceal and disguise the payment of kickbacks she made in exchange for patient referrals for admission to Esformes Network facilities and another Miami-area hospital," the office said.

Esformes and his co-conspirators are alleged to have further enriched themselves by receiving kickbacks in order to steer Medicare beneficiaries to other health-care providers—including community mental health centers and home health-care providers—who also performed medically unnecessary treatments that were billed to Medicare and Medicaid, the office said.

"In order to hide the kickbacks from law enforcement, these kickbacks were often paid in cash, or were disguised as payments to charitable donations, payments for services and sham lease payments, court documents allege," according to prosecutors.

Payments to escorts and a basketball coach to provide private lessons to Esformes' son also were used to disguise the illicit transactions, authorities said.

The indictment claims that Esformes used money from "bribes and kickbacks he received from co-conspirators" to fund travel and transportation for two escorts, whom he separately "met with" at the Ritz-Carlton Hotel in Orlando, Florida, on different dates in February and March 2014.

"Financial analysis to date has revealed that Esformes is significantly funded by his fraudulent Medicare business," prosecutors said in a court filing. "Our analysis has revealed that monies traced directly to Medicare accounts have allowed Esformes to withdraw cash of over $4.8 million, lease private jets in the amount of $2.1 million, lease luxury vehicles in the amount of $2.4 million, purchase watches in the amount of $360,000 and $600,000 respectively and paid over $8.9 million in credit card bills."

The federal officials noted that in 2006, "Esformes paid $15.4 million to resolve civil federal health-care fraud claims for essentially identical conduct, namely unnecessarily admitting patients from his assisted living facilities into a Miami-area hospital." A press release issued at the time by the Justice Department indicates that Esformes settled that fine with two doctors who had owned the hospital, as he did, along with Philip's father, a rabbi named Morris Esformes.

"However, [Philip] Esformes and his co-conspirators allegedly continued this criminal activity—adapting their scheme to prevent detection and continue their fraud after the civil settlement," said the U.S. attorney's office on Friday.

The Chicago Tribune, in an August 2013 article, reported that Philip and Morris Esformes agreed in principle to pay the U.S. government $5 million to settle claims that they "took kickbacks related to the sale" for $32 million of a pharmacy partially owned by Philip to pharmaceutical giant Omnicare. Earlier that same year, the Tribune reported, Ominicare had agreed to pay $17.2 million to the government to settle its part of a lawsuit filed by a whistleblower related to the alleged kickbacks.

Esformes' lawyer Marissel Descalzo could not be immediately reached for comment. But in an email statement to the Bloomberg news service, Descalzo said that Esformes "adamantly denies these allegations and will fight hard to clear his name."

"Mr. Esformes is a respected and well-regarded businessman," said Descalzo in the email to Bloomberg. "He is devoted to his family and his religion. The government allegations appear to come from people who were caught breaking the law and are now hoping to gain reduced sentences."

Descalzo's reference to such law-breakers apparently refers to the brothers Guillermo and Gabriel Delgado, who, while not being charged in the indictment, are accused in it of conspiring with Esformes to defraud Medicare. The Delgado brothers, in their own prior criminal case in 2014, were charged with selling the names of Medicare patients to a crooked pharmacist, the Miami Herald previously reported in 2015.

After agreeing to plead guilty in 2015, Guillermo Delagado was sentenced to nine years in prison for conspiring to distribute Oxycodone and other narcotics, while Gabriel was sentenced to 4-and-1/2 years after pleading guilty to conspiring to commit money laundering, the Herald reported. The newspaper noted at the time that the brothers' lawyer had said in court papers that "they have turned over numerous financial and legal documents of significant value to the government" and also that they "have participated in undercover operations."

Dan Mangan, Reporter.

These cases serve as examples of fraud perpetrated by physicians. For a summary of 2017, see "Examples of Healthcare Fraud Investigations—Fiscal Year 2017."[8]

There are other areas of corruption within the medical profession costing the system money that time and space do not allow addressing. Here is a partial list:

1. Defensive medicine that drives up costs

2. Unnecessary medicine or surgery
3. Abuse of antibiotics and the rise of drug resistance
4. Obstruction of the growth of telemedicine
5. Yielding to Pharma TV advertising
6. Opposition to the development of the electronic medical record rather than working to improve it
7. Loss of traditional logical diagnostic evaluation process (ordering imaging without a working diagnosis)

In June 2016, the Medicare Fraud Strike Force conducted a nationwide health-care fraud takedown,[9]

> which resulted in criminal and civil charges against 301 individuals, including 61 doctors, nurses and other licensed medical professionals, for their alleged participation in health care fraud schemes involving approximately $900 million in false billings.

No one knows for sure, but a conservative estimate is that from the Medicare Fraud Strike Force data,[10] physician *Medicare* fraud alone is $10 billion. Improper *Medicaid* payments in 2011, according to the GAO,[11] was $21.9 billion of which physician fraud is estimated to be 10 percent or $2.3 billion. Combined Medicare/Medicaid = *$12.3 billion*.

Prices Controlled by Big Pharma.

> *Drug prices are not realistic,*
> *They tend to be on the whole oligopolistic.*
> > The Author (with a
> > bow to Ogden Nash)

Large Complex Market.

The pharmaceutical industry is a global enterprise. In 2014, total pharmaceutical revenues worldwide had exceeded one trillion US dollars for the first time.[1]

North America is responsible for the largest portion of these revenues, due to the leading role of the U.S. pharmaceutical industry. However, as in many other industries, the Chinese pharmaceutical sector has shown the highest growth rates over previous years.

Still, the leading pharmaceutical companies come from the United States and Europe. Based on prescription sales, NYC-based Pfizer is the world's largest pharmaceutical company. In 2016, the company generated some 52.8 billion U.S. dollars in pure pharmaceutical sales. Other top global players from the United States include Johnson & Johnson, Merck and AbbVie. Novartis and Roche from Switzerland, GlaxoSmithKline and AstraZeneca from the United Kingdom, and French Sanofi are the European big five.

Branded, patented medicines by far make up the largest share of pharmaceutical revenues. Humira, an anti-inflammatory drug, generated over 16 billion U.S. dollars of revenue worldwide in 2016. Oncologics continue to be one of the three leading therapeutic classes based on revenue. In 2015, cancer drugs made almost 79 billion U.S. dollars of revenue globally. Other major therapy classes were pain drugs, antihypertensives and antidiabetics.

More than any other industry, the pharmaceutical sector is highly dependent on its research and development segment. Some pharmaceutical companies invest 20 percent and more of their revenues in R&D measures. The United States is a traditional stronghold of pharmaceutical innovation. The origin of most new substances introduced to the market can be traced back to the United States. Because of the steady loss of patent protection, the invention of new drugs is of vital importance for the pharmaceutical industry. Revenue losses due to patent expiry often are very significant, as can be seen with Pfizer's Lipitor from 2012 on.

The worldwide market for pharmaceuticals is projected to grow from around $1 trillion in 2015 to $1.3 trillion by 2020, representing an annual growth rate of 4.9 percent.[2] Several global demographic and economic trends are driving pharmaceutical consumption, including a rapidly aging world population and an associated rise in chronic diseases, increased urbanization and higher disposable incomes, greater government expenditure on healthcare and growing demand for more effective treatments.

The five top export countries for US pharmaceuticals in 2015 were, Belgium ($6.4B), Netherlands ($4.2B), Canada ($3.8B), UK ($3.7B) and Japan ($3.5B).

Challenges include:

1) Regulatory approval: Many regulatory agencies lack adequate training and resources to review submissions in a timely and consistent manner, creating enormous backlogs, approval uncertainty and market access delays.

2) Patent approval: patent backlogs and long, uncertain approval timelines are common

problems worldwide. Because the term of a patent usually begins on the date an application is filed, approval delays can greatly reduce the value of granted patents.

3) Patentability: Whether through regulations or court decisions, many countries prohibit patents on important pharmaceutical innovations, such as new dosage forms or combinations that make it easier for patients to take medicines.

That is the global picture—large, complex, and populated by several very big international companies. The very structure of such a market makes understanding of pricing product difficult. Several characteristics that other markets may not have come to mind. Creation and approval of a new product creates a monopoly with a time line of protection. In this time line, the manufacturer must recoup all costs and turn a profit from which 20 percent or thereabouts can be allocated to research to start the process over again. Another characteristic is that buying a prescription drug is not like buying a car.[3]

When you buy a car, you are the decision-maker. You are the customer, you choose what car you want, and it's up to you whether or not you want to pay whatever it costs. You go to a dealership and buy a car. With pharmaceuticals, the customer—the patient—is rarely the decision-maker. Usually, the physician makes the decisions. And the patient doesn't pay the cost directly either. The patients aren't usually writing the check. There may be a copay or coinsurance, but the majority of the cost is usually covered by the insurer.

Drugs are divided into two main groups of legally and economically different products[4]:

- Over-the-counter (OTC) Drugs, which can be acquired as a result of the autonomous decision of the purchaser, without requiring any authorization.
- Prescription-only drugs, which may only be acquired and sold based on a written prescription by a doctor authorized for the purpose.

However, in many Latin American countries, there is full freedom of access to many or all obligatory prescription-only medicines.

In Latin American countries, prescription-only medicines make up 70% of the total supply, while OTC drugs comprise only 30%. In other regions of the world OTC medicines have a relatively smaller market share (18% of the world market, 12% in the U.S.A. and Canada, 19% in Europe).

Another aspect of the global market is that the supply of medicines comes from a diminishing number of transnational producers.[5]

In recent years, there have been an increasing number of mergers of large multinational firms, and smaller ones and national companies have disappeared. Increasingly, therefore, the drug supply is oligopolistic.

This, by definition, means that it is not a balanced competitive market but obviously favors the large few sellers. From the economics of pharmaceuticals,[6] it is clear that the characteristics of the pharmaceutical market are markedly different from other markets and products which means that there are recognized weaknesses in the way this market functions. It has been argued that to remedy these defects, the State should play a specific role in establishing controls and regulatory mechanisms designed to overcome information imbalance, moral risks and adverse choices, seeking to guarantee the right to health and access to the drugs required to ensure this.

From an economics point of view, the United States has done a reasonably good job in regulating the market, having a limited formulary which clearly establishes which drugs must be available, maintaining a high level of quality, and encouraging the generic market. That is the economic side. The political side considers other issues.

The aggregate spent on lobbying by pharma and health-care products in 2017 was $279,113,483, with Pfizer and Amgen the leading contributors.[7] They've traditionally supported Republican candidates, as they have received 64 percent of industry contributions on average since the 1990 election cycle.[8] The most recent posting (2018) was

House Members	Ave. Received	Σ Contribution
Democrats 156	$11,055	$1,724,603
Republicans 153	$16,918	$2,588,488
Independents 0		
TOTAL 309	$13,958 [avg]	$4,313,091

House of Representatives has 435 members and Five non-voting delegates.
Totals may exceed 440 due to mid-term replacements.

==

Senate Members	Ave. Received	Σ Contribution
Democrats 45	$19,428	$874,284
Republicans 39	$18,833	$734,509
Independents 2	$2,595	$5,190
TOTAL 86	$18,767	$1,613,983

The Senate has 100 members.
Totals may exceed 100 due to mid-term replacements.

==

The top ten recipients were

1. Hatch, Orrin G (R-UT) Senate $228,699
2. Ryan, Paul (R-WI) House $169,925
3. Walden, Greg (R-OR) House $153,500
4. McCarthy, Kevin (R-CA) House $109,750
5. Barrasso, John A (R-WY) Senate $104,350
6. Gillibrand, Kirsten (D-NY) Senate $101,001
7. Brady, Kevin (R-TX) House $86,750
8. Casey, Bob (D-PA) Senate $79,924
9. Lance, Leonard (R-NJ) House $77,500
10. Heitkamp, Heidi (D-ND) Senate $69,155

We might compare this information with the amount spent by the vitamin/supplement lobbying which spent $6,768,000 in 2017,[9] which was two and a half times the amount spent in 2016.

The bottom line is the simple conclusion. Don't look to the congress for meaningful reform in drug pricing anytime soon.

The lobbying obviously paid off in 2003 when congress passed, and President George W. Bush signed Medicare Part D, a voluntary insurance program for prescription drugs for people on Medicare. It was a huge giveaway favoring the pharmaceutical industry because *it did not allow Medicare to negotiate drug prices*. Instead, prices are worked out between drug makers and the dozens of large and small Part D drug plans run by commercial insurers.[10] If reform is ever to come, that "middle-man" market might be the place to start. (See reference to PBMs above.)

There is another disturbing development in recent years, and that is the number of lawsuits brought against drug companies for hiding information about unsafe drugs. These suits are settled out of court according to planetdrugsdirec.com[11]:

> This avoids negative publicity by having the matter settled out of court and the drug companies write off these settlements as a cost of doing business. What ends up happening is that because the drugs are so expensive and in such high demand, pharmaceutical companies can sell as much of a drug as they want even if they know it is unsafe. By the time anyone figures it out and starts to sue, the companies have made millions or billions of dollars and don't mind having to pay some of this profit in settlements to the hurt consumers. This pattern is repeated over and over and demonstrates that Big Pharma has no regard for the patients it claims to want to help. They are only concerned with lining their own pockets and if some people get hurt or even die in the process then so be it.

A huge loophole that needs to be addressed is that generic drug makers cannot be held liable for damages. This same reference points out,

> If someone is hurt from complications due to using generic drugs, they have no legal recourse to pursue a claim. Since over 80 percent of the drugs on the market are generic, this leaves all

but a few consumers with even the legal option to retaliate against a drug company.

And further points out the control of Big Pharma over the FDA:

> The FDA approves 96 percent of all new drugs that are created. There is no way that there are no problems with such a high percentage of new drugs. The FDA is in bed with the pharmaceutical companies because both industries feed off of one another. The FDA gets more funding and publicity by bringing new drugs to the market and Big Pharma gets more money by having their drugs approved. It is essentially a corrupt system where the group that is supposed to be safeguarding the public has no financial incentive to do so. And the group producing the drugs therefore has no motivation to keep the public safe.

The top five companies[12] prosecuted for fraud in recent years are

1). GlaxoSmithKline;
> The number one spot for Big Pharma fraud unquestionably goes to GlaxoSmithKline. They have the most drugs that have been investigated for negative health effects to date. They also have a track record for the most insidious types of fraud. This includes bribing doctors to prescribe their drugs, using fraudulent research papers to cover up dangerous side effects and allowing the FDA to continue to let them manufacture their products. They also have marketed their medicines for ailments that they were never approved to treat. GlaxoSmithKline paid $3 billion in settlements

for their line of antidepressants alone including Paxil, Welbutrin, and Avandia. Since then the company has done little to mend its ways and seems to be undeterred as more and more profits from newly approved drugs continue to fill its bank account.

2). Merck;

Merck was forced to pull Vioxx from the shelves in 2004 when it was discovered through clinical trials that it doubled the risk of stroke, heart attack, and death. They have awarded over $4.85 billion to plaintiffs since 2008. While it may seem strange that such a dangerous drug could slip past the watchful eye of regulators, this is par for the course when it comes to the insufficient research that is done on these drugs.

3). Takeda;

Takeda is a Japanese drug company responsible for the manufacture of Actos, a diabetes treatment. While marketed to help reduce the need for insulin and as a way to lower a patient's A1C, the pharmaceutical giant neglected to mention the increased risk of developing cancer while on the drug. In 2015 the company stopped a trial midway and settled out of court with two plaintiffs who had developed bladder cancer as a result of taking Actos. Takeda has agreed to pay out $2.3 billion in settlements for all of the others who have been negatively affected.

4). Johnson & Johnson;

The blood thinning drug Xarelto has been linked to major bleeding and has resulted in at least 65 deaths according to recent court documents. Since the drug has no known antidote this made it especially dangerous and essentially gave anyone with major bleeding while on the drug a death sentence even if they received immediate medical attention. They also withheld information from the public on the disturbing tendency of the antipsychotic drug Risperdal to grow female breasts in male patients. Not surprisingly as outrage mounted this drug was quickly targeted for lawsuits as well. In total, Johnson and Johnson has been required to pay back $2.2 billion in 2013 in order to resolve criminal and civil investigations.

5). Bayer;

The birth control drugs Yaz and Yasmin were marketed as being more effective than other birth control methods. They were also said to provide the added benefits of reducing acne and severe menstrual pain. Instead many users experienced the extremely dangerous side effect of having blood clots. These blood clots increased stroke risk and are life threatening if not treated properly. What is particularly devious about this instance of Big Pharma fraud is that all oral contraceptives tend to increase acne and bloating. So, to say that these symptoms will be reduced by taking Yaz was particularly misleading. In total Bayer settled out of court for the sum of $1.4 billion for the damage done to those affected.

There are a considerable number of personal injury legal firms that use their websites to cater to whistleblowers who report fraud. One such example is Pintas & Mullins, a Chicago firm.[13] Their report (dated 2015) on their website may be summarized:

In the largest drug fraud settlement in history, J&J (Johnson and Johnson) was directed to pay $2.2 billion for breaking the law in marketing Risperdal. A whistle-blower testified that J&J had engaged a ghostwriter to produce articles for physician medical journals, claiming "safety and efficacy" of Risperdal. Risperdal, originally approved to treat adults with schizophrenia, was then marketed for children with various behavior disorders, originally without FDA approval. In following years, very serious side effects appeared.

There were also federal lawsuits claiming the manufacturers paid kickbacks in exchange for physician prescribing the drug often for off-label prescriptions.

And speaking of Wall Street, one of touted stocks in early 2018 has been PRAH (PRA Health Sciences), which is a clinical research organization (CRO), with operations in more than eighty countries. PRAH helps Pharma get their drugs to market by conducting Phase I-IV clinical trials, indicating that the drug makers are now turning to outsourcing the critical trial testing process. PRAH has conducted over 3,500 clinical studies leading to FDA or international regulatory approval for over seventy-five drugs.[14]

As Investor's Business Daily concluded recently,[15]

> One minute Merck might be doing battle with Bristol-Myers-Squib over cancer drugs. The next, Amgen and Sanofi are tussling in court over the fate of cholesterol-busting drugs. Gilead Sciences might be raked over the coals in Congress for charging $1000 a day to treat hepatitis.
>
> It's a brave—and contentious new world for pharmaceutical and biotechnology companies. It's a realm where science is trying to develop landmark medicines that cure cancer, hepatitis and other life-threatening illnesses.
>
> All the while it does a delicate dance with Wall Street and regulators—balancing public health issues and the demands of shareholders.

Investors will find it tricky to navigate the sector, as companies can rise and fall at the drop of a hat.

This may all look like free enterprise and open markets at work, but the problem remains. As the Center for Research on Globalization observes, Big Pharma controls the tilt of the playing field.[16]

USA Today's Editorial Board reported in 2017 that the FDA had received about 150 letters that generic companies sent to brand-name companies complaining about access to doses (supply) of a drug needed for their studies. FDA chief Dr. Scott Gottlieb[17] charged that

> drug makers "game the rules" through a patient safety program that allows them to keep generic drug companies from getting enough doses of their branded drug. Generic drug makers need 5,000 doses to do the studies needed to prove their products are truly equivalent, according to Gottlieb, who plans to stop what he said are anti-competitive actions by brand-name pharmaceutical companies that keep prices high.

These tactics force poor public policy and contribute to costing consumers millions, if not billions, of dollars. If drugs are to become more affordable in this country, the public must get involved and press their legislators who already have Big Pharma's money in their pockets. An uphill battle indeed!

From a study reported in 2016 in the *Health Affairs Journal*[18]

> Researchers have concluded that the federal government could save $15.2 billion to $16 billion annually if it negotiated with drug manufacturers and achieved the same prices as those paid by Medicaid or the Veterans Health Administration (programs that receive mandatory rebates on drug prices).

We can only imagine how much more we might save if our government was on the side of the people rather than Big Pharma.

Medicare Advantage Fraud

As a senior or disabled consumer, you get your Medicare coverage through original Medicare, or a Medicare Advantage Plan. If you have just Medicare, the government pays the benefits. Medicare Advantage Plans, sometimes called "Part C" or "MA Plans," are offered by private companies approved by Medicare. Medicare pays these companies to cover your Medicare benefits.[1]

> If you join a Medicare Advantage Plan, the plan will provide all your Medicare Part A (Hospital Insurance) and Medicare Part B (Medical Insurance) coverage. This is different than a Medicare Supplement Insurance (Medigap) policy. A Medigap policy is private insurance that helps supplement Original Medicare. This means it helps pay some of the health care costs that Original Medicare doesn't cover. These are "gaps" in Medicare coverage.

Recall that the initial Medicare legislation provided for coverage of 80 percent of "fair and reasonable" costs, and the consumer paid the remaining 20 percent.

> If you have Original Medicare and a Medigap policy, Medicare will pay its share of the Medicare-approved amounts for covered health care costs. Then your Medigap policy pays its share. A Medigap policy is different from a Medicare Advantage Plan (like an HMO or PPO) because those plans are ways to get Medicare benefits, while a Medigap policy only supplements the costs of your Original Medicare ben-

efits. There are the different types of Medicare Advantage Plans:

- Health Maintenance Organization (HMO) plans—In most HMOs, you can only go to doctors, other health care providers, or hospitals in the plan's network, except in an urgent or emergency situation. You may also need to get a referral from your primary care doctor for tests or to see other doctors or specialists.

- Preferred Provider Organization (PPO) plans—In a PPO, you pay less if you use doctors, hospitals, and other health care providers that belong to the plan's network. You usually pay more if you use doctors, hospitals, and providers outside of the network.

- Private Fee-for-Service (PFFS) plans— PFFS plans are similar to Original Medicare in that you can generally go to any doctor, other health care provider, or hospital as long as they accept the plan's payment terms. The plan determines how much it will pay doctors, other health care providers, and hospitals, and how much you must pay when you get care.

- Special Needs Plans (SNPs)—SNPs provide focused and specialized health care for specific groups of people, like those who have both Medicare and Medicaid, live in a nursing home or have certain chronic medical conditions.

- HMO Point-of-Service (HMOPOS) plans—These are HMO plans that may allow you to get some services out-of-network for a higher copayment or coinsurance.

- Medical Savings Account (MSA) plans—These plans combine a high-deductible health plan with a bank account. Medicare deposits money into the account (usually less than the deductible). You can use the money to pay for your health care services during the year. MSA plans don't offer Medicare drug coverage. If you want drug coverage, you have to join a Medicare Prescription Drug Plan. For more information about MSAs, visit Medicare.gov/publications to view the booklet "Your Guide to Medicare Medical Savings Account Plans."Most Medicare Advantage Plans include Medicare prescription drug coverage (Part D). New Medigap policies don't offer prescription drug coverage. If you want prescription drug coverage, you must get a stand-alone Medicare Prescription Drug Plan that works with Original Medicare, or you can leave Original Medicare and join a Medicare Advantage Plan that offers drug coverage.

Medicare Advantage is a popular alternative to traditional Medicare. The privately-run health plans have enrolled more than 18 million elderly and people with disabilities—about a third of those eligible for Medicare—at a cost to taxpayers of more than $150 billion a year.

These Medicare Advantage Plans have grown in recent years and enjoy strong support in Congress.[2]

They have been the target of at least a half-dozen whistleblower lawsuits alleging patterns of overbilling and fraud. In most of the prior cases, Justice Department officials have decided not to intervene, which often limits the financial recovery by the government and by whistleblowers, who can be awarded a portion of recovered funds. A decision to intervene means that the Justice Department is taking over investigating the case, greatly raising the stakes.

Congress created Medicare Advantage as a risk adjustment payment program that pays insurers more for sicker beneficiaries.[3]

Payers in Medicare Advantage now receive a yearly fee for each enrolled member and monthly risk adjustment payments for each enrolled beneficiary, based partly on the person's health status. This means a person with diabetes and other chronic health conditions will bring a larger monthly reimbursement than someone who needs few services.

Such a program is open to fraud. CMS (Center for Medicare Services) estimated that it overpaid $14.1 billion in 2013 to MA organizations. Medicare Advantage payers received about $160 billion in 2014 for approximately 16 million beneficiaries. CMS estimated about 9.5% of those payments were improper.

The U.S. Department of Justice (DOJ) is involved in two high-profile False Claims Act cases involving one of the largest health insurers. The DOJ joined two lawsuits involving UnitedHealth Group (UHG), which is the largest Medicare Advantage payer with more than 50

Medicare Advantage and drug prescription plans. (About 25% of the market)

The lawsuits allege UHG overcharged the federal government for Medicare Advantage. In 2016, CMS reportedly paid UnitedHealth $56 billion for covering 3.6 million Medicare Advantage beneficiaries.

The fraud of Medicare Advantage Plans can take many forms.[4]

1). Upcoding members' diagnoses to exaggerate the severity of the members' condition (claiming that they are sicker than they really are) in order to submit to CMS a diagnosis code that risk adjusts or a more serious diagnosis code that risk adjusts at a higher rate (i.e., has a higher risk score or larger risk multiplier), and thereby allows the Medicare Advantage plan to improperly increase the amount of the per member per month (pm/pm) capitation rate it receives for such members.

2). Conducting or hiring an outside vendor to conduct "chart audits," "chart reviews," or "chart mining" in which the chart reviewers upcode diagnoses and/or only look for new risk adjustment claims and fail to correct invalid, inaccurate or unsupported diagnoses that were improperly submitted to CMS.

3). Training, incentivizing and otherwise encouraging doctors, independent practice associations (IPAs), hospitals or other healthcare providers to upcode and submit diagnosis codes for diseases that risk adjust but which the member does not have or for which the member was not treated that year (such as diagnoses that only appear on the member's problem list), including submissions through "at risk" or "capitated" reimbursement arrangements.

4). Asking coders to look beyond the physician-documented diagnoses and attempt to identify diagnoses based on other evidence in medical charts (e.g., medications, laboratory test results, radiology reports, rule-out diagnoses or problem lists).

5). Failing to properly filter the diagnosis codes and other data the Medicare Advantage plan submits to CMS to generate risk adjustment claims, including failing to remove diagnoses that were not made during a face-to-face visit with a qualifying health care provider, such as a doctor or hospital.

6). Performing an internal audit of the validity of risk adjustment diagnoses the Medicare Advantage or PACE plan submitted to CMS—e.g., a mock risk adjustment data validation (RADV) audit—and failing to submit to CMS delete codes for the erroneous diagnoses identified in the audit or to investigate and correct any coding or data submission problems the audit may have uncovered.

There are even companies that provide Medicare Advantage plans with retrospective chart review services. Many contractors market their services by their high return on investment, not accuracy, as law firm Phillips & Cohen points out.[5]

Furthermore, instead of being paid hourly, some contractors have contingency fee arrangements with the Medicare Advantage plans, which pay them based on the number of new diagnosis codes they find for the plan. This type of arrangement gives the contractors a perverse incentive to focus on finding and adding to the Medicare Advantage or PACE plan's submission to CMS as many diagnosis codes as possible, whether or not the codes are valid, as opposed to ensuring the accuracy of the codes submitted.

Kaiser Health Care News[6] reported in 2017 that the federal government made more than $16 billion in improper payments to private Medicare Advantage health plans the previous year.

James Cosgrove, who directs health care reviews for the Government Accountability Office, told the House Ways and Means oversight subcommittee that the Medicare Advantage improper payment rate was 10 percent in 2016, which comes to $16.2 billion.

Adding in the overpayments for standard Medicare programs, the tally for last year approached $60 billion—which is almost twice as much as the National Institutes of Health spends on medical research each year.

Standard Medicare has a similar problem making accurate payments to doctors, hospitals and other health care providers, according to statistics presented at the hearing. Standard Medicare's payment error rate was cited at 11 percent, or $41 billion for 2016.

This represents Quackonomics in big numbers. "When trying to understand how much fraud is in Medicare, the answer is simply we don't know," subcommittee Chairman Vern Buchanan (R-Fla.) is quoted as saying.[7]

The National Health Care Anti-Fraud Association is the leading national organization focused exclusively on the fight against health-care fraud.[8]

Founded in 1985 by several private health insurers and federal and state government officials, the association is a private-public partnership—members comprise nearly 90 private health insurers and those public-sector law enforcement and regulatory agencies having jurisdiction over health care fraud committed against both private payers and public programs. Through their NHCAA Institute for Health Care Fraud Prevention, the mission is to protect and serve the public interest by increasing awareness and improving the detection, investigation, civil and criminal prosecution and prevention of health care fraud and abuse.

Their mission is to protect and serve the public interest by increasing awareness and improving the detection, investigation, civil and criminal prosecution and prevention of health care fraud and abuse.

In the list of members in the NHCAA Institute for Health-Care Fraud Prevention, it is noted that there are several national health insurance companies. Consumers can hope that an element of self-regulation and integrity will prevail rather than costly litigation.

Meanwhile, the 2016 year *$16.2 billion* quoted above can be the growing fraud generated by this little-known middleman called Medical Advantage Plans. Yes, the middleman strikes again!

Hospital Quackonomics

In reviewing hospital fraud, the following recent headlines were uncovered by simply googling "hospital fraud":

Auditor: 15-bed Missouri hospital at heart of $90M billing fraud scheme.[1] Putnam County Hospital allegedly acted as a shell company by submitting claims for other labs and funneling the insurance payments through the hospital.

Ex-California Hospital Owner Sentenced for $600M Fraud Plan[2] Prosecutors said that for at least 15 years, the owner paid more than $40 million to dozens of doctors, chiropractors and other medical professionals in return for referring thousands of patients to his hospital for spinal surgeries.

Bozeman Deaconess Hospital Fraud?[3] The heart of the lawsuit brought by radiologists is that "Bozeman Health maintained monopoly power over radiologic imaging in Bozeman and the surrounding area."

Patient Who Had Parts of Her Organs Removed Sues KU Hospital for Fraud[4] The once-anonymous patient at the center of a whistleblower action filed against KU Hospital by one of its own pathologists is now suing the hospital herself for fraud, negligence and civil conspiracy.

Lawsuit against 70 Indiana hospitals includes fraud.[5] Two South Bend lawyers say that 70 Indiana hospitals reported false claims. The hospitals allegedly cost the federal government and the state of Indiana more than $324 million dollars.

LA Hospital Pays $42M to Settle Healthcare Fraud, Kickback Case.[6] According to a Department of Justice, PAMC Ltd and Pacific Alliance Medical Center Inc, which together run the acute care hospital, reportedly submitted false claims to Medicare and MediCal programs.

Florida Whistleblower Lawsuit Accuses Hospital Software of Billing Fraud

The lawsuit alleges Epic Systems Corp.'s software, used by four South Florida hospitals and hundreds more across the U.S., double-bills for anesthesia.[7]

In June 2015, a former chief financial officer of Shelby Regional Medical Center in Texas, was ordered to pay $4.5 million and sentenced to 23 months in prison after pleading guilty to receiving nearly $800,000 from CMS after lying about meaningful use of electronic health records.[8]

Reference: At a glance: Medicare fraud in hospitals.[9]

These were cases picked at random, some settled, and some pending. The message is that despite hospital boards of directors and supposedly competent legal advice, hospitals can be predatory and greedy and quite without conscience. True, they are, thankfully, in a small minority, but as public institutions, they require the vigilance of the public. What the annual cost of hospital fraud is can only be estimated by extrapolating from the examples given above. It is estimated to be in 2018 over *$2 billion.*

This figure does not include gaming the system of hospital rating reports made popular by various publications and outside organizations,[10] which is just another intangible.

Celebrity Quackonomics

You are entitled to your own opinion. But you are not entitled to you own facts.
—*Daniel Patrick Moynihan*

Steve Jobs

The story of how Steve Jobs, the brilliant CEO of Apple, refused to follow medical (scientific) advice in favor of alternative medicine is a sad study in personal delusion.[1] His biographer, Walter Isaacson, recounts that the diagnosis of a pancreatic tumor was made in October of 2003 following a CAT scan to evaluate kidney and ureter areas because of a history of kidney stones, followed by a biopsy that revealed the tumor to be an uncommon neuroendocrine variety.[2] His doctors advised surgery as the only course. He refused. His biographer Isaacson called it "the dark side of his reality distortion field."[3] Jobs treated his cancer with a strict vegan diet supplemented with large doses of carrot and fruit juices, rounds of acupuncture, herbals, and visits to a psychic and natural healing clinic in southern California. Does this story sound familiar to believers in Complementary and Integrative "Medicine"?

The biopsy showing a neuroendocrine tumor is much less common than an adenocarcinoma, which is quite malignant. If Jobs had suffered the most common form of pancreatic cancer, adenocarcinoma, the chances are, he would have died soon after his 2003 diagnosis.

> Pancreatic neuroendocrine tumors (pancreatic NETs or PNETs) account for about 6% of all pancreatic tumors. They may be benign or malignant and they tend to grow slower than exocrine tumors. They develop from the abnormal growth of endocrine (hormone-producing) cells in the pancreas called islet cells.

Although I have no information on the original CAT scan, it is reasonable to conclude that the choice of immediate surgery would have been curative.

> According to Cleveland Clinic gastroenterologist Maged Rizk, MD, there's an overall 80% to 90% chance of 5-year survival.[4]

Despite urging of friends and experts such as Andy Grove, founder and CEO of Intel, and Dr. Dean Ornish, a leader in alternate medicine, he delayed surgery until July 31, 2004. The next day, he e-mailed that his tumor was a 1 percent type and that he was cured. What he was told by his surgeons, I do not know, but during the operation, three liver metastases were found. This was clearly an indication that the cancer had spread and was probably no longer curable by surgery. In August of 2011, Jobs stepped down as CEO of Apple and died on October 5, 2011,[5] eight years from the original diagnosis.

The tragic lesson is that Steve Jobs was a wizard at design and marketing but was not a student of science. As he once said, "I like living at the intersection of humanities and technology." He grew up in the 1970s amid a fugue of cultural conflicts and believed he was able to control everything by the force of his will—what he called his "magical thinking."

We have a tendency today in our culture to regard our celebrity leaders as possessors of superior knowledge in all matters and let down our own guard of skepticism when it comes to critical thinking, particularly in the science of health care. Jobs once said, "Be a yardstick of quality. Some people aren't used to an environment where excellence is expected."[6] In the end, Steve Jobs regretted, in his own mind, that lack of excellence.

Linus Pauling

The Linus Pauling story is one of a brilliant scientist who got carried away into the la-la land of pseudoscience. Pauling is the only person ever to win two unshared Nobel prizes, one in chemistry and one in peacemaking.[1]

> In 1996, Pauling, on a trip, began taking vitamin C. He thought that he felt better and that he experienced fewer colds. In time, vitamin C became "his obsession." He published a book in 1970, Vitamin C and the Common Cold. He expanded his advice to include other vitamins and supplements, and went so far as to claim the result to be "free of diseases."

> A Cochrane review concluded that Vitamin C reduced length of colds by about 8% (about ten hours).

Pauling's career could be roughly divided into before and after 1960. Dr. Paul Offit, listed his accomplishments before 1965.[2]

By age thirty, Linus Pauling had won a Nobel Prize in chemistry and a full professorship to Caltech. A paper in 1949 clarified unique properties of hemoglobin in Sickle cell anemia. In 1951 he used the term helix to describe a series of amino acids, two years before Watson and Crick. In addition, he was active politically on the international stage as a leading peace advocate, opposed the Vietnam War and in 1962 won a Nobel Peace prize plus a bucket-load of honorary degrees.

Then came the change. In 1966, as noted, he began his ventures into vitamin C. It was downhill from there. His claims became ridiculous, as Paul Offit recounts in 2013.[3]

> Pauling claimed that vitamin C, when taken with massive doses of vitamin A (25,000 international units) and vitamin E (400 to 1,600 IU), as well as selenium (a basic element) and beta-carotene (a precursor to vitamin A), could do more than just prevent colds and treat cancer; they could treat virtually every disease known to man. Pauling claimed that vitamins and supplements could cure heart disease, mental illness, pneumonia, hepatitis, polio, tuberculosis, measles, mumps, chickenpox, meningitis, shingles, fever blisters, cold sores, canker sores, warts, aging, allergies, asthma, arthritis, diabetes, retinal detachment, strokes, ulcers, shock, typhoid fever, tetanus, dysentery, whooping cough, leprosy, hay fever, burns, fractures, wounds, heat prostration, altitude sickness, radiation poisoning, glaucoma, kidney failure, influenza, bladder ailments, stress,

rabies, and snakebites. When the AIDS virus entered the United States in the 1970s, Pauling claimed vitamins could treat that, too.

Although studies had failed to support him, Pauling believed that vitamins and supplements had one property that made them cure-alls, a property that continues to be hawked on everything from ketchup to pomegranate juice and that rivals' words like natural and organic for sales impact: antioxidant.

As discussed earlier, more antioxidants are not better nor make one healthier, because of damage and abundance of free radicals upsets an internal balance.Dr. Offit's reference recounts many other vitamin studies that reported the opposite of what you might expect.

In 1994, the National Cancer Institute, in collaboration with Finland's National Public Health Institute, studied 29,000 Finnish men, all long-term smokers more than fifty years old. This group was chosen because they were at high risk for cancer and heart disease. Subjects were given vitamin E, beta-carotene, both, or neither. The results were clear: those taking vitamins and supplements were more likely to die from lung cancer or heart disease than those who didn't take them—the opposite of what researchers had anticipated.

In 1996, investigators from the Fred Hutchinson Cancer Research Center, in Seattle, studied 18,000 people who, because they had been exposed to asbestos, were at increased risk of lung cancer. Again, subjects received vitamin A, beta-carotene, both, or neither. Investigators ended the study abruptly when they realized that those who took vitamins and supplements were dying from cancer and heart disease at rates 28 and 17 percent higher, respectively, than those who didn't.

In 2004, researchers from the University of Copenhagen reviewed fourteen randomized trials involving more than 170,000 people who took vitamins A, C, E, and beta-carotene to see whether antioxidants could prevent intestinal cancers. Again, antioxidants didn't live up to the hype. The authors concluded, "We could not find evidence that antioxidant supplements can prevent gastrointestinal cancers; on the contrary, they seem to increase overall mortality." When these same researchers evaluated the seven best studies, they found that death rates were 6 percent higher in those taking vitamins.

In 2005, researchers from Johns Hopkins School of Medicine evaluated nineteen studies involving more than 136,000 people and found an increased risk of death associated with supplemental vitamin E. Dr. Benjamin Caballero, director of the Center for Human Nutrition at the Johns Hopkins Bloomberg School of Public Health, said, "This reaffirms what others have said. The evidence for supplementing with any vitamin, particularly vitamin E, is just not there. This idea that people have that [vitamins] will not hurt them may not be that simple." That same year, a study published in the Journal of the American Medical Association evaluated more than 9,000 people who took high-dose vitamin E to prevent cancer; those who took vitamin E were more likely to develop heart failure than those who didn't.

In 2007, researchers from the National Cancer Institute examined 11,000 men who did or didn't take multivitamins. Those who took multivitamins were twice as likely to die from advanced prostate cancer.

In 2008, a review of all existing studies involving more than 230,000 people who did or did not receive supplemental antioxidants found that vitamins increased the risk of cancer and heart disease.

On October 10, 2011, researchers from the University of Minnesota evaluated 39,000 older women and found that those who took supplemental multivitamins, magnesium, zinc, copper, and iron died at rates higher than those who didn't. They concluded, "Based on existing evidence, we see little justification for the general and widespread use of dietary supplements."

Two days later, on October 12, researchers from the Cleveland Clinic published the results of a study of 36,000 men who took vitamin E, selenium, both, or neither. They found that those receiving vitamin E had a 17 percent greater risk of prostate cancer. In response to the study, Steven Nissen, chairman of cardiology at the Cleveland Clinic, said, "The concept of multivitamins was sold to Americans by an eager nutraceutical industry to generate profits. There was never any scientific data supporting their usage." On October 25, a headline in the Wall Street Journal asked, "Is This the End of Popping Vitamins?" Studies haven't hurt sales. In 2010, the vitamin industry grossed $28 billion, up 4.4 percent from the year before. "The thing to do with [these reports] is just ride them out," said Joseph Fortunato, chief executive of General Nutrition Centers. "We see no impact on our business."

What happened? What is the lesson here? The answers are apparent. No matter how brilliant you are or how many honorary degrees you have, if the scientific community with careful science is unable to duplicate the claims, then the claims do not stand. What happened in Linus Pauling's brain after early 1960s is grounds for speculation. The lesson is that Pauling's legacy of the false science of mega doses of vitamin C and antioxidants lives on. Here is a quote to follow:

> When an old and distinguished person speaks to you, listen to him carefully and with respect—but do not believe him. Never put your trust into anything but your own intellect. Your elder, no matter whether he has gray hair or has lost his hair, no matter whether he is a Nobel laureate—may be wrong. The world progresses, year by year, century by century, as the members of the younger generation find out what was wrong among the things that their elders said. So, you must always be skeptical—always think for yourself.

The author of this quote? You guessed it—Linus Pauling (1901–1994).

Endnotes

Part III
Fraud Found along the Way
Corruption in the System
Fraud in the Science Literature
1 https://www.nih.gov/about-nih/what-we-do/budget.
2 https://ori.hhs.gov/historical-background.
3 Richard Harris, *Rigor Mortis: How Sloppy Science Creates Worthless Cures, Crushes Hope, and Wastes Billions* (New York: Basic Books, 2017), 7–28.
4 https://www.gbsi.org/about/who-we-are/.
https://sites.google.com/site/fakeresearchjournalpublishers/home.

⁵ https://www.raps.org/news-articles/news-articles/2017/9/
fda-s-woodcock-the-clinical-trials-system-is-broken.

⁶ https://en.wikipedia.org/wiki/John_Ioannidis.

⁷ Ibid., Harris, 218.

⁸ http://www.pnas.org/content/109/42/17028.full.

⁹ https://scholarlykitchen.sspnet.org/2017/09/07/
confusion-journals-pubmed-now.

¹⁰ https://beallslist.weebly.com/.

¹¹ https://sites.google.com/site/fakeresearchjournalpublishers/home.

¹² Gina Kolata, "He Promised to Restore Damaged Hearts. Harvard Says His Lab
Fabricated Research," *New York Times*, October 29, 2018.

¹³ https://www,nytimes.com/2018/12/08/health/medical-journals-conflict-of-in-
terest.html.

¹⁴ https://www.hopkinsmedicine.org/research/resources/offices-policies/OPC/
Research_Integrity/index.html.

Pharma and Associates Corruption
1. Reporting of Adverse Drug Events

¹ https://www.fda.gov/Drugs/GuidanceComplianceRegulatoryInformation/
Surveillance/AdverseDrugEffect

² https://fis.fda.gov/sense/app/777e9f4d-0cf8-448e-8068-f564c31baa25/
sheet/7a47a261-d58b-4203-a8aa-6d3021737452/state/analysis.

³ https://www.aasld.org/sites/default/files/documents/2012/2012%201A-1_
PaulsN.pdf.

⁴ https://www.acponline.org/system/files/documents/advocacy/current_policy_
papers/assets/fda.pdf4].

⁵ Ibid., ref. 2 above.

⁶ https://www.ncbi.nlm.nih.gov/pmc/articles/PMC3853675/.

⁷ https://jamanetwork.com/journals/jama/fullarticle/2585977.

⁸ https://www.ncbi.nlm.nih.gov/pmc/articles/PMC4321074/.

2. Price Gauging

¹ http://heinonline.org/HOL/LandingPage?handle=hein.journals/
clro102&div=4&id=&page=.

² https://www.usnews.com/news/articles/2016-09-21/
mylan-head-defends-epipen-price-gouging-in-capitol-hearing.

³ https://www.marketwatch.com/story/whats-wrong-with-price-gouging-for-
epipens-nothing-and-everything-2016-09-02.

⁴ https://www.webmd.com/allergies/news/20170112/cvs-price-epipen-generic.

⁵ https://www.google.com/search?rlz=1C1LOQA_enUS627US655&bi-
w=1292&bih=628&ei=1CdyWvPzHI6B5wKbo5KACg&q=CVS+and+pric-
ing+E.

6   https://www.forbes.com/sites/kennethdavis/2016/06/03/a-market-fix-for-ge-neric-drug-price-gouging/#68183cfa6f21.

7   https://www.vox.com/policy-and-politics/2018/1/30/16896434/trump-drug-prices-year-one.

8   http://www.centerforbiosimilars.com/news/drug-makers-raise-prices-on-more-than-30-products-for-2018.

9   http://www.modernhealthcare.com/article/20171228/NEWS/171229930.

10 https://www.andruswagstaff.com/blog/big-pharma-has-higher-profit-margins-than-any-other-industry/.

11 https://www.yardeni.com/pub/sp500margin.pdf.

12 https://yourbusiness.azcentral.com/average-profit-margin-pharmaceuti-cals-20671.html.

13 https://www.investopedia.com/ask/answers/031215/what-average-range-prof-it-margin-company-financial-services-sector.asp.

14 https://www.yardeni.com/pub/sp500margin.pdf.

15 http://fortune.com/2017/06/07/fortune-500-companies-profit-apple-berk-shire-hathaway/.

16 https://www.fool.com/investing/2016/07/31/12-big-pharma-stats-that-will-blow-you-away.aspx.

3. Lack of Independence of the FDA

1   https://en.wikipedia.org/wiki/History_of_the_Food_and_Drug_Administration.

2   https://www.pbs.org/wgbh/pages/frontline/shows/prescription/hazard/independent.html.

3   https://www.fda.gov/OHRMS/dockets/AC/07/briefing/2007-4329b_02_01_FDA%20Report%20on%20Science%20and%20Technology.pdf.   (This website reference has been taken down from the time of writing to publication and without explanation.)

4   https://www.fda.gov/ForConsumers/ConsumerUpdates/ucm050803.htm.

4. Surrogate Endpoints / Unapproved Uses

1   https://www.cancer.gov/publications/dictionaries/cancer-terms/def/surrogate-endpoint.

2   https://www.students4bestevidence.net/surrogate-endpoints-in-ebm-what-are-the-benefits-and-dangers/.

3   Gabe Alpert, "Wake-up Call for the FDA," *Barron's* (December 5, 2016): 12.

4   https://www.reuters.com/article/us-health-cancer-drugs/cancer-drugs-may-re-main-approved-despite-lack-of-benefit-idUSKBN13Q5UD.

5   Naci H, Smalley KR, Kesselheim AS. Characteristics of Preapproval and Post approval Studies for Drugs Granted Accelerated Approval by the US Food and Drug Administration. JAMA. 2017 Aug 15;318(7):626-636.doi:10.1001/

jama.2017.9415.PubMed PMID: 28810023; PubMed Central PMCID: PMC5817559.

6 https:www.reuters.com/article/ushealth-fda-appovals-idUSKCN1AV23K

7 https://academic.oup.com/eurheartj/article/36/33/2212/2465947

5. Generic Drugs and Biosimilars

1 https://en.wikipedia.org/wiki/Drug_Price_Competition_and_Patent_Term_Restoration_Act.

2 Thomas G. Donlan, "Monopoly of Power: The Complex Markets for Pharmaceuticals Challenge the Force of Law," *Barron's* (August 14, 2017): 31.

3 Jerome A. Greene, *Generic: The Unbranding of Modern Medicine* (Baltimore: Johns Hopkins Press, 2014).

4 Ibid., ref. 2 above.

5 Sydney Lupkin, "Delayed Generics Have Cost Medicare, Medicaid Billions," *USA Today*, May 28, 2018.

6 https://www.congress.gov/bill/116th-congress/senate-bill/340/all-info.

7 https://www.ajmc.com/newsroom/5-things-to-know-about-the-creates-act.

8 https://www.fda.gov/downloads/Drugs/DevelopmentApprovalProcess/HowDrugsareDevelopedandApproved/ApprovalApplications/TherapeuticBiologicApplications/Biosimilars/UCM581282.pdf.

9 http://www.amgenbiosimilars.com/the-basics/biosimilars-versus-generics/.

10 Canny Hakim, "The Humira Play: Raise High Prices, Steadily," *New York Times*, January 7, 2018.

11 Ibid.

12 https://www.thebalance.com/biobetter-definition-3895896.

13 https://bblsa.com/documents/Back-Bay-US-Biosimilars-2018.pdf.

14 Allison Gatlin, "The Boon and Bane of Biosimilars," *Investor's Business Daily* 35, no. 24 (September 11, 2018).

15 https://www.stock-analysis-on.net/NYSE/Company/AbbVie-Inc/Ratios/Profitability#Gross-Profit-Margin.

6. Pharmacy Benefit Mangers (PBMS)

1 https://www.google.com/search?q=Pharmacy+Benefit+Managers&rlz=-1C1LOQA_enUS627US655&oq=P&aqs=chrome.4.69i60j69i61j69i60.

2 http://www.ncpanet.org/advocacy/pbm-resources.

3 Bill Alpert, "The Next Drug Wars," *Barron's* (July 25, 2016).

4 https://en.wikipedia.org/wiki/Pharmacy_Benefit_management.

5 https://www.statnews.com/2018/08/27/pharmacy-benefit-managers-good-or-bad/.

6 https://www.healthcarelawtoday.com/2019/02/01/hhs-proposes-new-rules-to-eliminate-drug-rebates-and-encourage-direct-discounts-for-federal-beneficiaries/.

7 Ibid., ref. 3 above.

7. The Opioid Crisis

[1] https://www.northwell.edu/about/news/publications/spotlight-opioid-crisis/volume-1-2017/the-opioid-crisis-is-born.

[2] https://www.nytimes.com/interactive/2017/08/03/upshot/opioid-drug-overdose-epidemic.html.

[3] https://www.theexaminernews.com/holding-big-pharma-accountable-for-opioid-crisis/.

[4] Ibid.

[5] https://www.medscape.com/viewarticle/881215.

[6] https://www.nytimes.com/interactive/2017/08/03/upshot/opioid-drug-overdose-epidemic.html.

[7] https://www.ncbi.nlm.nih.gov/pmc/articles/PMC2622774/.

[8] http://www.nytimes.com/2007/05/10/business/11drug-web.html.

[9] https://www.stamfordadvocate.com/business/article/Report-Purdue-to-end-opioid-promotion-to-doctors-12603949.php.

[10] https://www.vox.com/policy-and-politics/2017/10/30/16339672/opioid-epidemic-vermont-hub-spoke.

[11] Ibid.

[12] https://www.vox.com/policy-and-politics/2018/2/8/16988236/congress-federal-budget-opioid-crisis.

[13] https://www.cnn.com/2017/10/26/politics/donald-trump-opioid-epidemic/index.html.

[14] https://www.annualreviews.org/doi/abs/10.1146/annurev-publhealth-031914-122957.

[15] https://www.whitehouse.gov/sites/whitehouse.gov/files/images/The%20Underestimated%20Cost%20of%20the%20Opioid%20Crisis.pdf.

[16] http://newsok.com/article/5572873.

Medical Device Fraud

[1] https://www.healthcaredive.com/news/recognizing-and-preventing-medical-device-fraud/430686/.

[2] https://www.justice.gov/opa/pr/former-owner-and-operator-california-medical-equipment-supply-company-sentenced-their-roles.

[3] https://www.prnewswire.com/news-releases/olympus-has-fallen-false-claims-act-whistleblower-lawsuit-prompts-medical-device-titan-to-strike-a-record-623m-settlement-kenney-mccafferty-announces-300228799.html.

[4] http://www.usfraudattorneys.com/healthcare-fraud/medical-device-fraud/.

[5] http://www.washingtonpost.com/sf/national/2014/08/16/a-medicare-scam-that-just-kept-rolling/.

[6] http://www.healthcarefinancenews.com/news/university-california-oks-85-million-payout-spine-surgery-cases.

[7] https://www.mddionline.com/1-fraud-and-accounting-problems.

8 https://www.gao.gov/products/GAO-13-213T.
9 http://www.thewhistleblowerlawyer.com/medical-equipment-fraud/.
10 https://oig.hhs.gov/fraud/enforcement/index.asp.
11 http://abcnews.go.com/Politics/medicare-funds-totaling-60-billion-improper-ly-paid-report/story?id=32604330.

Elimination of the Office of Technology Assessment

1 https://www.sciencedirect.com/science/article/pii/S0040162596001679.
2 https://link.springer.com/chapter/10.1057/9781137359056_7.
3 https://books.google.com/books?id=U6p-sCwKAC4C&pg=PA32&lpg=PA32&dq=elimination+of+the+OTA&source=bl&ots=mc1hw63UIt&sig=tPaiEBOszwiCmClNn5NZqTACHlM&hl=en&sa=X&ved=0ahUKEwiruKO66rfZAhVD0VMKHc_fDn84ChDoAQgzMAM#v=onepage&q=elimination%20of%20the%20OTA&f=false.
4 https://en.wikipedia.org/wiki/Office_of_Technology_Assessment#cite_note-2.

Fraud by the States

1 https://www.cdc.gov/tobacco/data_statistics/sgr/history/index.htm.
2 https://profiles.nlm.nih.gov/ps/retrieve/Narrative/NN/p-nid/60.
3 https://www.surgeongeneral.gov/library/reports/50-years-of-progress/full-report.pdf.
4 https://www.nolo.com/legal-encyclopedia/tobacco-litigation-history-and-development-32202.html.
5 Ibid.
6 Ibid.
7 Jim Estes, "How the Big Tobacco Deal Went Bad," *New York Times*, October 6, 2014, 1–3.
8 https://www.tobaccofreekids.org/what-we-do/us/statereport.
9 https://www.propublica.org/article/top-tobacco-bond-banker-departs-barclays.
10 https://www.surgeongeneral.gov/library/reports/50-years-of-progress/fact-sheet.html.
11 https://www.tobaccofreekids.org/problem/toll-us.

Continuous Pressures on the FDA

1 https://www.google.com/search?q=Responsibilities+of+the+FDA&rlz=-1C1LOQA_enUS627US655&oq=Responsibilities+of+the+FDA&aqs=chrom.
2 https://en.wikipedia.org/wiki/Criticism_of_the_Food_and_Drug_Administration#cite_ref-IndI_7-1.
3 Ibid.
4 Ibid.
5 https://www.ucsusa.org/our-work/center-science-and-.democracy/promoting-scientific-integrity/drug-companies-inf.

6   https://www.opensecrets.org/lobby/agencysum.php?id=135.

7   https://www.ucsusa.org/our-work/center-science-and-democracy/ promoting-scientific-integrity/fda-survey-shows-p.

8   https://www.nytimes.

9   https//www.google.com/search?riz=enUS627US655&ei=HjqoWtGaHq2c_ QbVy4uQB&q=https%3A%2F%2Fnyt.ms%2F2BRilka&o.

10 Beth Macy, *Dopesick: Dealers, Doctors and the Drug Company that Addicted America*, (New York: Little, Brown & Co., 2018), 185.

11 "Warren Says F.D.A. Chief Joining is a Conflict." The New York Times 7 July. 2017.

Within the Medical Profession
Invasion of CIM into Scientific Medicine

1   https://my.clevelandclinic.org/departments/functional-medicine.

2   https://sciencebasedmedicine.org/quackademia-update-2014/.

3   Ibid.

4   Ibid.

5   https://www.holisticprimarycare.net/topics/topics-a-g/functional-medi- cine/1772-facing-huge-demand-cleveland-clinic-doubles-its-functional-medi- cine-center.ht.

6   https://www.ifm.org/find-a-practitioner/.

7   https://www.huffingtonpost.com/john-weeks/mt-sinai-merger-shuts- new_b_14748672.html.

8   https://www.nutraceuticalsworld.com/issues/2017-05/view_columns/ are-we-at-the-end-of-the-integrative-medicine-era/.

9   http://sfsbm.org/index.php?option=com_content&view=arti- cle&id=32&Itemid=545.

Complicity in the Opioid Epidemic

1   https://www.wsls.com/opioids-epidemic/ what-role-have-doctors-played-in-creating-the-opioid-crisis.

2   https://blogs.wsj.com/experts/2017/09/14/ how-doctors-have-contributed-to-and-can-help-reverse-the-opioid-epidemic/.

3   https://prahs.com/blog/2017/02/03/now-is-the-time-to-solve-the-opioid-epi- demic/.

4   Ibid.

5   Maggie Haberman, Abby Goodnough, and Katharine Q. Seelye, "Trump Offers Tough Talk but Few Details in Unveiling Plan to Combat Opioids," *New York Times*, March 20, 2018.

6   John Fritze, "Administration Late on Opioid Plan Required by Law Months Ago," *USA Today* (2018), 2B.

Abusing Medicare/Medicaid Billing

1 http://www.ncsl.org/research/health/medicaid-fraud-and-abuse.aspx.
2 https://en.wikipedia.org/wiki/Medicare_fraud.
3 http://abcnews.go.com/Politics/medicare-funds-totaling-60-billion-improperly-paid-report/story?id=32604330.
4 http://www.healthcarefinancenews.com/news/oklahoma-physician-hit-580000-settlement-resolve-false-medicare-billing-allegations.
5 http://www.healthcarefinancenews.com/news/texas-doctor-slapped-35-year-sentence-and-268m-restitution-massive-fraud-scheme.
6 https://www.csmonitor.com/USA/Society/2017/0621/An-epic-case-of-medical-fraud-and-the-agent-who-cracked-it.
7 https://www.cnbc.com/2016/07/22/1-billion-alleged-medicare-fraud-money-laundering-scheme-leads-to-florida-arrests.html.
8 https://www.irs.gov/compliance/criminal-investigation/examples-of-healthcare-fraud-investigations-fiscal-year-2017.
9 https://www.cms.gov/Newsroom/MediaReleaseDatabase/Fact-sheets/2017-Fact-Sheet-items/2017-01-18-2.html.
10 https://www.justice.gov/criminal-fraud/health-care-fraud-unit.
11 GAO, "Improper Payments: Remaining Challenges and Strategies for Government-Wide Reduction Efforts," GAO-12-573T, March 28, 2012.

Prices Controlled by Big Pharma
Large Complex Market

1 https://www.statista.com/topics/1764/global-pharmaceutical-industry/.
2 https://www.trade.gov/topmarkets/pdf/Pharmaceuticals_Executive_Summary.pdf.
3 http://www.newsweek.com/prescription-drug-pricing-569444.
4 http://apps.who.int/medicinedocs/en/d/Jh3012e/3.3.html.
5 Ibid.
6 http://apps.who.int/medicinedocs/en/d/Jh3012e/6.html.
7 https://www.opensecrets.org/industries/indus.php?ind=H4300.
8 Ibid.
9 https://www.opensecrets.org/industries/lobbying.php?ind=H4600.
10 http://www.politifact.com/wisconsin/statements/2012/sep/04/tammy-baldwin/uncle-sam-barred-bargaining-medicare-drug-prices-s/.
11 https://www.planetdrugsdirect.com/articles/big-pharma-big-fraud.
12 Ibid.
13 https://www.pintas.com/.
14 Matthew Galgani, "No. 1-Ranked Drug-Trial Stock and IBD 50 Member Examines Buy Zone," *Investor's Business Daily*, Mar 15 2018.
15 https:www.investors.com/news/technology/biotech-and-pharma-indusstry-and-stock-news-merk-bristol-myers-amgn-gilead/.
16 https://www.globalresearch.ca/the-evils-of-big-pharma-exposed/5425382.

17 Jayne O'Donnell, "FDA Chief Slams Drug Makers Who Are 'Gaming the System,'" *USA Today*, August 16, 2017.
18 https://www.healthaffairs.org/do/10.1377/hblog20160201.052912/full/.

Medicare Advantage Fraud

1 https://www.medicare.gov/Pubs/pdf/11474.pdf.
2 https://www.publicintegrity.org/2017/03/28/20782/justice-department-joins-suit-alleging-massive-medicare-fraud-unitedhealth.
3 https://www.healthcaredive.com/news/doj-sends-warning-shots-on-medicare-advantage-overpayments/444542/.
4 https://www.phillipsandcohen.com/medicare-advantage-fraud-risk-adjustment/.
5 Ibid.
6 https://khn.org/news/fraud-and-billing-mistakes-cost-medicare-and-taxpayers-tens-of-billions-last-year/.
7 Ibid.
8 https://www.nhcaa.org/about-us/who-we-are.aspx.

Hospital Quackonomics

1 https://www.beckershospitalreview.com/finance/auditor-15-bed-missouri-hospital-at-heart-of-90m-billing-fraud-scheme.html.
2 https://www.usnews.com/news/best-states/california/articles/2018-01-12/ex-california-hospital-owner-sentenced-for-huge-fraud.
3 http://centurycity.news/bozeman-hospital-fraud-p1181-181.htm.
4 http://kcur.org/post/patient-who-had-parts-her-organs-removed-sues-ku-hospital-fraud#stream/0.
5 http://www.abc57.com/news/lawsuit-against-70-indiana-hospitals-includes-fraud.
6 https://revcycleintelligence.com/news/la-hospital-pays-42m-to-settle-healthcare-fraud-kickback-case.
7 https://www.law.com/dailybusinessreview/sites/dailybusinessreview/2017/11/10/florida-whistleblower-lawsuit-accuses-hospital-software-of-billing-fraud/?slreturn.
8 https://www.healthcaredive.com/news/at-a-glance-medicare-fraud-in-hospitals/404860/.
9 Ibid.
10 https://www.statnews.com/2016/08/02/hospital-ratings-skepticism/.

Celebrity Quackonomics
Steve Jobs

1 https://www.telegraph.co.uk/technology/apple/8841347/Steve-Jobs-regretted-trying-to-beat-cancer-with-alternative-medicine-for-so-long.html.
2 Walter Isaacson, *Steve Jobs* (New York: Simon & Schuster, 2011), 453.

[3]   Ibid., 454.

[4]   https://blogs.webmd.com/breaking-news/2011/10/steve-jobs-pancreatic-cancer.html.

[5]   http://abcnews.go.com/Health/CancerPreventionAndTreatment/steve-jobs-pancreatic-cancer-timeline/story?id=14681812.

[6]   Leander Kahney, *Inside Steve's Brain* (New York: Penguin Group, 2008), 68.

Linus Pauling

[1]   https://www.vox.com/2015/1/15/7547741/vitamin-c-myth-pauling.

[2]   https://www.theatlantic.com/health/archive/2013/07/the-vitamin-myth-why-we-think-we-need-supplements/277947/.

[3]   Ibid.

Summary-of-the-Cost Questions

*Healthcare is expensive enough without unscrupu-
lous people trying to defraud the taxpayer.*
—*Thomas Dinapoli,
New York State comptroller*

A N ESTIMATE OF the cost of Complementary and
Integrative Medicine in the United States in an up-to-date
year may be based initially on a survey done every five years
by National Health Interview Survey.[1] The most recent survey was
completed in 2017 but will not be analyzed and reported until 2019,
according to NIH sources. The most complete data is from 2007 as
the 2012 is incomplete.[2]

In the 2007 National Health Interview
Survey (NHIS), approximately 38 percent of
adults reported using complementary and alternative medicine (CAM) in the previous 12
months. Eighty-three (83) million adults spent
$34 billion out-of-pocket on CAM.

Of the total out-of-pocket expenditures on CAM, US adults
spent approximately $12 billion specifically on CAM professional
services, according to a study by Davis and Weeks.[3]

In looking at these 2007 and 2012 reports, I cannot find out
why the government reporting system uses the category "out-of-

pocket" expenses, rather than determining the exact amount charged and reporting that number in a straightforward manner. The most recent reference on insurance coverage for CAM users is a NCHS Data Brief published in 2016[4] covering the three most commonly used complementary approaches: acupuncture, chiropractic, and massage. The findings were as follows:

> While 60% of adults who saw a practitioner for chiropractic had at least some health insurance coverage, far fewer (25%) adults seeing a practitioner for acupuncture or massage therapy (15%) had coverage for these approaches.

NO COVERAGE: PARTIAL: COMPLETE
CHIROPRACTIC: 39.9% 41.418.7
ACUPUNCTURE: 75.0% 16.58.5
MASSAGE: 84.7% 8.3 7.0

It is of interest that no cost information was found anywhere in this reference. Nonetheless, the value of coverage data is that we can check the accuracy of our estimate for gross cost of each of the three approaches by multiplying the noncoverage percentage to get the out-of-pocket figures, and when we do, they agree with the NHIS out-of-pocket data quite closely.

If $34 billion is the out-of-pocket, the next question is, how much insurance coverage can be added to estimate the gross cost? Since we can only add for "complete" coverage, the calculation would be 1.12 billion for chiropractic, 0.3 billion for acupuncture, and 0.9 billion for massage. Therefore, the sum added would be $2.32 billion + $34 billion = $36.32 billion. We can estimate that for the other 22 CAM modalities noted above, some may have partial insurance, so we might round out the total gross amount to be $37 billion by the 2007–2012 data. As a comparison, independent Deloitte Healthcare Solutions[5] reports the cost to be $34.66 billion from the 2012 data. We can then, assuming about a 3 percent annual growth, extrapolate to the 2018 number at *$40 billion.*

Tallying up the aggregate costs the systemic corruption found along the way extrapolated to 2018 is as follows:

Cost of Corruption in the System
Fraud in the science literature .... $22.6 B
Pharma and Associates Corruption
1. Adverse effects .... $25 B
2. Gauging .... $50 B
3. Lack of FDA independence .... ——
4. Surrogate endpoints .... ——
5. Generics and biosimilars .... $15.2 B
6. PBMs .... $25 B
7. Opioid Crisis .... $504 B
$\Sigma = 619.2$ B → 619.2 B
Medical Device Fraud .... $9.6 B
Elimination of OTA .... ——
States Fraud .... $331 B
Pressures on the FDA .... ——
The Medical Profession
Invasion of CIM into Scientific Medicine .... ——
Complicity in the Opioid crisis $5B
Abusing Medicare/Medicaid billing .... $12.3 B
$\Sigma = 17.3$ B → 17.3 B
      Prices Controlled
      by Big Pharma .... $15.2 B
      Medicare Advantage Fraud .... $16.2 B
      Hospital Quackonomics .... $2 B

—————

$\Sigma = \$114.11$ B

Combining $40 billion of unscientific medicine with $102 billion wasted by fraud, we can estimate the quackonomics of the year 2018 at over *$142 billion*.

Endnotes

Part IV
Summary of the Cost Questions

[1] https://nccih.nih.gov/research/statistics/costs.

[2] https://nccih.nih.gov/news/camstats/costs/costdatafs.htm.

[3] Matthew A. Davis and William B. Weeks, "Concentration of Out-of-Pocket Expenditures on Complementary and Alternative Medicine in the United States," *Alternative Therapies* 18, no. 5 (September/October 2012): 37.

[4] R. L. Nahin, P. M. Barnes, B. J. Stussman, "Insurance Coverage for Complementary Health Approaches among Adult Users: United States, 2002 and 2012," NCHS Data Brief no. 235 Hyattsville, (Maryland: National Center for Health Statistics, 2016).

[5] https://www2.deloitte.com/content/dam/Deloitte/us/Documents/life-sciences-health-care/us-lshc-hidden-costs-inforgraphic-111214.pdf.

PART V

Epilogue

Noncooperation with evil is as much
a duty as cooperation with good.
                    —Gandhi

THIS BOOK WAS not intended to be all-inclusive but to be thought-provoking. That is why I reviewed origins and a brief history of the scientific method. Health information in the United States is a thunderous tsunami. The reasons we have trouble managing it is traced in our history of anti-intellectualism, a stagnant education system, and loss of trust resulting in anti-science, allowing the erosion of medicine by complementary and integrative fraud. What I have shown is the need for a more educated and skeptical consumer, more educated in science to understand and regain trust in science-based medical care, and more critical skepticism to identify corruption in the delivery system costing billions of dollars.

I have noted that quackery has a larger meaning beyond medicine in our moral perspective and intellectual discourse, not just in monetary consequences. Fake news is bad enough! We cannot allow ourselves to be buried in "fake medicine." We must develop a method of analysis to make us more discriminating consumers. In a larger sense, it is a fundamental responsibility of citizenship.

In an age of expanding knowledge in science other than medicine—of big data centers, artificial intelligence, deep learning, and massive NASA astronomical projects, why do we employ false science on ourselves? Perhaps we can take money saved from avoiding medical nonscience and put it to work researching in-utero causes of obesity and autism. We must fund and strengthen the standards of the FDA, both for drug approval and high-risk medical devices. Accelerated approval processes and outsourcing must be closely monitored to avoid missing data and bias.

The patient-healer relationship will forever be a source of dialogue. We all must work on improving it. When you look up a medical condition on the internet, you get information that is dated. It often has bias you cannot identify. As you probably noticed, the information that I have given you in this book is spread over a ten-year span. It is near impossible to get up-to-date government information on the cost of health care.

The prescribing of Cannabis-derived drugs will require much more research. Indeed, the legalizing of marijuana should be further researched before national legalization. Education and strict restrictions of usage before age twenty-one is imperative. We must define exactly what the term "medical marijuana" so as to avoid the current confusion in political discussions and legislative efforts. There is evidence that cannabis can be helpful, for example, in controlling seizures, especially for difficult-to-control conditions like Lennox-Gastaut syndrome (LGS) in children and adults and Dravet syndrome in children.[1] We have done reasonably well in tobacco control and should not drop the ball with a hell-bent liberality toward marijuana. We must learn from the mistakes we made with the national tobacco settlement.

I have stressed the need for better sourcing of reported health news. This includes improved search engines, media reporting of exact literature sources, and improved availability of the primary source papers with understandable abstracts. It would help the consumer if a reader could always go from a newspaper or magazine story to a website and directly to the original source with clear bottom-line conclusions. Creating higher standards for peer review of medical literature would ensure elimination of "in-house" medical research as the sole basis of approving pharmaceuticals.

Of all the fraud uncovered along the way, the most disturbing to me, is finding the erosion of legitimacy of medical science journals. Knowing that Pub Med, for example, one of our main sources of medical journalism has a flawed peer review process, can lead to disaster. Decisions in clinical practice are founded on integrity of the medical literature and of the contributors, not to mention the general public's dependency on daily access to this information through government sponsored websites! The growth of polluting predatory publishing has spread to nearly every field and has become a global disgrace.

We must have an accounting of the responsibility of testing whether alternative or functional medicine has any science. Placing this responsibility within the NIH may prove to be an illusion.

You have noted that I have not let the medical profession off the hook. A lax understanding of the pharmacology of opioids stands as a critical indictment yet to be answered. Drug manufacturers may have made the opioids, but it was the physicians that wrote the prescriptions.

I have pointed out the role insurance companies must follow to prevent taxpayers from being charged for nonscience. The industry must join forces with our government to examine this growing cost of the "middleman" in covering Medicare costs. Specifically, we must investigate the funding sources, and determine if Medicare Advantage Plans really save the federal government any money. Where there is a middleman, there is middle money. Controlling the cost of drugs must start with legislating the obligation of government to bargain with Big Pharma on price for all programs.

Education is a forever challenge. We need a course in pharmacology at the high school level and a K–12 curriculum on substance abuse. We will have to educate our teachers to the next level, so all will know the scientific method and how to understand a medical "study." We need further education of our public policy makers before legalizing substances that we do not know enough about. A nation that is antiscience is not smart enough to regain a lost democracy.

Improvement in the integrity of the professional medical literature is an ongoing effort and must be supported. As reported in 2013,

In the New England Journal of Medicine RCTs (Randomized Clinical Trials) published over the past decade that purportedly should have changed medical practice showed that 46% were subsequently reversed. An accompanying, highly provocative editorial stated, "After 65 years of randomized trials, ineffective, harmful, expensive medical practices are being introduced more frequently now than at any other time in the history of medicine. [Eric Topol, MD <Medscape@mail.medscape.com>., Sept 4,2013.

I am confident that much has been done to improve the situation since that time.

To tackle the fraud in the system that I have found along the way on this journey, we must fund better governance. The *Economist* reports that health-care fraud in the United States is $271 billion "swindle,"[2] essentially twice what I have uncovered.

Finally, we must all vote to build a Congress that is on the side of the people. We must demand of candidates for office, a basic education in and appreciation of science in the public square. Opposition to the reality of science and making government smaller is not a formula for a better future.

Endnotes

Epilogue

[1] https://www.epilepsy.com/learn/treating-seizures-and-epilepsy/other-treatment-approaches/medical-marijuana-and-epilepsy.

[2] https://www.economist.com/news/united-states/21603078-why-thieves-love-americas-health-care-system-272-billion-swindle.

ACKNOWLEDGMENTS

THANKS GOES TO the late Dr. Robert Joynt, former dean of the University of Rochester School of Medicine, whose early encouragement was much appreciated; Werner Library staff at Rochester Regional Health; especially Elizabeth Mamo, Dir. and Cathy Carey, the late Bernard "Bernie" Weiss, PhD, professor of Environmental Medicine at the University of Rochester; Kathy Pieper, a guiding adviser; Lucretia McClure, former Harvard and University of Rochester librarian Manish Madan, MD and Jenifer Matic PhD; and Jill Ryan of Montreal for their critical reading of the manuscript. I also thank friends Ted Richman and Lynne Herndon for their support and suggestions. Finally, thanks to my wife, Janet, and our four children—Anne, Ellen, Matt, and Maggie—for their continued support.

SUGGESTED READING

Mooney, Chris, and Kirshenbaum, Sheril. *Unscientific America*. New York: Basic Books, 2009.

Harrington, Anne, ed. *The Placebo Effect*. Cambridge: Harvard UP, 2000.

Winchester, Simon. *The Man Who Loved China*. New York: Harper, 2008.

Pigliucci, Massimo. *Nonsense on Stilts, How to Tell Science from Bunk*. Chicago: University of Chicago Press, 2010.

Gower, Barry. *Scientific Method: An Historical and Philosophical Introduction*. London and New York: Routledge, 1997.

Bausell, R. Barker. *Snake Oil Science: The Truth about Complementary and Alternative Medicine*. Oxford: Oxford University Press, 2007.

Greene, Jeremy A. *Generic: The Unbranding of Modern Medicine*. Baltimore: Johns Hopkins University Press, 2014.

Wooton, David. *Bad Medicine: Doctors Doing Harm Since Hippocrates*. New York: Oxford University Press, 2006.

Rovelli, Carlo. *The First Scientist: Anaximander and His Legacy*. Yardley, PA: Westholme Publishing, 2007.

Park, Robert L. *Voodoo Science: The Road from Foolishness to Fraud*. Oxford: Oxford University Press, 2000.

Park, Robert L. *Superstition: Belief in the Age of Science*. Princeton: Princeton University Press, 2008.

Harris, Richard. *How Sloppy Science Creates Worthless Cures, Crushes Hope and Wastes Billions.* New York: Basic Books, 2017.

Offit, Paul A., MD. *Do You Believe in Magic? The Sense and Nonsense of Alternative Medicine.* New York: Harper, 2013.

Conrad, Peter. *The Medicalization of Society.* Baltimore: Johns Hopkins University Press, 2007.

Berezow, Alex B., and Campbell, Hank. *Science Left Behind, Feel-Good Fallacies and the Rise of the Anti-Scientific Left.* New York: Public Affairs, 2012.

Freely, John. *Aladdin's Lamp How Greek Science Came to Europe through the Islamic World.* New York: Vintage Books, 2010.

Shih-Chen, Li. *Chinese Medicinal Herbs: A Modern Edition of a Classic Sixteenth-Century Manual.* Mineola, NY: Dover Publications, 1973.

Goldacre, Ben. *Bad Science, Quacks Hacks, and Big Pharma Flacks.* New York: Faber & Faber, 2008.

Institute of Medicine. *Complementary and Alternative Medicine in the United States.* Washington, DC: National Academy Press, 2005.

Ernst, Edzard. *Healing, Hype, or Harm? A Critical Analysis of Complementary or Alternative Medicine.* UK: Societas, 2008.

Isaacson, W. *Leonardo Da Vinci.* New York: Simon & Schuster, 2017.

Rosenthal, Elisabeth. *An American Sickness: How Healthcare Became Big Business and How You Can Take It Back.* New York: Penguin Press, 2017.

Angell, Marcia, MD. *The Truth about the Drug Companies.* New York: Random House, 2005.

Goldacre, Ben, MD. *How Drug Companies Mislead Doctors and Harm Patients.* New York: Farrar, Straus, and Giroux, 2013.

Welch, Gilbert H., Schwartz, Lisa M., and Woloshin Steven. *Overdiagnosed: Making People Sick in the Pursuit of Health.* Boston: Beacon Press, 2011.

Harris, Richard. *Rigor Mortis: How Sloppy Science Creates Worthless Cures, Crushes Hope, and Wastes Billions.* New York: Basic Books, 2017.

Kendrick, Malcolm. *The Great Cholesterol Con.* London: John Blake Publishing, 2007.

Whorton, James. *Nature Cures: The History of Alternative Medicine in America.* Oxford: Oxford University Press, 2001.

Kendrick, Malcolm. "A Statin Nation". London: John Blake Publishing, 2018.

ABOUT THE AUTHOR

E THAN L. WELCH M.D. (retired), is Emeritus Professor of Surgery from the University of Rochester School of Medicine and Dentistry. A graduate of Harvard College and Johns Hopkins Medical School, he trained at Bellevue Hospital in NYC and served as a lieutenant commander in the USPHS. He practiced and taught vascular surgery in Rochester, New York, for over thirty years. He lives in Rochester with his wife, Janet.

CPSIA information can be obtained
at www.ICGtesting.com
Printed in the USA
BVHW032331050323
659706BV00006B/128